York Manuscript and Early Print Studies
Volume 7

Medieval Manuscripts, Readers and Texts

Medieval Manuscripts, Readers and Texts

Essays in Honour of Kathryn Kerby-Fulton

Edited by Misty Schieberle
with the assistance of Amanda Bohne

THE UNIVERSITY *of York*

YORK MEDIEVAL PRESS

© Contributors 2024

All rights reserved. Except as permitted under current legislation no part of this work may be photocopied, stored in a retrieval system, published, performed in public, adapted, broadcast, transmitted, recorded or reproduced in any form or by any means, without the prior permission of the copyright owner

First published 2024

A York Medieval Press publication
in association with The Boydell Press
an imprint of Boydell & Brewer Ltd
PO Box 9, Woodbridge, Suffolk IP12 3DF, UK
and of Boydell & Brewer Inc.
668 Mt Hope Avenue, Rochester, NY 14620-2731, USA
website: www.boydellandbrewer.com
and with the Centre for Medieval Studies, University of York

ISBN 978-1-914049-28-6

A CIP catalogue record for this book is available
from the British Library

The publisher has no responsibility for the continued existence or accuracy of URLs for external or third-party internet websites referred to in this book, and does not guarantee that any content on such websites is, or will remain, accurate or appropriate

Contents

List of Illustrations	vii
List of Contributors	ix
Acknowledgments	x
List of Abbreviations	xi

Introduction   1
Misty Schieberle

1. The Trevisa-Gower Scribe: Another London Literary Scribe of the Early Fifteenth Century   8
Linne R. Mooney

2. Telling Tails: Pursuing the Trail of the Minstrel-Scribe in Manuscripts of *Sir Isumbras*   28
Andrew W. Klein

3. Ars Codicis: Marginalia, Meaning and the Manuscript Book(s) of Chaucer's *House of Fame*   54
Sarah Baechle

4. Editing Chaucer's Works: Coherence and Collaboration   74
Christopher Cannon and James Simpson

5. The Pleasures of Plainness: Ordinary Manuscripts in Extraordinary Traditions   105
Siân Echard

6. A Dream of John Bale? The *Catalogus Vetus* and the Lives of Ralph Strode   121
Thomas Goodmann

7. Women's St Edmund: Envisioning a Saint and his Contemplative Legacy   144
Jocelyn Wogan-Browne

8.	Three English Otherworld Visions: Toward a Spirituality of Parish Life	167
	Barbara Newman	
9.	Recognizing the Clerical Proletariat: Evidence from Late Medieval London Wills	190
	Misty Schieberle	
10.	Langland's Government Scribes at Home and at Work: A Brief Comparison of the HM 114 Scribe and the Fortescue Family	212
	Karrie Fuller	
11.	Function, Form and *The Lay Folks' Mass Book*	231
	Jeremy J. Smith	
12.	Professional Reading Networks and The Reception of Nicholas Love's *Mirror of The Blessed Life of Jesus Christ*: Opportunities and Consequences	253
	John J. Thompson	
	Kathryn Kerby-Fulton: The Making of a Medievalist	270
	Rosalynn Voaden	
	Kathryn Kerby-Fulton: List of Publications	274
	Karrie Fuller and Misty Schieberle	
	Index of Manuscripts	279
	General Index	282
	Tabula Gratulatoria	292

Illustrations

'The Trevisa-Gower Scribe: Another London Literary Scribe of the Early Fifteenth Century', *Linne R. Mooney*

1.1 Oxford, Bodleian Library, MS Bodley 693, fol. 48vb. Reproduced by the kind permission of the Bodleian Library in accordance with Creative Commons license CC-BY-NC 4.0. Illustration of the hand of the Trevisa-Gower Scribe. 12

1.2 Oxford, Bodleian Library, MS Laud Misc. 609, fol. 122va. Reproduced by the kind permission of the Bodleian Library in accordance with Creative Commons license CC-BY-NC 4.0. Illustration of the hand of the Trevisa-Gower Scribe. 13

1.3 Tokyo, Senshu University Library, MS 1, fol. 16rb. Reproduced by the kind permission of the Librarian of Senshu University Library. Illustration of the hand of the Trevisa-Gower Scribe. 14

1.4 Princeton, NJ, Princeton University Library, MS Taylor 5, fol. 8r. Reproduced by the kind permission of the Princeton University Library. Illustration of the hand of the Trevisa-Gower Scribe. 15

1.5 Princeton, NJ, Princeton University Library, MS Taylor 5, fol. 4r. Reproduced by the kind permission of the Princeton University Library. Illustration of the hand of the second scribe of the manuscript, whose work survives on folios 4–7 of the first quire. 18

'Telling Tails: Pursuing the Trail of the Minstrel-Scribe in Manuscripts of *Sir Isumbras*', *Andrew W. Klein*

2.1 Edinburgh, National Library of Scotland, MS Advocates' 19.3.1 (Heege Manuscript), fol. 56v. Image is in the public domain and is reproduced by the kind permission of the National Library of Scotland in accordance with the Creative Commons Attribution 4.0 International License. 40

'A Dream of John Bale? The *Catalogus Vetus* and the Lives of Ralph Strode', *Thomas Goodmann*

6.1 Oxford, MCR 4.16 (*Catalogus Vetus*), fol. 64v. Reproduced by kind permission of The Warden and Fellows of Merton College. 125

6.2 Oxford, Bodleian Library, MS Selden Supra 64, fols. 204v. Reproduced by kind permission of the Librarian and Executive of the Bodleian Library. 127

The editor, contributors and publisher are grateful to all the institutions for permission to reproduce the material to which they hold copyright. Every effort has been made to trace the copyright holders; apologies are offered for any omission, and the publisher will be pleased to add any necessary acknowledgement in subsequent editions.

Contributors

Sarah Baechle   Assistant Professor, Department of English, University of Mississippi

Amanda Bohne   Senior Lecturer, Department of English, University of Illinois at Chicago

Christopher Cannon   Bloomberg Distinguished Professor of English and Classics, Johns Hopkins University

Siân Echard   Professor and Distinguished University Scholar, Department of English Language and Literatures, University of British Columbia

Karrie Fuller   Independent Scholar

Thomas Goodmann   Associate Professor, Department of English, University of Miami

Andrew W. Klein   Associate Professor, Department of English, St Thomas University

Linne R. Mooney   Professor Emerita of Medieval English Palaeography, Department of English and Related Literatures and Centre for Medieval Studies, University of York

Barbara Newman   John Evans Professor of Latin and Professor of English, Classics, and History, Northwestern University

Misty Schieberle   Professor, Department of English, University of Kansas

James Simpson   Donald P. and Katherine B. Loker Research Professor of English, Harvard University

Jeremy J. Smith   Senior Research Fellow and Professor Emeritus, English Language and Linguistics, University of Glasgow/Honorary Professor, University of St Andrews

John J. Thompson   Professor Emeritus, Department of English, Queen's University, Belfast

Rosalynn Voaden   Professor Emerita, Department of English, Arizona State University

Jocelyn Wogan-Browne   Thomas F. X. and Theresa Mullarkey Chair in Literature Emerita, Fordham University

Acknowledgments

We wish to thank the International Medieval Congress at Kalamazoo, MI, for supporting two sessions in honour of Kathryn Kerby-Fulton in May 2018, Sarah Baechle and Amanda Bohne for organizing them and Karrie Fuller for further planning that led to this volume. For providing images from manuscripts in their care and granting permission for their reproduction, we are grateful to the Bodleian Library, the National Library of Scotland, the Princeton University Library, the Tokyo Senshu University Library and the Warden and Fellows of Merton College, Oxford. We acknowledge the generosity of the University of Notre Dame Medieval Institute and Department of English for funding the color portrait of Kathryn Kerby-Fulton, and of Matt Cashore, Senior University Photographer at the University of Notre Dame, for permitting the reproduction of his photo. We also thank the British Library for permission to use the image from MS Royal 19 C. ii, on the cover of this book, and the University of Kansas Department of English for funding the cover image. We are grateful to Professor Peter Biller, General Editor of York Medieval Press, to Dr Holly James-Maddocks and Dr Orietta Da Rold, Series Editors, and to the anonymous reader for suggestions that have strengthened our essays. Amanda Bohne's assistance was invaluable: she formatted the essays according to press guidelines and prepared the index. We owe a debt of gratitude to Caroline Palmer, Laura Bennetts and all the staff at Boydell & Brewer for their thorough and painstaking work producing this volume. The editors and contributors take responsibility for any errors or omissions.

Abbreviations

AND	Anglo-Norman Dictionary: https://anglo-norman.net
ANTS	Anglo-Norman Text Society
BHO	*British History Online*: https://www.british-history.ac.uk
BL	British Library, London
Bodl.	Bodleian Library, Oxford
Cal. Wills	*Calendar of Wills Proved and Enrolled in the Court of Husting, London*, ed. R. R. Sharpe, 2 vols (London, 1889–90).
ChR	*Chaucer Review*
Dean	R. J. Dean with M. B. M. Boulton, *Anglo-Norman Literature: A Guide to Texts and Manuscripts*, ANTS OPS 3 (London, 1999).
DIMEV	*Digital Index of Middle English Verse*: https://www.dimev.net/Search.php
DLB	*Dictionary of Literary Biography*
DMLBS	*Dictionary of Medieval Latin from British Sources*: https://logeion.uchicago.edu/
DNB	*Dictionary of National Biography, 1885–1900*: https://en.wikisource.org/wiki/Dictionary_of_National_Biography,_1885-1900
EEBO	Early English Books Online
EETS OS	Early English Text Society, Original Series
HR	The Husting Rolls of Deeds and Wills (LMA)
LALME	*A Linguistic Atlas of Late Medieval English*, ed. A. McIntosh, M. L. Samuels and M. Benskin (Aberdeen, 1986)
LFMB	*Lay Folks' Mass Book*
LGM	K. L. Scott, *Later Gothic Manuscripts, 1390–1490*, 2 vols, in *A Survey of Manuscripts Illuminated in the British Isles*, gen. ed. J. J. G. Alexander (London, 1996)
LP	linguistic profile (in *LALME*)

LMA	London Metropolitan Archives (City of London)
MED	*Middle English Dictionary*, ed. R. E. Lewis et al. (Ann Arbor, 1952–2001). Online edition in Middle English Compendium, ed. F. McSparran et al. (Ann Arbor, 2000–18): http://quod.lib.umich.edu/m/middle-english-dictionary
MLQ	*Modern Language Quarterly*
MS	manuscript
NIMEV	*A New Index of Middle English Verse*, ed. J. Boffey and A. S. G. Edwards (London, 2005)
ODNB	*Oxford Dictionary of National Biography Online*: https://www.oxforddnb.com/
PMLA	*Publications of the Modern Language Association*
SAC	*Studies in the Age of Chaucer*
TLS	*Times Literary Supplement*
VCH	*Victoria County History*
VLT	*Vernacular Literary Theory from the French of Medieval England: Texts and Translations c. 1120–c. 1450*, ed. J. Wogan-Browne, T. Fenster and D. W. Russell (Cambridge, 2016)
YLS	*Yearbook of Langland Studies*

Introduction

MISTY SCHIEBERLE

Kathryn Kerby-Fulton's research has been foundational to the study of medieval manuscripts, scribes and readers, particularly in the areas of Middle English devotional literature, clerical writing and women readers and patrons. Her scholarly talents are matched only by her commitments to mentoring and collaboration. As a result, she has produced not only wide-ranging and impressive scholarship but also the indispensable pedagogical resource *Opening Up Middle English Manuscripts* (co-produced with Maidie Hilmo and Linda Olson) and the compassionate analogy of the current state of academic employment to the late medieval clerical crises in *The Clerical Proletariat*.[1] Many of her publications are collaborative – either with co-authors or, as in *Voices in Dialogue*, designed to put scholars at various stages of their careers in conversation. To her students and colleagues, only a small fraction of whom it was possible to represent in this volume, she is a thoughtful, caring mentor and friend. Her capacious generosity and commitment to creating community among scholars are inseparable from her scholarship, which has inspired, energized and supported so many over the years.

This volume of tributes focuses on the centrality of manuscript and cultural contexts to understanding not only medieval texts but also the very shape of our field of study. Over her career Kathryn has contributed to the shift away from studying singular authors toward seeking to understand literary texts in relation to the persons and networks that produced, read and preserved them, from the medieval era forward. Such investigations shed new light on professional scribes, lay scribes and readers, manuscript marginalia, images (regardless of their quality), individual manuscript witnesses, book production and local engagements with literary texts. The manuscript that once was regarded as a poor copy of Chaucer can now be viewed as offering valuable insights into the processes of reading, copying and interpreting literature. Archival documents offer new evidence about the social, ecclesiastical, educational and other cultural conditions in which the poets we study lived and wrote. Thus, the literary studies we embark on in this volume consider not only the traditional literary

---

[1] K. Kerby-Fulton, M. Hilmo and L. Olson, *Opening Up Middle English Manuscripts: Literary and Visual Approaches* (Ithaca, 2012); K. Kerby-Fulton, *The Clerical Proletariat and the Resurgence of Medieval English Poetry* (Philadelphia, 2021).

text but also the material and historical circumstances in which that text was produced, read, circulated and passed down to us, circumstances that – in any number of fascinating permutations – might be affected by the author, scribe, compiler, patron, audience and later readers and editors. In this productive and interdisciplinary matrix, as Kathryn has shown time and again, even the smallest detail can open up vital new discoveries and directions for study.

This book is loosely organized around three groupings of essays, though there are no formal divisions, in order to keep open the rich conversations occurring among and across various essays. The first grouping of essays focuses on scribal activities (Mooney, Klein, Baechle). The second demonstrates how manuscript and archival evidence can help us both interrogate and expand scholarly and editorial perspectives (Simpson and Cannon, Echard, Goodmann). The last set engages devotional manuscripts, texts and practices from around the thirteenth century, through the Ricardian era and up to the eve of the Reformation (Wogan-Browne, Newman, Schieberle, Fuller, Smith, Thompson). There are several thematic through-lines that engage with research topics that Kathryn has emphasized throughout her career: attention to multiple features of the manuscript page; an interest in archival sources, especially neglected ones; and a commitment to exploring manuscripts and variant copies of texts for evidence of late medieval literary and religious practices. The resulting essays demonstrate how manuscript and archival studies energize interdisciplinary scholarship on such varied topics as authority, reader reception, modern editorial practices, gender and religious practices. The contributors address canonical and lesser-studied works afresh by analyzing scribal practices, professional readers' activities, manuscripts and layouts, archival evidence and complex manuscript traditions and variants. All are bound together by a fierce commitment to manuscript and archival evidence, and many invite us to rethink scholarly practices in productive and provocative ways.

The collection begins with essays that explore the details of the manuscript page. Linne Mooney's essay offers the first full description of the hand of the Gower-Trevisa scribe and places his work within the contexts of other early fifteenth-century London scribes. As she shows, he must have worked as a professional scribe, and his hand is found alongside 'Scribe D' (about whom Kathryn has written). Mooney argues for a strong likeness of script in several manuscripts that suggests that, just as we have evidence of a project to distribute high-quality copies of John Trevisa's works, so, too, is there evidence of a similar project, involving some of the same scribes, to produce high-quality copies of Gower's *Confessio Amantis*.

Sarah Baechle assesses an imagined authorial community in her essay, which reconsiders the glosses in *House of Fame* manuscripts as part of Chaucer's fraught exploration of creative and textual authority. She builds on

Kathryn's characterization of Chaucer's glossing practices to argue that these glosses, like those in the *Canterbury Tales* and *Troilus*, ought to be regarded as the work of the poet himself. Because the glosses direct readers toward often competing intertextual *auctoritates*, Baechle sees them as part of Chaucer's interrogation of the concept of authority; rather than offering evidence of the anxiety of influence, they show Chaucer embracing the impossibility of reconciling different classical *auctores*, which creates a generative space in which he can practice his art free from Fame's judgment. Baechle theorizes a 'poetics of the codex' in which the book becomes a structuring metaphor and invites scholars to imagine new possibilities for the poet's authorial self-fashioning and complex relationship to prior authorities.

The layout of the manuscript page also animates Andrew Klein's contribution, which explores *mise-en-page* practices of medieval scribes and later editors of *Sir Isumbras* to highlight the importance of visualizing the graphic tail-rhyme form. Klein argues that the graphic tail-rhyme layout emphasizes the storytelling and performative mode of *Sir Isumbras*, and he shows how scribes made purposeful decisions about when to represent visually the graphic tail-rhyme or instead resort to columnar layouts. With evidence that the graphic layout should be taken seriously as a literary device, Klein calls for its restoration in modern editions to immerse readers in the form that Chaucer's *Sir Thopas* may have parodied but that some medieval scribes felt was important to preserve in their copies of tail-rhyme romances. Klein demonstrates a searching interest in the choices made by medieval scribes and modern editors (see also Smith, later in the volume).

The co-authored essay by Christopher Cannon and James Simpson likewise considers the challenges faced by editors, as they develop a new editorial approach that they call pragmatic editing, based on their recent experiences editing the works of Chaucer. Pragmatic editing emphasizes building an edition based on textual coherence (rather than on shared errors in textual witnesses) and results from collaboration among author, scribe and modern editor, 'where the editor supplies what scribes do not'. Although their practice might be conflated with a new form of eclecticism, Cannon and Simpson demonstrate a search for consistency and an editorial restraint that distinguishes their approach from true eclecticism, remaining grounded in the textual tradition while resisting the exaltation of the written text as the sole repository of truth. The results of their innovative approach are illustrated in the essay's dramatic and persuasive emendations of oft cited and familiar Chaucerian lines.

Siân Echard reflects on another challenge that scholars face when we are fortunate enough to have many manuscript exemplars of a single text: neglected, 'ordinary' manuscripts that do not carry the 'best text' but are nevertheless crucial witnesses to individual and local engagements with a popular literary text. Her assessment of neglected manuscripts of Geoffrey of Monmouth's *Historia regum Britannie* shows how their evidence creates a fuller matrix in which we can appreciate the larger textual tradition, recover medieval reader responses and help scholars better understand the physical manuscript features that we choose to notice or overlook. Attending to ordinary manuscripts, Echard shows, gives us new access to physical evidence of a complex and lively medieval past that goes beyond the 'best' copies of literary works. By thus widening our view, we notice new things about texts, readers and our own scholarly practices.

Thomas Goodmann's essay revisits the once-contentious scholarly debate about whether the Oxford philosopher, poet and London prosecutor identified as Ralph Strode were the same one individual. Goodmann traces the documentary evidence that suggests that there were at least two separate individuals who first coalesced into a single persona in the works of John Bale (1495–1563). Early scholarship only cautiously linked them, and their identities were the subject of much debate among early twentieth-century scholars. Yet since the 1980s, the field seems to have silently adopted the assumption that the two Ralph Strodes were one and the same. Goodmann reflects on not only the documentary records and plausible identification(s) of Ralph Strode(s) but also the possibilities for career change in late medieval England and the kinds of investments we make as readers in the lives of those we study.

Jocelyn Wogan-Browne's contribution turns to devotional texts to explore a different, crucial investment of readers in their topic of study. She argues convincingly that St Edmund of Canterbury owes much of his reputation to women of both cloister and court who engaged with the living saint and his textual legacy. She first reevaluates historical and literary sources, tracing the women in Edmund's life and the ways they envisioned and disseminated his legacy. Wogan-Browne then considers where and for whom the *Mirour de seinte eglyse*, a French translation of Edmund's thirteenth-century Latin *Speculum religiosarum*, was made, suggesting rich possibilities for its association with women at Lacock Abbey and at the court of Queen Eleanor of Provence. Wogan-Browne ultimately challenges the modern view of the *Mirour* as restricting contemplation and instituting a divide between what was appropriate content for men or women, religious or lay audiences. Instead, she develops a sense of the French text as transmitting inclusive models of meditation and contemplation that depend on the reader's capability, not status.

Lay spirituality takes centre stage in Barbara Newman's essay, which brings together three understudied visionary texts, provides information on their textual milieux and manuscript traditions and argues for these texts' importance as examples of lay spirituality mediated through clerical writers. She investigates what such visions tell us about relationships among laity, monks and clerics in a genre that combines folklore with Latin learning to transmit 'popular' piety within a deeply monastic milieu. More specifically, for the first time, Newman teases out an emerging spirituality of parish life, a difficult task for which her three otherworld visions provide neglected evidence. These Latin narratives recorded by monks and clerics emphasize standard doctrine and lay salvation but also convey profoundly personal glimpses of the laity at work in the parish world. Such visionary texts invite us to reconsider Chaucerian pilgrims, Langlandian figures and late medieval social attitudes toward peasants and clerics.

My own contribution likewise examines lay participation in spiritual matters and builds on Kathryn's *Clerical Proletariat*, which showed how the precarious employment circumstances of late medieval clerks acutely affected writers such as Hoccleve, Langland and Audelay. During the same time that Middle English poets objected to clerical corruption and the lack of advancement for devout priests, London merchants were also expressing concerns about the clerical proletariat in what might be the only document these Londoners ever authored: their wills. Exploring the wills' representations of clerks and students helps to put literary accounts into perspective and to understand London merchant assessments of clerical careers. By analyzing bequests to underfunded members of the spiritual economy (lay clerks, students and stipendiary priests), I show that the London merchant community was sympathetic to the occupational crises affecting their local churches and the underemployed men who operated in and around them – men who were very likely relatives, friends or at least clerks from less-privileged status groups than most beneficed clergy.

Karrie Fuller's essay draws inspiration from Kathryn's research on lay government scribes and *Piers Plowman*. Fuller considers the efforts of two government scribes, working about 100 years apart: the scribes of San Marino, CA, Huntington Library, MS HM 114 and of Oxford, Bodleian Library, MS Digby 145. As a result of these manuscripts' overlapping but distinct readings of *Piers*, Fuller argues that their scribes share certain reformist tendencies influenced not only by individual circumstances but also by their respective occupations in offices tied to the royal and/or City governments. Fuller focuses on their treatment of friars, particularly in textual interpolations and annotations in the last passūs, where both scribes demonstrate interests in antimendicant discourse. Their distinct religious climates may put different pressures on these scribes, but Fuller shows them to be united by a broad investment in ecclesiastical reform, both in fifteenth-century and in Reformation-era England.

The final two essays offer further perspectives on late medieval religious cultures and texts near the eve of the Reformation. Jeremy Smith analyzes the manuscript tradition of the versified prayer book *The Lay Folks' Mass Book* (*LFMB*) and reexamines the 1879 edition by Thomas Frederick Simmons. Smith demonstrates that the variations among extant versions of the *LFMB* reflect dynamic social situations, in which 'speakers'/'scribes' and 'audiences'/'readers' interacted in complex and creative ways. Although the early edition has been criticized by modern scholars for its antiquarian and ecclesiastical perspectives, Smith contextualizes Simmons's efforts within evidence that fifteenth- and sixteenth-century textual producers viewed the *LFMB* as a living text that could be transmitted in bespoke fashion for individuals who wished to respond to the liturgy in their own personal and complex ways. Similarly, Smith argues, the antiquarian, ecclesiastical and local interests on display in Simmons's edition and notes may be taken as a precursor of cultural mapping: Simmons's approach to the medieval past is diachronically linked to his own time, place and cultural practices. Smith's essay ultimately shows that Simmons embraces the ways that medieval manuscripts reflected their texts' individualized devotional functions, something that cleaner, more 'objective' modern editorial processes tend to obscure.

John J. Thompson's essay concludes the collection but also hearkens back to earlier essays' interests in assessing manuscript traditions and late medieval professional readers and copyists. Thompson evaluates the earliest surviving and often expensively produced manuscripts of Nicholas Love's *Mirror of the Blessed Life of Jesus Christ*, with an interest in the activities of the copyists and their ambitions for the work. Thompson argues for viewing these copyists as professional readers and as part of an important early reading network associated with Love, Mount Grace Priory and nearby areas that had a profound influence on the earliest reception and reputation of Love's *Mirror*. He also considers the ways that later manuscripts offer insight into the activities of professional metropolitan readers and copyists a generation after Love completed the work. While Thompson cautions that analysis of such networks may not always offer a fully reliable guide to late medieval reading and textual production habits, such research nevertheless calls attention to the importance of Love's *Mirror* as an example of English pseudo-Bonaventuran writing between the early fifteenth century and the Reformation.

Read together, the essays in this volume employ careful attention to manuscripts and archival sources, literary and historical contexts and devotional practices to celebrate the scholarly revelations that develop from intense investigation of material and cultural contexts for literary texts. Some essays originated in two sessions at the 53rd International Medieval Congress at

Kalamazoo (2018) in Kathryn's honour, organized by Amanda Bohne and Sarah Baechle, on 'Visionary Literature' and 'Middle English Manuscripts and Their Professional Readers'. While I have served as main editor, I cannot take full credit for the volume's origins. In a fitting echo of Kathryn's model of scholarly collaborations, the book owes its existence to conversations with and efforts by Fuller, Baechle, Bohne and Marjorie Harrington, with supportive encouragement from many others. Contributors generously laboured and patiently endured delays brought on by the COVID pandemic and its aftermath (as it turns out, the midst of a worldwide pandemic is a terrible time to launch a volume that relies heavily on far-flung archival resources). We hope these collected essays will honour Kathryn's contributions to the field and serve as a small sign of our appreciation for our colleague, mentor and friend.

1

The Trevisa-Gower Scribe: Another London Literary Scribe of the Early Fifteenth Century

LINNE R. MOONEY

Several early fifteenth-century scribes in London wrote more than one copy of John Gower's *Confessio Amantis*.[1] One of these was the so-called 'Scribe D' identified by Malcolm Parkes and Ian Doyle in their ground-breaking article, 'The Production of Copies of the *Canterbury Tales* and the *Confessio Amantis* in the Early Fifteenth Century', where he is called 'Scribe D' because he was the fourth hand in the manuscript of Gower's *Confessio Amantis* that was the focus of their article.[2] They listed ten manuscripts besides his portion of Cambridge, Trinity College, MS R.3.2 that they believed to be written by this hand, to which has been added a further manuscript of Gower's *Confessio* since publication of their article.[3] The added manuscript brings to eight the

---

[1] I am grateful to Ralph Hanna, Joel Fredell, Bob Yeager and Peter Nicholson for reading drafts of this article and offering useful suggestions for its improvement. The ideas and arguments set out here, and any errors, are nevertheless my own.

[2] A. I. Doyle and M. B. Parkes, 'The Production of Copies of the *Canterbury Tales* and the *Confessio Amantis* in the Early Fifteenth Century', in *Medieval Scribes, Manuscripts and Libraries: Essays Presented to N. R. Ker*, ed. M. B. Parkes and A. G. Watson (London, 1978), pp. 163–210, esp. pp. 174–82; repr. in M. B. Parkes, *Scribes, Scripts and Readers: Studies in the Communication, Presentation and Dissemination of Medieval Texts* (London, 1991), pp. 201–48 (pp. 212–20). Further references to this work will give pages for only the original publication.

[3] Cambridge, Trinity College, MS R.3.2 (581), fols. 66ra–73vb, 113rb–153vb, Gower's *Confessio Amantis*; London, British Library, MS Additional 27944, fols. 2–7v, 196–335v, Trevisa, *De proprietatibus rerum*; London, British Library, MS Egerton 1991, Gower, *Confessio Amantis*; London, British Library, MS Harley 7334, Chaucer, *Canterbury Tales*; London, University of London, Senate House MS Sterling V.88, Langland, *Piers Plowman*; New York, Columbia University Library, MS Plimpton 265, Gower, *Confessio Amantis*; Oxford, Bodleian Library, MS Bodley 294, Gower, *Confessio Amantis*; Oxford, Bodleian Library, MS Bodley 902, fols.

number of *Confessio Amantis* manuscripts to which he contributed all or part of the text. Doyle and Parkes also identified another scribe, whom they called 'Scribe Delta', whose handwriting has now been identified in six manuscripts, including one of the *Confessio Amantis* and three of John Trevisa's *Polychronicon*.[4] Delta's hand, they said, was 'remarkably close' to that of their Scribe D, so close that they went on to say that 'the correspondences between the hands of these two scribes … are so close that it is difficult to accept that this similarity was the result of independent, uncoordinated efforts by the two scribes to achieve this new style'.[5]

In *Scribes and the City*, Estelle Stubbs and I briefly mentioned another scribe who copied multiple manuscripts of Gower's *Confessio Amantis* and one of Trevisa's *Polychronicon*, whom we called 'The Trevisa-Gower Scribe', and this scribe will be the focus of my article in this collection.[6] He makes an appearance only in a chart in *Scribes and the City*, where we were drawing attention to the number of early copies of Gower's *Confessio Amantis* that were written by scribes who were in some way associated with the London Guildhall. The Trevisa-Gower Scribe was included there because a hand I would now

---

2–16v, Gower, *Confessio Amantis*; Oxford, Christ Church, MS 148, Gower, *Confessio Amantis*; Oxford, Corpus Christi College, MS 67, Gower, *Confessio Amantis*; and Oxford, Corpus Christi College, MS 198, Chaucer, *Canterbury Tales*; to which Jeremy Griffiths added Princeton, NJ, Princeton University Library, MS Taylor 5, fols. 9–190, Gower, *Confessio Amantis*. See J. Griffiths, '*Confessio Amantis*: The Poem and its Pictures', in *Gower's Confessio Amantis: Responses and Reassessments*, ed. A. Minnis (Cambridge, 1983), pp. 163–78 (see p. 170, n. 19).

4 Doyle and Parkes, 'Production of Copies', pp. 206–8. The five manuscripts identified by Doyle and Parkes (p. 206) as written by scribe Delta were as follows: Cambridge, St John's College, MS H.I (204), Trevisa's *Polychronicon*; London, British Library, MS Additional 24194, Trevisa's *Polychronicon*; London, British Library, MS Royal 18 C.xxii, Gower's *Confessio Amantis*; Oxford, Brasenose College, MS 9, Love's *Mirror of the Blessed Life of Jesus Christ*; and Paris, Bibliothèque Nationale, MS anglais 25, Guy de Chauliac's *Cyrurgie* (first scribe), to which has since been added Princeton, NJ, Princeton University Library, MS Garrett 151, another copy of Trevisa's *Polychronicon*.

5 Doyle and Parkes, 'Production of Copies', pp. 206–8 (pp. 207–8). They proposed three possible means to achieve this similarity of script: 1, 'the stimulus of commercial competition upon independent practitioners in the same neighbourhood to produce similar results'; 2, both scribes worked in a single scriptorium that observed a 'house style'; 3, a 'master-apprentice relationship existed' (p. 207). Doyle and Parkes discarded the second two possibilities because no manuscripts have yet been found in which both hands appear, so they opted for the first, commercial pressures acting to influence both scribes to write in a similar style.

6 L. R. Mooney and E. Stubbs, *Scribes and the City: London Guildhall Clerks and the Dissemination of Middle English Literature, 1375–1425* (York, 2013), p. 136.

characterize as only *similar* to his had shared the writing of Oxford, Bodleian Library, MS Bodley 902 of Gower's *Confessio Amantis* with Doyle and Parkes's Scribe D, whom Estelle had identified as John Marchaunt, Chamberlain of the City 1381–99 and Common Clerk 1399–1417.[7] In this manuscript Bodley 902, the first two quires were written by Marchaunt and the remainder of the manuscript was written by two other scribes, though their handwriting is so similar that they may alternatively be a single scribe writing at different times and from different exemplars.[8] The second scribe writes folios 17–80 and the third scribe writes the remainder of the manuscript, folios 81–184. However, among the manuscripts attributed on our chart to the Trevisa-Gower scribe, the hand(s) of this one or two similar scribes show the greatest variation from the standard Trevisa-Gower scribe style, and I would no longer attribute the manuscript to him.[9] So too I would now characterize the hand of the London, University College London, MS Frag. Angl. 1 of Gower's *Confessio Amantis* as only *similar* to that of the Trevisa-Gower scribe and would not attribute the manuscript to him.[10] On the other hand, as I cast doubts on his contribution to two manuscripts of the *Confessio*, one partly written by Marchaunt, I shall examine another manuscript of Gower's *Confessio* written mostly by Scribe D, or John Marchaunt, in which one of the contributing hands is very similar to that of the Trevisa-Gower Scribe. This is Princeton, NJ, Princeton University Library, MS Taylor 5, in which the first hand of the manuscript is the one that is very similar to that of the Trevisa-Gower Scribe, writing only folios 1r–v and 8r–v, copying the text of the *Confessio*, Prologue, lines 1–153 and Book I,

---

[7] Mooney and Stubbs, *Scribes and the City*, pp. 38–65.

[8] Jeremy Griffiths told Derek Pearsall he also thought these two scribes might be one: see D. Pearsall and L. Mooney, *A Descriptive Catalogue of the English Manuscripts of John Gower's Confessio Amantis* (Cambridge, 2021), p. 192.

[9] Dated by Macaulay to the first quarter of the fifteenth century, and belonging to the family of manuscripts he called 'First Recension, Revised', I(a). See G. C. Macaulay, *The English Works of John Gower*, 2 vols (London, 1901–2), I, cxxxviii–cxxxix. Pearsall and Mooney, *A Descriptive Catalogue*, p. 192, included the third scribe of this manuscript as the same one who copied the manuscripts that I here attribute to the Trevisa-Gower Scribe, following the chart in Mooney and Stubbs, *Scribes and the City*, p. 136. After further study I would now not attribute the manuscript to this scribe.

[10] This manuscript was unknown to Macaulay. Pearsall and Mooney, *A Descriptive Catalogue*, pp. 344–5, date it to the first quarter of the fifteenth century. Too little of the text survives (it consists of only two bifolia) to place it in any of Macaulay's families or recensions. Pearsall and Mooney attribute its writing to the Trevisa-Gower Scribe, citing the chart in Mooney and Stubbs, *Scribes and the City*, p. 136.

lines 146–317.[11] In 2001, Kathryn Kerby-Fulton and Stephen Justice wrote a long article focused on Scribe D and this manuscript, so it seems appropriate to include my arguments about the scribe in this volume of essays gathered together in Kathryn's honour.[12]

The manuscripts I would now identify as clearly written by the Trevisa-Gower Scribe comprise two copies of Gower's *Confessio Amantis* and one of John Trevisa's translation of Higden's *Polychronicon*:

- Oxford, Bodleian Library, MS Bodley 693 (SC 2875), *Confessio Amantis*
- Oxford, Bodleian Library, MS Laud Misc. 609, *Confessio Amantis*
- Tokyo, Senshu University Library, MS 1 (*olim* Schøyen 194, *prior* Sotheby's December 8, 1981, lot 80; December 6, 1988, lot 45), Trevisa's *Polychronicon*

Written by a very similar hand is:

- Princeton, NJ, Princeton University Library, MS Taylor 5, fols. 1r–v and 8r–v, *Confessio*

Jeremy Griffiths identified the two Oxford *Confessio* manuscripts, Bodley 693 and Laud Misc. 609, as having been written by the same hand as the Senshu *Polychronicon* in his description of the *Polychronicon* manuscript for the Sotheby's Sale Catalogues for December 8, 1981, Lot 80 and December 6, 1988, Lot 45.

The characteristics of the handwriting of the Trevisa-Gower scribe begin with its aspect as a textura semiquadrata script: very upright, with letters within a word crammed together and frequent biting curves. Ascenders and descenders are short, so that they do not impinge on the space of lines above or below. There is not quite but almost a bold appearance to the script. There are very short thick approach strokes or capping strokes at the tops of ascenders; and the bases of letters have rounded feet (e.g., Figure 1, line 1, 'believued').

---

[11] Princeton MS Taylor 5 has not been studied in relation to its place among *Confessio Amantis* manuscripts because it was only very briefly examined by Macaulay, and not examined by Doyle and Parkes, writing in 1978. Jeremy Griffiths first brought it to the attention of Gower scholars in his 1983 article, '*Confessio Amantis*: The Poem and its Pictures', pp. 163–78, where he included his opinion that the third hand, writing most of the manuscript, matched that of Doyle and Parkes's Scribe D of the Trinity MS R.3.2 (p. 170, n. 19).

[12] K. Kerby-Fulton and S. Justice, 'Scribe D and the Marketing of Ricardian Literature', in *The Medieval Professional Reader at Work: Evidence from Manuscripts of Chaucer, Langland, Kempe and Gower*, ed. K. Kerby-Fulton and M. Hilmo (Victoria BC, 2001), pp. 217–37.

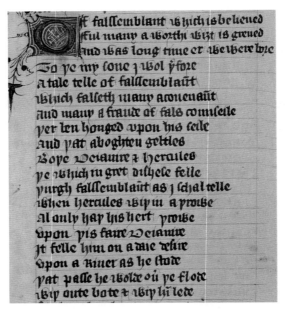

Figure 1.1 Oxford, Bodleian Library, MS Bodley 693, fol. 48vb. Reproduced by the kind permission of the Bodleian Library in accordance with Creative Commons licence CC-BY-NC 4.0. Illustration of the hand of the Trevisa-Gower Scribe.

These establish the aspect of the hand. In terms of letter forms, the scribe uses two-compartment **g** and **a**, unlooped **d**, 8-shaped **s** and long **s** standing on or just below the baseline. The z-shaped **r** is the most frequent form of this letter, though the form resembling modern **r** also occurs; never the anglicana long **r**. The rounded minim-height lobes, or bowls, of many letters are squared, or sometimes hexagonal. These characteristics distinguish the version of textura semiquadrata script used by the scribe. In general, textura handwriting of the late fourteenth and early fifteenth centuries is so formal, and therefore written so similarly by its users, that individual scribes are difficult to distinguish.[13]

In such circumstances, then, we turn to habits that might vary among writers of this script. These habits include punctuation, which for this scribe consists of adding a punctus or punctus with hairline curl creating something like an upside-down comma at the end of some lines (e.g., Figure 2, end of

---

[13] See K. E. Kennedy's description of distinguishing characteristics of a scribe writing textura quadrata, the so-called 'dog-head scribe', in 'Hunting the Corpus *Troilus*: Illuminating Textura', *SAC* 44 (2022), 133–63 (pp. 136–7).

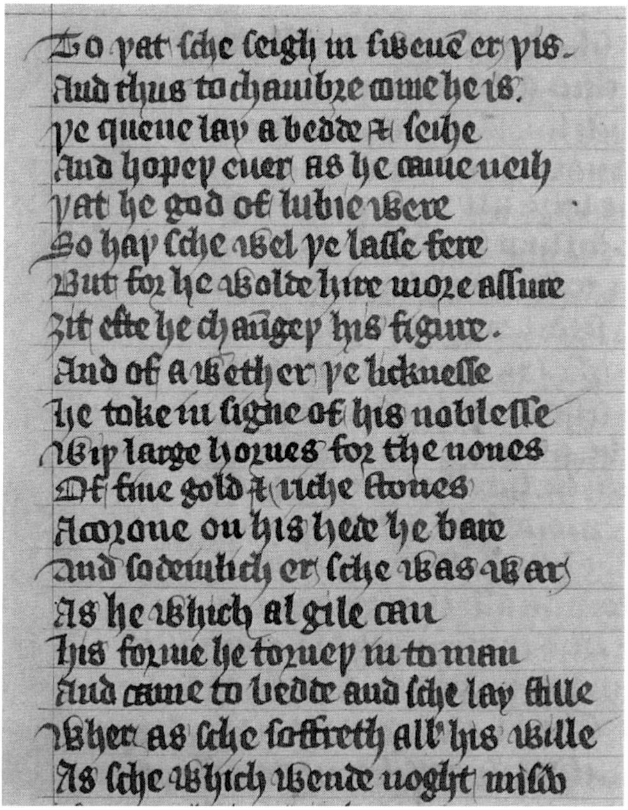
So þat sche seigh in heuene er þis.
And thus to chambre come he is.
Þe queene lay a bedde & seihe
And hopeþ euer as he came neih
Þat he god of lubie were
So haþ sche wel þe lasse fere
But for he wolde hire more assure
Ȝit efte he changeþ his figure.
And of a wether þe likenesse
He toke in signe of his noblesse
Wiþ large hornes for þe nones
Of fine gold & riche stones
Acorone on his heede he bare
And sodeinlich er sche was war
As he which al gile can
His forme he torneþ in to man
And came to bedde and sche lay stille
Wher as sche soffreth all his wille
As sche which wende noght misdo

Figure 1.2 Oxford, Bodleian Library, MS Laud Misc. 609, fol. 122va. Reproduced by the kind permission of the Bodleian Library in accordance with Creative Commons licence CC-BY-NC 4.0. Illustration of the hand of the Trevisa-Gower Scribe.

lines 1, 2 and 8). He occasionally uses a punctus to mark a significant break within a line of verse. He also very often writes a slanting hairline above the letter to dot an **i**. In his writing, heights of minims are sometimes irregular when several occur together, in a series or in **m** (e.g., Figure 1, line 6, 'many'). The anglicana **g** has spikes projecting to the right from both the upper and lower lobes.

These habits occurring together suggest the scribe's handwriting, but there are also a few letter forms that are less common that, when occurring together, point to his hand. First and most distinctive is a **w** with either an approaching curve from the left to a short minim-height first stalk or sometimes just a

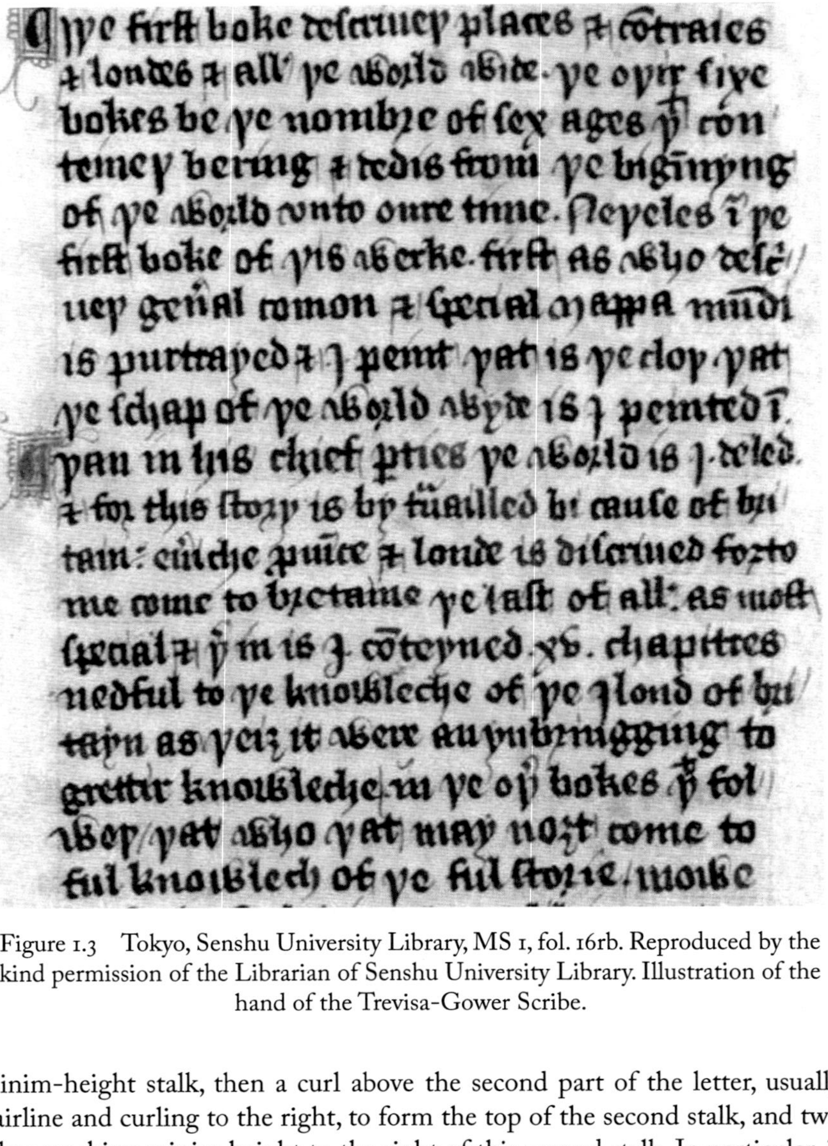

> The first boke descriueþ places & cõtraies
> & londes & all þe worlde abite. þe oþer fiue
> bokes be þe nombre of sex ages þt cõ-
> teineþ bering & redis from þe biginyng
> of þe worlde vnto oure tyme. ¶ey cles ĩ þe
> first boke of þis werke. first as who desc-
> riueþ genāl comon & spēciāl a mappa mūdi
> is purtrayed & I peint þat is þe clop þat
> þe schap of þe worlde abyde is I peinted ī
> þan in his chief pties þe worlde is I teled.
> & for this story is by tuailled bi cause of bri-
> tain: eũiche puīce & londe is discriued for to
> me come to bretaine þe last of all. as most
> specīal & þ m is I cõteyned xv. chapitres
> nedful to þe knowleche of þe ylond of bri-
> tayn as yet; it were aumbrigging to
> grettur knowlech in þe oþ bokes þ fol-
> wen þat who þat may no3t come to
> ful knowlech of þe ful storie, worche

Figure 1.3   Tokyo, Senshu University Library, MS 1, fol. 16rb. Reproduced by the kind permission of the Librarian of Senshu University Library. Illustration of the hand of the Trevisa-Gower Scribe.

minim-height stalk, then a curl above the second part of the letter, usually hairline and curling to the right, to form the top of the second stalk, and two lobes reaching minim height to the right of this second stalk. In particular, it is the tops of the ascenders pointing in different directions that is the distinguishing feature. (See Figure 1, line 3, 'was'; Figure 2, line 6, 'wel'; Figure 3, line 2, 'world'.) Both of scribes 2 and 3 of MS Bodley 902 share this unusual graph with the Trevisa-Gower scribe, as does the scribe of the fragment of *Confessio Amantis* in University College London. Second, the graph of **d** has an unlooped ascender that points at an angle toward the left that, together

The Trevisa-Gower Scribe 15

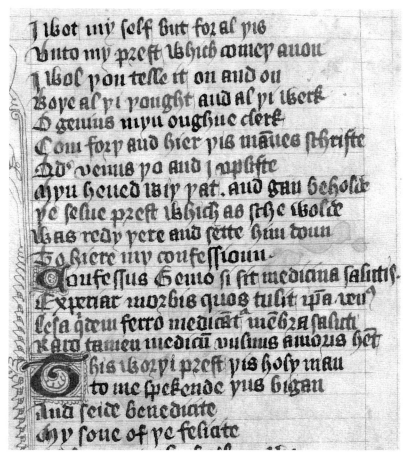

Figure 1.4　Princeton, NJ, Princeton University Library, MS Taylor 5, fol. 8r. Reproduced by the kind permission of the Princeton University Library. Illustration of the hand of the Trevisa-Gower Scribe.

with the squared lobe, often gives it the appearance of an opened box; in some samples the ascender box-top has a slight **s**-bend. (See Figure 1, line 2, 'greved'; Figure 2, line 3, 'bedde'; Figure 3, line 10, 'world'.) Third, the descender of **y** is usually of hairline width, tapering off or curling sharply to the right. (See Figure 1, line 4, 'my'; Figure 2, line 3, 'lay'; Figure 3, line 4, 'biginnyng', but also when not a hairline, line 9, 'wyde'.) Although a few scribes may use some of these distinctive forms, their occurring together in these samples point to a single hand. One of these forms alone might not be sufficient to identify the Trevisa-Gower scribe, which is why I have now questioned my earlier identification of the Bodley 902 and London University College manuscripts as written by his hand.

Each of these details can be found in the hand of the first scribe of Gower's *Confessio Amantis* in Princeton MS Taylor 5, writing only folios 1r–v and 8r–v. (See Figure 4, the **w** in line 3, 'wol'; the **d** in line 3, 'and'; the **g** in line 5, 'oughne'; the **y** in line 5, 'myn'; frequent use of the hairline stroke as a 'dot' above **i**.) The script in the Senshu manuscript and in the two leaves of the Taylor manuscript is slightly less formal than that in the two Bodleian manuscripts, so there are fewer biting curves, and more lateral spread. On the other hand, in the Taylor manuscript, the scribe extends the foot of **f** and long-**s** slightly below the line, whereas in the other manuscripts it sits on the line, and the foot is also straight whereas it curls to the right in the other three manuscripts. These small differences may indicate the same scribe writing less formally or at a different time in his career; or they may be enough to convince you that the leaves of MS Taylor 5 are written by a different scribe. I shall investigate the relationship of the manuscript with others by the Trevisa-Gower Scribe later in this essay.

First, it may be useful to examine the first scribe's part in producing the Taylor manuscript as it stands today. Although his is the first hand one encounters, and so is called 'the first scribe' of this manuscript, his contribution was probably last of the three scribes. This manuscript is mostly written by the prolific Scribe D, or John Marchaunt, whom Kerby-Fulton and Justice credit with organizing or overseeing the re-writing of the outer bifolium of the first quire, which had probably been originally written with a Ricardian introduction in the Prologue.[14] Gower's *Confessio Amantis* survives in three major families of manuscripts, the first and third being based primarily on changes that the author made to lines at the beginning describing Richard II as the instigator of the work to lines instead praising his successor Henry IV, and changing lines at the end to omit lines of Venus in praise of Chaucer and to alter lines at the very end, again in praise of Henry IV.[15] The second family of manuscripts lies between these in terms of its beginnings and endings, but

---

[14] For changes to the Prologue and the ending of Book VIII relating to King Richard II or King Henry IV, see Pearsall and Mooney, *A Descriptive Catalogue*, pp. 2–3. For discussion of the first quire of Princeton MS Taylor 5, see Kerby-Fulton and Justice, 'Scribe D and', pp. 219–20.

[15] As Pearsall and I note in the Introduction to *A Descriptive Catalogue*, pp. 2–3, Macaulay's recensions wrongly imply a chronological order for production of the surviving manuscripts, whereas surviving manuscripts might be copied from earlier or later exemplars, and there were apparently several versions circulating at the same time: the recensions identified by Macaulay are more useful for identifying families of textually-related manuscripts.

also contains lines not found in either of the other two families. Given these three families of manuscripts, one would characterize the first quire of Princeton MS Taylor 5 as having probably been of the first family (or 'recension' as Macaulay called his groupings of manuscripts), and the contribution of the Trevisa-Gower Scribe, if it was him, was to change the prologue from a first recension manuscript to a third recension one.

Kerby-Fulton and Justice argue that Scribe D, Marchaunt, had acquired or was given the first quire of a text of the *Confessio* and was commissioned to write the remainder of the text to append to this one quire. Either he or his patron also 'stripped off the first [outer] bifolium to send to the man [they were] calling Scribe 1'.[16] They argue that the bifolium was re-written in order to add the beautiful miniature of the man of precious metals at the beginning of the text,[17] but it seems more likely that it was sent to be re-written to change from a Ricardian to a Lancastrian Prologue, since the miniature takes up thirteen lines of the first column. Therefore, its addition to a quire that had not had a miniature would have thrown off the lineation in the rest of the quire, already written by the second scribe of the manuscript as it now stands. This first quire of eight leaves is missing its second and third leaves, so as it stands at present only six of its leaves survive. Of these, folios 1 and 8 are written by the hand very similar to that of the Trevisa-Gower Scribe, while 2–3 are missing and 4–7 are written by the second hand, a contemporary scribe, whose contribution to the manuscript came first (see Figure 5). The missing text of folios 2–3v comprises 356 lines of English (Prol. 154–509) and sixteen lines of Latin (ten after Prol.192 and six after Prol.498), a total of 372 lines. The first quire of Taylor 5 as it survives is written throughout with 46 lines per column, except folio 7r–v written with 47 lines per column. It is likely that folio 2 also had 47 lines per column, as it would be the other half of the bifolium with folio 7, and that folio 3 had 46 lines per column, for a total exactly matching the missing text, 372 lines.[18] Therefore, if the bifolium was only replaced to add a miniature at the beginning, the line-count would be thirteen lines off, but it is not: it matches exactly the pattern of 46 lines per column except the bifolium 2 and 7, with 47 lines per column. The original first quire, probably entirely written by the second scribe, must have included space of thirteen lines for a miniature, so the only reason for re-writing the bifolium would have been to change the Prologue to the new version favouring Henry IV.

[16] Kerby-Fulton and Justice, 'Scribe D and', p. 220.
[17] Kerby-Fulton and Justice, 'Scribe D and', p. 220.
[18] I thank Peter Nicholson for suggesting this to me (personal communication, July 2021).

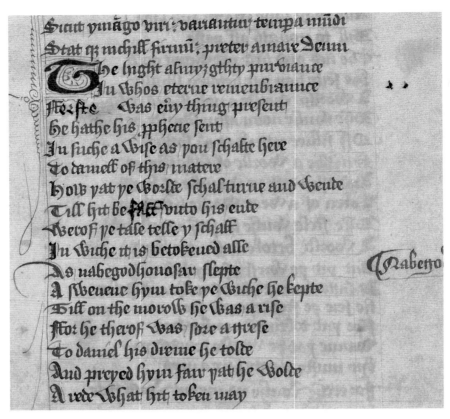

Figure 1.5 Princeton, NJ, Princeton University Library, MS Taylor 5, fol. 4r. Reproduced by the kind permission of the Princeton University Library. Illustration of the hand of the second scribe of the manuscript, whose work survives on folios 4–7 of the first quire.

In MS Taylor 5, the miniature of Nebuchadnezzar's dream of the man of precious metals appears at the top of the first column of folio 1r, and there is also a historiated initial and border below in that column at the beginning of the English text, so it is possible that the scribe of folios 1 and 8 worked in the artist's workshop, adding text to leaves illustrated by the limners.[19] The second hand, writing folios 4–7 of this first quire, wrote a slightly less formal script than our scribe, including some influence from secretary (see Figure 5). This second scribe apparently applied his own flourishing to the initial letters of his quire, because it differs in style from that used in the rest of the manuscript;

[19] Kerby-Fulton and Justice, 'Scribe D and', p. 220, also make this suggestion.

but folios 1 and 8 are flourished in a style similar to the remainder of the manuscript, folios 9 to 193v, written by John Marchaunt. It may be that both the scribe of folios 1 and 8 or the limner's shop and the premises where John Marchaunt worked used the same or a very similar style of flourishing, or it may be that the illuminated bifolium was returned to the milieu of John Marchaunt where its flourishing was added by the same hand as had done folios 9 to 193v. Either way, the flourishing on folios 1 and 8 is a tie to Marchaunt, who wrote the remainder of the manuscript.[20]

This manuscript, Princeton MS Taylor 5, therefore illustrates a manuscript being updated with a new Prologue to appeal to an audience more sympathetic to Henry Earl of Derby, Duke of Lancaster and then Henry IV, King of England. The first quire, originally written by the second scribe (whose work survives only on folios 4–7), must have recorded the earlier, Ricardian form of the Prologue. Until now Oxford, Bodleian Library, MS Fairfax 3, with its erasures and re-written text, has been thought to be the only manuscript to illustrate this early state of the text of *Confessio Amantis* where a Ricardian Prologue was replaced by a Lancastrian one.

We must now consider the evidence for dating the addition of the miniature and historiated initial on folio 1 to get a date for the revisions to the outer bifolium of this first quire. Kathleen Scott's dating of the two illustrations on folio 1 recto confirms that the first leaf written by our scribe was very early among *Confessio* manuscripts, between 1395 and 1410. She writes that the haircuts of the men illustrated on folio 1r, 'short or half-way up the head', are characteristic of the late fourteenth century, and in the left border 'it is notable that the stem of the decoration begins inside the frame: this is a fourteenth-century usage'.[21] Furthermore, she argues that the artist was trained in the fourteenth century, and the artwork of three important fourteenth-century manuscripts 'had an effect on his work' in that he adopted some of their traits in illustrating the first folio of Taylor 5. In the Sherborne Missal (Alnwick, Alnwick Castle, MS 82), dated by Scott between 1396 and 1407, 'we find a figure rendered outside of an important illustration on a column, as in Taylor 5, and the picture [is] enclosed by a decorative frame of scrollwork'.[22] The second influencing manuscript is the Lovell Lectionary (London, British

---

[20] Kerby-Fulton and Justice, 'Scribe D and', pp. 219–21, argue for his overseeing the rewriting of the first quire, pointing to signs of his marginal corrections to the text written by the second hand on fols. 4–7.
[21] K. L. Scott, personal communication, October 2021.
[22] See K. L. Scott, *Later Gothic Manuscripts 1390–1490*, in *A Survey of Manuscripts Illuminated in the British Isles*, gen. ed. J. J. G. Alexander, 2 vols (London, 1996), numbers 45, 48, 50, 51.

Library, MS Harley 7026), which she dates also to between 1396 and 1407: 'Again, a column or columns with figures have been placed outside of the miniature'.[23] The third manuscript, 'equally important', is Oxford, Bodleian Library, MS Bodley 264, containing *Alexander and Dindimus* and Marco Polo, *Le Livres du Graunt Caan*, which Scott dates *c*. 1400–10: '[h]ere slender architectural frames with a capital enclose long curled strands of scrollwork',[24] and Scott notes, 'These elegant treatments of design also occur in Taylor 5 (almost to looking out of place!)'. She concludes that '[i]t seems as if the artist was trying to upgrade his work by imitating the remarkable decoration of the[se] three manuscripts'.[25]

The illuminated border on folio 1 also suggests an early date, toward the end of the period Scott assigns to the miniatures, around 1410, since it features spikey-lobed acanthus leaves wrapped around the bar of the bar-border, and sprays originating from the tips of these acanthus leaves, similar to borders in London, British Library, MS Arundel 38 of Hoccleve's *Regiment of Princes* which Scott dates to 1410–13.[26] The miniature artist may have been trained in the fourteenth century and influenced by fourteenth-century styles while the border artist, probably a younger artist in the same atelier, was more up-to-date in creating the borders.

The manuscript's early date is also suggested by its ties with other manuscripts of the *Confessio* whose early date has already been established. Princeton MS Taylor 5 shares the positioning of the miniature of Nebuchadnezzar's dream of the man of precious metals at the beginning of the Prologue with Oxford, Bodleian Library, MS Fairfax 3; London, British Library, MS Harley 3869 and San Marino, CA, Huntington Library MS EL 26.A.17 (most manuscripts with illustrations place this image near the description of the dream in the Prologue, around line 594).[27] Fairfax 3 and the Huntington manuscript (nicknamed 'Stafford') are considered the two earliest surviving manuscripts of the *Confessio*, standing at the heads of two families of manuscripts, Macaulay's second and third recensions, and Harley 3869 is copied from Fairfax.

The question of dating also depends upon the changing of the Prologue of *Confessio Amantis* from the Ricardian to the Lancastrian version of the

---

[23] Scott, *LGM*, number 9, illustrations 59, 60.

[24] Scott, *LGM*, illustrations 62, 65.

[25] Scott, personal communication, November 2021.

[26] See K. L. Scott, *Dated and Datable English Manuscript Borders, c. 1395–1499* (London, 2002), p. 42, plate VIII. I thank Joel Fredell for drawing my attention to these details.

[27] See also J. Fredell, *Fictions of Witness in the Confessio Amantis* (Cham, 2023), pp. 15–17.

Prologue. Offering detailed evidence from manuscripts of the *Confessio*, Terry Jones concluded that 'we simply have no reliable evidence that Gower rededicated the *Confessio Amantis* before Henry's usurpation'.[28] The original first quire of Taylor 5 may have been written before 1399 but the outer bifolium with changed dedication to Henry, folios 1 and 8, would most likely date from after Henry had become king in late 1399. This date, combined with the dating on the basis of the artwork on folio 1ra, shows that the revision to folios 1 and 8 of this manuscript would have been executed around 1407–10, in other words, during Gower's lifetime or shortly after his death in 1408.

Nevertheless, evidence for the relative dating of the first quire and the rest of the manuscript is mixed. Borders at the beginning of Books II and IV–VIII in the main portion of the manuscript (fols. 9–193v) are in a style typical of the first decade of the fifteenth century, of simpler design and with kidney-shaped leaves and white highlighting.[29] The style of the flourishing on folios 4–7 written by the second scribe is of an earlier style to that on folios 1 and 8 and folios from 9 onwards. All in all, one could argue from the decoration and illustration that the first quire in its original state was the earliest portion of the manuscript, while the revised outer bifolium of that first quire and the bulk of the manuscript written by Scribe D, Marchaunt, are of approximately the same date, still in the first decade of the fifteenth century, possibly with Marchaunt's completion of the text slightly antedating the change to folios 1 and 8. Any way you look at it, Taylor 5, including Marchaunt's completion of the text and the first scribe's alteration of the beginning, must have been a very early manuscript of the *Confessio Amantis*.[30]

As Kerby-Fulton and Justice argue, either John Marchaunt or the patron who commissioned him to complete the text of *Confessio Amantis* from a single first quire must be responsible for either employing the first scribe directly to rewrite the outer bifolium, or providing the limner with an exemplar from which the scribe, working for the limner, could write the revised pages.[31] Was

[28] T. Jones, 'Did John Gower Rededicate his *Confessio Amantis* before Henry IV's Usurpation?', in *Middle English Texts in Transition: A Festschrift dedicated to Toshiyuki Takamiya on his 70th Birthday*, ed. S. Horobin and L. Mooney (York, 2014), pp. 40–74 (p. 56).

[29] I thank Joel Fredell for pointing out these details to me.

[30] See also L. Mooney, 'The Production of Trinity College, Cambridge, MS R.3.2 Revisited', *Journal of the Early Book Society* 24 (2021), 11–35, arguing that Trinity MS R.3.2 was copied directly from Taylor 5, both being written at the same time.

[31] Kerby-Fulton and Justice, 'Scribe D and', p. 220, argue that it was Scribe D who was responsible for this, but it could equally have been the person who commissioned his work on the manuscript who hired the Trevisa-Gower Scribe and the limner to convert folios 1 and 8 to the new-style Prologue.

the scribe of folios 1 and 8 an independent scrivener or text-writer, or was he employed in a limner's shop? Or in what way do relationships between this manuscript and others establish whether the scribe was the Trevisa-Gower Scribe or not?

The other three manuscripts now attributed to the Trevisa-Gower Scribe may offer clues to his dates and place of work. Oxford, Bodleian Library, MS Bodley 693, a copy of Gower's *Confessio Amantis*, was written entirely by the hand of the Trevisa-Gower Scribe. In his description of the manuscript, G. C. Macaulay dates this manuscript to the first quarter of the fifteenth century, and classifies it as one of the group of manuscripts he calls 'First Recension, Unrevised' (Ic).[32] In terms of illustration, it includes a small illustration of the man of precious metals from Nebuchadnezzar's dream, squeezed into space of eight lines after Prologue, line 594, alongside the Latin gloss that is normal at this position; and it also includes inside an initial letter 'T' after I.202 on folio 8vb, an illustration of the lover confessing to Genius.[33] On folio 1ra, at the very beginning of the poem, inside the initial 'T' of the Latin text, a coat of arms has been added later, with the Garter around it and a crest in the margin beside it, pointing towards ownership by Charles Brandon, Duke of Suffolk, *c.* 1484–1545, who became a Knight of the Garter in 1513. The manuscript later belonged to James I, as seen by his arms stamped on the cover, and was later owned by Dr John King, Dean of Christ Church, 1605–11, who left it to the Bodleian.[34] The illuminated bar borders are in the style of the Hermann Scheerre school of artists, according to Spriggs, and are close to those of two other copies of the *Confessio*, Bodley 294 and Bodley 902,[35] the former written entirely by Scribe D, Marchaunt, and the latter having the first two quires, fols. 1–16v, written by him. These three manuscripts show that both Marchaunt and the Trevisa-Gower Scribe (whether directly or through their patrons) had their manuscripts decorated by the same artists.

The second manuscript in my list of works copied by the Trevisa-Gower Scribe is another copy of the *Confessio Amantis*, Oxford, Bodleian Library, MS

---

[32] Macaulay, *The English Works of John Gower*, I, cxlix–cl. There is a good summary of Macaulay's recensions in the Introduction to Pearsall and Mooney, *A Descriptive Catalogue*, pp. 2–3.

[33] See G. M. Spriggs, 'Unnoticed Bodleian Manuscripts illuminated by Herman Scheerre and his School', *Bodleian Library Record 7*, No. 4 (1964), pp. 193–203 (see pp. 198–9, plates XIIc, XIId); and S. Drimmer, *The Art of Allusion: Illuminators and the Making of English Literature, 1403–1476* (Philadelphia, 2019), p. 91; colour plate 9 illustrates the lover and Genius (fol. 8v).

[34] Pearsall and Mooney, *A Descriptive Catalogue*, p. 186, give references to several scholars who have written on these additions.

[35] Spriggs, 'Unnoticed Bodleian Manuscripts', p. 194.

Laud Misc. 609, which Macaulay also dates to the first quarter of the fifteenth century, and classifies as 'First Recension, Unrevised' (Ic), like Bodley 693. Also like Bodley 693, it contains two illustrations, at the same positions in the text but with slight differences. The miniature after Prol.595 illustrates both king Nebuchadnezzar lying in bed and the man of precious metals appearing to him, and the image of the Lover confessing to Genius after I.202 is a ten-line miniature rather than being squeezed inside a historiated initial. Spriggs attributed the illustration of this manuscript to the Scheerre workshop, but Kathleen Scott attributes the miniatures to the Pentecost Master of the Neville Hours at Berkeley Castle.[36] The borders are very much in the style of Scheerre, however.

The third manuscript by the Trevisa-Gower Scribe preserves the text of Trevisa's translation of Ranulph Higden's *Polychronicon*, now Tokyo, Senshu University Library, MS 1 (*olim* Schøyen 194), which Jeremy Griffiths dated to *c*. 1420.[37] I have outlined the characteristics of the script above, which match those of the Senshu manuscript scribe (see references to Figure 3). As in the first quire of the Taylor 5 manuscript, the text in the Senshu manuscript begins (fol. 15r) with a historiated initial depicting the author, in this case Ranulph Higden, portrayed in the black robe of a Benedictine monk. The only other illustration in the huge volume is a drawing of two versions of Noah's ark, on folio 55r, that often appears at this place in manuscripts of *Polychronicon* alongside the debate in the text about the style of the ark. The illuminated borders of this manuscript are (once again) attributed to the workshop of Hermann Scheerre.[38] The text of this copy, entirely written by the Trevisa-Gower Scribe, is closely related to the copies in London, British Library, MS Additional 24194; Cambridge, St John's College, MS 204 and Princeton, Princeton University Library, MS Garrett 151, all three written by Scribe Delta and dated to the first quarter of the fifteenth century, and all four were illustrated in Scheerre's workshop. The same illuminator is also responsible for the borders in a copy of Trevisa's translation of Bartholomeus Anglicus's *De proprietatibus*

---

[36] See Macaulay, *The English Works of John Gower*, I, cxlix and Pearsall and Mooney, *A Descriptive Catalogue*, pp. 208–9 for details of the recension and illustration, and Scott, *LGM*, II, 94 for attribution to the Pentecost Master.

[37] See Sotheby's Sale Catalogues, December 8, 1981, Lot 80 and December 6, 1988, Lot 45.

[38] Spriggs, 'Unnoticed Bodleian Manuscripts', pp. 193–203. For further details of this and the following attributions and comparisons, see also L. R. Mooney, 'Introduction', in Ranulph Higden translated by John Trevisa, *Polychronicon: Tokyo, Senshu University Library, MS 1*, a facsimile produced under the direction of Tomonori Matsushita (Tokyo, 2010), pp. v–viii; and R. Hanna III, 'Sir Thomas Berkeley and his Patronage', *Speculum* 64 (1989), 878–916.

rerum, London, British Library, MS Additional 27944, for which the table of contents (fols. 2–7v) and second half of the text (fols. 196rb, line 9, to the end on 335v) were written by Scribe D, John Marchaunt. Ralph Hanna has suggested that the multiple copies of Trevisa's translations produced in London, by a small number of scribes including Scribe D, Scribe Delta and the Trevisa-Gower Scribe, and all decorated in the workshop of Hermann Scheerre, seems a deliberate project to distribute high-quality copies of Trevisa's works, perhaps instigated by Sir Thomas Berkeley, Trevisa's patron.[39]

A similar argument can be made for one family of early manuscripts of Gower's *Confessio Amantis*. The two manuscripts entirely written by the Trevisa-Gower Scribe are closely related textually, and they are also closely related to other manuscripts of Gower's *Confessio* written by Scribe D (John Marchaunt) and Scribe Delta. Bodleian Library, MSS Bodley 693 and Laud Misc. 609, written by the Trevisa-Gower Scribe, present the text of that family of manuscripts Macaulay called 'First Recension, Unrevised'. As the name he assigns to this family suggests, Macaulay believed that these manuscripts preserved the earliest version of the text. Besides the two manuscripts written by the Trevisa-Gower Scribe, both of Macaulay's 'First Recension, Unrevised' family, four other manuscripts of the *Confessio Amantis* that fit Macaulay's classification as 'First Recension, Unrevised' – London, British Library, MS Egerton 1991; Oxford, Christ Church, MS 148; Oxford, Corpus Christi College, MS 67 and New York, Columbia University Library, MS Plimpton 265 – were copied by Scribe D, John Marchaunt, while a seventh of this family, London, British Library, Royal 18 C.xxii, was copied by Scribe Delta. As with the production of Trevisa's works by a small group of London scribes, we find in the early manuscripts of Macaulay's 'First Recension, Unrevised' classification a group of manuscripts of related texts of the *Confessio Amantis* copied by the same small group of scribes, Scribe D (John Marchaunt), Scribe Delta and the Trevisa-Gower Scribe, but in this case there is also a fourth scribe involved: John Carpenter, Common Clerk of the City of London 1417–37.[40] Carpenter's manuscripts of the *Confessio*, Cambridge, University Library, MS Dd.8.19 and Philadelphia, The Rosenbach, MS 1083/29, also preserve

---

[39] Hanna, 'Sir Thomas Berkeley', pp. 909–12.
[40] See Mooney and Stubbs, *Scribes and the City*, pp. 86–106 for Carpenter as scribe of three literary manuscripts, Cambridge, University Library, MS Dd.8.19 (*Confessio*); Philadelphia, The Rosenbach, MS 1083/29 (*Confessio*) and New York, Morgan Library and Museum, MS M.817 (Chaucer, *Troilus and Criseyde*). While doubting the other attributions, L. Warner, *Chaucer's Scribes: London Textual Production 1384–1432* (Cambridge, 2018), pp. 108–11, accepted that the Cambridge MS was written by Carpenter. For dating, see Pearsall and Mooney, *A Descriptive Catalogue*, p. 308.

Macaulay's 'First Recension, Unrevised' version of the text. The second of these, the one in Philadelphia, includes an author portrait in a historiated initial at the beginning of the text. Jeremy Griffiths noted that among manuscripts of the *Confessio* only Princeton, MS Taylor 5 and Philadelphia, The Rosenbach, MS 1083/29 have a picture of the author in the initial to the Prologue at line 1, though he had not identified the Trevisa-Gower Scribe as responsible for writing folios 1 and 8 of Princeton MS Taylor 5 nor John Carpenter as having written the Rosenbach copy of the *Confessio*.[41] In fact these two are the only manuscripts of the *Confessio* to have a stand-alone image of the author, and in the positioning within the first initial they are parallel with the portrait of Ranulph Higden in the historiated initial at the beginning of the Trevisa-Gower Scribe's copy of *Polychronicon* now known as Senshu University MS 1. These details connect the manuscripts by John Carpenter to the others copied by Marchaunt, Delta and the Trevisa-Gower Scribe.

Manuscripts of Macaulay's 'First Recension, Unrevised' (Ic), written before 1425:[42]

- Cambridge, University Library, MS Dd.8.19 (Ic) John Carpenter
- London, British Library, MS Egerton 1991 (Ic) Scribe D (John Marchaunt)
- London, British Library, MS Royal 18 C.xxii (Ic) Scribe Delta
- New York, Columbia University, MS Plimpton 265 (Ic) Scribe D (John Marchaunt)[43]
- Oxford, Bodleian Library, MS Bodley 693 (Ic) Trevisa-Gower
- Oxford, Bodleian Library, MS Laud Misc. 609 (Ic) Trevisa-Gower
- Oxford, Christ Church, MS 148 (Ic) Scribe D (John Marchaunt)[44]
- Oxford, Corpus Christi College, MS 67 (Ic) Scribe D (John Marchaunt)

---

[41] Griffiths, '*Confessio Amantis*: The Poem and its Pictures', pp. 163, 176–77.

[42] Others in this family written later are London, College of Arms, MS Arundel 45 (mid-fifteenth century); Oxford, Bodleian Library, MS Arch. Selden B.11 (mid- to third quarter fifteenth century); Oxford, Bodleian Library, MS Ashmole 35 (mid- to third quarter fifteenth century) and Chicago, Newberry Library, MS +33.5 (second half fifteenth century).

[43] Not known to Macaulay but classed as Ic by J. H. Fisher, *John Gower: Moral Philosopher and Friend of Chaucer* (New York, 1964), Appendix A, p. 305.

[44] Not known to Macaulay but classed as Ic by Doyle and Parkes, 'Production of Copies', p. 195, n. 76.

- Philadelphia, The Rosenbach, MS 1083/29 (Ic) John Carpenter
- New York, Morgan Library and Museum, MS M.690 (Ic) very early fifteenth century, written by two unidentified scribes[45]
- Cambridge, Pembroke College, MS 307 (Ic) written *c*. 1420–30 by the 'Petworth Scribe' who was a clerk of the Skinners' Company of London)[46]

Since the manuscripts thus far identified as being written by the Trevisa-Gower Scribe fit this closely-knit group, the argument for his hand being that of two leaves in Princeton MS Taylor 5 is somewhat compromised. However, his small contribution to the manuscript, only two leaves recording Prol.1–153 and Book I.146–317, might have originated in a second or third recension exemplar supplied by the limner, supervisor or Marchaunt.[47] While we can fit Marchaunt with the group that copied most of the manuscripts of the 'First Recension, Unrevised' family, he also wrote one complete manuscript of the second recension, Oxford, Bodleian Library, MS Bodley 294, and contributed to the Cambridge, Trinity College, MS R.3.2 manuscript of the *Confessio*, a second recension manuscript which I have argued was copied directly from Taylor 5, with Marchaunt organizing the work of the other four scribes.[48] The Trevisa-Gower Scribe might have been just as open to copying varying versions of Gower's text. While the argument is nevertheless weakened by the class of the manuscript to which he contributed in this case, the argument from likeness of script remains quite strong.

In the two *Confessio Amantis* manuscripts clearly written by the Trevisa-Gower Scribe, he clearly fits with this small group of London scribes copying almost all of the early manuscripts of one version of Gower's *Confessio Amantis*, three of whom copied almost all of the earliest manuscripts of John

---

[45] Not known to Macaulay but classed as Ic by Fisher, *John Gower*, Appendix, p. 305.

[46] See J. Griffiths, 'Thomas Hingham, Monk of Bury and the Macro Plays Manuscript', *English Manuscript Studies* 5 (1995), 214–19 (p. 214).

[47] Macaulay, *The English Works of John Gower*, I, clvi. Macaulay apparently examined the manuscript only briefly when it was still in the Phillipps collection at Cheltenham, Thirlestaine House, MS 8192. He notes that the text of Taylor 5 is close to that of British Library, MS Additional 12043, but cites only Prol.14, 22, 115 and 127, in other words, lines written by the scribe of folios 1 and 8. The manuscripts of the second recension might have either form of the Prologue and end of Book VIII but differ from Recensions I and III in that they introduce new lines in Books V and VII and move around lines in Book VI. See Macaulay, *The English Works of John Gower*, I, cxxviii–cxxix and Pearsall and Mooney, *A Descriptive Catalogue*, p. 2.

[48] See Mooney, 'The Production of Trinity College, Cambridge, MS R.3.2 Revisited'.

Trevisa's works. Kerby-Fulton and Justice noted that works of Gower and Trevisa dominate the texts of surviving manuscripts attributed to the hands of Scribes D and Delta (twelve of seventeen manuscripts);[49] but if we add to these the manuscripts by the Trevisa-Gower Scribe (two more *Confessio Amantis* texts and one more *Polychronicon*), and those of John Carpenter (two more *Confessio Amantis* plus one of Chaucer's *Troilus and Criseyde*), the dominance becomes more pronounced still. Furthermore, Kerby-Fulton and Justice had not pointed out the dominance of this group in copying a single early version of the *Confessio Amantis*, Macaulay's 'First Recension, Unrevised' family of manuscripts. As Hanna said of the production of early manuscripts of high quality of John Trevisa's works,[50] we might conclude that this same small group of scribes (plus John Carpenter) were involved similarly in a deliberate strategy to produce very high-quality copies of the *Confessio Amantis* of John Gower at the beginning of the fifteenth century.

---

[49] Kerby-Fulton and Justice, 'Scribe D and', p. 223.
[50] Hanna, 'Sir Thomas Berkeley', p. 910.

2

Telling Tails:
Pursuing the Trail of the Minstrel-Scribe in Manuscripts of *Sir Isumbras*

ANDREW W. KLEIN

One of the funniest jokes in all of Chaucer's *Canterbury Tales* is the genre parody of *Sir Thopas*.[1] Most readers today recognize the banal tropes for what they are, and Chaucer's vicious yet ironic self-parody in having himself attempt to tell, badly, a romance that is then interrupted in exasperation by the host of the company is a self-deprecating touch that emphasizes the parody itself, not just of popular stories but also of story-tellers. Part of the parody's humour derives from its form: standard tail-rhyme stanzas, long identified as a particularly English vehicle for medieval romance.[2] Less consistently discussed is how much the poem's parody relies on layout – *mise-en-page* – in some of the best manuscripts of the *Canterbury Tales* like Aberystwyth, National Library of Wales, MS Peniarth 392 D ('Hengwrt') or San Marino, CA, Huntington Library, MS EL 26.C.9 ('Ellesmere'); this aspect of the parody has received more attention occasionally,[3] but taking layout's contribution to the parody

---

[1] I have Kathryn Kerby-Fulton to thank for first introducing me, at the time a first-year graduate student at the University of Notre Dame, to the world of manuscript studies and to the Ellesmere manuscript of the *Canterbury Tales* in particular. This essay takes much of its inspiration from what Kathryn has taught me over the years since.

[2] The foundational study of tail-rhyme in English is R. Purdie, *Anglicising Romance* (Cambridge, 2008). The idea that 'the tail-rhyme *romance* is, as far as we know, unique to Middle English' is central to her study (p. 1).

[3] See especially R. Purdie, 'Implications of Manuscript Layout in Chaucer's *Tale of Sir Thopas*', *Forum for Modern Language Studies* 41.3 (2005), 263–74 and *Anglicising Romance*, pp. 66–78; J. Brantley, 'Reading the Forms of *Sir Thopas*', *ChR* 47.4 (2013), 416–38; K. Kerby-Fulton and A. W. Klein, 'Rhymed Alliterative Verse in *Mise en page* Transition: Two Case Studies in English Poetic Hybridity', in *The Medieval Literary: Beyond Form*, ed. C. Sanok and R. J. Meyer-Lee (Cambridge, 2018), pp. 87–118; but see also J. Tschann, 'The Layout of *Sir Thopas* in the Ellesmere,

seriously demands that we consider afresh the implications of scribes' uses of *mise-en-page*. In some of the better-known manuscripts of the *Canterbury Tales*, *Sir Thopas* displays a particular layout of the tail-rhyme stanza that sets the rhyming tails, every third line of the six-line stanzas (*aabccb*), to the right in what Rhiannon Purdie has helpfully described as the 'graphic tail rhyme'.[4] Despite being a distinct part of Chaucer's parody, the layout appears in no modern editions, or for that matter, in editions of other poems that exist in graphic tail-rhyme in their manuscripts. Editors seem to have found the untidy layout of the graphic tail-rhyme less preferable than a regular columnar presentation of text.

Chaucer's ridicule of the style may well have contributed to its disappearance, but it also suggests the prominence of the graphic tail rhyme for the medieval scribe through satirical example. Regardless of how niche the joke is, there needs to be a formal pattern that has gained broad acceptance for any parody to work. We ought to consider the implications of the particular form of *Sir Thopas* in its manuscripts; even if the number of *Thopas* manuscripts with this layout are relatively few, and even if Chaucer did not have a hand in determining the layout, the graphic tail-rhyme form was widely recognized.[5] Although the variety of generic attributes being mocked does not help us make sense of the baggy term 'romance', an irresolvable generic category, it does provide a rare positive, contemporary set of criteria for what we now call 'tail-rhyme romance' that includes the graphic tail-rhyme in its most elaborate manuscripts.

Of course, some medieval copyists experimented with and even eschewed the form, but in what follows, I argue that modern erasure of the form where we find it has been a mistake. Rather than an example of poor scribal planning, the graphic tail-rhyme form deeply connects to and supports the signifying, story-telling power of its poems; in this essay, I wish to point out particularly that scribes contribute to a poem's meaning by suggesting a positionality for the reader who, by voicing a narrative, adopts the role of storyteller. By analyzing the *mise-en-page* of the romance *Sir Isumbras* across manuscripts and early printed editions, I suggest that medieval scribes saw the artistic potential of the graphic tail-rhyme form, and that we can see evidence for scribes appreciating the form in the manuscripts containing *Isumbras*, a tail-rhyme romance that is particularly well-attested. Reading *Isumbras* in its manuscript context

---

Hengwrt, Cambridge Dd.4.24 and Cambridge Gg.4.27 Manuscripts', *ChR* 20 (1985), 1–13.

[4] Purdie, *Anglicising Romance*, p. 7.
[5] See Purdie, 'Implications of Manuscript Layout'; few Chaucer manuscripts and only one printing (Wynkyn de Worde's) use the graphic layout.

can subsequently inform our sense of the orality, aurality and even musicality of this verse form, so that the performative suggestiveness and potential interpretive benefits of layout provide compelling evidence that we should take the graphic tail-rhyme seriously as a literary device. This essay argues that graphic tail-rhyme romances represent medieval scribes' artistic attempts to signify the orality and aurality of a text and calls for modern editors to consider restoring the dynamism of the *mise-en-page* of popular medieval poetry.

The problem with the graphic tail-rhyme form, in particular the confusion in reading and delivery that it causes, might indicate that it was an ill-suited form for any poetry. Yet, as Purdie observes, the persistent recurrent discovery of the form 'indicates the force of the tradition behind it: this is clearly what tail-rhyme poetry was supposed to look like in manuscript, even if it often did not in practice'.[6] The form's persistence raises a simple question: Why? What benefit is there, when there are so many drawbacks to this layout? Other commentators of *Sir Thopas* have notably argued for the benefits of restoring the poem in our modern editions to its medieval *mise-en-page*, observing that we 'miss some of the fun' or a good portion of the joke from Chaucer by editing it out.[7] While I whole-heartedly endorse this position, viewing the graphic tail-rhyme simply as a means of understanding a good joke stops short of what we might gain by restoring the graphic layout. There is evidence that original scribes of *non*-satirical romances valued the graphic layout, and we might discover some of the benefits and appropriateness of the form by considering tail-rhyme romances that unironically profit from the graphic layout.

One benefit of the form implied by certain instances of *Sir Isumbras*'s reception is that it reflects the continuation of oral delivery and the aural culture of early romance and minstrel stylings amidst the rising program to establish a higher 'literary' value for English literature that was being advanced by the likes of Chaucer. There is little doubt among scholars of Middle English romance at this point that the tail-rhyme romance was performed. In her extensive assessment of the metrical qualities of the tail-rhyme romance, Linda Marie Zaerr identifies the tail-rhyme as the 'best evidence for musical performance of Middle English Romance'.[8] Ad Putter has recently concluded, using tail-rhyme as his primary test case, that Middle English romance exhibits convincing internal and external signs that it was sung.[9] Authors composed

---

[6] Purdie, *Anglicising Romance*, p. 265.
[7] Tschann, 'Layout of *Sir Thopas*', p. 10.
[8] L. M. Zaerr, *Performance and the Middle English Romance* (Cambridge, 2012), p. 128.
[9] See A. Putter, 'The Singing of Middle English Romance: Stanza Forms and *Contrafacta*', in *The Transmission of Medieval Romance: Metres, Manuscripts and Early*

and scribes copied with this eventual mode of delivery in mind; this was an issue of authorial and scribal creation that attracted persistent negotiating and renegotiating on the page. Joyce Coleman argues that the fourteenth century, a time most ripe for the tail-rhyme romance, was a 'crucial period … of growing sophistication of *both* private and public reading'.[10] Coleman demonstrates that the primary modality of literary engagement in late medieval England was reading aloud in a group setting – what she terms 'aurality'. This situation is unique from a typically imagined 'oral' culture:

> Although writing for performance, the author had time to compose the text at his own pace and alone, knowing that it would be preserved in written form and that this written form would visibly dominate the group experience, in a way that no oral or memorial author's text could do. The audience's awareness of the book before them entailed an increased awareness of the fixity and authority of the text, and of the author's role as mediator of the traditions that text represented.[11]

To this description, I wish to add that scribal participation is a key component of the development of the aural culture Coleman outlines. In this essay, I draw attention to the variety of ways in which scribes deployed the power of *mise-en-page* to participate in the oral/aural reading environment of their texts. Keeping in mind that, as Daniel Sawyer has observed, only with extreme caution should particular manuscripts be read as definitive 'authoritative rulings', the manuscript and print history of *Isumbras* does indicate different schools of thought in *what* exactly these poems represented.[12] And in fact we ought

---

Prints, ed. A. Putter and J. A. Jefferson (Cambridge, 2018), pp. 69–90, who concludes: 'There is strong external evidence for the musical performance of medieval romances by minstrels, and this evidence is consistent with the internal evidence of the romances themselves. A number of these romances show signs of having been transmitted from memory, and some … call themselves songs. Although these "minstrel tags" are often dismissed as literary conventions, the affinity of medieval romances with medieval song is borne out by the striking fact that they use the same stanza forms' (p. 90). K. Reichl, 'Comparative Notes on the Performance of Middle English Popular Romance', *Western Folklore* 62.1–2 (2003), 63–81, following a different tack that uses Turkish traditions of epic poetry as a comparison, also argues that medieval English romances were sung. Reichl focuses on works called 'gestes' but makes the case for romance orality more generally throughout.

[10] J. Coleman, *Public Reading and the Reading Public in Late Medieval England and France* (Cambridge, 1996), p. 2.

[11] Coleman, *Public Reading*, p. 28.

[12] As D. Sawyer, *Reading English Verse in Manuscript, c. 1350–c. 1500* (Oxford, 2020), p. 156, explains, 'Taking past reading seriously entails imagining past readers

not look to any one version of *Isumbras* as an 'authority' on the poem: a key feature of manuscript culture is that, 'because of the constantly shifting nexus of agents involved in manuscript production, literary and textual authority in the later Middle Ages was largely decentralized'.[13] Observing the poem in its manuscripts with an eye to how scribes handle the tail rhyme can help us, if speculatively, grasp how various medieval audiences – scribes, readers and listeners – thought of the text. *Isumbras* provides a particularly apt test case for such a literary shift; as Purdie observes, 'some of the earliest and latest references to *Isumbras* place it in the context of oral performance' citing the mid-fourteenth-century *Speculum Vitae* which condemns the 'mynstraylles and iestours / þat mas carpyne in many place / Of Octouyane and Isambrase'.[14] Such positions on the Middle English romance and minstrel entertainment make each recording of *Isumbras* a site of surprisingly tense negotiation over literary form.

The eight late medieval *Isumbras* manuscripts, then, each deserve some consideration. All but the earliest date from the fifteenth century, so they offer a sense of how various scribes approached one romance in a century when the genre's cultural saturation had reached such a point that it had, at least in Chaucer's notorious example, become ripe for parody, and authors had not yet begun to privilege private reading over public reading, 'dividuality over aurality'.[15] I argue that the manuscripts of *Isumbras* provide evidence that tail-rhyme romance, and its occasional deployment of the graphic tail-rhyme style, underwent changes as a result of a scribe's sense of the form's proximity to, and evocation of, oral literature and the aural reading experience. By examining

---

    capable of disagreeing with each other, of objecting to each other's formalisms, of disappointing the poets whose work they transmitted'.

[13] M. Johnston and M. Van Dussen, 'Introduction: Manuscripts and Cultural History', in *The Medieval Manuscript Book: Cultural Approaches*, ed. M. Johnston and M. Van Dussen (Cambridge, 2015), p. 9.

[14] *Speculum Vitae*, ed. R. Hanna, 2 vols, EETS OS 331 (Oxford, 2008), ll. 38–40, qtd. in R. Purdie, 'Sir *Isumbras* in London, Gray's Inn, MS 20: A Revision', *Nottingham Medieval Studies* 55 (2011), 249–84 (p. 268).

[15] See Coleman, *Public Reading*, pp. 218–20 (p. 218) for the eventual sixteenth-century tipping of the scales in favour of private reading (although by no means the disappearance of public reading). For dates of copies, see Purdie, 'Gray's Inn', p. 254. The ninth manuscript of *Isumbras*, Oxford, Bodleian Library, MS Douce 261, fols. 1r–7v, dates to 1564 and derives from a print edition. There is little to say of this late manuscript in the present context that differs from what I say about its print contemporaries (below). See also A. Wiggins, 'Romance in the Age of Print', in *The Romance of the Middle Ages*, ed. N. Perkins and A. Wiggins (Oxford, 2012), pp. 121–49.

the manuscripts, we see how some scribes attempted to copy the form, how the layout could coincide with shifts in the audience, altering the performative nature of the oral tradition for a likely private reading audience, and how some like Thornton discarded it despite its attractions. In the case of two of the manuscripts – London, Gray's Inn, MS 20 and Oxford, University College, MS 142 – *Isumbras*'s fragmentary versions suggest how the poem lived as an oral/aural artifact that was initially preserved in the graphic tail-rhyme style. The manuscript context and layouts of two other manuscripts of *Isumbras*, the Heege manuscript (Edinburgh, National Library of Scotland, MS Advocates' 19.3.1) and Oxford, Bodleian Library, MS Ashmole 61, appear to encourage fifteenth-century readers to engage in performative minstrel-play. On the other hand, manuscripts that avoid the graphic tail-rhyme layout appear to do so as part of a general desire to remove the performative aspects of *Isumbras*, namely Naples, Royal Library, MS XIII.B.29, and London, British Library, MS Cotton Caligula A.ii. Finally, I give special attention to Cambridge, Gonville and Caius College, MS 175 and the Thornton Manuscript (Lincoln, Lincoln Cathedral Library, MS 91), because in my reading of their manuscript structure and compilation, they show scribes torn between modes of literary reproduction. Surveying the manuscript evidence prepares us to understand better not only scribes and readers but also the options available to early modern printers. Because the graphic tail-rhyme was not preserved in the print era, when it was clearly an option considered by scribes preserving the image of the minstrel in romances like *Isumbras*, this essay asks us in the end to consider what interpretive possibilities have been obscured by its loss.

In two ephemeral examples of *Isumbras*, the Gray's Inn and the Oxford University College manuscripts, even the disposable qualities of the text indicate the poem's life as an oral production. The offhand nature with which the Gray's Inn *Isumbras* is cast in the graphic tail-rhyme style implies that scribes were habituated to the style to the extent that it was a natural choice for the genre. In that earliest fragmentary manuscript, the romance bears the signs of transience one would expect for a text circulating orally and received aurally.[16] The manuscript itself compiles mid-thirteenth-century Latin homilies, but a fragment of *Isumbras* was used as a pastedown and has since been rebound near the manuscript's end and dated to *c.* 1400.[17] Even in its current derelict state, the faded page clearly shows the scribe was not particularly neat or careful in his copying. Spacing fluctuates as does the hand itself, in part

---

[16] I acknowledge with gratitude Abigail Cass, librarian at Gray's Inn, who provided me with manuscript images.

[17] Purdie, 'Gray's Inn', p. 254.

because the scribe employs the graphic tail-rhyme layout. The scribe marks tail rhyme out at times with the graphic bracket that connects the couplet on the left to the tail on the right. The tail rhyme, with its associations with an oral, even musical medium of minstrel delivery, is simultaneously preserved and discarded here, perhaps as the result of the well-documented practice of live transcription.[18] The scribe may use the graphic tail-rhyme style, but the poem and its chaotic format was apparently of little value as *written* text to an owner since it is 'preserved' only as a pastedown.[19] It strikes me that interest in *Isumbras*, a text serially updated by various performers and scribes, was much depleted in the eyes of the medieval compiler concerned here with preserving Latin homilies, despite *Isumbras*'s reputation as a 'devotional romance'. The graphic tail-rhyme may also have marked the content as disposable in the eyes of the binder of these sermons.

A similarly ephemeral exemplar of seventeen lines of *Isumbras* occurs in Oxford, University College, MS 142, tentatively dated to the late fifteenth century, a copy altogether so slapdash that it would seem to contain little literary value.[20] Yet its slapdash character highlights *Isumbras* as an exemplary oral/aural text in the same vein as the Gray's Inn manuscript and shows the long-lasting life of that tradition. The Oxford University College fragment has never received much attention, but both Carleton Brown and Purdie acknowledge its obvious connection to orality.[21] The fragment is scribbled on a flyleaf of a manuscript containing the *Prick of Conscience* and some theological texts; the scribe does not use the graphic tail-rhyme, and, in fact, at several places, he runs two lines together. Judging from its quality, the scribe was not taking pains to preserve the romance for other readers – so there is little reason to expect an attempt to generate a minstrel-like feeling with the

---

[18] See M. B. Parkes, *Scribes, Scripts and Readers: Studies in the Communication, Presentation and Dissemination of Medieval Texts* (London, 1991), pp. 19–33; for reference to the practice in a dramatic setting, see T. Stern, *Making Shakespeare: From Stage to Page* (London, 2004), pp. 46–7.

[19] As H. Ryley, 'Waste Not, Want Not: The Sustainability of Medieval Manuscripts', *Studies in Ecocriticism* 19.1 (2015), 63–74, observes, works that became unfashionable or no longer current – such as legal texts – were often reused as pastedowns and flyleaves. For further analysis of pastedowns, flyleaves and the ephemeral uses to which scribes put these oft-overlooked manuscript spaces, see H. Ryley, *Re-using Manuscripts in Late Medieval England: Repairing, Recycling, Sharing* (York, 2022), especially pp. 61–103.

[20] My thanks to Philip Burnett and Elizabeth Adams, librarians at University College, for providing an image of this fragment.

[21] C. Brown, 'A Passage from *Sir Isumbras*', *Englische Studien* 48 (1914), 329; Purdie, 'Gray's Inn', p. 268.

graphic tail-rhyme. Even so, Brown acknowledges that the fragment demonstrates 'the freedom with which minstrel romances like *Isumbras* were altered in their phrasing as they passed from mouth to mouth'.[22] This idly copied fragment shows how audiences committed these romances to memory – perhaps in the same way one commits, with little effort, a popular song-lyric to memory today and might scrawl it down in a vacant moment; or perhaps it reflects live transcription at the moment it was heard. The opening line of the fragment is also unique; although it draws on the 'Hende in hall' incipit, the Oxford fragment instead reads 'All þat wyllyn þys romonse here / Of lords þat before ous were …', removing the courtly reference ('hall') and therefore broadening the audience. The shift in audience accords with scholars' sense of *Isumbras* and other tail-rhyme romances as family entertainment, as has been suggested of the Thornton, Ashmole and Heege manuscripts. While the messiness and popular nature of the *Isumbras* fragment may seem at odds with the manuscript's primary religious content, Michael Johnston has brilliantly demonstrated that *Isumbras* was here copied out not by the experienced scribe of the *Prick of Conscience* but by a servant employed in the kitchens, offering 'powerful evidence for what may once have been a vibrant and widespread culture of reading and listening to texts like *Amis and Amiloun* and *Isumbras*'.[23] It makes sense that this servant-cum-scribe heard a version of the text directed not to the elite but to anyone willing to listen, and as such, I see his impulse to record what he heard as a convincing example of *Isumbras* as a text deeply connected to the aural existence of tail-rhyme romance and as a text that encouraged listeners to engage in a kind of 'minstrel-play' themselves, a kind of 'pseudo-minstrelsy'.[24]

Two other manuscripts, the Heege manuscript and Ashmole manuscript – classic examples of the 'library *in parvo*', little library or 'household book'[25] – suggest that *Isumbras* was not just a poem that evoked and encouraged oral

---

[22] Brown, 'A Passage', p. 329.

[23] M. Johnston, 'New Evidence for the Social Reach of "Popular Romance": The Books of Household Servants', *Viator* 43.2 (2012), 303–32 (pp. 315, 324), observes that *Sir Isumbras* (fols. 126r–128v) is copied following the *Prick of Conscience*, along with various signatures of household servants like William Slywright, a 'kitchen slave', and reasonably assumes that the messy, fragmentary text was written by someone from the same group. This supports, too, the suspicion by A. Taylor, 'Fragmentation, Corruption, and Minstrel Narration', *The Yearbook of English Studies* 22 (1992), 38–62 (p. 52), that rather than a move from oral to textual reading of romances, there was a shift in which classes were enjoying the oral texts.

[24] On such minstrelsy, see Taylor, 'Fragmentation', p. 62.

[25] P. Hardman, 'A Mediaeval "Library *in parvo*"', *Medium Aevum* 47 (1978), 262–73, is the foundational text for this formulation.

performance but also one that allowed readers to enter into the role of musical minstrel, connecting the act of reading *Isumbras* with the performance of an imaginary past of minstrel-filled romance. Although such manuscripts are known for their miscellaneous character, the shared potential of their texts' aurality,[26] speaking to a household and in a group setting, gives us reason to consider especially their performative character. Oxford, Bodleian Library, MS Ashmole 61, dated to the last quarter of the fifteenth century, is a narrow manuscript penned by a scribe who signs himself 'Rate'. The manuscript contains five romances, along with various pious tales, instructional verse and debate poetry. Rate writes *Isumbras* consistently with rhyming brackets, which lay out the tail-rhyme nature of the stanza at a glance in six-line groupings.[27] While rhyming brackets in themselves are not the graphic tail-rhyme, they effectively communicate to a reader quickly the form of the narrative, providing opportunities for impromptu changes in emphasis and differing cadence. In fact, the manuscript seems designed with performance in mind. The strange long and narrow format (420 x 145 mm) of Ashmole 61 accommodates only one column of text per page, resembling a so-called 'holster-book', designed with portability and perhaps minstrel performance as its purpose. Andrew Taylor has convincingly discredited this idea in part because the manuscript is so large, but I am not prepared to fully depart from analysis of the shape.[28] That is, although there are a number of other long, narrow books (e.g., ledgers), as Taylor observes, this shape remains the 'format most often used for Tudor prompt books' and allows for easy reference in oral presentation.[29] The book's shape itself evokes performance and the at-a-glance functionality of prompt books; even if the overall bulk of Ashmole 61 might make it prohibitively cumbersome, as a family book designed to bring to mind the history, or even the romance, of English poetic performance – that is, minstrelsy – it serves well.[30] In fact, George Shuffelton has gone so far as to argue that Ashmole's

---

[26] Understood especially as defined by Coleman, *Public Reading*, p. xi: 'the reading of books aloud to one or more people'.

[27] On the six-line stanza, as opposed to what is often thought to be a twelve-line stanza, see Purdie, *Anglicising Romance*, pp. 85–7.

[28] A. Taylor, 'The Myth of the Minstrel Manuscript', *Speculum* 66.1 (1991), 43–73 (pp. 57–60). More recently, Taylor reassesses the evidence for so-called 'minstrel manuscripts', observes the 'wishful thinking' involved in such identifications and notes that Ashmole 61 offers 'perhaps the most extreme misapplication of this dubious term'; see R. Rastall with A. Taylor, *Minstrels and Minstrelsy in Late Medieval England* (Woodbridge, 2023), pp. 241–9 (pp. 243, 245).

[29] Taylor, 'Myth', pp. 57–8.

[30] On its potential family associations, see L. S. Blanchfield, 'The Romances in MS Ashmole 61: An Idiosyncratic Scribe', in *Romance in Medieval England*, ed. M.

defining trait is 'a deep investment in oral entertainment as the centerpiece of domestic life',[31] while Myra Seaman comments that 'the performative outlook of the collection, with its verse-only texts and its abundant references to minstrels and minstrelsy, is one distinct feature of its materiality'.[32] Part of enjoying romance has always been generating nostalgia for a fantasy-past; as Taylor has recently observed, medieval romance frequently evokes the 'harper in the hall' trope, so that 'those listening to a young man or woman reading aloud from a book and hearing themselves addressed as "seigneurs" or "lordings" could imagine themselves part of [an] idealized aristocratic society ... [such romances] evoke a legendary past'.[33] Similarly, copyists might be called 'minstrel-scribes' because their role involves retelling the romance. The contents of Ashmole 61 certainly suggest that adopting the minstrel-role was part of the reading experience: of the 41 items contained in the manuscript, I count 19 marked for oral delivery by their minstrel-style incipit.[34] Most texts not marked out by such incipits are prayers or psalms, already an identifiably oral genre. Those texts that begin with such minstrel-style incipits are also much longer, so that the majority of the manuscript appears marked with the recommendation for oral delivery. Minstrelsy and orality can even explain Rate's fondness for insertion of rough, if endearing, illustrations of fish between his texts, including his romances. Olson, citing Mary Carruthers, observes that

---

Mills, J. Fellows and C. M. Meale (Cambridge, 1991), pp. 65–87; M. Johnston, *Romance and the Gentry in Late Medieval England* (Oxford, 2014), pp. 114–15.

[31] G. Shuffelton, 'Is There a Minstrel in the House? Domestic Entertainment in Late Medieval England', *Philological Quarterly* 87.1–2 (2008), 51–76 (p. 69).

[32] See M. Seaman, *Objects of Affection: The Book and the Household in Late Medieval England* (Manchester, 2021), p. 11.

[33] Rastall with Taylor, *Minstrels*, p. 257.

[34] See 'MS Ashmole 61', *Medieval Manuscripts in Oxford Libraries*, accessed April 1, 2023, https://medieval.bodleian.ox.ac.uk/catalog/manuscript_359. Some incipits call for listeners to pay attention and hear what is being said or sung, but several poems contain these calls a few lines further in. I admit that mention of 'hearing' or 'listening' does not necessarily connote a 'performance text'; however, the specific styling of the minstrel incipit establishes an imaginary situation of the court storyteller that also frequently includes an implied performance situation. Narrators refer to their 'song' or, for instance, Ashmole 61's *The Ten Commandments* begins, 'Herkyns syrys that standys abowte' (fol. 16v.). Coleman, *Public Reading*, pp. 57–62 and chapters 5–7, deals with the argument against seeing such 'minstrel tags' as indications of a performance environment in her discussion of 'fictive orality' where she argues forcefully that those that attribute such signs of performance to 'fictive orality' inevitably engage in circular reasoning that relies on an unnecessary binary of orality and literacy, ignoring 'the read-aloud book' in between.

fishing was a metaphor for memorization and lesson learning.[35] Here, Rate's fish can evoke the practice of recitation, perhaps an encouragement to set some rhymes to memory for better performance in the 'minstrel style' suggested by both *Isumbras*'s narrative incipit and the format of the manuscript.

Isumbras in the Heege manuscript, another late fifteenth-century example, is particularly notable for its graphic tail-rhyme, also indicating a desire for adopting a 'minstrel style' as suggested above.[36] That *Isumbras* shows up in this manuscript at all supports the notion that *Isumbras* inhabits that space between the oral and the literary. James Wade points out that 'the whole book, taken together, has a strong flavour of the functional and popular' and outlines how particularly the first booklet bears signs that, although circumstantial, cumulatively make a strong case for its minstrel origins.[37] Although Wade places *Isumbras* among the texts in the Heege manuscript that partake of a robust culture of '*textual* exchange and vernacular (often amateur) book compilation',[38] there is little doubt that the poem, with its 'minstrel tags' and tail-rhyme, is invested with a similar performative energy. The graphic tail-rhyme persists throughout the duration of the poem, and although the scribe cannot avoid the cramping of such a layout, the presentation is relatively consistent and orderly. In fact, Heege, the primary scribe who copied all the romances, uses a secondary bracket to connect the rhyming tail-rhymes as well when he is able, an addition to this style that often leads to messy and inconsistent layouts (see, for instance, fol. 56v, Figure 1), and the page surely resembles the performative style Chaucer satirizes in *Thopas*. However, the style of graphic tail-rhyme chosen for *Isumbras* is unique in the Heege manuscript. Deciding to try something a bit neater for the other tail-rhyme romances *Sir Gowther* and *Sir Amadas*, Heege uses a different graphic representation that uses a bracket for

---

[35] See M. Carruthers, *The Book of Memory: A Study of Memory in Medieval Culture* (Cambridge, 1990), pp. 247, 345 n. 67; and L. Olson, 'Romancing the Book: Manuscripts for "Euerich Inglische"', in K. Kerby-Fulton, M. Hilmo and Olson, *Opening Up Middle English Manuscripts* (Ithaca, 2012), pp. 116–39 (p. 112). Seaman, *Objects of Affection*, pp. 25–6, also suggests several ways of considering the fish (along with the floral) illustrations in the text as a 'signature-equivalent' that also becomes part of the poetry. Later, Seaman proposes that Rate favoured the consistent use of the fish as a way of uniting the miscellany of texts in the manuscript; without a uniting thematic among them, the persistent fish prompts the reader to generate such connections upon reflection (pp. 255–9).

[36] 'Adv.MS.19.3.1', *National Library of Scotland: Early Manuscripts*, accessed April 1, 2023, https://digital.nls.uk/134162905.

[37] J. Wade, 'Entertainments from a Medieval Minstrel's Repertoire Book', *Review of English Studies* 74 (2023), 605–18 (p. 607).

[38] Wade, 'Entertainments', p. 608 (emphasis mine).

the *aa* lines of his stanzas but places the tail-rhyme underneath the couplet, marked out with simple, interlacing line filler.[39]

The variation in Heege's *mise-en-page* recalls similar layout discrepancies in the Lincoln Thornton Manuscript, discussed below. Like that manuscript, the Heege manuscript was produced in fascicules, indicated by quire signatures and different paper-stock between them, as well as individual quire *compilation*.[40] Unfortunately, we cannot determine the order in which Heege composed his fascicules, but it seems plausible that, like Thornton, Heege was determined to preserve that lively minstrel style in his layout. Although Heege's *Isumbras* successfully renders a full graphic tail-rhyme format, each folio still appears inevitably cramped – Heege's altered layout for the other tail-rhyme poems may well have been chosen after his experiment with *Isumbras*.

Messy though the Heege manuscript may be, its scribes do seem conscious of layout's potential to contribute to a poem's meaning. For instance, 'The Complaint of God to Man', a dialogue between humankind and the divinity, marks out speaking parts with the marginal annotation *homo* and *jhc* respectively (fols. 158–70). Throughout the manuscript, the scribes are consistent in marking out rhyming couplets with brackets, and tail-rhyme is, at a glance, observable thanks to the line-fillers found in poems like 'The Hunting of the Hare' (fols. 1–7) and others. Other contents and layouts of the Heege manuscript demonstrate that it was of interest to those who were musically inclined. Later scribes added to the Heege manuscript a variety of musical texts including several lyrics and carols with refrains. Although the layouts for these are not particularly remarkable, the lullaby 'This lovely lady sat and sang' (210v–211r) is marked off with a refrain indicated to the right of the stanzas. The musical inclinations of later scribes show up particularly at the end of the manuscript (fol. 246v) where musical notation accompanies the hymn or troped kyrie 'Deus creator omnium'. Perhaps even more interesting is that midway through the manuscript (fol. 175v), there is a large full-page illustration of a Guidonian hand (a mnemonic for the degrees of a musical scale) – along with some sketched musical notation. These bits of music added to Heege's collection demonstrate that a community of musician-scribes were subsequent users of the manuscript and contribute to the overall notion that the book, if not a 'minstrel book', was connected to performance, and so it is no surprise to see graphic tail-rhyme at home among performance texts.

[39] On the use of 'line-fillers', see C. Tuck and Y. Liu, 'Line-fillers', *Medieval Codes*, April 21, 2016, accessed April 1, 2023, http://www.medievalcodes.ca/2016/04/line-fillers.html.

[40] Discussion of the collation of the Heege manuscript can be found in P. Hardman, ed., 'Introduction', *Heege Manuscript: A Facsimile of National Library of Scotland Ms. Advocates 19.3.1* (Leeds, 2000), pp. 1–16.

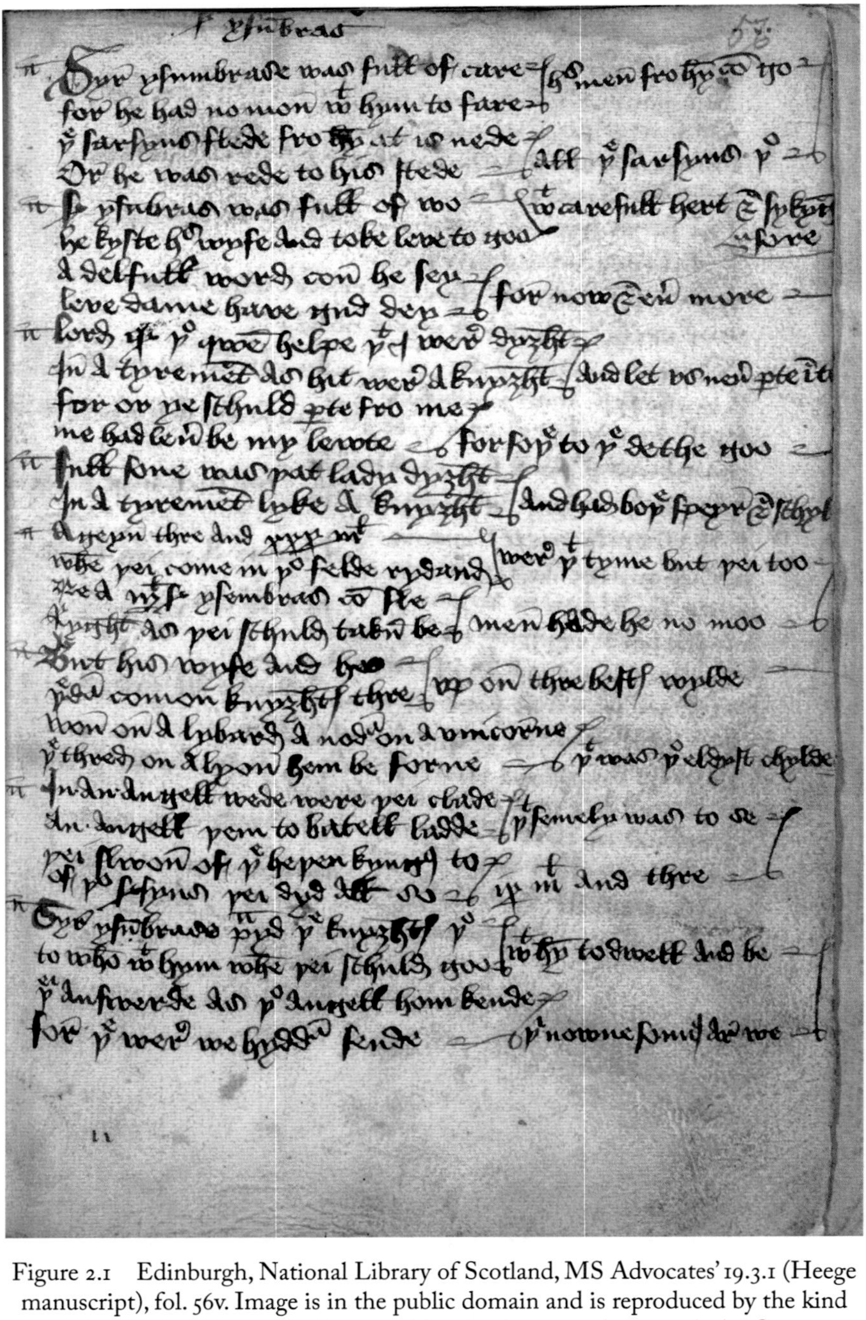

Figure 2.1 Edinburgh, National Library of Scotland, MS Advocates' 19.3.1 (Heege manuscript), fol. 56v. Image is in the public domain and is reproduced by the kind permission of the National Library of Scotland in accordance with the Creative Commons Attribution 4.0 International License.

The 'performative mode' suggested by graphic tail-rhyme romance can be partly supported, ironically enough, by looking at other texts of *Isumbras* that do *not* use the graphic layout, the Naples and Cotton manuscripts, which share an otherwise unique incipit.[41] The less analyzed version of *Isumbras* found in Naples, Royal Library, MS XIII.B 29, fols. 114–15, preserves only the poem's opening 122 lines; the manuscript also contains two other well-known romances *Bevis of Hampton* and *Libeaus Desconus*, Chaucer's 'Clerk's Tale' (removed from its *Canterbury Tales* context), the hagiographical *Of Seint Alex of Rome* and 137 medical recipes.[42] The medical recipes occupy the first section of the manuscript and fill its pages with little margin; there are several blank leaves separating this section from the following romance material, which is then neatly laid out in two columns. The portions of the manuscript dedicated to poetry, although not ornate, are all carefully and tidily written in clearly ruled pages with a generous margin, all by one scribe who dates the manuscript's composition to 1457 on the last page of the manuscript.

The Naples scribe's decision *not* to write *Isumbras* in graphic tail-rhyme is unsurprising given that the codex's medicinal contents could suggest that the compiler had little interest in oral delivery. More tellingly, the opening lines – unique to the Naples and Cotton manuscripts – dispense with the common invocation of a live audience. The typical invocation, based here on the Cambridge manuscript, reads:

Hende in halle and ye wole her } That lyfede in are thede
Off eldres that before us wer

Jhesu Cryst hevene kynge } And hevene unto oure mede[43]
Geve hem alle hys blessyng

In contrast the Naples manuscript offers:

He þat made both hevyn and erthe
And all þis worlde in deyes seuen
That is full of myȝte

---

[41] Brantley, 'Reading the Forms', p. 435, posits, through comparison with a variety of genres, in particular drama, that the graphic tail-rhyme signifies not *genre* on its own but the 'performative mode'.

[42] See R. Cioffi et al., 'Il Codice Napoli, Biblioteca Nazionale, MS XIII.B.29. Studio ed Edizione Digitale', in *I Longobardi in Italia: Lingua e Cultura*, ed. C. Falluomini (Edizioni dell'Orso, 2015), pp. 349–76. My thanks to the librarians at Biblioteca Nazionale di Napoli for images.

[43] Quoted text comes from *Sir Isumbras* in *Four Middle English Romances*, ed. H. Hudson (Kalamazoo, 1995); I have formatted lines in a graphic tail-rhyme layout and removed punctuation.

> Sende vs alle his blessynge
> Lasse and more olde and ȝynge
> And kepe vs day and nyȝte[44]

Although the general sense of asking for a blessing is the same, there is a clear difference in the way the scribe situates the narrator and audience relationship. The Naples and Cotton versions both dispense with the illusion of a live audience. A number of missed rhymes in the Naples manuscript suggests that the scribe was not even reading their copy out loud from the beginning, since the opening couplet, 'He þat made both hevyn and erthe / And all þis worlde in deyes seuen', badly botches the rhyme found correctly in the Cotton version (which is not the Naples copy's exemplar).[45] The graphic tail-rhyme, which connects with the oral nature of medieval romance, could hardly be further from this scribe's mind. His exemplar likely did not employ it either, and the manuscript then represents a further movement away from the 'performance mode' of minstrel-telling days idealized in these types of poems.

The Cotton manuscript (London, British Library, MS Cotton Caligula A.ii) is a contemporary of the Neapolitan, and its nearly identical incipit likewise removes the poem from the immediate context of a performative production. The multi-text manuscript is squarely written in a two-column layout by a single hand. There are no brackets, and the only decoration, apparatus or marginalia are paraph marks indicating a six-line stanza break. Although this manuscript contains eight romances, none receives any variance in *mise-en-page* except for the alliterative poems, which are written in long lines even though the scribe knew of the graphic tail-rhyme's existence: he uses it for a prayer, 'Jhesu for þy blod þat þu bleddest' (fol. 70v). The layout of this prayer, again, feels connected to the orality of the medium – a prayer after all has always been a strongly oral genre.[46] The choice to keep all tail-rhyme romances in the manuscript in simple columns along with the different incipit suggests that this scribe also did not have the poem's orality at the forefront of his mind. Indeed, the scribe of this manuscript seemed more interested in crafting a

---

[44] Naples MS, fol. 114.

[45] Cotton MS, fol. 130r, reads: 'God þat made both erthe and hevene / And all þis worlde in deyes seuen …'.

[46] The only other poem in this manuscript to deviate from the straight-forward *mise-en-page* is the first text *Susannah* (or the *Pistel of Susan*), written in a more elaborate alliterative verse form of the 'bob-and-wheel' sort, with the 'bob' and last line of the 'wheel' set off to the right. For a diplomatic transcription, see D. C. White, 'BL Cotton Caligula Aii, Manuscript Context, the Theme of Obedience, and a Diplomatic Transcription Edition' (unpublished Ph.D. dissertation, Georgia State University, 2012).

uniform vision of the tail-rhyme stanza, regularizing the layout in 'an obvious desire to present some twelve-line stanzas in six-line reading units'.[47] As J. J. Thompson observes, this scribe briefly seems to have attempted a different long-line layout for *Octavian* but quickly abandoned it in favour of the two-column layout applied consistently in every other tail-rhyme romance in the manuscript.[48] This scribe was clearly concerned with *mise-en-page*, but his preferred *mise-en-page* sought to create a uniformity of presentation among the set of romances that was not chiefly concerned with the playful, often messy layout of the graphic tail-rhyme.[49]

Final, extended consideration needs to be given to those manuscripts that fascinatingly reveal the internal struggle of scribes unsure how best to represent *Isumbras*. In Cambridge, Gonville and Caius College, MS 175, fols. 98–107, an early fifteenth-century manuscript, the scribe appears to have attempted to use the graphic tail-rhyme for *Isumbras* but only partially. As observed by Purdie, this copy 'has only every second tercet in graphic tail-rhyme and the scribe drops the layout altogether after the first page', though, technically, the scribe misses the initial tail-line.[50] Throughout, the scribe has drawn brackets to connect rhymes in the manuscript, a practice that was fairly common, but the tail-rhyme lines are cramped in the margin and not easily read. The layout apparently was abandoned because of the inconvenience of squashing the tail-line in the margin, which, as Purdie has argued, 'makes any attempt to use it significant'.[51] What is signified here? One might impulsively assume that the scribe of the Cambridge manuscript was simply careless and began using the graphic tail-rhyme only to be discouraged by the mess, but that would not explain why twenty or so folios later, another popular tail-rhyme romance gets the exact same treatment. The scribe similarly begins writing *Bevis of Hampton* (fols. 131–56) in the graphic layout but abandons it on the verso

---

[47] J. J. Thompson, 'Looking Behind the Book: MS Cotton Caligula A.ii, Part 1, and the Experience of its Texts', in *Romance Reading on the Book: Essays on Medieval Narrative presented to Maldwyn Mills*, ed. J. Fellows, R. Field, G. Rogers and J. Weiss (Cardiff, 1996), pp. 171–87 (p. 181).

[48] Thompson, 'Looking Behind the Book', p. 181.

[49] What the principles of compilation were in this manuscript remains an open question, although scholars have made intriguing connections among texts that suggest interests ranging from the devotional to interest in contemporary events. See Thompson, 'Looking Behind the Book', pp. 185–7; M. Edlich-Muth and C. Edlich-Muth, 'The Reader at Large: A Computational Approach to London, British Library, Cotton Caligula A.ii (Part One)', *Anglia* 139.1 (2021), 154–80.

[50] Purdie, *Anglicising Romance*, p. 69. Many thanks to Mark Statham, College Librarian at Gonville and Caius College, for assisting me with MS 175.

[51] Purdie, *Anglicising Romance*, p. 70.

of the first folio.[52] Furthermore, other evidence from the manuscript shows signs of a single thoughtful scribe who made deliberate choices in decoration and layout.[53] The scribe likely sought to indicate visually both a genre and, perhaps, an approach to the poem grounded in a history of oral performance.[54] Whether or not the poem was performed, the layout effectively announces 'this is an English romance'.[55] Having established this local tone and marked the tail-rhyme romances as distinct from other texts in the manuscript, the scribe drops the inconvenient layout and resorts to more straightforward columns. The scribe found it meaningful, in more than one case then, to preserve his readers' awareness of the graphic layout, even as he chose to copy the rest of the folios to match the linear layout of the rest of the book.

Of course, layout is highly idiosyncratic and even arbitrary, but the Cambridge and Thornton manuscripts in particular reveal the conscious minds of scribes debating how to suit the page to the poem and vice versa. The famous mid-fifteenth-century Thornton manuscript (Lincoln, Lincoln Cathedral Library, MS 91) depicts just such a debate.[56] Robert Thornton (*c.* 1418–56) was an amateur scribe, a hobbyist keen on collecting what appealed to his or his household's tastes, and he copied out nearly the entire manuscript.[57] Linda Olson has observed the enthusiasm with which Thornton appears to have designed a portion of his book as a collection of romances, and it is now generally accepted that the 'romance section' was initially compiled as its own booklet.[58] What we might detect as the enthusiasm of a 'fan' of the genre should

---

[52] In a striking parallel, *Bevis* in London, British Library, MS Egerton 3862 is composed partly in tail-rhyme stanzas, and those initial stanzas are depicted in graphic form. Later, the same scribe copies out the tail-rhyme romance *Eglamour* without the graphic layout. See M. Bateman, M. Edlich-Muth and C. Edlich-Muth, 'Disrupted Plans: Negotiating *Bevis of Hampton* in the Shifting Framework of British Library Egerton MS 2862', *Philological Quarterly* 101.3 (2022), 163–87 (p. 167).

[53] See M. J. Evans, *Reading Middle English Romance: Manuscript Layout, Decoration, and the Rhetoric of Composite Structure* (Montreal, 1995), pp. 68–9.

[54] Cf. scribes of the *Canterbury Tales* who likewise evoked graphic tail-rhyme for parodic effect.

[55] It is worth considering how similar choices in formatting-signification remain common today, for example, the employment of small caps in the opening line of a chapter.

[56] I have consulted *The Thornton Manuscript, Lincoln Cathedral MS. 91*, ed. D. S. Brewer and A. E. B. Owen (London, 1975).

[57] See Olson, 'Romancing the Book', pp. 116–39.

[58] Olson, 'Romancing the Book', pp. 117–24. The notion that Thornton approached this manuscript initially as two 'booklets', one containing romances and one containing primarily devotional texts, has found wide support and 'these speculations

inspire us to attend to Thornton's choices with some seriousness and consider that even his scribal missteps might be revealing. Although Thornton did *not* write *Isumbras* in graphic tail-rhyme, strikingly, another tail-rhyme romance that appears later in the 'romance section', *Sir Degrevant*, is written completely in consistent graphic tail-rhyme stanzas. I argue that this discrepancy in fact aligns with Thornton's process of acquiring paper stock and exemplars, and it reveals his attempt *initially*, following his intuitions about the genre, to accommodate the graphic tail-rhyme before relinquishing it when he copied out his version of *Sir Isumbras*.

The quires of this section of the manuscript present nine verse romances in a row (with a few shorter works to fill space in between) which employ various *mise-en-page* indicating a scribe trying out different forms.[59] Thornton's choices may have been informed by his exemplars, but they display a sense of manuscript aesthetic, too. For instance, the alliterative *Morte Arthure* that initiates the romance portion of the manuscript has large rubricated initials, caesuras and brackets connecting every fourth line throughout the poem. However, these brackets serve no obvious metrical or poetic purpose – they do not connect lines that alliterate or rhyme with one another. The appearance in the margin, however, of these interlinked brackets creates a visual cascading effect not dissimilar to the aural effect of alliteration, and we can see that Thornton was fond of brackets in various places in his manuscript. Thornton follows the *Morte* with, in order, *Octovyane*, *Ysambrace* (*Isumbras*) and *Dyoclociane* (fols. 98v–121v), all tail-rhyme romances that do not display the graphic tail-rhyme; immediately afterward, Thornton employs the full graphic tail-rhyme in *Degrevant* for the duration of the poem (fols. 130r–138r). The layout for *Degrevant* becomes increasingly cramped and messy as the poem progresses, suggesting that Thornton did not plan the layout carefully. Subsequent tail-rhyme romances in the manuscript *Eglamour* and *Percyvelle* do not attempt the graphic tail-rhyme layout (fols. 138v–147r, 161r–176r). Thornton chose instead to copy *Percyvelle* in standard columns but with brackets connecting the rhymes throughout. In copying *The Awentyrs of Arthure at the Terne Wathelyne* (fols. 154r–161r), Thornton employs a less complex graphic bob-and-wheel layout with more success, with the 'bob' line set to the right of the 'wheel' and connected by a bracket.

---

have almost hardened into fact' over the years. See G. R. Keiser, 'Robert Thornton: Gentleman, Reader and Scribe', in *Robert Thornton and His Books: Essays on the Lincoln and London Thornton Manuscripts*, ed. M. R. Johnston and S. Fein (York, 2014), pp. 67–108 (p. 77).

[59] Keiser, 'Robert Thornton', describes Thornton throughout as a scribe experimenting with letter forms in particular.

Approaching the quire structure for these romances can help us see how Thornton grappled with the graphic tail-rhyme and perhaps provide clues to the order in which he copied the texts. Thornton was clearly familiar with these types of tales, and he likely took care in considering which layout was appropriate for each composition. The romance section begins in Quire 4 with the alliterative *Morte Arthure*, which continues into Quire 6. *Octavian* finishes the sixth quire and continues on to Quire 7, which includes *Ysambrace* and *Dyoclicyan* to end that quire. All three tail-rhyme romances – *Octavian*, *Ysambrace*, *Dyoclicyan* – have the same columnar layout. Quire 8 begins with the *Vita Sancti Christofori* and then the tail-rhyme romances *Degrevant* and *Eglamour*; *Eglamour* continues on to Quire 9. *Percyvalle* and other romances in Quires 9 and 10 conclude the 'romance' portion. Of all the tail-rhyme romances, only *Degrevant* employs the graphic tail-rhyme layout. Michael Johnston takes *Degrevant*'s unique layout as an indication that Thornton was replicating his exemplar here, as 'there is no conceivable reason he would not have copied *Sir Degrevant* with the same layout as the previous three romances, which fit onto the page much more nicely'.[60] However, *Degrevant* is the first tail-rhyme romance in Quire 8, and there is reason to believe that Thornton copied it before any of the other tail-rhyme romances. Thus *Degrevant*, not the other three romances that precede it in the book's current form, plausibly represents Thornton's initial experiments with genre and form.

I maintain that we can detect how Thornton viewed the graphic tail-rhyme by understanding his process of compilation and production. Because his collection of romances was likely compiled as its own booklet, I examine Thornton's compilation practices as they apply to the quires running from fols. 53–178. Using Ralph Hanna's analysis of watermarks and the paper-stock used for the fascicular compilation of the Lincoln manuscript, we can determine the likely copying order of the *texts*. Hanna argues that Thornton began the romances for his manuscript early on; the scribe used one stock of paper (B) for the first quires (4–5) of the *Morte Arthure* before finishing that poem with stock L (Quire 6). In Quire 6 *Octavian* begins on paper-stock L but finishes in Quire 7 on paper-stock G; *Ysambrace* and *Dyoclicyan* follow on paper-stock G, C and M.[61] However, in Quire 8, which contains the *Vita Sancti Christofori*, *Degrevant* and *Eglamour*, Thornton has written on only L

---

[60] Johnston, *Romance and the Gentry*, pp. 175–83 (p. 179).

[61] R. Hanna III, 'The Growth of Robert Thornton's Books', *Studies in Bibliography* 40 (1987), 51–61 (pp. 52, 57). For the initial watermark analysis of this manuscript, see S. M. Horrall, 'The Watermarks of the Thornton Manuscripts', *Notes and Queries* 27 (1980), 385–6.

stock, the same stock that he used to complete the *Morte Arthure*. Hanna has suggested that Thornton copied multiple texts simultaneously, and the particular arrangement of paper-stock suggests that he added or acquired new stocks of paper as he went.[62] This compilation history is further supported by the oft-observed notion that *Octavian*, *Ysambrace* and *Dyoclicyan* likely come from a single exemplar so that Thornton treated these texts in a single stint of copying and acquired new paper stock while he had access to that exemplar.[63] Despite the compilation's final arrangement, my reading of Hanna's watermark analysis places *Degrevant* as the first tail-rhyme romance Thornton copied.

Thornton's *Morte Arthure* begins the romance booklet and concludes on paper stock L, and I propose that around the time that he finished this text, he began copying the *Vita Sancti Christofori* and *Degrevant* on that same paper-stock L in the graphic tail-rhyme form. Only after he completed *Degrevant* and struggled to maintain the complex graphic layout did he embark on copying other tail-rhyme romances, for which he used a simpler layout. All of the *Vita Sancti Christofori*, *Degrevant* and *Eglamour* are on stock L, but only the beginning of *Octavian* is – the portion that completes the quire containing the *Morte*. If we follow the same logic of Hanna's widely accepted analysis in which Thornton seems to change paper stock only when he has depleted his store, then there is little reason to believe that Thornton would abandon stock L in the middle of copying the *Octavian* text and change to stock G but save enough of stock L to begin the Quire 8 texts and *Degrevant* at a later time.[64] The more logical solution is that Thorton copied Quire 8 when he had plenty of stock L and copied *Octavian* at a later date, using up his remaining stock L, then finishing *Octavian*, *Ysumbrace* and *Dyoclician* on G stock. In other words, Thornton had already tried his hand at the graphic tail-rhyme form with *Degrevant* when he decided to add *Octavian* to the same quire as the *Morte* and copy a trio of tail-rhyme romances in an easier layout. This mode of copying means that the *Vita Sancti Christofori* and *Degrevant* may have

---

[62] R. Hanna, 'The London Thornton Manuscript: A Corrected Collation', *Studies in Bibliography* 37 (1984), 122–30 (p. 127), suggests that Thornton likely wrote several fascicules or collections of quires simultaneously, looking for the right fit as he borrowed exemplars and as they became available.

[63] A. McIntosh, 'The Textual Transmission of the Alliterative *Morte Arthure*', in *English and Medieval Studies Presented to J. R. R. Tolkien on the Occasion of His 70th Birthday*, ed. N. Davis and C. L. Wrenn (London, 1962), pp. 231–40, makes this argument primarily on linguistic grounds. The claim is accepted by Hanna, 'Growth', and various scholars in *Robert Thornton and His Books: Essays on the Lincoln and London Thornton Manuscripts*, ed. M. R. Johnston and S. Fein (York, 2014).

[64] Hanna, 'Growth', p. 56.

been bound after the other romances in the codex, but the above-described sharing of paper-stock among the *Morte*, *Octavian* and the quire containing *Degrevant* implies that Thornton chronologically copied *Degrevant* as the *first* of his tail-rhyme romances.

Recalling that *Degrevant* alone exhibits the graphic tail-rhyme, Thornton's process tells us that from the outset, like the scribe of the Cambridge manuscript, he saw the graphic tail-rhyme as an important feature of the English romance genre but was disappointed in his ability to preserve that aspect in practice. The process outlined in these two manuscripts indicates that those who enjoyed English tail-rhyme romances associated them with the graphic style and felt it worth preserving the tail rhyme, even if they later changed course. Thornton's amateur attempt at displaying the graphic tail-rhyme in *Degrevant* begins fairly neatly and only falters later, as the tail-rhymes continually bleed into the second primary column of the page, perhaps displaying some of the 'scribal fatigue' Johnston observes elsewhere in the manuscript's handling of romances.[65] Plausibly dissatisfied with his inability to reproduce graphic tail-rhyme consistently in *Degrevant*, Thornton settles for single columns with rhyme brackets (and no tail rhyme to the right) in the following poem, *Eglamour* (fol. 138v). They too result in a mess, seen in the bracket cutting into the next column in the eleventh line of the poem; the frustrated Thornton then abandons the layout when he acquired and copied a set of three more tail-rhyme romances, *Octavian*, *Ysambrace* and *Dyoclicyan*. Thornton's *mise-en-page* was not arbitrary at all but rather a conscious result of trial and error. Given that he was an amateur hobbyist scribe, he likely felt no obligation to be particularly consistent. That Thornton, a collector of romances, felt the need to try to represent the first tail-rhyme romance he likely copied, *Degrevant*, in graphic arrangement at all should inform our notion of how to read these romances. The variety of scribal idiosyncrasies he displays have been attributed to the use he likely intended for these texts: John Ivor Carlson suggests, 'If one remains open to the possibility that Thornton … intended either to read his texts aloud for friends and family or have them read by another, his copying style begins to make better sense'.[66] Carlson's point is that Thornton was thinking about performance when copying, as it seems likely most scribes of household books were.[67] I argue that this is particularly relevant in

---

[65] Johnston, *Romance and the Gentry*, p. 177.
[66] J. I. Carlson, 'Scribal Intentions in Medieval Romance: A Case Study of Robert Thornton', *Studies in Bibliography* 58 (2007–8), 49–71 (p. 61).
[67] In Coleman, *Public Reading*, the main thrust is that aurality – reading aloud to a group – was the 'modality of choice' in England and France in the fourteenth and fifteenth centuries (p. 1 and passim).

Thornton's approach to tail-rhyme romance, a genre that employs the graphic layout because its representation of the poem communicated an aspect central to its form, that is, its bouncy, 'performative mode' suggested by several of the manuscripts already discussed.

The collection of *Isumbras* manuscripts discussed above reveals, then, that although there was *not* wide agreement on how to translate the energy of oral, musical storytelling of English romance to the page for public or private reading, capturing that energy was part of scribal consideration. Looking at tail-rhyme poems in their manuscripts reveals a quiet dispute over the relationship between the page and the story – a dispute that results in a dynamic range of methods of presenting the tail-rhyme text in which the graphic tail-rhyme takes centre stage. And although it does not include that graphic layout, what is perhaps most striking is that our latest medieval copy of *Isumbras*, Oxford, University College, MS 142, in its ephemeral state, indicates that the lower classes had an important role in preserving tail-rhyme romance as an oral medium while more experienced scribes attempted to capture that orality on the page. As amateur scribes, Thornton and Heege were perhaps also motivated to communicate that orality, and so initially turned to the *graphic* tail-rhyme. Carlson has concluded that many of Thornton's choices in syntax and style hint that 'Thornton consciously crafted the vernacular romances in his miscellanies for spoken delivery', and, given what we see in other manuscripts of *Sir Isumbras*, I see Thornton's experiments with *mise-en-page* as further indication of that orality.[68]

Like the early printers of Chaucer's *Thopas*, however, the printers of *Isumbras* found the graphic tail-rhyme more of a hassle than it was worth and chose the columnar layout. While there must be some truth to the often-held notion that early printers wanted their books to look like manuscripts, new media demand new methods, and there are obvious changes in the regularity of layout introduced by the press that limited the dynamism of the written page.[69] And while various examples of graphic layouts in print do exist,[70]

---

[68] Carlson, 'Scribal Intentions', p. 65.

[69] On this, see D. McKitterick, *Print, Manuscript, and the Search for Order, 1450–1830* (Cambridge, 2003), p. 37.

[70] A survey of de Worde's prints on EEBO provides many examples, ranging from tables of contents, block print illustrations, capitals, and marginal annotations and chapter headings, as well as multi-column layouts. Brantley, 'Reading the Forms', p. 433, presents an excellent example of graphic tail-rhyme in de Worde's printing of Stephen Hawes, *Conuercyon of swerers* (London, 1509), STC 12943, sigs. A3v–A4. Many other Scottish prints employ analogous forms; see, for instance, the Myllar and Chepman 1508 print of *Gologras and Gawane* discussed in A. W. Klein, 'Scots

the general rule was to keep things simple and keep costs down.[71] No early printing of *Isumbras* or any other tail-rhyme romances attempted the graphic tail-rhyme.[72] However, unlike the manuscripts discussed above, in print, the lack of any graphic representation of rhyme scheme does not preclude the 'minstrel call' incipit. All print versions of *Isumbras* begin 'Hende in hall …'. By this time, doubtless as print became the more common way to encounter romance texts, the idea of a court minstrel reciting romance was itself becoming a part of the genre, a fantasy rather than a reality of oral storytelling. That is, the minstrel call becomes a part of the story, an important aspect of creating the atmosphere that is divorced from memorial performance even if a reading performer might have felt emboldened to adopt the 'minstrel style' by the opening lines.

The foregoing pursuit of *Sir Isumbras*'s tail-rhyme manuscript history demonstrates that early 'editors' – that is, scribes – considered and experimented with *mise-en-page* as an element of a text's literary art connected to its narrative voice. The scribal variations in tail-rhyme presentation, and the difficulties they indicate, were a prelude to how early printers would attempt to broaden Middle English romance's marketability. Considerations of cost aside, the complete erasure of the graphic tail-rhyme from English romance represents, I suspect, a last attempt by those secret enjoyers of such texts to preserve verse romance despite the upper class preference for long continental-style prose romances that Caxton printed;[73] removal of the graphic tail-rhyme obscures the genre's connection to bygone, oral performance and tidies up the genre by making it and its narrative voice more presentable, more

---

take the Wheel: The Problem of Period and the Medieval Scots Alliterative Thirteen-line Stanza', *Studies in Scottish Literature* 43.1 (2017), 15–21.

[71] McKitterick, *Print*, pp. 43–5.

[72] See J. Sánchez-Mardí, 'The Printed History of the Middle English Verse Romances', *Modern Philology* 107.1 (2009), 7–9 (pp. 6–7), for a list of known romances printed by de Worde. The early prints of *Isumbras* are Oxford, Bodleian Library Douce fragment f 37; London: Wynkyn de Worde or W. Copland, 1530? 1550? (*STC* 14281), one leaf; Oxford, Bodleian Library 1119. London: William Copland?, *c.* 1530 (*STC* 14282), one leaf; London, British Library C 21c61, Garrick Collection. London: William Copland, *c.* 1530 (*STC* 14282), fifteen leaves; Boston, Harvard University Library. London: John Skot, *c.* 1525 (*STC* 14280.1), eight leaves; Boston, Harvard University Library. London: I. Treveris, *c.* 1530 (*STC* 14280.2), one leaf. I also consulted Oxford, Bodleian Library, MS Douce 261 (1564), fols. 1r–7v, a late manuscript based on a printed edition. See n. 15 above.

[73] Wiggins, 'Romance in the Age of Print', p. 124, describes how Caxton sought to appeal to courtly appetites by emulating continental trends.

regular, more conservative and, if the parodic *mise-en-page* failure of Chaucer's *Sir Thopas* is any indication, more fluidly delivered when read aloud.[74]

Before the era of true mass production, early print books were still prestige items. This sense of prestige clashes with the populism of the Middle English romance, a populism evidenced by the Oxford fragment of *Isumbras*. In Caxton's initial printings, his reticence to print Middle English tail-rhyme romance can even be seen in his decision to remove the graphic tail-rhyme from Chaucer's *Thopas*. Early prints of texts like *Isumbras* demonstrate that scribes and then printers crystalized a sense of romance that conformed to a notion of textuality and literacy still predominantly available to the elite. Similarly to how printers regularized spelling to make rhymes precise for the reading eye rather than for the listening ear,[75] printers regularized their verse romance layouts to avoid unduly challenging a readerly audience. Although Wynkyn de Worde, Caxton's heir to printing in England, would begin publishing English metrical romances, including *Isumbras*, as a way of 'enhancing the genre's market penetration', like any savvy marketer, de Worde wanted to appeal to as broad an audience as possible.[76]

By comparison, all of the examples of *Isumbras* in graphic tail-rhyme come from family or 'household books' or ephemera. We see, then, a movement away from a more oral and loosely organized literary culture towards a greater separation of the 'elite' textual literature from the 'popular' oral one even while an aural culture persisted, a movement ushered in by Caxton's first print runs – his canon. This statement should be nuanced by acknowledging the oral culture of the ballads of centuries to follow as well as continued and increasing public readings of published fiction. Nonetheless, a shift had occurred in romance reading, precipitated in part it would seem by the conventions of print. In looking closely at the material history of *Isumbras*, I highlight the other side to the tension Andrew Taylor observes between performance and private reading in searching for the realities of minstrel narration in medieval England.[77] While, as Taylor points out, there is little actual evidence to suggest any sort of clean

---

[74] After all, Chaucer's Host derides *Sir Thopas* as 'drasty riming' then asks for something in prose instead: L. D. Benson, gen. ed., *The Riverside Chaucer*, 3rd ed. (Oxford, 1987), 7.930–1.

[75] A. Putter, 'Metre and the Editing of Middle English Verse: Prospects for Tail-Rhyme Romance, Alliterative Poetry, and Chaucer', *Poetica* 71 (2008), 29–47 (p. 31).

[76] J. Sánchez-Mardí, 'The Printed Transmission of the Medieval Romance from William Caxton to Wynkyn de Worde, 1473–1535', in *The Transmission of Medieval Romance: Metres, Manuscripts and Early Prints*, ed. A. Putter and J. A. Jefferson (Cambridge, 2018), pp. 170–90 (p. 190).

[77] Taylor, 'Fragmentation', pp. 48–54.

transition occurred from oral, minstrel performance to private, textual reading, I am here identifying how a text with obvious connections to oral transmission demonstrates scribal attempts to work with and transmit an oral, minstrel text in what was a largely aural environment.[78] Rather than piecing together the realities of the minstrel, I consider the workings of 'minstrel-scribes', scribes who would adopt the position of pseudo-minstrel when it came time to copy the text, expanding on the now generally accepted combination of oral and scribal activities involved in transmission of English romance.[79] This survey of manuscripts of *Sir Isumbras* has been a prolegomenon to reading the graphic tail-rhyme as literary device. As I have suggested, scribes employed the graphic tail-rhyme purposefully, so we ought to take the style seriously in our attention to the formal poetics of a text. Yet, the graphic tail-rhyme is an important feature of the minstrel-scribe role that has been obscured since the first English prints, and we must consider what we lose when it disappears.

To return to Chaucer's great joke: assessing and recontextualizing the history of tail-rhyme in a poem like *Isumbras* helps us see Chaucer's satire as more broad than usually supposed. Nobody doubts that Chaucer satirizes himself, the 'elvyssh ... popet', in the text.[80] However, once we recognize the strength of that satire against the formal conventions of not just stories but also *storytelling*, extending that to forms both aural and visual, we gain a richer sense still of Chaucer's irony when in *Sir Thopas* and *Melibee*, he presents two ends of a still-growing spectrum. I join an increasing number of critics who see that much has been overlooked in our attempts to 'tidy up' medieval English literature, and that genres that have traditionally been seen as less sophisticated, like the tail-rhyme stanza, are at greatest risk of suffering by comparison to other texts that have received closer critical attention.[81] However, I assert that print essentially closed the door on the graphic tail-rhyme prematurely; remarkably, de Worde, who showed such interest in reviving the verse romance Caxton eschewed, printed only Chaucer's *Sir Thopas* in graphic tail-rhyme.[82]

---

[78] *Isumbras* is typically cited as an example of how at least some tail-rhyme romances must have been transmitted orally (Purdie, 'Gray's Inn', p. 268).

[79] On this combination, see A. Putter, 'Introduction', in *The Spirit of Medieval English Popular Romance*, ed. J. Gilbert and A. Putter (New York, 2000), p. 13.

[80] For Chaucer's satire of self, see L. Patterson, '"What Man Artow?": Authorial Self-Definition in *The Tale of Sir Thopas* and *The Tale of Melibee*', SAC 2 (1989), 117–35.

[81] For an assessment of the issues pertaining to metrics, with some emphasis on tail-rhyme, see Putter, 'Metre and the Editing of Middle English Verse', pp. 29–33.

[82] See Sánchez-Mardí, 'The Printed History', pp. 7–9; J. Sánchez-Mardí, 'The Publication of English Medieval Romances after the Death of Wynkyn de Worde,

De Worde was certainly aware of the layout's importance to Chaucer's parody, and so preserved it, and yet Chaucer's parody appears to have been almost too successful, convincing de Worde that this *mise-en-page* styling in particular was laughable, or at least unnecessary. Yet manuscripts such as those detailed here and others, including the Findern manuscript (Cambridge, University Library, MS Ff.1.6), show clearly that a variety of graphic layouts and *mise-en-page* were thought natural by readers and amateur scribes late into the fifteenth century. De Worde also printed texts with relatively complex apparatus, images and layouts which indicates printing the graphic tail-rhyme would not have produced difficulties. I must conclude that de Worde and his printshop made a conscious choice to set the type of verse tail-rhyme romances into cleaner columns with no graphic tail-rhyme layout, establishing the form for centuries of readers to come, as their primary encounter with this medieval form became written and not sung. But I maintain that we can best understand graphic tail-rhyme as an imaginative feature of the form, not an obstacle to comprehension. Restoring the graphic tail-rhyme to the general reading experience could restore important elements of its poetic power that mark such poetry as a distinct artifact occupying a space between the oral and the written. The poetic contours of these artifacts remain as yet unexplored. Recognizing these aspects of manuscript form would go some way towards recuperating the tail-rhyme's poetic achievements.

1536–1569', in *Early Printed Narrative Literature in Western Europe*, ed. B. Besamusca, E. de Bruijn and F. Willaert (Boston, 2019), pp. 144–5. See also C. M. Meale, 'Caxton, de Worde, and the Publication of Romance in Late Medieval England', *The Library* 14.4 (1992), 283–98; T. Adams, 'Printing and the Transformation of the Middle English Romance', *Neophilologus* 82 (1998), 291–310; Y. Wang, 'Caxton's Romances and Their Early Tudor Readers', *Huntington Library Quarterly* 67 (2004), 173–88; Wiggins, 'Romance in the Age of Print'.

3

Ars Codicis: Marginalia, Meaning and the Manuscript Book(s) of Chaucer's *House of Fame*

SARAH BAECHLE

In the indispensable *Opening Up Middle English Manuscripts*, Kathryn Kerby-Fulton sets forth the first compelling interpretation of the authorial *Canterbury Tales* glosses as hermeneutic, rather than editorial detritus.[1] The glosses from *Against Jovinian* in the Wife of Bath's Prologue dramatize a conflict between competing sacred *auctores* on the nature of marriage, sexuality and gender, simultaneously pitting scripture itself – particularly the Pauline epistles – against their polemical use in Jerome's text. Each differently recontextualizes the vernacular, unrestrainedly proliferating multiple competing interpretations of the Wife, without assigning authority to any particular one. This hermeneutic practice is found, as well, in two manuscripts of *Troilus and Criseyde* with authorial glosses, suggesting that Chaucer engaged, over at least some portion of his career, in a sustained practice of deliberate obfuscation accessible to varying tiers of readers and embraced interpretive complexity and uncertainty over ethical orthodoxy.[2]

This essay explores the lifespan of this practice: how, I ask, is the hermeneutic of ambiguity present in the meta-literary texts of Chaucer's early career? My purpose is to trace how the material tradition of the *House of Fame*, Chaucer's complex meditation on the problems of literary authority and the nature of poetic practice, unfolds an *ars poetica* embracing precisely this hermeneutic. This early Chaucerian work, a meta-literary dream vision, is a poem deeply

---

[1] K. Kerby-Fulton, 'Professional Readers at Work: Annotators, Editors, and Correctors in Middle English Literary Texts', in K. Kerby-Fulton, M. Hilmo and L. Olson, *Opening Up Middle English Manuscripts: Literary and Visual Approaches* (Ithaca, 2012), pp. 207–44.

[2] S. Baechle, 'Multi-Dimensional Reading in Two Manuscripts of *Troilus and Criseyde*', *ChR* 51 (2016), 248–68.

concerned with the literary foundations upon which the edifice of Chaucer's text is both literally and figuratively constructed. As the poet grapples with identifying his place in classical tradition, the poem unravels, and while it is tempting for modern readers to see in the text a performance of the anxiety of influence, a writer measuring himself against the poets of 'gret auctoritee' (l. 2158) and finding it impossible to compare, the poem's display of skepticism for poetic *auctoritas* enacts instead a heuristic that accords with the codicological evidence of the Chaucerian textual tradition and the hermeneutic complexity which Kerby-Fulton describes.[3] Rather than seeking solutions to the impossibilities of differing classical *auctores* that the text raises, Chaucer identifies precisely this impossibility and difference as generative, a font from which poetic practice emerges complexly and free of the fickle influence of Fame's judgment. Moreover, I argue, this poetic is embraced in the Latin source glosses of all three extant manuscripts of the *House of Fame*, glosses whose unknown author, I wish to suggest, is Chaucer himself.

Although they are less known than the glosses in the *Tales* or in *Troilus*, a small set of marginal glosses appears in some form in all three of the surviving manuscripts of the *House of Fame*: Oxford, Bodleian Library, MSS Fairfax 16 and Bodley 628, and Cambridge, Magdalene College, MS Pepys 2006.[4] Their presence within each of the extant copies suggests those manuscripts' reliance upon an earlier exemplar for the glosses; that they span two different textual families – the α group, consisting of Fairfax 16 and Bodley 628, and the β, which includes Pepys 2006 and the Caxton and Thynne editions – necessitates the glosses' presence early in the text's stemma, and arguably from the theorized original copy.[5] This apparatus includes a set of source and citation glosses that direct readers toward often competing intertextual *auctoritates* for the poem's fraught exploration of creative and textual authority. Building on Kerby-Fulton's characterization of the glossing apparatus in the manuscripts of the *Tales* and drawing into account both the relationships of the manuscripts to one another and the text's invocation of the *ordinatio* of the manuscript

---

[3] Kerby-Fulton, 'Professional Readers at Work'; all Chaucer quotations are from L. D. Benson, gen. ed., *The Riverside Chaucer*, 3rd ed. (Boston, 1987).

[4] Available online at 'Bodleian Library MS. Fairfax 16', *Digital Bodleian*, accessed May 8, 2023, https://digital.bodleian.ox.ac.uk/objects/ee2d3617-5696-4ec8-9e4d-a99d0c485019/, and 'Bodleian Library MS. Bodl. 638', *Digital Bodleian*, accessed May 8, 2023, https://digital.bodleian.ox.ac.uk/objects/720cc562-25c9-4a5f-8200-8784e12066f8/.

[5] See M. C. Seymour, *A Catalogue of Chaucer Manuscripts, vol. 1: Works Before the Canterbury Tales* (Aldershot, 1995), and the discussion of base text in *The Riverside Chaucer*, p. 1139.

page in the *House*'s literary architecture, I argue that these glosses, like those in the *Tales* and *Troilus*, ought to be regarded as the work of the poet himself.

As the *House of Fame* watches the authority of classical texts deteriorate until both that authority and the poem itself fall apart, the source glosses from the classical tradition appended to the English exploration of their destabilization underscore the poem's depiction of rapidly disintegrating *auctoritas*. The *House of Fame*'s manuscript setting, often elided from discussions of the text, thus witnesses a material context that both reinforces the central dilemma of the text and mimics – or perhaps, more accurately, prefigures – the hermeneutic processes of the Chaucerian apparatus that Kerby-Fulton sets forth.[6] These glosses' fitness, both within the specific context of the *House of Fame* and the wider context of other Chaucerian glosses, argues strongly for the poet's authorship. Understanding, moreover, these glosses as authorial and thus as part of a lifelong interest in the potential of the manuscript page invites Chaucer scholars to reimagine the poet's authorial self-fashioning.[7] It allows us to theorize a poetics of the codex, under whose rubric Chaucer engages the material book not merely as writing support or engine of literary circulation but also as structuring metaphor, aestheticizing the book object in order to mediate simultaneously metaliterary and very literal exploration of the (im)possibility of poetic *auctoritas*.

Tempered Textuality: The Poetics of Synthesis in the *House of Fame*

Scholarship on the *House of Fame* has long recognized the poem's abiding mistrust of *auctoritas* and of Fame 'understood as the body of traditional knowledge that confronted the educated fourteenth-century reader'.[8] Yet the scholarship that acknowledges Chaucer's engagement with this conflict seeks likewise to find a way to ameliorate it: Chaucer is imagined, for example, as presenting faith – the superior faculty to logic – as a means of adjudicating interpretation in weighing conflicting authors, or as placing the authority for interpretation in the hands of the reader, who is imagined to weigh *auctores* and

---

[6] Kerby-Fulton, 'Professional Readers at Work'.

[7] R. Davis, 'Fugitive Poetics in Chaucer's *House of Fame*', *SAC* 37 (2015), 101–32, argues for the *House of Fame*'s poetics as a kind of 'theoretical General Prologue to the *Canterbury Tales*', foregrounding not only its status as *ars poetica* but also its metaliterary *and* formal ties to the later work.

[8] S. Delany, *Chaucer's House of Fame: The Poetics of Skeptical Fideism* (Gainesville, 1994), p. 3.

identify a correct, ethical reading.⁹ Even for scholarship receptive to Chaucer's skepticism towards classical poetics, the poet still works from a position of anxiety about authority and conflict. For David Lyle Jeffrey, although the fallen human reader – and presumably poet – cannot themself arrive at a singular, unified 'truth' of historic and poetic meaning, such meaning does exist, and its desirability is unquestioned, with Jeffrey terming humanity's foreshortened perspective a 'problem' of interpretation that demands 'ultimate judgement' to determine literary truth.[10] Laurel Amtower and Katherine H. Terrell, both receptive to Geffrey's (and Chaucer's) abdication of poetic authority, relocate the responsibility to readers. For them, the *House of Fame*'s metapoetics still demands *some* resolution to the conflicts generated by disagreeing *auctores*: Amtower imagines readers 'sifting' potential interpretations to determine how to properly understand a text, while Terrell observes that the 'burden of interpretation falls to the reader' when faced with conflicting *auctores*.[11] Crucially, these accounts imagine such ambiguity as a crisis demanding resolution – a problem, for Jeffrey, and a burden, in Terrell's phrasing – all readings that lean into scholars' sense that medieval theories of authorship fostered anxiety on the part of poets attempting to find their place in the canon. Sarah Powrie, whose reading of the poem most visibly distances Chaucer's enterprise from received notions of authority and truth, observes his joy in the playful potential of this polysemy, identifying it as a 'creative principle and generator of potential meaning' – a process, though, that ultimately still returns to the necessity of hermeneutic authority, again invested in readers who here launch the text into the ambit of Fame.[12] I want to advocate still further movement from the sphere of interpretation and into that of generation: that the *House*

---

[9] For discussions of the *House of Fame* as meta-poetic, see L. Amtower, 'Authorizing the Reader in Chaucer's *House of Fame*', *Philological Quarterly* 79 (2000), 273–91; J. C. Fumo, 'Chaucer as *Vates*?: Reading Ovid through Dante in the *House of Fame* Book 3', in *Writers Reading Writers: Intertextual Studies in Medieval and Early Modern Literature in Honor of Robert Hollander*, ed. J. L. Smarr (Newark DE, 2007), pp. 89–108; D. L. Jeffrey, 'Sacred and Secular Scripture: Authority and Interpretation in the *House of Fame*', in *Chaucer and Scriptural Tradition*, ed. D. L. Jeffrey (Ottawa, 1979), pp. 207–28; S. Powrie, 'Alan of Lille's *Anticlaudianus* as Intertext in Chaucer's *House of Fame*', *ChR* 44 (2010), 246–67; R. J. Meyer-Lee, 'Literary Value and the Customs House: The Axiological Logic of the *House of Fame*', *ChR* 48 (2014), 374–94; K. H. Terrell, 'Reallocation of Hermeneutic Authority in Chaucer's *House of Fame*', *ChR* 31 (1997), 279–90.

[10] Jeffrey, 'Sacred and Secular', p. 228.

[11] Amtower, 'Authorizing the Reader', p. 283; Terrell, 'Reallocation of Authority', pp. 284–5.

[12] Powrie, '*Anticlaudianus* as Intertext', p. 257.

of Fame shows Chaucer invested ultimately not in how poetry means what it does (right or wrong) or in how it will be apprehended but rather how this ambiguity provides the locus for vernacular authors to generate – to *do* poetry, as it were. However, as the *House of Fame* progresses through a series of metapoetic explorations, I argue, we see an invitation for radical departure from the need for adjudication and a refusal of differentiation, for Chaucer locates his poetic not in the choice between conflicting *auctores* but in the ability to hold them simultaneously together in conflict, asserting, ultimately, not division and 'right' selection, but fusion, a mutually shared *auctoritas*.

The *House of Fame* begins from the spectre of misreading, as its narrator, Geffrey, curses all who might 'mysdeme' the dream he is about to recount (ll. 93–101), giving voice to the concerns of classical exegesis, aligning authorship, authority and truth – to *mis*read presumes the existence of a correct reading to misapprehend. These anxieties shape the first locus of exploration within the *House*, as Geffrey navigates the textual edifice of the *Aeneid*, synecdochic emblem of this classical tradition and realized as the Temple of Venus, engraved all over with images of the text's narrative. Contained within its walls, he encounters a poetic tradition that appears reliant on stability – engraving, 'graven', both to write and to etch into metal as the gold of Venus's Temple (ll. 121–2) produces a static, fixed text – and functions through a kind of ekphrastic mnemonic reading. A brass tablet with the opening lines of the *Aeneid* locates the narrative (ll. 142–8), but this plaque offers the sole point of textual access, with the narrative unfolding visually, Geffrey filling in its peregrinations as he wanders through illustrations of its pivotal scenes.[13] The text is recounted collaboratively, Geffrey's witnessing, in repeated iterations of 'sawgh I'/'I saugh', spinning a recapitulation of its events that rely upon cued recollection of the correct narrative. Literally occupying and moving through the text, he is dwarfed by tradition, which holds space for him only as he acts

---

[13] On ekphrastic reading in *House*, see M. Bridges, 'The Picture in the Text: Ecphrasis as Self-Reflectivity in Chaucer's *Parliament of Fowles, Book of the Duchess* and *House of Fame*', *Word and Image* 5 (1989), 151–8; A. Cook, 'Creative Memory and Visual Image in Chaucer's *House of Fame*', in *Chaucer: Visual Approaches*, ed. S. Fein and D. Raybin (University Park PA, 2016), pp. 22–38; J. L. Simmons, 'The Place of the Poet in Chaucer's *House of Fame*', *MLQ* 27 (1966), 125–35. See also B. Rowland, 'The Art of Memory and the Art of Poetry in the *House of Fame*', *Revue de l'Université d'Ottawa* 51 (1981), 162–71; and D. Coley, '"Withyn a temple ymad of glas": Glazing, Glossing, and Patronage in Chaucer's *House of Fame*', *ChR* 45 (2010), 59–84. On theories of authorship and exegesis, see A. Minnis, *Medieval Theory of Authorship: Scholastic Literary Attitudes in the Later Middle Ages* (London, 1984); A. Minnis and I. Johnson, eds, *The Cambridge History of Literary Criticism, vol. 2: The Middle Ages* (Cambridge, 2005).

as conduit between the story – accessing and communicating a preexisting truth – and his own audience.

Yet, as Chaucer recognizes, this is inherently problematic, for multiple stories about the fall of Troy, Aeneas's journey and the founding of Italy circulate in the Middle Ages, with some, like Virgil and Ovid, both cited here, telling very different versions of the same story. As Geffrey perambulates the narrative, reproducing its contours in increasing depth, moving from narrative recapitulation to the renarration of Dido's address to Fama, he pauses to directly address his – and Chaucer's – readers. 'Whoso to knowe [her story] hath purpos', he commands his audience, 'Rede Virgile in Eneydos / Or the Epistle of Ovyde' (ll. 377–9), following this exhortation with a brief abstract of the *Heroides*'s contents (ll. 388–426). This interlude (for Geffrey then returns to narrating Virgil's text) reminds readers that the assumptions undergirding mnemonic reading are tenuously held. The authoritative text at the centre is not the only version that readers might access; indeed, it stands in distinct conflict with another, equally authoritative author, for whom Dido occupies the centre of the text and Aeneas is treated more critically. Geffrey observes, citing Ovid, that many books record 'the harm, the routhe / That hath betyd for such untrouthe' as Aeneas's (ll. 383–4). The type of reading structured by the Temple of Venus fantasizes a textual fixity that cannot work when it encounters a reader; indeed, the narrative interruption which dilates focus on this conflict – that is, the brief of the Ovidian intertext – must be resolved, and Geffrey turns back to the graven *Aeneid*, dismissing the crisis of conflicting *auctorites*. But this is a model of textuality that, for all its 'noblesse' (l. 471) and all its 'richesse' (l. 472), is ultimately sterile. Geffrey departs the Temple to search for signs of life, and we realize how truly empty the textual edifice has been, inhabited by him alone. Emerging through its doors, he looks around:

> Then sawgh I but a large feld,
> As fer as that I myghte see,
> Withouten toun, or hous, or tree,
> Or bush, or grass, or eryd lond;
> For al the feld nas but of sond
> ....
> Ne no maner creature
> That ys yformed by Nature
> Ne sawgh I, me to rede or wisse. (ll. 482–91)

Geffrey defines the landscape by its fundamental lack: seeking another living being, he encounters the utter lack of presence, encapsulated in a catalogue of absences – the markings of civilization, from the communal town to the individual home, cannot be found as far as Geffrey can see.[14] He characterizes this absence as fundamentally barren; nothing grows, not a single tree breaks up the expanse of sand, and his declaration that no 'eryd' [arable] land exists around the Temple both underscores the infertility of the space and links it to the metapoetics that undergird the text – to 'eren' is to plow, to prepare for sowing, but also to inscribe, the act of writing which creates the 'graven' text inside the edifice.[15] Geffrey's framing 'sawgh I' as he exits the Temple follows sixteen prior iterations that define the reading of the *Aeneid*'s visual text, conflating the authoritative text that Geffrey sees with the wasteland in which he finds himself, and this furnishes a crisis of both interpretation and authorship. This desert proffers no human to explicate the text, to instruct Geffrey in its particularities – he wonders at its authorship, its creation – or anyone to read him, for 'reden' indexes both teaching, advising and the act of reading itself in its manifold forms.[16] Indeed, within this barren field, Geffrey encounters the Jovian eagle who diagnoses his malaise: Chaucer's narrator *wishes* to write, labours at poetry, but lacks appropriate matter, labouring over others' books rather than enditing from 'tydynges' of his subject (ll. 620–60). The sterility that defines Venus's Temple and the text upon which it very literally rests precludes literary generation. The engraved golden Virgilian text transforms into barren sand, leaving no room for further production, constructed as an act simultaneously of reading or interpreting and crafting.

As the dream progresses, Geffrey discovers that the very architecture itself on which this classical tradition is written is unstable. His abduction by an eagle who reminds Geffrey of his failure as an aspiring poet leaves him deposited in the territories of Fame, where the architecture of Venus's Temple is echoed in the first building he encounters, set on a foundation on which the names of famous men are inscribed, the glass and gold and brass of the temple diminished to ice and the names written on half partially melted, irretrievably lost. As Geffrey enters into Fame's house, home to literal monuments to the

---

[14] Scholarship typically associates this absence with a rejection of the poetry of Venus. See P. Boitani, *Chaucer and the Imaginary World of Fame* (Cambridge, 1974), p. 60; Delaney, *Chaucer's House*, p. 58; B. Koonce, *Chaucer and the Tradition of Fame: Symbolism in the House of Fame* (Princeton, 1966), pp. 127–8.

[15] *MED*, s.v. 'eren' v. (1). See also Davis, 'Fugitive Poetics', pp. 111–17. In contrast to my own reading, Davis's, which briefly surveys other scholarship on the desert, identifies the desert as a shore, a transitional space between traditions that is fundamental to creative generation. S. Meecham-Jones, 'Betwixen Hevene and Erthe and See: Seeing Words in Chaucer's *House of Fame*', in *Unity and Difference in European Cultures*, ed. N. Thomas and F. Le Saux (Durham, 1998), pp. 155–71 (p. 164), also characterizes it as a potential space of inspiration or 'spiritual enlightenment'.

[16] *MED*, s.v. 'reden' v. (1).

auctores and a place of distortion in which things are not what they seem, he encounters Fama herself, fluctuating in size from less than a cubit until her feet reach the earth, distorting reality as she doles out praise and censure in ways untethered to the deeds or the people in question, divorcing *auctoritas* from merit according to her whims. Here, Geffrey witnesses new models of circulation and multiplication, which he soundly rejects. Asked if he, too, has come to seek approbation from Fama, Geffrey denies any desire for such a 'name' or for the chance to petition Fama herself:[17]

> Sufficeth me, as I were ded,
> That no wight have my name in honde.
> I wot myself best how y stonde;
> For what I drye, or what I thynke,
> I wil myselven al hyt drynke,
> Certeyn, for the more part,
> As fer forth as I kan myn art. (ll. 1876–82)

Geffrey's desired outcome of this journey to Fama's territory is not reputation founded on participation in *auctoritas*, but on the 'new tydynges' that he was promised when scooped up by Jove's eagle. These tidings – the promised comfort or solution to Geffrey's abysmal performance as a poet – foreground novelty: as news, gossip, announcements, revelation, 'tidinge' encompasses language that, in contrast to the sterility of the Virgilian textual desert, foregrounds generation.[18] Geffrey finds these tidings in Dedalus's house, a house of diverse twigs that 'whirleth … aboute' 'as swyft as thought' – so quickly that one cannot enter without a guide to show one the way (ll. 2006, 1924). Yet the twig house is remarkably stable, for although it is built from 'tymber of no strengthe / yet hit is founded to endure' (ll. 1980–1). Its ligneous origins recall the sterility of the wasteland in which no single tree can be seen, relieved in the living, green (and red, yellow and white) fertile material of Dedalus's house (ll. 1936–7, 1920). Its 'founding' stresses creation as well as stability, because 'founden' means to create or to establish by building a sound basis or beginning, connotations that are affirmed in the contrasting doublet that bookends this act of construction.[19] Although not physically strong, the house is lasting, hardened, resistant, rivalling, it seems, classical *auctoritas* in one of

---

[17] See also J. Burrow, 'Geffrey's Credo: *House of Fame*, Lines 1873–82', *ChR* 48 (2014), 251–7, which notes that nothing further comes of Geffrey's rejection of Fame, and A. Minnis, 'Chaucer Drinks What He Brews: *The House of Fame*, 1873–82', *Notes and Queries* 61 (2014), 187–9.

[18] *MED*, s.v. 'tidinge' n.

[19] *MED*, s.v. 'founden' v. (2); s.v. 'enduren' v.

the criteria for determining authority: its ability to last, wood withstanding where ice cannot. Wooden twigs, more pliable than the sterile gold of Venus's Temple or the slowly melting foundations of Fame's house, both endure and reproduce in ways the other two cannot.

Inside this space, Geffrey finds a new model for textual circulation, the house abuzz with the new tidings covering a lengthy list of topics – amongst which subjects one finds the *materia* of Chaucer's later corpus, though the list is holistic enough to support alignment with a great many vernacular poet's works (ll. 1959–76). This model operates through its very audience, who immediately become authors themselves, each hearing some gossip and passing it along to the next person they see, always magnifying its content, increasing it beyond its origins:

> Whan oon had herd a thing, ywis,
> He com forth ryght to another wight,
> And gan him tellen anon-ryght
> The same that to him was told,
> Or hyt a forlong way was old,
> But gan somwhat for to eche
> To this tydynge in this speche
> More than hit ever was. (ll. 2060–7)

Language circulates, within this house, beyond the kind of control fantasized about in the mediated text of Venus's Temple, but for Geffrey, this process appears generative. Propelled by a kind of audience consumption and replication in which tidings, once heard, are circulated by the hearer, this process is imagined as accretive, increasing the original 'text' of the tiding until it becomes 'more', a quantitative and qualitative measure suggesting both material expansion – the text grown through a kind of amplification or augmentation – and improvement, bettering.[20] A sonic instead of visual process of reading, tidings in the twig House of Dedalus are mediated through 'speche' and increased ('eche', from 'eken') through sound, the homophonically invoked echo rebounding from speaker to speaker.[21] This auditory nature affirms the novelty, the immediacy of the tiding as text, foregrounding the process of its generation: we witness its repeated creation and circulation, without denying its literariness, as 'speche' indexes the written word as well as the verbal.[22]

[20] *MED*, s.v. 'mor(e' adj. (comparative).
[21] *MED*, s.v. 'eken' v., but also s.v. 'ecco' n. See also L. K. Arnovick, '"In Forme of Speche" is Anxiety: Orality in Chaucer's *House of Fame*', *Oral Tradition* 11 (1996), 320–45.
[22] *MED*, s.v. 'speche' n.

Dedalus's House proffers a site of fundamentally literary production, the circulating 'tydynges' presented as texts themselves.

The result is that, as in circulation-by-Fama, the story is distorted, this time through each member of its audience, until again, conflicting versions of a story face one another:

> And somtyme saugh I thoo at ones
> A lesyng and a sad soth sawe
> That gonne of aventure drawe
> Out at a wyndowe for to pace;
> And, when they metten in that place,
> They were achekked bothe two,
> And neyther of hem moste out goo
> For other, so they gonne crowde,
> Til ech of hem gan crien lowde,
> 'Lat me go first!' 'Nay, but let me!
> And here I wol ensuren the,
> Wyth the nones that thou wolt do so,
> That I shal never fro the go,
> But be thyn owne sworen brother!
> We wil medle us ech with other,
> That no man, be they never so wrothe,
> Shal han on [of us] two, but bothe
> At ones …'. (ll. 2088–105)

In the space of Dedalus's House, expressly contrasting statements butt up against one another, 'metten', a capacious verb that can suggest not merely encountering one another but also joining with, engaging, potentially with martial connotations as well as coincidental ones, meeting specifically by chance.[23] These layers of signification collapse the central concerns of the *House of Fame*'s metapoetics: the clash that occurs beyond control or prediction is reinforced in the meeting 'of aventure' between conflicting sources, and it is resolved not by exclusion, as in the return to Virgilian orthodoxy in the Temple of Venus, but by union. The 'lesyng', the lie or falsehood, and the sober 'soth' that encounter one another both witness this clear conflict and summon the terms of anxiety that underlie constructions of authorship as authority, introducing truth to the terms of textual production.[24] But, in the whirling

---

[23] *MED*, s.v. 'meten' v. (4).
[24] On truth and falsehood, see R. W. Hanning, 'Chaucer's First Ovid: Metamorphosis and Poetic Tradition in *The Book of the Duchess* and the *House of Fame*', in *Chaucer and the Craft of Fiction*, ed. L. A. Arrathoon (Rochester MI, 1986), pp. 121–63 (pp.

twig house of new tidings, this conflict requires no adjudication; rather, both lie and truth bind themselves to one another as 'sworn brethren', promising to 'medle' with one another so that in the future, all who hear them shall never have one or the other but encounter both at once. The use of 'medle' here is telling, suggesting not merely a simple binary pairing, each side identifiable and divisible, but rather a mixture of the two disparate parts: 'medlen' means to conflict, to fight with – underscoring the disparity between texts – as well as to blend, to mix, but also to temper, an alchemical transformation that renders the resulting substance stronger and more flexible.[25] The increase, the echoing 'eke' that renders a tiding 'more', roots itself in this synthesis, in which the hearer must always have both texts, lie and truth at once, because they have ceased to exist independently of one another – however much the reader, potentially 'wrothe' with their union, might wish it otherwise.

Throughout, Geffrey stresses the crucial melding of the two conflicting texts, their merging framed by uses of 'at ones' (ll. 2088, 2105), which insist upon the simultaneity of truth and lie, always to be encountered in unison. The merging, described by the personified tidings themselves, stresses mutuality, a blending of 'ech with other' (l. 2102), equating the two grammatically and refusing to differentiate between them. The final product metrically centres this mutuality; the paradoxical union in which two tidings become one new union, doubled or increased in its decrease – two to one, a one that is now two – arrests readerly attention in its spondaic 'on two' (l. 2104), as the unamended line reads.[26] Metrical and grammatical equivalency – 'on' and 'two' equally stressed but also equally the object of 'han' – conspire to refuse differentiation between either tiding, authorizing the mutual 'bothe' that defines the reality an audience will encounter. This union itself adopts the legal-theological rhetorics of marriage's fleshly union: one (unidentified) tiding offers to 'ensuren', a formal pledge with legal registers, including marital vows, itself to the other *on the condition* of mutuality, that is, only if ('wyth the nones', l. 2099) the other consents as well.[27] Adducing marriage as a framing context – mutual consent being necessary for the formation of marriage in canon law – the bond between the two conflicting texts becomes disseverable, translating them into the single, indivisible flesh of conjugal union. The Temple of Venus deals

---

144–5); N. Haydock, 'False and Sooth Compounded in Caxton's Ending of Chaucer's *House of Fame*', *Atenea* 26 (2006), 107–29.

[25] *MED*, s.v. 'medlen' v.

[26] 'Shal han on two but bothe' is the Fairfax 16 reading (fol. 183r); 'of us' is an editorial emendation not witnessed in either manuscript text (Bodley has 'that oon'). See *The Riverside Chaucer* textual notes, p. 1142.

[27] *MED*, s.v. 'ensuren' v.

with its crisis of conflict through excision, purging the Ovidian spectre raised in Geffrey's acknowledgment of other *auctores* through its decisive return to the ekphrastic graven *Aeneid*. It affirms the division between two competing traditions and identifies a definitive winner to the contest. But the textual interplay in Dedalus's twig house refuses this severance entirely. One tiding, one text may be true and one false, but once 'meten', these divisions no longer exist; they cannot be extricated from one another.

In this form, each tiding, magnified and conflicting, circulates without need of Fame's judgment – they arrive in her house and are blown about the world without narrative recourse to the long process of appeals that Geffrey earlier witnessed. It appears, then, to be a successful model of publication, growing from the uncontrollable proliferation of ambiguous and contradictory tidings. The problems raised by Book I, exposing the inconsistencies of classical *auctores*, are addressed not by determining a method of choosing the correct interpretation but rather by insisting on holding both simultaneously together – and allowing them to circulate as the *materia* of the new poetic. It should not be surprising, then, that the Man of Gret Auctoritee does not appear, or that the poem cuts off: he has no place in this house of new tidings. This polyvalent poetic is familiar to readers of the *Canterbury Tales* and *Troilus* glosses, which literally, physically hold Chaucer and his multiple, conflicting sources together on the manuscript page. But these marginalia are not exclusive to the manuscript tradition of Chaucer's later poetry; the *House of Fame* itself is likewise accompanied by a short series of Latin source glosses, to which I now turn.

Marginal 'Medling': Practicing Poetics in the Manuscripts of the *House of Fame*

The *House of Fame* survives the Middle Ages in three manuscript copies, none complete, but all three accompanied by a shared apparatus of marginal glosses. The two Oxford manuscripts, Bodleian Library, MSS Fairfax 16 and Bodley 638, are members of the same textual family and contain essentially identical glosses, while Cambridge, Magdalene College, MS Pepys 2006 witnesses a circumscribed version, less complete but nonetheless shared where it includes a gloss. Like their counterparts in Chaucer's later texts, these glosses explore the potential immanent in the clashing authorities at the heart of the *House*'s metapoetics.[28] I address them here from their instantiation in Fairfax 16 – on

---

[28] Kerby-Fulton, 'Professional Readers at Work'; Baechle, 'Multidimensional Reading'.

the authority of both its earlier date and typical use as base text for modern editions[29] – where the text of the first book is accompanied by a series of glosses from the Latin *auctores* that inform the Trojan War history etched into the Temple of Venus. These glosses follow a narrative of divergence from their central Latin source of *auctoritas*: after an allusion to the stream of Lethe, a set of glosses spanning folios 156r to 159v grows out from the invocation of the beginning of the *Aeneid*. The brass plaque on the Temple's wall promises to 'synge, yif I kan / the armes and also the man' (ll. 143–4), echoing (in English) the first two lines-and-a-word of the *Aeneid*'s famous opening. The marginal text offers Virgil's Latinate counterpart:

Arma viru<u>m</u> <u>que</u> cano troie qui
pri<u>mus</u> ab horia . Italia<u>m</u> fato pro
fugus labina <u>que</u> venit litora .

[I sing the arms and the man, who first from the borders of Troy, exiled by Fate, came to Italy and the Lavinian shores.][30]

The Latin and vernacular cleave closely to one another; what Chaucer has written in English is what he has found in Virgil, endlessly repeating in gloss, text, engraven Temple image, all appearing to accord with one another. The next several glosses also draw on extracts from the *Aeneid* Books I–IV, and they typically agree with Chaucer's vernacular version. The gloss observes that the story of Polites's death can be found, just as we have read – or seen in the ekphrasis on the Temple – in Virgil, which the manuscript quotes briefly in the margins. Chaucer observes that the ghost of Creusa appears to her now-widower and commands him to look after their son, and the gloss offers readers Book II's wording of her request. Chaucer narrates, almost whimsically, how Achate met with Venus dressed quaintly as a huntress, and the gloss writes up the details of Venus's attire from Book II.

At folio 159r, however, text and gloss begin to interact in more complicated ways. Three glosses march down the right-hand margin. Two are taken at least partially from the *Aeneid*: in one, Dido blames Anna for encouraging her to look kindly on Aeneas; in the other, Chaucer holds forth on the swiftness of Fama, as Dido, speaking from her graven image on the walls of Venus's temple, laments (ironically, given she speaks only in circulating text) the spread of her reputation:

---

[29] See J. Norton-Smith, 'Introduction', in *Bodleian Library MS. Fairfax 16* (London, 1979), pp. vii–ix.

[30] Fairfax's gloss reads 'horia' where Bodley, more correctly, has 'horis'; I translate from this reading. All translations mine except where otherwise indicated.

> For thorgh yow is my name lorn
> And alle myn actes red and songe
> Over al thys lond, on every tonge.
> O wikke Fame! – for ther nys
> Nothing so swift, lo, as she is!
> O, soth ys, every thing ys wyst,
> Though hit be kevered with the myst. (HF, ll. 346–52)

The margins include a source gloss reading, 'Virgilius Fama mal<u>um</u> qua no<u>n</u> / veloci<u>us</u> vllu<u>m</u> Nichil occultu<u>m</u> / quod non reueletur' [Virgil No other evil thing travels faster than Fama / Nothing [is] hidden that may not be revealed] (Fairfax 16, fol. 159r), which is drawn from two source texts, the *Aeneid* and the Bible:

> Extemplo Libyae magnas it Fama per urbes –
> Fama, malum qua non aliud velocius ullum;
> mobilitate viget, viresque adquirit eundo,
> parva metu primo, mox sese attollit in auras,
> ingrediturque solo, et caput inter nubila condit.
>
> [Immediately, Fama races through the great cities of Libya – No other evil thing travels faster than Fama; strengthened by speed, and gaining strength as she goes, small at first through fear, soon she raises herself up into the air, and she advances, with her head hidden among the clouds.] (*Aeneid* IV.173–7)

> Ne ergo timueritis eos. Nihil enim est opertum, quod non revelabitur: et occultum, quod non scietur. Quod dico vobis in tenebris, dicite in lumine: et quod in aure auditis, prædicate super tecta.
>
> [Therefore do not fear them. There is nothing hidden that shall not be revealed: and nothing secret, that shall not be known. What I say to you in the shadows, say in the light: and what you have heard in your ear, preach from the rooftops.] (Matthew 10:26–7)

The manuscript gloss begins with the appropriate excerpt from *Aeneid*, Book IV: Dido bemoans Fama's velocity, and Virgil offers further detail into the mechanisms of her travel, a perpetual motion machine of speed and strength that increases her size in proportion with her influence. Yet this Dido does not merely ventriloquize her own authors; rather, she speaks in competing *auctores*, splicing Virgil with Matthew's warning that those things which are hidden will be revealed.[31] Both source texts are weighed in the gloss: only a capital letter, at the beginning of a new sentence, marks the change of source. Each offers a different field within which to set Dido's lament: the gloss from the *Aeneid* provides (like the earlier glosses) fuller descriptive context, the lengthy revelation of Fama's monstrous body with its thousand prying eyes, straining ears and gossiping tongues. Rumour and revelation are horrifying things, circulating through this terrible form and wounding innocent victims like Dido. The Gospel of Matthew, the second intertext, frames the problem of knowledge and circulation rather differently, as a simultaneous comfort and admonition to the persecuted: they need not fear their persecutors, those who kill the body but not the soul, for their wicked deeds will be revealed, however they may try to hide them. The spread of information is a balm, and the good Christian is encouraged, then, to preach this message from the rooftops, taking on for themselves the role of Fama and dispersing news through the sacred Christian body, rather than its monstrous counterpart. Here, amusingly, even Fama herself is subject to the vicissitudes of reputation's uncontrolled circulation and interpretation beyond one's origins.

Sandwiched between these two Virgilian glosses on folio 159r is the third, a brief, uncited gnomic statement in Latin. Dido observes ruefully that her future actions will come under scrutiny, interpreted in terms of her marriage to Aeneas:

> I shal thus juged be:
> 'Loo, ryght as she hath don, now she
> Wol doo eft-sones, hardely'
> Thus seyth the peple prively. (HF, ll. 357–60)

Here, the margins read, 'Cras poterunt turpia / Fieri sicut heri' [tomorrow the same foulness will be done as yesterday] (Fairfax 16, fol. 159r), a textual excerpt locatable in multiple texts:

> 'Rumor de veteri faciet ventura timeri;
> Cras poterunt fieri turpia sicut heri'.
>
> [From old things, Rumour will cause what is to come to be feared; tomorrow the same foulness will be done as yesterday.] (*Carmina burana*, Carmen 101)

> Calcant archipraesules colla cleri prona,
> Et extorquent lacrimas ut emungant dona;
> Nec, si ferunt miseri pauca, vel non bona,

---

[31] To my knowledge, only J. Griffiths, *Diverting Authorities: Experimental Glossing Practices in Manuscript and Print* (Oxford, 2014), p. 58, discusses these paired glosses.

Aequis accipient animis, donantve corona.
Si de contumelia caeperit quis conqueri,
Statim causse porrigunt aurem, manum muneri;
Si semel acceperint rem pluralis numeri,
Cras poterunt fieri turpia sicut heri.
Diligit episcopus hilarem datorem,
Fas et nefas ausus post muneris odorem,
Nescius resumere, post lapsum pudorem,
Ejectum semel attrita de fronte ruborem. (*Contra avaros*)

[The archbishops tread under foot the necks of the clergy, and extort tears in order that they may be dried by gifts; nor, if the poor wretches bring few or not good ones, do they take them in good part, or acknowledge them with favour. If anyone begins to complain of an injury, they immediately stretch their ear to the cause, their hand to the gift; if they once receive a thing of the plural number, tomorrow the same basenesses may be done as yesterday. The bishop loves a cheerful giver, and dares either right or wrong after the smell of a bribe, unable to resume, after he has thrown shame aside, the blush once rejected from his worn brow.][32]

The gloss, which echoes Dido's complaint, has no Ovidian or Vergilian origins; rather, it is taken from a couplet alluding to Helen of Troy that is witnessed in multiple sources and that circulated widely in the Middle Ages as 'the so-called Versus magistri Hildeberti, a short elegiac poem on Troy'; as 'Pergama flere volo' in the *Carmina Burana*; as an excerpt in Caxton's 1464 *Recuyell of the Historyes of Troye* (a translation of Raoul le Fèvre's 1464 compendium of 'dyuerce books' on the subject) and as a proverb. It is, moreover, witnessed in the Harley 978 political poem 'Contra avaros', a 'Song on the Corruptions of the Time', which abstracts the couplet from its Trojan context entirely.[33] Instead, it is marshalled into the service of a lengthy critique of archbishops who abuse the clergy to extract bribes.

The couplet, which Chaucer places in Dido's mouth, has undergone a process of unrestrained proliferation, magnified beyond its criticism of Helen of Troy into radically different contexts, which conflate *luxuria* and *cupiditas*, Helen's promiscuity and the earthly greed of grasping bishops unable to stop sinning once they have tasted its rewards. Dido inserts herself into an ambiguous tradition in which her mistake in loving Aeneas might be read intertextually

---

[32] 'Contra avaros', in *The Political Songs of England*, ed. and trans. T. Wright (London, 1839), p. 29; available online at *Project Gutenberg*, accessed May 11, 2023, https://www.gutenberg.org/files/61511/61511-h/61511-h.htm.

[33] *The Riverside Chaucer*, pp. 980–1.

alongside a far more expansive array of vices. The gloss facilitates this process by refusing to disclose a source: whereas excerpts from Virgil and Ovid are frequently identified as such (including the first Virgilian source quotation on this folio), the origins of this gloss are left unclear, allowing any – or all – of its sources and contexts to speak with authority about Dido's reputation.

The glosses in *House of Fame* conclude on folio 159v, with a flurry of source quotations from Ovid that pit the two central *auctores* of Dido's story against one another. Chaucer instructs readers who want to know more to 'Rede Virgile in Eneydos / Or the Epistle of Ovyde' (ll. 378–9), and as he outlines the lives of other mistreated women below, the glosses present source quotations from Ovid's versions, which, too, begin to fill in details from one source of *auctoritas* – Chaucer notes vaguely that a number of classical men were false to women: Achilles to Briseis, Jason to Medea, Theseus to Ariadne. Each is accompanied by an excerpt of the opening lines of each woman's letter in the *Heroides*, outlining the particulars of the *ways* in which each woman has been mistreated: Briseis identifies herself as 'rapta'; Medea remembers securing Jason's safety in her native land; Ariadne accuses Theseus of savagery worse than wild beasts. In and of themselves the glosses simply fill in further narrative detail. But in their context as the concluding set of glosses in the *House of Fame*, they offer a means of following Chaucer's advice in the text to read Virgil *or* Ovid: one can read both. The Ovidian intertext, glossing a narrative emerging from the ekphrastic narration of Virgil's text, holds the two together simultaneously, a solution to the problems of competing authority that Chaucer raises continually throughout the *House of Fame*. The Temple of Venus affirms textual orthodoxy, effecting a return to a single narrative's authority, and the glosses both underscore this choice, disappearing when Geffrey resumes his ekphrastic reading, and foreshadow the resolution he imagines will generate literary production in the merging of conflicting tidings.

I want to conclude by addressing the unspoken question implied in the discussion of these marginalia: the problem of their authorship. There are two possibilities: either they reflect the work of a later reader, or they, like the source glosses in manuscripts J and Gg of *Troilus and Criseyde* and those in the *Canterbury Tales* tradition, may be the work of Chaucer himself. Both suggestions are equally, if differently, significant: they could show later readers responding to the *House of Fame* in a way that brings full-circle the hermeneutic of ambiguity that Chaucer's corpus explores. Or they might provide evidence of an earlier iteration of Chaucer sorting out his marginal practice. It is with this latter possibility that I wish to conclude. For, if Chaucer's, they settle his early poetry among a robust tradition of authorial macaronic textual play among the poet's Ricardian contemporaries. John Gower affixed an elaborate apparatus of Latin material to his *Confessio Amantis*, including Latin elegiac verses, prose summaries and occasional marginal citations of authorities and explanations of allusions in the English text; these are generally understood as Gower's 'attempt ... to provide for his own works that apparatus which medieval readers believed to be appropriate to an *auctor*'.[34] William Langland's *Piers Plowman* incorporates numerous in-text Latin quotations, whose often conflicting relationship to the surrounding vernacular verse parallels that of the *Troilus* and *Tales* glosses, and Sarah Wood demonstrates the likelihood of archetypal glossing in all three textual versions of *Piers*.[35] But while Chaucerians have long accepted the poet's likely responsibility for the glosses in *Troilus* and the *Tales*, marginalia in his earlier poems have escaped this accounting, truncating our picture of his material practice and the expression of his metapoetics.

These glosses are witnessed in some form in all three manuscripts, and though their likely composition history, post-dating Chaucer's death, offers only circumstantial evidence, there are persuasive reasons to locate their composition within the sphere of the poet's creation. Fairfax 16 itself is dated to the middle of the fifteenth century, but the *House of Fame* concludes the first booklet of the manuscript, dated to not earlier than 1425, but whose compilation as a possible scriptorium exemplar is dated earlier: John Norton-Smith, citing the presence of early Lydgate in the booklet, gives it a *terminus post quem* of 1412, just over a decade after Chaucer's death.[36] Its text, though imperfect, is typically considered authoritative. Although these details cannot date the glosses conclusively, they suggest that their instantiation in Fairfax 16 sits perhaps somewhat nearer Chaucer than the manuscript's date might suggest. More compellingly, the existence of the glosses in Bodley 638 (ascribed to the α, the same textual family as Fairfax 16) as well, announces their derivation from a shared textual ancestor, while the preservation of a subset of the glosses in Pepys 2006 (classified within the β textual group), locates the glosses at a point early enough in the text's history to predate this branch in the

---

[34] Minnis, *Theory of Authorship*, p. 275. Derek Pearsall observes that Gower's glosses are markedly different from those in the *Canterbury Tales* manuscripts. D. Pearsall, 'Gower's Latin in the *Confessio Amantis*', in *Latin and Vernacular: Studies in Late-Medieval Texts and Manuscripts*, ed. A. Minnis (Cambridge, 1989), p. 14. See also Kerby-Fulton, 'Professional Readers at Work', pp. 220–1. Gower's *Traitié Selonc Les Auctours Pour Essampler Les Amantz Marietz* is likewise glossed.

[35] J. A. Alford, *Piers Plowman: A Guide to the Quotations* (Oxford, 1995); Kerby-Fulton, 'Professional Readers at Work', pp. 223–34; S. Wood, *Piers Plowman and Its Manuscript Tradition* (York, 2022), pp. 43–4.

[36] Norton-Smith, 'Introduction', p. viii.

text's transmission. Wood's extensive discussion of *Piers Plowman* marginalia observes that scribes and readers might respond to similar passages of a text, producing similar corpora of glosses, and her reminder that widely attested texts accrete layers of material whose origins can never be clear provides a necessary caution to readers of the *House of Fame*'s manuscript tradition. In the case of the *House* glosses, however, the three manuscripts witness nearly identical source quotations, appended without citation to the same passages in each manuscript, differing only in the truncation of Pepys's glosses.[37] This shared history does not prove Chaucerian authorship, but it does suggest a point of origin that does not automatically post-date the poet's lifetime.

More intriguing are the possibilities raised in the content and function of the glosses themselves. As Jane Griffiths observes, the first two glosses in the text, from the Morpheus episode in the *Metamorphoses*, are taken from the episode that also features significantly in the beginning of the *Book of the Duchess* and functions particularly well as an intertextual site of anxiety about the nature of working with authority.[38] It is a particularly Chaucerian source, in other words, one that appeared to occupy an enduring place in his early literary imagination and one that is particularly well suited to the larger questions that the *House of Fame* attempts to answer. The visible presence of Virgil and Ovid on the manuscript page underscores and illustrates precisely the struggle that Geffrey addresses; it is curious that, of all of the moments of classical *auctoritas* in Book I, the glosses zero in on the moments when *auctores* clash, picking up easily on a meta-poetic question that is incredibly complexly and convolutedly sketched out across the poem. Indeed, perhaps this is why the glosses disappear at the conclusion of Book I – as the poem increasingly enacts the more generative poetics Chaucer explores in the latter books of the *House*, these conflicting texts are drawn increasingly into the narrative itself, their eventual meeting and mixing occupying the focus of the main text. They need no longer appear in the margins; they have become the centre.

---

[37] Wood, *Manuscript Tradition*, pp. 56–63. Pepys 2006 includes the same Ovidian quotations on Lethe and the land of the Cimmerians which append the invocation to Morpheus but not the remainder of the glosses. Given the identical nature of the quotations, it would be a fairly sizable coincidence for them to be the product of two separate glossators; given their identical format to the remainder of the source glosses, it seems more likely to me that Pepys, lacking multiple lines of the text, has similarly shed its later glosses rather than that Fairfax and Bodley accreted new, hermeneutically harmonic ones, but it is of course impossible to say for sure.

[38] Griffiths, *Diverting Authorities*, pp. 56–9, suggests, albeit in passing, these glosses' potential Chaucerian origins. She, however, accords with early scholarship on the *Canterbury Tales* glosses, treating them as memoranda for further revision rather than a deliberate part of the material project of the *House of Fame*.

Likewise, we should not dismiss the significance of their paralleling, hermeneutically, the effects of the later and likely authorial glosses in *Troilus and Criseyde* and the *Canterbury Tales*, which Kerby-Fulton's exegesis in *Opening Up Middle English Manuscripts* sets forth fruitfully.[39] We lack, in this case, the clear patterns of shared textual error that link these latter marginalia to the same copies from which the English text was composed.[40] Yet the balance of similarities suggests two possibilities. The first is that a later reader adopted a particularly Chaucerian practice of annotation, one rooted in the classical materials most enduringly influential on the poet's earliest works and acutely perceptive about problems of textual interpretation whose complexity continues to challenge the poem's readers centuries later. The second, and more intriguing, is that they owe their compatibility with Chaucer's hermeneutic to their origin from his own pen, not as editorial detritus, but rather as the expression of his ongoing experimentations with a poetic of indeterminacy.

---

[39] K. Kerby-Fulton, 'Professional Readers at Work'.

[40] See, for example, J. P. Brennan, 'Reflections on a Gloss to the *Prioress's Tale* from Jerome's *Adversus Jovinianum*', *Studies in Philology* 70 (1973), 243–51; G. D. Caie, 'The Significance of the Early Chaucer Manuscript Glosses (with Special Reference to the *Wife of Bath's Prologue*)', *ChR* 10 (1976), 350–60; G. Dempster, 'Chaucer's Manuscript of Petrarch's Version of the Griselda Story', *Modern Philology* 41 (1943), 6–16 (p. 6); R. E. Lewis, 'Glosses to the *Man of Law's Tale* from Pope Innocent III's *De Miseria Humane Conditionis*', *Studies in Philology* 64 (1967), 1–16; S. Partridge, 'Glosses in the Manuscripts of the Canterbury Tales: An Edition and Commentary' (Ph.D. dissertation, Harvard University, 1992), pp. 1–26; R. A. Pratt, 'Chaucer and the Hand that Fed Him', *Speculum* 41 (1966), 619–42; and D. S. Silvia Jr., 'Glosses to the *Canterbury Tales* from St. Jerome's *Epistola Adversus Jovinianum*', *Studies in Philology* 62 (1965), 28–39.

4

Editing Chaucer's Works: Coherence and Collaboration[1]

CHRISTOPHER CANNON AND JAMES SIMPSON

There are at least three received methods of editing texts written in Middle English: by recension, by best text and eclectically.[2] Recension, formulated by Karl Lachmann (1793–1851), would have the editor detect genealogical, stemmatic relations among witnesses by filiations of shared error. This method was regarded, since the later nineteenth century, as the most 'scientific'.[3] Best text editing was proposed by Joseph Bédier (1864–1938) as an answer to logical fallacies inherent in the supposedly 'scientific' method of stemmatics.[4] Bédiér's method gave the editor a certain liberty in choosing a 'good' text plausibly close to the original, but also limited editorial liberty by having the editor stick to the best text unless it was demonstrably erroneous. From the 1960s best text editing was itself challenged for Middle English editing by George Kane (1916–2008). Kane formulated forceful arguments in favour of eclecticism. An editor's judgment, by this method, should bring to bear the evidence of textual witnesses, variant by variant, and sift that evidence so as to restore the poetic genius that scribal habits had flattened; an eclectic editor should attempt to restore an authorial reading even, if necessary, by

---

[1] We dedicate this essay to Kathryn Kerby-Fulton, in admiration for her extraordinary scholarship no less than for her exceptional mentorship and friendship.

[2] For a crisp summary of these three approaches, see R. Hanna III, '(The) Editing (of) the Ellesmere Text', in *The Ellesmere Chaucer: Essays in Interpretation*, ed. M. M. Stevens and D. Woodward (San Marino CA, 1995), pp. 225–43 (pp. 225–6). For a more extensive account, see A. Hudson, 'Middle English', in *Editing Medieval Texts: English, French, and Latin Written in England*, ed. G. Rigg (New York, 1977), pp. 34–57.

[3] For the history of stemmatics, see S. Timpanaro, *The Genesis of Lachmann's Method* (Chicago, 2005), pp. 45–89.

[4] J. Bédier, 'La tradition manuscrite du *Lai de l'Ombre*: réflexions sur l'art d'éditer les anciens textes', *Romania* 54 (1928), 161–96 (pp. 321–56). See also P. F. Dembowski, 'The "French" Tradition of Textual Philology and Its Relevance to the Editing of Medieval Texts', *Modern Philology* 90 (1993), 512–32.

conjectural emendation (i.e., by adopting a reading without support of witnesses).[5] In this essay, we present and defend a fourth method, which derives directly from our practice in our recent edition of the works of Chaucer.

A method that firmly rejects the application of any *a priori* theory must be advanced as a model, rather than as a set of principles applicable to any and every set of texts. Indeed, the fundamental premise of our method is that those principles can only be discovered *a posteriori*, after sufficient immersion in the textual environment of surviving witnesses. We have chosen to call this method 'pragmatic' because, at root, it consists of the aggregation of decisions necessitated by the specificities and the irreducible state of the surviving witnesses and their readings of Chaucer's texts. We nonetheless call our practice a 'method' because it finally elevates those decisions into a set of principles that governs the distillation of the best reading from a pool of variants.

'Pragmatic' is a term that could be stretched to describe editing by recension (in the absence of an 'original' text the editor makes the practical decision to make do with that text's surviving traces), and it certainly applies to 'best text' editing (since, again in the absence of an 'original' text, the editor makes the practical decision to rely on the witness that seems 'best'), but we press on the importance of 'practice' to the term insofar as we claim that, while our method could be used for turning other witnesses of other poets into an edition, the principles governing it in this instance only apply to the editing of the works of Chaucer.

A method so practical is itself embedded in the thousands of decisions that we have recorded as fully as possible in the *apparatus criticus* of *The Oxford Chaucer*.[6] But it is equally true that we have found, both in the course of editing and then very clearly in retrospect, that our pragmatism in this edition was governed by two simple and fundamental principles: coherence and collaboration.

We define our model of textual coherence by contrast with the model of shared error as used in editing by recension. In elucidating collaboration, we define a practice of editing as work that sits between the efforts of author and scribe, where the editor supplies what scribes do not. We recognize how much

---

[5] For various explications of eclecticism, see the following essays by G. Kane: 'Conjectural Emendation', in his *Chaucer and Langland: Historical and Textual Approaches* (London, 1989; first published 1966), pp. 150–61; '"Good" and "Bad" Manuscripts: Texts and Critics', in his *Chaucer and Langland* (Berkeley, 1989), pp. 206–13; W. Langland, *Piers Plowman: the A-Version*, ed. G. Kane, rev. ed. (London, 1986; originally published 1960), pp. 115–72; and W. Langland, *Piers Plowman: The B Version*, ed. G. Kane and E. T. Donaldson, rev. ed. (London, 1988; originally published 1975), pp. 128–220.

[6] *The Oxford Chaucer*, ed. C. Cannon and J. Simpson, 2 vols (Oxford, 2024).

our method sounds like a form of eclecticism, although we reject the association since we make none of eclecticism's necessary claims. We set out to do the following in this essay: (i) briefly demonstrate how recension is inapplicable to many of the textual environments of the surviving witnesses of Chaucer's works; (ii) make the case for pragmatic editing by defining the textual coherence and editorial collaboration in a series of examples that demonstrate the clarity such principles provide.

The Impossibility of Recension

The problems John Manly and Edith Rickert encountered in trying to edit the *Canterbury Tales* by recension are well known, but our explication here uses another well-attested work in the Chaucer canon to explore the difficulties involved in attempting to establish a hierarchy of manuscript groups in the editing of *any* work by Chaucer.[7] The process of learning how to edit Chaucer's works begins, as we have already said, with immersion in the surviving witnesses of the works, rather than with any pre-formed theory. Demonstrating the perils of employing recension in all of the textual environments of Chaucer's works is potentially a huge task. Doing so exhaustively for even a single textual environment can often itself turn out to be a large task. We have supplied copious evidence for such cases in the Textual Notes of our edition.[8] We focus here, by way of example, on the issues of shared error and of convergent variation in the witnesses of *The Parlement of Foules* (hereafter *PF*).

IA: Shared error

There are 15 authoritative witnesses for *PF*, 14 manuscripts and 1 early print.[9] The textual relations of these witnesses defy any attempt to sort them into

---

[7] For a concise critique of their method see G. Kane, 'John M. Manly (1865–1940) and Edith Rickert (1871–1938)', in *Editing Chaucer: The Great Tradition*, ed. P. G. Ruggiers (Norman, 1984), pp. 207–29, 289–91.

[8] See 'Textual Notes', in *The Oxford Chaucer*, ed. Cannon and Simpson.

[9] They are as follows: B = Oxford, Bodleian Library, MS Bodley 638, fols. 96–109; Cx = Caxton's edition (1477–8), fols. 1–16v; D = Oxford, Bodleian Library, MS Digby 181, fols. 44–52; F = Oxford, Bodleian Library, MS Fairfax 16, fols. 120–9; Ff = Cambridge, University Library, MS Ff.1.6, fols. 29–44v; Gg = Cambridge, University Library, MS Gg.4.27, fols. 480v–90v; H = London, British Library, MS Harley 7333, fols. 129v–132; Hh = Cambridge, University Library, MS Hh.4.12 (fragmentary lines 1–365), fols. 94v–9; J = Oxford, St John's College, MS 57, fols. 226–237v; L = Oxford, Bodleian Library, MS Laud 416 (fragmentary lines 1–142), fols. 288–9v; Lt = Warminster, Longleat House, MS Longleat 258, fols. 85–101; P = Cambridge, Magdalene College, MS Pepys 2006, fols. 127–42; R = Cambridge,

easily intelligible genealogical relations. We explicate the state of surviving witnesses for just four representative lines. The exercise reveals the impossibility of grouping all the witnesses of *PF* on the grounds of shared error. These lines are chosen to exemplify an argument, to be sure, but very many lines, not only in *PF*, but in all of Chaucer's works, would serve as well.

In our edition, line 54 of *PF* reads thus: 'Nis but a maner deth, what wey we trace'. The surviving witnesses reproduce the line in the following ways (we list the witnesses in order of their likelihood of being authorial, starting from most likely and moving to least; where possible we arrange them, therefore, in what look like potential groups):

	PF, 54
Gg	Nys but a maner deth what weye we trace
Cx	Nis but a maner deth what way we trace
J	In a manere dethe what wey wee trase
F	Meneth but a maner dethe what wey we trace
B	Meneth but a maner deth what wey we trace
Lt	Meneth but a manere dethe what wey we trace
H	Menyth but a maner deth what wey we trace
R	Meneth but a maner dethe what wey we trace
Ff	Meneth bot a manere deth what may we trace
T	Menith but a man deth what wey we trace
D	Mornyth but a maner deth what wey we trace
L	Ment but a maner deth what wey we trace
P	Ment but a maner deth what wey we trace
Hh	Ment but a maner deth what we trace
S	Was but a moment here quat weye we trace

Setting aside for the moment the overall effect of poor and centrifugal results – both semantic and metrical – by the scribes here, we restrict ourselves to location of groupings of shared error. Putting the matter thus immediately exposes, of course, the unavoidable vulnerability of recension: in order to locate error, one must locate shared error; but to locate shared error, one must locate

---

Trinity College, MS R.3.19, fols. 17–24; S = Oxford, Bodleian Library, MS Arch. Selden B.24, fols. 142–52; T = Oxford, Bodleian Library, MS Tanner 346, fols. 120–31.

error. The practice presupposes, that is, what it aims to isolate (i.e., error).[10] We do not regard this as in itself a disabling vulnerability, since location of obvious and likely error is often uncontentious, and some form of circularity is in any case inevitable in all hermeneutic practice.[11] Thus the clearly erroneous S reading of 'moment', for example, presumably derives from 'ment', and S's whole line in fact unpersuasively tries to make better sense of the uncertain sense of 'ment' in L, P and Hh. It is, in any case, unequivocally erroneous.

We assume that 'ment' derives from 'meneth'. However 'meneth' and 'ment' arose, they too are likely errors, given the fragility of sense they produce. One group of shared error is B, D, F, Ff, H, Lt, R and T. Another sub-group is Hh, L and P, with S as plausibly a derivative from this sub-group. This leaves Cx and Gg as the likeliest authorial forms, with J an erroneous derivative. We cannot, however, designate Cx and Gg as a 'group', since their identity is not one of shared error, but of likely shared correctness, which proves nothing about the dependence of one witness on the other.[12]

---

[10] The point about the circularity of stemmatics is often made. See, for example, R. Hanna III, 'On Stemmatics', in his *Pursuing History: Middle English Manuscripts and their Texts* (Palo Alto, 1996), pp. 83–96 (p. 85). See also Langland, *Piers Plowman: The B Version*, ed. Kane and Donaldson, pp. 17–18, n. 10. A. E. Housman (d. 1936) supplies a succinct example: 'The MSS are the material on which we base our rule, and then, when we have got our rule, we turn round upon the MSS and say that the rule, based upon them, convicts them of error. We are thus working in a circle, that is a fact that there is no denying' (cited in Kane, 'Conjectural Emendation', p. 159).

[11] That interpretation generally is necessarily a circular process is an old point, first stated as such by F. Schleiermacher (1768–1834); see, for example, his *Hermeneutics and Criticism and Other Writings*, ed. and trans. A. Bowie (Cambridge, 1998), pp. 109, 231–3. For contemporary application of the point, see J. Simpson, 'Faith and Hermeneutics: Pragmatism versus Pragmatism', *Journal of Medieval and Early Modern Studies* 33 (2003), 215–39.

[12] It may be worth underscoring here that, just as the convergence of scribes on a given variant can make it impossible to group manuscripts on the basis of error, the faithful copying that is the norm (and any scribe's aspiration) almost always makes it impossible to do so on the basis of shared correctness. As the axiom goes, 'manuscripts must be weighed and not counted' (*ponderandi non numerandi*), which is to say that the agreement of Cx and Gg here – or their agreement with any number of other manuscripts of *PF* – may mean they are equivalent to a *single* witness, since we cannot know if they are correct because they represent a genealogy of accurate copying or are correct because they were *all* copied directly from a single exemplar. We derive the language of the axiom from E. J. Kenney, *The Classical Text: Aspects of Editing in the Age of the Printed Book* (Berkeley, 1974), p. 44, who quotes from Lucas de Bruges in his edition of the Vulgate (1574). See also J. Mann, *The Poetics of Editing: In Memory of George Kane* (London, 2011), pp. 3–4.

Analysis of this kind about a single line only gains traction, however, when set in the context of identical analyses of other lines. What happens when we turn to line 237 (which in our edition reads thus: 'And on the temple, of doves white and faire')?

The 14 witnesses (L ends before this line) report this line in the following ways:

	PF, 237
Gg	And on the temple of dowis white and fayre
Hh	And on the temple of doves white and fayre
S	And on the temple of dowis quhite and fayre
H	And on the temple of dofes white and fayre
J	And on the tempill of dovis white and feire
Ff	And on the temple of dowfs whyte and fayre
R	And on the temple of douys whyte and fayre
Cx	And on the temple of duuves whyt and fayr
P	And the temple of dowves whyte and faire
B	And on the temple saugh I white and faire
D	And on the temple sawe I white and faire
F	And on the temple saugh I white and faire
Lt	And on the temple sawe I white and faire
T	And on the temple saugh I white and feir

We can be sure that the grouping B, D, F, Lt, T is a grouping of shared error, since in line 238, the next line in these texts ('Of doves white many a hundred paire') repeats information given in line 237. That would leave Gg, Hh, S, H, J, Ff, R and Cx as plausibly authorial, with P as a corrupted derivative from that group.

A third line's variation, line 383 (in our edition, 'Foules, tak hede of my sentence, I preye') has 13 surviving witnesses (Hh and L end before this line). The variants read thus:

	PF, 383
D	Foules take hede of my sentence I praye
H	Foules take hede of my sentence I pray
T	Foulis take hede of my sentence I praye
R	Fowles take hede of my sentence I prey
Gg	Foulis tak hed of myn centence I preye

J	Foulis takithe hede of my sentence I prey
S	Foulis take hede to my sentence I preye
P	Fowles take hede of my sentence I yow praye
B	Foules take of my sentence I prey
F	Foules take of my sentence I prey
Lt	Foules take of my sentence I prey
Cx	Fowlis take kepe of my sentence I preye
Ff	Foules take kepe to my sentence I prey

In this case the shared error groupings look like this: B, F, Lt (an error in each case because the transitive verb 'take' is missing its object); and Cx, Ff (with the likelihood, though not certainty, of 'hede' being earlier and therefore more likely authorial). The group of most plausibly authorial readings is D, H, T, R and Gg (with J, S and P being slightly erroneous derivatives).

Our final sample is line 604 (in our edition 'For foul that eteth worm and seide blive'). There are 12 surviving witnesses (in Hh, L and S, the line is either missing [Hh, L] or spurious [S]).

	PF, 604
F	For foule that eteth worme and seyde blyve
B	For foule that etith worme and seide blive
Lt	For foule that etith worme and sede blyve
Gg	For foule that etith werm and seyde blythe
T	For foule that eteth worm and seide blyue
J	For foule that etithe worm and sede blive
D	For fowle that etith worme and saide blyve
Cx	For fowlis that eten worme and said by lyve
H	For foule that etithe wormes and saide belive
R	For fowle that eteth wormes and seyde by lyfe
P	For fowle that etith worms and blive
Ff	For fowel that ittith worme as blyve

'Blyve' must be correct (it rhymes exactly with 'stryve' at line 606). Therefore Gg ('blythe') is erroneous. Ff is metrically deficient. Cx, H and R are plausibly a group sharing error, as are P and Ff. All the other witnesses are either plausibly correct or mildly erroneous derivatives of a correct reading. The plausibly correct are B, D, F, J, Lt, P and T.

We can now see the alignment of groupings of error or shared error in the four lines adduced so far. The grid below is presented so as to be able to see the separate groupings of shared error for the same line (in 3 cases there are two groupings of shared error in the same line). Horizontal lines are labelled A–G for ease of reference. (Here we do not include single erroneous readings whose derivation cannot be detected, since such errors cannot be used to establish recensions one way or the other.)

(X = manuscript ended)

A	54	B		D	F	Ff	H			Lt		R		T		
B	54							Hh	L			P		S		
C	237	B		D	F					X	Lt			T		
D	383	B			F				X	X	Lt					
E	383		Cx			Ff			X	X						
F	604		Cx				H		X	X		R				
G	604					Ff			X	X		P				

The key, if provisional, finding from this tiny sample is that the groupings of shared error do not hold steady. A large grouping of erroneous texts for A.54, for example, does not hold as one moves down the grid. To be sure, B, D, F and Lt maintain reasonably but not completely steady vertical lines of shared error, but H, R and T do not maintain such vertical lines of shared error. Where H appears again (at F.604), it appears in a different horizontal grouping. Where Cx appears in a grouping (at E.383 and F.604), it appears in conjunction with different groupings of shared error. Whereas Ff appears in A.54, it fails to hold its shared error with other members of A.54, and appears again twice (E.383 and G.604), each time with one other, different partner in error. From this small sample, at least, one cannot say that new groupings of shared error form and hold as copying of each witness progresses.

The point of this tiny sample is, obviously, not to make every effort to establish such genealogical groupings as are possible for the entire existing textual environment of the witnesses of *PF*. The grids suggest a reliably steady grouping of error for B, D, F and Lt. That, however, does not help the editor much, since the real value of even such a small sample is to reveal that the effort to elucidate and solidify vertical groupings of stable error is beyond rational capacity. Had we access now to every witness ever made of *PF* in the century or so after its composition, we would surely be able to establish iron-hard genealogical groupings. Such, however, is not the case with the surviving witnesses of *PF*; it simply must be the case that too many links in the chain are lost for recovery of historical relations among witnesses.

Previous editors felt more confident in the application of stemmatic analysis to *PF*. Thus in 1902 Eleanor Hammond, in addition to isolating the shared error grouping so far isolated in this essay (i.e., B, F, T and D, to which she adds Lt), isolates other groups as genealogical, notably Gg and Ff, and H, R, S, Hh and Cx. These extra groups are, however, not at all groupings of shared error, but of shared plausible correctness. To describe a 'group' of readings with plausibly shared correctness as a genealogical 'group' is a fundamental error in stemmatic analysis, since groupings of likely shared correctness cannot be counted as genealogically-descended groups. Their identity may derive from coincidental overlap between one tradition or another, or from scribal convergence.[13] Shared error may also, of course, be coincidental, but is much less likely to be so. In sum, we have one plausible group of shared error, whose vertical filiations are unstable, and no other groups. Stemmatic analysis is inoperable.

Another way of making the same point is to consider a grid of variant agreements with MS B of what are regarded, by us at least, as shared errors, for the first 100 lines of the poem. B is chosen because it is a member of the one definite group of shared error. (Where the same line is cited in the left-hand column, that indicates a second variant grouping within that same line):

Line											
7	B		F				L	Lt			T
9	B		D	F	Ff			J	Lt	P	
24	B	Cx				H		J	Lt	P	R
28	B		F						Lt			T
30	B		F			H			Lt		R	
30	B		F						Lt			
31	B		F									
32	B		F						Lt			
43	B		F						Lt			
46	B		D	F								
49	B		F						Lt			
50	B	Cx	F			H	Hh	J	Lt	P	R	T
53	B		F					J	Lt			T
53	B		F									T

[13] E. P. Hammond, 'On the Text of Chaucer's *Parlement of Foules*', *The Decennial Publications of the University of Chicago* 7 (1902), 3–25. Derek Brewer accepts Hammond's analysis of the textual evidence; see Chaucer, *The Parlement of Foulys*, ed. D. Brewer (Manchester, 1972), p. 58. The point about 'groups' of shared correctness not being evidence for a group at all is made by V. di Marco in Chaucer, *The Riverside Chaucer*, 3rd ed., gen. ed. L. D. Benson (Boston, 1987), p. 1147.

55	B			F				Lt			T
64	B			F				Lt			T
65	B		D	F	Ff						
70	B		D	F				Lt		S	T
71	B			F			J				T
72	B			F				Lt			
75	B			F				Lt			
77	B		D	F	Gg			Lt			T
79	B	Cx		F							T
82	B			F				Lt			
91	B			F	Gg			Lt			T
95	B	Cx		F	Ff			Lt	P		T
98	B			F				Lt			

Unlike our four samples across the entire work of *PF*, this collation of some shared error for lines 1–100 does produce a very strong vertical sharing of B, F, Lt and T. It also produces, however, horizontal oddities that find vertical confirmation: at line 50, for example, B's reading agrees with Cx, F, H, Hh, J, P, R and T. This nearly squares with the B agreements of rejected readings for line 24, and finds more than faint echo in line 95. These echoes suggest more than coincidence. Making sense of overlaps with these witnesses (classed by previous editors as belonging to different groups) as non-coincidental is not possible with the evidence available. And that impossibility is part of the larger impossibility of establishing robust genealogical relations between all 15 witnesses. One group of shared error doth not a full stemma make.

IB: Convergent variation

The shared errors that produce such varying groupings of the witnesses of *PF* might be explained by convergent variation. That is unlikely in most of the cases presented so far, but entirely likely in the instances of final -e given below. Convergent variation was indeed a phenomenon that (as they noted) particularly bedevilled Manly and Rickert's attempt to sort the manuscripts of the *Canterbury Tales* genealogically.[14] Scribes are well known to make certain

---

[14] Manly and Rickert's acknowledgement of the possibility of convergent variation is as devastating to their method as it is subsequently ignored in its formulation and execution: they cite, with approval, Moore's view that 'the more striking the variant the greater chance there is of its being created independently by different scribes' (E. Moore, *Contributions to the Textual Criticism of the Divina Commedia* (Cambridge,

kinds of errors with frequency (skipping a word or line, say) or to be led into a particular error by the near-homonym that allows the line to make some sense ('belive' for 'blive', as above, for example). It is always therefore possible that two or more scribes will make the same mistake in copying independently of one another. What we want to describe here, however, is a variation in which neither alternative (nor any of the alternatives) found in the manuscript record can fairly be called an 'error'. Our experience of editing Chaucer has everywhere suggested that the ideas of 'convergence' hide not only instances, but also a general pattern, in which Chaucer's scribes were unaware of making anything like a change in the text they copied because they were unaware that a form they substituted was, in fact, different.

We are familiar with something like this process in instances where we note the influence of a scribe's dialect in a copy, but we believe that editors of Middle English have never fully absorbed the implications of the widely accepted view that the grammaticality of final -e was unstable because rapidly evolving in the fourteenth century. That evolution is necessarily relevant to any copy of a Middle English poem written in this period, where there is a significant temporal distance between the poem's writing and that copy. The phenomenon is particularly acute for copies of the poems of Chaucer since it is also widely believed that Chaucer took advantage of this change, 'ma[king] use of inflexional -e in a way that was already becoming archaic in its own day' and expecting final -e to be sounded or silent depending on its metrical position.[15] If this view is true, only a scribe with a clear understanding of Chaucer's metrical practice could copy these instances of final -e aright, but

---

1889)), but then take this view as warrant for relying on 'multitudinous minor variations' for their classifications (that is, the very variations most subject to convergence and least likely to represent shared error). See *The Text of the Canterbury Tales: Studied on the Basis of All Known Manuscripts*, ed. J. M. Manly and E. Rickert, 8 vols (Chicago, 1940), pp. 2, 22–3. Convergent variation, or 'coincident variation', was regularly acknowledged as a phenomenon in the manuscripts of *Piers Plowman* in the Athlone Press editions, and Lee Patterson's analysis revealed the surprising extent to which Kane's recognition of this phenomenon lay at the heart of his characterization of the *usus scribendi* fundamental to his eclectic editorial method. On convergent variation see Langland, *Piers Plowman: The A-Version*, ed. Kane, pp. 61–4; Langland, *Piers Plowman: The B Version*, ed. Kane and Donaldson, pp. 57–61; *Piers Plowman: The C Version*, ed. G. Russell and G. Kane (London, 1997), pp. 57–9 (hereafter referred to as 'Kane-Russell'). The relationship of 'coincident variation' to the 'distinguishing of original from unoriginal variants' is clearest (in all of the Athlone Press editions) in Kane's A-text introduction (p. 61). See also L. Patterson, 'The Logic of Textual Criticism and the Way of Genius', in his *Negotiating the Past: the Historical Understanding of Medieval Literature* (Madison, 1987), pp. 77–114 (esp. pp. 84–6).

15 D. Pearsall, *John Lydgate* (London, 1970), p. 61.

it is also unclear how anyone other than a person who heard Chaucer recite his poems could fully understand his practice, since all the manuscripts we have of Chaucer's poems differ in their disposition of final -e and, therefore, the instruction they might provide in that practice. The most likely (if not inevitable) case is that a scribe for whom either a given -e, or final -e generally, was differently inflexional would delete or add such an -e to a word when copying with no sense at all that he was making a mistake. Indeed, for any given scribe, what would appear to be the random disposition of -e in the text he was copying would necessarily conceal Chaucer's metrical practice while acting as an invitation to ignore or add final -e at will.

No distinction could seem so trivial at the level of a given line than the deletion or addition of an -e, but none is more consequential for Chaucer's verse, since the regularity of a preponderance of his lines depends on an -e to provide an unstressed syllable, and, on the same grounds, will be confounded if an unnecessary -e is introduced. An example ready to hand here is the -e on 'weye' in line 54 of the *Parlement* (our first example, above). Gg's version of this line has a final -e on 'weye', as does S, while Cx, F, B, Lt, H, R, T, D, L and P lack it. There is, in fact, no etymological reason to pronounce this -e,[16] and for this reason alone, Skeat, Robinson and the *Riverside* print 'wey' without comment.[17] We find it a mistake to be so casual, however, since the pronunciation of an inorganic -e is not uncommon in Middle English.[18] Although 'wey' is the reading in the preponderance of witnesses, we do not print the word in this form on these grounds. If we regard the -e as a scribal error, then it assembles yet another manuscript grouping for these lines (here Gg and S), but we do not regard this -e as an error, because the preponderance of evidence in *all* the lines in *PF* suggests that such -e's were not important to any of these scribes.

We will discuss that evidence more below, but here we offer three other lines (again as they appear in Gg) that demonstrate the consequences of ignoring the disposition of final -e and the degree to which convergent variation ensures that it will always remain undetected by recension:

---

[16] See *MED*, s.v. 'wei' n. (1).

[17] See *The Complete Works of Geoffrey Chaucer, Edited from Numerous Manuscripts*, ed. W. W. Skeat, 7 vols (Oxford, 1894–7), 1, p. 337; Chaucer, *The Works of Geoffrey Chaucer*, ed. F. N. Robinson, 2nd ed. (Boston, 1957), pp. 311 and 903; and *The Riverside Chaucer*, pp. 371 and 1148.

[18] On this phenomenon see S. Barney, *Studies in Troilus: Chaucer's Text, Meter, and Diction* (East Lansing, MI, 1993), p. 78 n. 1, and D. Minkova, 'The Prosodic Character of Early Schwa Deletion in English', in *Papers from the 7th International Conference on Historical Linguistics*, ed. A. G. Ramat et al. (Philadelphia,1987), pp. 445–57.

> Than shewed he him the litel erthe, that heer is (line 57)
> For me to stonde so ful was al the place (line 315)
> And seyde myn sone the choys is to yow falle (line 406).

In the first example 'erthe' confounds the meter (placing two unstressed syllables next to one another ('-e' and 'that'), and, in this case, the confounding -e has historical warrant. The same is true of the -e on 'stonde' in line 315 which also confounds the line's meter (with two successive unstressed syllables on '-e' and 'so') and also has historical warrant. Finally the -e on 'seyde' as well as the '-e' on 'sone' in line 406, while equally historical, if pronounced, give us a line of 12 syllables and a sequence of successive unstressed syllables ('-e' and 'myn' and then '-e' and 'the').[19] We remove the -e's from all of these lines and print them with regular meter as follows:

> Than shewed he him the litel erth, that heer is (line 57)
> For me to stond, so ful was al the place (line 315)
> And seid, 'My son the chois is to yow falle (line 406)

In all of these cases, we reject the preponderance of our witnesses and any groupings the shared error might seem to assemble because they are entirely inconsistent. The variants in each case are as follows:

Line 57	erth B P S T	erthe Cx D F Gg H Hh J L Lt R *om* Ff
Line 315	stond R J	stonde B Cx D F Ff Gg H Hh P T stande Lt stand S
Line 406	seid B Cx D Ff T	seide F Gg Lt P R *out* Hh L saide H
Line 406	son D H J P R	sone B Cx F Ff Gg Lt S T *out* Hh L

One further example shows best why these patterns make a different point about stemmatics than our first four (again given as in Gg):

> That made me to mete that he stod ther (line 108)

The -e on 'mete' (or 'mette') here is again historical and to pronounce it is, again, to produce a line with two successive unstressed syllables ('-e' and 'that'), but the regularizing form 'met' is nowhere to be found in any of the extant witnesses.[20] We discuss below the principles according to which we delete this -e, but our point here is that no care taken with variants or their analysis will offer the necessary guidance to do so. Indeed, setting the

---

[19] For the inflectional forms see *MED*, s.v. 'erthe' n. (1), 'stonden' v. (1), 'seien' v. (1) and 'sone' n.

[20] See *MED*, s.v. 'meten' v. (3). S, it should be noted, has the metrically helpful reading 'think'.

confounding presence of the final -e in all extant copies of this line beside the many other lines in the *Parlement* where all extant witnesses agree in copying a metrically unnecessary -e (or in lacking a metrically necessary -e) make abundantly clear that recension can detect neither convergence of error in the crucial case of final -e nor the changing shape of Middle English that makes such detection crucial.

The pervasiveness of convergent variation in the manuscripts of *PF* is yet another instance of the impossibility of producing meaningful groupings of witnesses by means of shared error for the purpose of editing Chaucer. As a result, we have found it unnecessary to move beyond a core of relatively early witnesses in editing every poem of Chaucer. In so doing, we wholly reject stemmatic analysis, not because it is an inadequate method for the editing of Chaucer, but because it is an impossible one. With the possible exception of the *Boece* (as acknowledged, but also critiqued below), Chaucer's texts are not susceptible to robust stemmatic analysis.

Rejected Alternatives

If recension is inoperable, then what is an editor to do?

One editing 'method' we have not so far mentioned is diplomatic reproduction of texts. The editor of a diplomatic text aims to reproduce the text exactly as it appears in a given manuscript, down even to exact reproduction of antiquated letter forms such as, in Middle English, thorn and yogh.[21] This practice expresses one of the dreams of textual criticism (authentic reproduction of the past) by renouncing another (editorial decision-making that mediates a text to a new audience). The editor thereby withdraws and lets the reader make all the decisions.[22] More recently this expensive practice for print has become technologically and economically imaginable by digital technology, with the wonderful possibility of digital facsimiles of the manuscripts themselves. Some projects propose, indeed, to make thus available every manuscript, facsimile and transcription of a given work.[23] In some (by no means all) cases this presentation is underwritten by Barthesian persuasions about the oppressive, authoritarian and idealizing presuppositions of the single author and his or

---

[21] Though the self-damaging practice of reproducing thorn and yogh survives much higher up the scholarly scale.

[22] Hudson, 'Middle English', p. 38, puts the point thus: 'This method exalts palaeography as sole editor'.

[23] See, for example, *The Wife of Bath's Prologue on CD-ROM*, ed. P. Robinson (Cambridge, 1996), and *The Piers Plowman Electronic Archive*, accessed April 8, 2023, https://piers.chass.ncsu.edu/.

her intention. Such presuppositions, the Barthesian argument would have it, putatively suppress the historicity both of the making of the work by multiple hands,[24] and of the variousness of the work as it was delivered into history by the practice of scribes.[25] The task of the 'editor' is to dissolve him or herself, by bringing the multiplicity of the text's making and reception to light, and to replicate that multiplicity by presenting not the work, but all texts of the work. In the editing of the *Canterbury Tales*, the most extreme and perhaps facetious offshoot suggestion from this tradition was that of Derek Pearsall, who floated the notion that the ideal 'edition' of the *Tales* would be a folder with fascicules for each tale that readers would compile into orders as they saw fit.[26]

We have not mentioned diplomatic editing as a method because it is not, in our view, a method at all, so much as an abjuration of method. Of course the information it purveys is of value to scholars, but it is neither useful nor useable by anyone else. What might be called the eulogy of the variant reaches its apotheosis in a diplomatic edition of a well-attested text, but it is also fundamental to any critical edition that provides a corpus of all known variants (and here Manly-Rickert's *Canterbury Tales* will do nicely as an example). For us, in theory and on the basis of our editing of Chaucer, the assembling of such a corpus ignores the following:

- The fact that the vast majority of variants are wholly trivial errors that should not waste more time than is absolutely necessary;[27] historicity is crucial for many topics, but not for the production and recording of trivial error.
- Average brain size. Editions are destined for audiences with different competences and different levels of available time. Some editions, for example, are designed for other textual critics, some for university literary scholars

---

[24] A case most powerfully made by J. McGann, *A New Republic of Letters: Memory and Scholarship in the Age of Digital Reproduction* (Cambridge MA, 2014).

[25] B. Cerquiglini, *Eloge de la Variante: Histoire Critique de la Philologie* (Paris, 1989).

[26] D. Pearsall, 'Pre-empting Closure in The Canterbury Tales: Old Endings, New Beginnings', in *Essays on Ricardian Literature in Honour of J. A. Burrow*, ed. A. J. Minnis, C. C. Morse and T. Turville-Petre (Oxford, 1997), pp. 23–38 (p. 31). Pearsall first made the suggestion in 1985: see D. Pearsall, *The Canterbury Tales* (London, 1985), p. 23.

[27] There are, of course, exceptions, where scribal participation is so engaged as to blur the lines between author and scribe. See, for example, B. A. Windeatt, 'The Scribes as Chaucer's Early Critics', *SAC* 1 (1979), 119–41; D. Wakelin, *Scribal Correction and Literary Craft: English Manuscripts 1375–1510* (Cambridge, 2014), esp. pp. 304–7; and M. Fisher, *Scribal Authorship and the Writing of History in Medieval England* (Columbus OH, 2012), esp. pp. 6–7.

and students, and some for a general readership. But whatever the destined readership of a given edition, all editions will in fact be consumed by brains with no more than a certain, generally strong but inevitably limited human capacity. Most human brains have the time and patience inwardly to absorb one version of a given work at most; none can truly absorb more than, say, two. The task of editors is to make compromises between fidelity to the historical record on the one hand, and the needs, cognitive competences and resources of a readership on the other. This will usually mean (as it meant for us) moving from surviving witnesses to produce a single, ideal work.

If recension and diplomatic editing are, respectively, impossible or irrelevant, and we can see no reason to assemble a full corpus of variants for any text of Chaucer, then our question can be repeated. What method is an editor of the works of Chaucer to adopt? Eclecticism is one possibility. By eclecticism we refer to the method most fully articulated by George Kane in 1975, whereby editors rely wholly on their own judgment, ignoring groupings of shared error, the numbers of witnesses favouring a given reading, the antiquity of a witness and the claims of any witness to be the 'best text'.[28] The only ground of evidence is the variants themselves, arranged alongside each other, each with potentially identical claim, and where each set of variants constitutes a new and largely distinctive problem.[29] The eclectic editor will not exercise judgment adventitiously; by careful definition of the *usus scribendi* of the scribes, the editor will become able to descry scribal failure to replicate authorial practice.

---

[28] For references to Kane's accounts of his method see nn. 5 and 12 above. For sustained and penetrating critique of the Athlone editions, see C. Brewer, *Editing Piers Plowman: The Evolution of the Text* (Cambridge, 1996), Chapters 20 and 21, pp. 343–408. For an appreciation and trenchant critique, see Mann, *The Poetics of Editing*. For an exemplary instance of 'best text' editing of a Middle English text with the practicalities of using only 5 MSS of the 18 extant MSS of C described, see *Piers Plowman by William Langland: An Edition of the C-Text*, ed. D. Pearsall (London, 1978), pp. 20–3. We have, not incidentally, derived our own system for marking the manuscript that provided our chosen reading in our *apparatus criticus* from this edition. Pearsall's decision to emend his text using the corpus of variants in the Kane-Russell edition when he revised this edition in 2008 (see Langland, *Piers Plowman: A New Annotated Edition of the C-Text*, ed. D. Pearsall (Exeter, 2008), pp. 17–18) made it much more eclectic in method.

[29] 'The sole source of [textual] authority is the variants themselves, and among them, authority, that is originality, will probably be determined most often by identification of the variant likeliest to have given rise to the others', in Langland, *Piers Plowman: The A Version*, ed. Kane, p. 115. For reflection on this claim, see T. J. Farrell, 'Eclecticism and its Discontents', *Textual Cultures* 9 (2015), 27–45 (pp. 28–9).

There are, to be sure, textual environments where eclecticism may be unavoidable. Where, for example, *all* surviving witnesses are evidently both unsatisfactory in significant ways, and not susceptible of recension, then an editor may have no choice but to adopt an eclectic method. The method comes, however, with obvious dangers and even breath-taking risks.[30]

The obvious dangers have been remarked upon often enough not to be further belaboured, especially when they were obvious to begin with: the method invests the judgment of the editor with extraordinary power, asking of editors that they almost become their authors, against the scribes of those authors. The required levels of both intuitional perception (of the authorial mind) and of permanent distrust (of the scribes) are both extremely high. And if editors somehow 'become' their authors, then they do so, as they must (if they are to be taken seriously), by long immersion in the authorial and scribal practices perceptible in the witnesses. Setting aside the certainty of circularity here, there are two further dangers to an eclecticism joined to a comprehensive account of variants, as follows:

- Definition of the authorial *usus poetandi* (as one recent scholar has named it) is very likely to correspond to the criteria judged to be characteristic of poetic genius in the editor's own culture.[31] It is unlikely to be accidental, for example, that Kane's own definition of Langland's *usus poetandi* conforms exactly with New Critical criteria of literary excellence dominant in Anglo-American literary culture in the mid-twentieth century: 'vigorous, nervous, flexible and relatively compressed [style of the poet], made distinctive by characteristic mannerisms and figures'.[32] Such criteria are the opposite of the *usus scribendi* of the scribes, which Kane characterized thus: '... flat statement or crude overemphasis, diffuseness in denotation and loss of connotation, dilution of meaning and absence of tension, in general a bald, colourless and prosy expression'.[33] Chaucer's works exhibit a huge stylistic variety, including 'prosy expression', and including, after all, much prose itself. Kane's characterization of the style of *Piers Plowman* is itself doubtfully restricted. For a poet like Chaucer, so conscious of style, such definitions would need to be remade for each work.

---

[30] For sustained reflection on the potential perils of eclecticism specifically, see Farrell, 'Eclecticism and its Discontents'.
[31] For apt use of the phrase '*usus poetandi*', see Farrell, 'Eclecticism and its Discontents', p. 29.
[32] Langland, *Piers Plowman: The B Version*, ed. Kane and Donaldson, p. 130.
[33] Langland, *Piers Plowman: The B Version*, ed. Kane and Donaldson, p. 130.

- The empirical grounds of Kanian eclecticism are so deeply embedded in editorial judgment as to be forever elusive. Kane himself articulates the 'o altitudo' status of this ethereal knowledge thus: '[W]e admit to subjectivity, but it seems to us that editorial subjectivity, correctly understood in the circumstances of this text, is not merely an inevitable factor but a valuable instrument. The data are abundant; the editor's subconscious mind cannot fail to store so many impressions from comparison between readings strongly presumed original and readings evidently or almost certainly scribal that he will at length acquire, as we hope we may have done, some accuracy of feeling for the turns of speech and even of thought respectively characteristic of the poet and his scribes'.[34] The consequences of this elusive knowledge, gained only 'at length' and 'from so many [stored] impressions', are that every crux requires its own distinctive argument,[35] and that disproof of one such argument leaves the whole package quite untouched.[36]

We were unprepared for our editorial method to be buttressed by quite such dauntingly self-assured, elusive and effectively nominalist defences, and we will illustrate the perils we have just detailed for such eclecticism in one revealing instance in the editing of Chaucer.

We could refer here to the whole of Ralph Hanna and Traugott Lawler's edition of Chaucer's *Boece* in *The Riverside Chaucer*, which is unique in this collaborative edition for claiming that the text provided achieves a Lachmannian precision, approximating 'the ancestor of all surviving manuscripts' in its readings.[37] Here we focus only on the climactic passage at the centre of this

---

[34] Langland, *Piers Plowman: The B Version*, ed. Kane and Donaldson, p. 213.

[35] As noted by C. L. Wrenn, '*Piers Plowman*, The A Version by George Kane', *Modern Language Notes* 76 (1961), 856–63 (p. 860): '... Every crux is treated as uniquely problematic'.

[36] 'Nevertheless, that kind of discontent remains a wholly local argument about the application of Kane's logic to one crux. Such local critiques leave Kane's eclectic methodology untouched, because its central principle stands: recognizable scribal or metrical deficiencies may vitiate better-attested lections, rendering a poorly attested variant or a conjectural emendation the correct editorial choice' (Farrell, 'Eclecticism and its Discontents', p. 30).

[37] *The Riverside Chaucer*, p. 1151. The edition of the *Astrolabe* in the *Riverside* is the only other text arrived at with anything like the Lachmannian rigor of the method Hanna and Lawler use for the *Boece*, although this edition only represents itself as an attempt to get '*nearer* Chaucer's version' (p. 1193, our emphasis), not to reconstruct the 'original'. In general, the editorial method for each of the other texts in the *Riverside* is much less theoretically ambitious. The edition of the *Canterbury Tales*, for example, is described as 'eclectic', which means, in this case, that the copy-text (the 'Ellesmere' MS) is regularly emended with the 'Hengwrt' MS (p. 1120).

treatise, Book 3, prose 12, in which Philosophy finally reveals the 'forme of the devine substaunce' to Boethius. Given its formal and ideational centrality, it is no surprise that, at 207 lines (in the *Riverside*), it is one of the longest passages in this treatise, and therefore also provides abundant scope to illustrate the four key concerns we have raised.

The first is the overplus created by a full collation, since there are, in our view, only three substantive emendations on the basis of that collation in the whole of this prose passage: the substitutions in Cambridge, University Library, MS Ii.1.38 (hereafter C^1), the *Riverside*'s copy text, of 'wonnen' for 'woven', of 'Good' for 'God' and of 'quod' for 'that'. These differences are not individually trivial of course, but there is no doubt that, in 200 lines of prose, they represent a vanishingly small proportion of the text. It is worth noting, moreover, that these are, in every case, discrepancies that can be corrected by consulting only one additional manuscript, Cambridge, University Library, MS Ii.3.21 (hereafter C^2), which is, in fact, the most obvious manuscript to consult since it is the copy-text chosen by Skeat as well as by Robinson in his first and second editions.

To look at the apparatus of both stemma and collation on which Hanna and Lawler would have based these decisions is to see (as in our second objection above) just how difficult it is for the average brain to take in this data in a way that makes the grounds of this decision intelligible. There is an elegant parsimony in Hanna and Lawler's method such that the variation behind these three readings can be represented in three simple and short lines:

112 **quod**] þ^t
155–6 **woven**] C^2 only; *wonnen* α (-H) A^1; *wounded* H; *vonnen* Sal.
167 **God**] *good* C^1 H θ (-Th) ι Rob

But this simplicity is beguiling, in part because it requires a certain amount of research, even for the expert reader, to unpack this shorthand in even the simplest instance, such as the two forms provided for line 112. In fact, 'þ^t' is a shorthand meaning that this error only appears in C^1 and it is only the absence of other sigla that indicates that they all have 'quod'. The beginning of the note for lines 155–6 says very plainly that only C^2 has the reading 'woven' and the end of that note makes clear that 'H' (London, British Library, MS Harley 2421) has 'wounded' and 'Sal' (Salisbury, Salisbury Cathedral Library, MS Sarum 113) has 'vonnen'. But what about the Greek letters and the horizontal line in the middle of this note? It is not hard to work out that alpha ('α')

Its edition of *Troilus and Criseyde*, so far from a Lachmannian text, is in fact a textbook example of best text editing, based on one manuscript without 'full reports of variants' (p. 1162).

refers to a branch of the stemma, but it requires a few page turns to expand that grouping into its constituents (A^2, C^1, B, H, P, Cx, Th, C^2 and Hn).[38] It requires some intuition (because Hanna and Lawler nowhere guide the uninitiated) to realize that '-' is a subtraction sign so '-H' indicates that all of α with the exception H has this reading. The apparatus for line 167 may be shorter, but it is much the hardest of these notes to parse. It tells us that 'good' appears in C^1, H and θ, the last symbol of which a few page turns show to be a subsidiary branch of α containing P, Cx and Th, with '-Th' making clear that Th is the one witness lacking this in in θ. It is only the absence of any mention of that reading that makes clear Th must also have 'God'. The rest of the note tells us that subsidiary branch, ι, of the other branch in the stemma, β, which a few page turns reveal contains A^1, Sal and Auct, also reads 'good', as does Robinson in his first and second editions.[39] What this last note actually never specifies, however, is where 'God' appears: it is, as our own collation of just three manuscripts makes clear, in C^2, a solution that can only be revealed by noting which of the sigla does not appear in either this list or part of some branch of the stemma specified by this shorthand.

It may be unfair to describe such a method as confusing since it is a nomenclature standard to editing, if certainly less common in the editing of Middle English texts. But it should be noted too that the use of this apparatus *itself* requires collation of its constituent parts, first between the Greek sigla and the branches of the stemma, and then between two sections of the textual apparatus, one of which seems to contain substantive variations from the copy-text, and another labelled 'Additional corrections of C^1' which seems devoted to less important variants (although it is baffling to us that the very meaningful difference between 'good' and 'God' is placed in this section). If the quantity of information provided here seems far beyond anything that another editor of the *Boece* could or would want to assimilate, it is also our point that, in the case of Book 3, prose 12, it is wholly unnecessary in the production of this passage of Chaucer's text.

With all this variation at their disposal, Hanna and Lawler also fall through the trap door such evidence seems to create: they feel (as in our third criticism above) that they can work back to 'what Chaucer probably wrote', and that

---

[38] The additional sigla here refer to the following witnesses: London, British Library, MS Additional 16165 ('A^2'), Oxford, Bodleian Library, MS Bodley 797 ('B'), Cambridge, Pembroke College, MS 215 ('P'), Caxton's edition of *c.* 1478 ('Cx'), Thynne's edition of 1532 ('Th') and Aberystwyth, National Library of Wales, MS Peniarth 392 D ('Hn', formerly MS Hengwrt 328).

[39] The additional siglum here, 'Auct' refers to Oxford, Bodleian Library, MS Auctarium F.3.5.

this fall is abetted to the extent that (as our fourth concern, enumerated above) the judgments they use to work back to 'Chaucer' are thoroughly embedded in their method.[40] Tim Machan has described these problems already with precision. As he puts it, Lawler and Hanna prove C^1's proximity to Chaucer's holograph by a 'circular use of stemmatics' because the fundamental assumption of their method is that C^1 preserves the holograph's readings 'when [the other] witnesses disagree or when the received reading is judged inadequate'.[41] The consequence is the Kanian view that C^1 is 'one of three manuscripts most faithful to O', and, moreover, that there has been 'a substantial loss of harder authorial readings between O, Chaucer's autograph, and O′, the ancestor of all surviving manuscripts'.[42] The problem is, therefore, the typical one: C^1 is found to be the 'superior' text because it was initially thought to be so with the result that 'if C^2 or any other manuscript were predicated as superior, it would perforce be closer to [Chaucer's holograph]' by this same method.[43]

To be sure, that method produces an excellent edition with a comprehensive corpus of variants which makes the reconstruction of any given decision, if not easy, at least possible. And yet, the herculean effort involved in such editing actually makes each of its constituting decisions less rather than more sound. In fact, it is the very need to sift the flood of variants so as to justify them that produces the views that compromise the resulting text. Most problematic of all, the assurance that such a method will return us to a more 'accurate' text calls into question what an 'accuracy' so arrived at could mean.

Pragmatic Text Editing: Textual Coherence

Recension and eclecticism rejected, we were left, as the basis of our own method, with one of the received methods of editing Middle English texts, best text editing, re-thought – and, in our view, clarified methodologically – by the practical experience with all of the witnesses we consulted of the poetry and prose of Chaucer. We have called this 'pragmatic editing' because it is the mode and understanding of best text editing urged upon us by the state of the witnesses.

While the miniscule sample of variant readings offered above suggested that the road to recension was closed, that same evidence also produces a

---

[40] *The Riverside Chaucer*, p. 1152.
[41] T. W. Machan, 'The "Consolation" Tradition and the Text of Chaucer's "Boece"', *The Papers of the Bibliographical Society of America* 91 (1997), 31–50 (p. 48).
[42] *The Riverside Chaucer*, p. 1151.
[43] Machan, '"Consolation" Tradition and the Text', p. 48.

positive: it points us to plausibly authorial readings. For our four sampled lines, those witnesses that survived as plausibly authorial were as follows:

54		Cx			Gg						
237		Cx		Ff	Gg	H	Hh	J	P	R	S
383			D		Gg	H	X	J	P	R	S	T
604	B		D	F					P			T	Lt

Of course, the sample is far too small to be persuasive, but the fact that a pattern emerges even in such a small sample may be revealing: Gg appears in three of the four lines as plausibly authorial. As we argued above, this vertical consistency in no way points to a genealogical 'group', but it does point the editor in the direction of one manuscript. Our work on collating all the witnesses in fact substantially confirmed Gg as the most reliable text: for 670 of our 970 lemmata, we chose the Gg reading. As we have already noted in a few cases, there was no pattern in the agreements of witnesses that disagreed with the Gg reading. For lines 1–10 of *PF*, for example, the witnesses that offer a different reading from the adopted Gg reading are as follows (lines with more than one horizontal entry indicate separate lemmata):

Line	Sigla of witnesses disagreeing with Gg
1	R
1	L
2	Cx D F H Hh Lt R T
3	Lt T
3	Cx Ff H Hh L Lt T
3	Ff J
4	J
6	Ff
7	H Hh R T
8	R
9	J
9	B D F Ff J Lt P T
10	J L Lt

There were, however, many instances where Gg, our first port of call, disappointed, and we had recourse especially to F and Hh. We need not go into the detail of those decisions here, except to say that the textual environment of witnesses in this case necessitated that we adopt a pragmatic approach, that is, the choice of a best text corrected on the basis of the kind of judgment usually associated with eclecticism, but with a defining restraint (that is, no illusion that we were using shared error scientifically or our understanding of 'the style of the poet' to recover an 'original text', but, rather, reaching toward a coherence in our decisions on the whole).[44]

But by what principles did we isolate the best text on which our method was based?[45] Not surprisingly, Ralph Hanna speaks dismissively of best-text editing, thus: such a practice, he says,

> surrenders any effort to find an authorial text in the competing readings of multiple manuscript copies; instead – on bases that strike me as unclear and generally illogical – it designates a single copy as 'the best surviving witness' to the text and follows it as 'correct' at all points – sometimes making an exception where it is palpably not.[46]

This dismissive description is useful for prompting us to disagree with and correct almost every aspect of it. We do not 'surrender any effort to find an authorial text' (on the contrary, we claim our text as plausibly authorial); we do not abandon the search for accuracy among the 'competing readings of multiple manuscript [or early print] copies' (on the contrary, we consult either all or a judicious selection of such competing readings). And we do not regard the bases of our selection of the best text as 'unclear' or 'illogical', as we state below. The only point of Hanna's description with which we agree is the last one: that we do not observe the best text reading when it is palpably incorrect.

Let us, then, turn to a positive defence of best text editing according to the pragmatic grounds of *coherence* we have used when employing it for the editing of Chaucer. If editing by recension depends on the isolation of shared error, editing from a best text relies on the opposite form of attention from editors, as they settle on what the best text is. Looking for shared error demands that the editor spot where a scribe has diverged from what is then understood as a preceding text; it demands a permanent readiness to notice the *exceptional*. Isolating a best text, by contrast, demands attention to the *norm*, to the overall coherence of a given witness, or a given set of witnesses; it demands a synthetic attention to what is most consistent and plausibly right. Accuracy, in best text editing, is not embracing what is passively left over after one has isolated and

---

[44] The phrases are taken from the now classic formulation of the eclectic method in Langland, *Piers Plowman: The B Version*, ed. Kane and Donaldson, p. 130.

[45] This and the following six paragraphs overlap significantly with *The Oxford Chaucer*, ed. Cannon and Simpson, 'Editorial Introduction', 1.33.

[46] Hanna, '(The) Editing (of) the Ellesmere Text', pp. 225–6.

corrected error, as it is in editing by recension. Accuracy is instead an active principle that determines norms (notably syntactic and metrical) as intended by authors, and thereby serves to isolate some (if not all) errors.

Accuracy as an active principle clearly demands a spelling out of the principles by which 'accuracy' is determined. Editing on the basis of a best text generally, and, when best text evidently fails, editing eclectically, is not objective. It is, however, as we have practiced it, grounded on forms of coherence, which we articulate here.

The principle of coherence that underpins our refinement of best text editing has been defined at two levels, the macro and the micro. At the macro level, the surviving witnesses of Chaucer's works present a relatively solid state. To a much greater extent than, say, the surviving witnesses of *Piers Plowman*, the works of Chaucer survive for the most part in complete texts of what is evidently the same 'work'. Some manuscripts of Chaucer's works are unfinished; some contain lacunae;[47] some arrange the material in a different order;[48] some very few works are made whole by placing fragments from different witnesses together;[49] but only two works, the Prologue to the *Legend of Good Women* and the *Treatise on the Astrolabe*, exist in more than one distinct version.[50] For these texts it has been customary to preserve as much of the variation as possible not least because it seems likely that differences in the witnesses often reflect different versions of the text Chaucer produced. We too have included large blocks of text as different versions, either as a parallel texts, or as full transcriptions in our notes. But, in every other case, the surviving witnesses of the works of Chaucer are stable at this level, which means that it is not necessary to define the work itself by an editorial procedure.

At the micro-level of the individual line, however, the surviving witnesses are much less stable, and so our search for coherence also had to proceed word by word. There were, in every case, low levels of nonsensical substitution or omission, the obvious result of one form or another of scribal carelessness creating what could best be described as incoherencies in meaning. Coherence in meaning was the only principle that could be used on the prose works. But coherence in the 43,500 or so lines of Chaucer's verse was most persuasively measured by single, continuous features that encompassed each and every text, rather than by the local instances of conceptual incoherence that had to be

[47] Thus, for example, many manuscripts of *Troilus and Criseyde*.
[48] See, for example, the variant order of *exempla* in the Monk's Tale.
[49] For example, 'Truth' and *A Treatise on the Astrolabe*.
[50] B. Windeatt persuasively rejects the notion that *Troilus and Criseyde* exists in different versions; see Chaucer, *Troilus & Criseyde: A New Edition of The Book of Troilus*, ed. B. Windeatt (London, 1984), pp. 36–55.

relied on in editing Chaucer's prose. For us, the textual glue that bound whole verse texts most deeply together, and thereby rendered them most fully and persuasively coherent, was meter.

As we have noted, there is huge variation in the disposition of final -e. But the earliest manuscripts of Chaucer generally preserve a set number of stresses per line, and many are in fact scrupulous in the distribution of final -e so as not to upset the very small number of available metrical possibilities. As we have also demonstrated through example above, the rest of the texts we chose as 'best' lie just a minor adjustment or two away from such regularity.

We describe Chaucer's metrical practice in detail in our edition and will not replicate that presentation here. For the purposes of this discussion, suffice it to say that the basic patterns are, throughout, 4 or 5 pairs of alternating unstressed/stressed syllables, for the 4- and 5-stress lines respectively. The number of syllables in a Chaucerian line varies from 8 to 9 for the 4-stress lines, and from 10 to 11 for the 5-stress lines. The syllabic variability derives from the possibility of a final unstressed syllable, or not, at the end of the line. In the 4-stress line, Chaucer will frequently produce headless lines (lines starting, that is, on a stressed syllable). While many who study Chaucer's meter find evidence of so-called broken-backed lines (lines with adjacent, medial stressed syllables), we have found that simple emendations, particularly of final -e, eliminate almost all of these instances.[51] In the 43,500 lines of his verse, Chaucer's meter is accentual-syllabic and conforms to a very small set of possible patterns. It is, already, as it survives in some manuscripts, extraordinarily regular. Every edition is a hypothesis, of course, and our hypothesis here is that Chaucer's meter is regular.

We gained confidence in our understanding of Chaucer's meter from the fact that, wherever we claim to isolate a best text, that text also manifests a high and, among competitor witnesses, distinctive commitment to metrical precision. This is especially true of our best texts for both *Troilus and Criseyde* and the *Canterbury Tales*.

Pragmatic Editing: Best Text Editing as Collaboration

The three methods of editing so far considered, plus the non-method of diplomatic editing, can be graded thus according to levels of editorial intervention, from lowest level of intervention to highest: diplomatic, recension, best text, eclecticism. Best text editing commits itself to editorial intervention but does so respectfully with regard to the actual historical texture of the witnesses. That

---

[51] For the scholarship on Chaucer's metre, see 'Reading Chaucer', in *The Oxford Chaucer*, ed. Cannon and Simpson, 1:26, n. 23.

said, in our view best text editing should never be slavishly beholden to the witnesses. When the best text is palpably incorrect, we have therefore intervened. Metrical intervention is by far the most consistent kind of emendation we made. Here, too, however, we found that the rationale for intervention is actually embedded in Chaucer's works themselves.

We have already described the ways that our editorial is 'pragmatic' because it is so fully derived from and embedded in our practice, but we can also call our version of editing 'pragmatic' because Chaucer asks his scribes, and his readers, to practice what contemporary linguists would call 'pragmatism', an understanding dependent on the receiver's knowledge of the linguistic protocols assumed by the person making the utterance. Pragmatism, as defined in linguistics, posits that the meaning of an utterance is not at all wholly contained in its words. Full meaning is, instead, transmitted only through consensual understanding, by utterer and receiver, of the protocols within which the uttered words operate. 'Where's Bill?' someone might ask, to which the response might be 'There's a yellow VW outside Sue's house'.[52] The semantic content of the reply offers no response to the question; on the face of it, and by a positivist reading, the response is irrelevant to the question. We make these two statements a part of a single narrative, however, on the assumption that the respondent is in fact answering the question. The appearance of irrelevance merely provokes us to hypothesize relevance at a further level.

We infer many things, in fact: that the respondent is sane; that the answer is relevant; that the car had transported Bill, and that Bill is at Sue's house. None of these inferences is logically generated; they are, on the contrary, inferred simply from an expectation of conversational relevance. Meaning is produced collaboratively.

Chaucer himself frequently asks his readers to collaborate in the meaning of his narratives through what he calls 'correction'. At the end of *Troilus and Criseyde*, for example, he sends the work to Gower and Strode, asking that they 'vouchen sauf, ther nede is, to corecte, / Of your benignitees and zeles goode' (5.1858–9). Earlier in the poem, in Book 3, Chaucer addresses the lovers in his audience to fix the text as they see fit:

For mine wordes, here and every part,
I speke hem alle under correccioun
Of yow, that feling han in loves art,

[52] Simpson, 'Faith and Hermeneutics'. The example is drawn from S. C. Levinson, *Pragmatics* (Cambridge, 1983), p. 102. Pragmatics is itself dependent on the brilliant analysis of the relation between utterance and linguistic understanding by H. P. Grice, 'Logic and Conversation', in *Speech Acts*, ed. P. Cole and J. L. Morgan (New York, 1975), pp. 41–58.

> And putte it al in your discrecioun
> T'encresse or maken diminucioun
> Of my langage. (*Troilus and Criseyde*, 3.1331–6)

The kinds of 'correction' required here are, respectively, ethical and emotional. But Chaucer will also ask readers for more precisely linguistic and metrical correction from supportive audiences. Thus in the *House of Fame* he prays for metrical help from Apollo,

> ... for the rim is light and lewed,
> Yit make it sumwhat agreable,
> Though som vers faile in a sillable. (*House of Fame*, 1096–8)

Or in the *Romance of the Rose* translation, the God of Love is possibly asking his student to articulate the text with proper pauses so as to understand it accurately: 'For a reder that pointith ille / A good sentence may ofte spille' (2161–2).[53] These instances, not to speak of the broader hermeneutic license that Chaucer encourages his readers to exercise in his works generally,[54] imply a conversational understanding of text in context. The written text, with its every 'jot and tittle',[55] is not an absolute source of authority; it is fully pro-

---

[53] See *MED*, s.v. 'pointen' 1 (b), 'to make pauses in reading a text'.

[54] The phenomenon to which we point is, of course, but one of many categories of the hermeneutic power of the audience in Chaucer's works. See J. Mann, 'The Authority of the Audience in Chaucer', in her *Life in Words: Essays on Chaucer, the Gawain-Poet and Malory* (Toronto, 2014), pp. 102–16 (first published 1991).

[55] The history of philological textual fetishism has various tributaries, most obviously the early modern recovery of classical texts, but most consequentially in Biblical editing and translation. If the assumption is that the text is divinely written, and that the text underwrites every aspect of ecclesiastical dogma and governance, then textual accuracy of an exactingly high order, for both Biblical editions and translations, becomes literally a burning issue. These pressures rise with especial clarity in early modern Europe, precisely the moment that philology, not coincidentally, rockets in importance. The topic is large. See, for one revealing instance, William Tyndale's comment, in the Prologue to his translation of the Pentateuch (1530), about what we might call the textual fetishism of his hostile critics. His enemies, says Tyndale, have 'so narrowly looked on my translation, that there is not so much as one *i* therein if it lack a tittle over his head, but they have noted it, and number it unto the ignorant people for an heresy' (W. Tyndale, *Tyndale's Old Testament*, ed. D. Daniell (New Haven, 1992), p. 3). For the larger cultural stakes informing Biblical philology, see J. Simpson, *Burning to Read: English Fundamentalism and its Reformation Opponents* (Cambridge MA, 2007), pp. 142–83. For some penetrating reflections on the identification of written text and truth in the development of Humanist philology, see T. W. Machan, *Textual Criticism and Medieval Texts* (Charlottesville, 1994), pp. 9–38. For the early modern Biblical issues more broadly,

duced only through reception, according to consensual understandings shared between, or at least recognized by, author and readership.[56]

In some cases, this shared consensual understanding is ethical and emotional. In others, however, it is metrical. And here Chaucer is especially conscious of the need for readerly attention and co-operation, since the state of his language itself is in flux. Thus, as his great poem *Troilus and Criseyde* closes, he anxiously enjoins the scribes to participate actively in coherent replication of the semantic and metrical state of the authorial text:

> And for ther is so greet diversitee
> In English and in writing of our tonge,
> So preye I God that noon miswrite thee,
> Ne thee mismetre for defaute of tonge. (*Troilus and Criseyde*, 5.1793–6)

Chaucer as author felt this anxiety; later in the fifteenth century the scribe John Shirley (d. 1456) expressed the same anxiety to his readers:

> As for fayllinge of the scripture
> Of the meter or ortagrafyure
> Vouche save it to correct
> Elles of the defaute am I suspecte
> That thorugh your supportacion
> Yow list to make correcion
> Sith to such craffte I am not used.[57]

In our experience of scribal practice in all the witnesses of Chaucer's works, however, the scribes of most of Chaucer's manuscripts did not take Chaucer's appeal to heart; so it is *this* correction that the pragmatic editing of a best text supplies.

We conclude, then, with four examples of the occasionally dramatic consequences of our method. Each of these examples is a well-known line, canonized in a form we have decided to emend, and we are acutely aware in each case that our principles of editing are not only correcting the text but a tradition of commentary on the canonized form. The examples are most

---

see J. H. Bentley, *Humanists and Holy Writ: New Testament Scholarship in the Renaissance* (Princeton, 1983).

[56] Ian Cornelius posits the same contextual understanding of how meter worked for Middle English readers: 'Middle English spellings are a fuzzy record of speech forms: they cue the word, leaving readers to select the operative prosodic form'. See I. Cornelius, 'Language and Meter', in *What Kind of a Thing is a Middle English Lyric?*, ed. C. M. Cervone and N. Watson (Philadelphia, 2022), pp. 106–34 (p. 115).

[57] Cited from Wakelin, *Scribal Correction*, p. 30; letter forms have been modernized.

important, however, in showing how a pragmatic editing based on the principle of coherence works in the case of Chaucer.

We begin with line 8 of the General Prologue of the *Canterbury Tales* as printed in the *Riverside* and Robinson's two editions preceding it:

Hath in the Ram his half cours yronne.

This is a ten-syllable line, though the tenth of these (the -e at the end of 'yronne') is really extraneous to this count since it falls after the final stress. The line in this form could be described as a 'broken-backed' line because of the inevitable clash of stresses on 'half' and then 'cours'. 'Half' is the reading in the two excellent manuscripts from which the *Canterbury Tales* is normally edited, Aberystwyth, National Library of Wales, MS Peniarth 392 D (formerly Hengwrt 154, Hg) and San Marino, CA, Huntington Library, MS EL 26.C.9 (El), but the line is not a regular pentameter in either witness, and grammar itself immediately suggests a regularizing emendation, the -e we might expect on the weak adjective 'half', a reading that can in fact be found in London, British Library, MS Harley 7334 (Ha[4]). The change is small, but, at scale, it produces, by collaboration, a Chaucer whose meter is more coherent than in even the most careful editions of Chaucer to date.[58] This is not eclectic editing because it does not rely on some supposition about the quality of a given line; nor is it best text editing since we do not require a demonstrable error to choose the reading in another witness over the reading in our copy text. Rather, we appeal to the preponderance of lines in El and Hg, and their governing patterns, and the coherence that results in emending to conform with that pattern.

We take the next three examples together because we found them among the most challenging changes urged on us by our method – an overturning of settlements we were ourselves, sentimentally, reluctant to overturn. The three lines, all from the conclusion of *Troilus and Criseyde*, are edited in the *Riverside* thus:

Go, litel bok, go, litel myn tragedye (5.1786)
So sende might to make in som comedye! (5.1788)
To the and to the, philosophical Strode (5.1857)

All of these lines have 12 syllables if the final -e on the last word of the line is to be sounded, but the real difficulty in each of them is where to place five stresses appropriately and comfortably. One might reasonably start with the

---

[58] Chaucer, *The Canterbury Tales*, ed. J. Mann (London, 2005), is an important exception here. Mann emends on metrical grounds throughout (see her description of method, pp. lxii–lxv). In this case she emends 'half' to 'halve', a logical conjecture, unnecessary for us, since we accept a plausible reading where possible from the 9 witnesses on which we rely (and Mann relies only on El and Hg).

assumption that 'Go litel bok …' is a headless line since it is common for lines that begin with imperatives to begin in this way. But such an assumption throws a stress onto '-el' in 'litel' or puts a stress on 'bok', and then on 'go' (breaking the back of the line) at which point the line is well on its way to 8 stresses. This is ridiculous of course, but the problem is similar for 5.1788: assuming the -e in 'sende' sounds, it is hard to avoid 6 stresses. In 5.1857 it is hard to know where the second stress could actually go (on the second 'to'?) and *any* scanning of this line that begins with a presumption of alternating syllables becomes hopelessly tangled in 'philosophical' and, again, produces more than 5 stresses however that tangle is unwound. Of course, anyone familiar with these lines, and the extended possibilities of elision is likely to read the first two of them stressing the syllables below in bold:

Go, **li**tel **bok**, go, **li**tel myn **tra**gedye (5.1786)
So **sen**de **might** to **mak**e in som **co**medye! (5.1788)

This requires an abundance of elision which, if allowed in all possible cases in the last of our examples, collapses the line's 12 syllables into only 4 stresses:

To **the** and to **the**, philo**so**phical **Stro**de (5.1857)

To produce 5 stresses a reader would have to pronounce the line with something like the following emphases:

To **the** and to **the** phi**lo**so**phi**cal **Stro**de

Although the consensual tradition in the editing of these lines, with so many fine editors having accepted something similar to the *Riverside*'s forms, we felt that our method demanded that we emend these three lines as follows:

Go litel book, my litel tragedie.
So sende might to make som comedie!
To thee, and thee philosophical Strode

The third of these remains imperfect, still requiring that we stress 'philosophical' on the second and fourth syllables (phi**lo**so**phi**cal), but the example also shows that emendation for meter can improve a line without making it fully regular. We report in our textual apparatus a warrant for the substitution of 'my litel' for 'go litel myn' in London, British Library, MS Harley 1239 (H³). We report 'to make some' as a conjectural emendation found in none of our witnesses (though, in this case we were also informed by semantic coherence reported by the *MED*).[59] And we report that we find, in one of our preferred

---

[59] In the 91 instances of 'make', meaning 'compose', in the *MED*, s.v. 'maken', not one supports 'make in [a genre or mode]' and there are, by contrast many examples of 'make + direct object'.

manuscripts, New York, Morgan Library and Museum, MS M.817 (formerly Doncaster, Campsall Hall MS [Cl]), the omission of the pleonastic 'to' in the third of these lines, which moves it toward regularity.

We would not want to seem glib about the importance of discernment in editing (the judgment based on wide learning and a knowledge of other examples both within and beyond a given medieval poet's work), nor to suggest, on the other hand, that our process is in any way mechanical (the moment when Chaucer is edited as against *all* other lines in Chaucer simultaneously, with the metrical patterns in relation to grammatical structures digitally to hand is as yet beyond us). Our assumption that these or any of the lines of poetry in our edition survive in most or all extant witnesses in a corrupt form is not equivalent to the assumption that we have discerned in the metrical possibilities for this particular line the contours of an 'original' reading. We assume our method will move the meter in all of the works in this edition closer on the whole to the meter Chaucer wrote, but we abjure such valuations in any individual case and the kinds of texts that are their result. Rather, we emend these four lines – as we emend throughout our edition – so that they conform to the metrical pattern in the preponderance of lines in all of *Troilus and Criseyde* and all of Chaucer's other poetry as they survive in our witnesses. The premise of our method is, then, that error in surviving witnesses is pragmatically discernible in any significant deviation from the coherent metrical pattern constituted by the evidence of all of Chaucer's lines in all surviving witnesses. Our method is to move any given line toward that coherence rather than to leave it in the form it has in our copy-text.

5

The Pleasures of Plainness: Ordinary Manuscripts in Extraordinary Traditions[1]

SIÂN ECHARD

Many important medieval texts barely survived the Middle Ages. *Beowulf* exists in a single manuscript (London, British Library, MS Cotton Vitellius A.xv), and that manuscript was damaged in the Ashburnham House fire of 1731, so that some of our readings today depend on the transcriptions made by and for the late eighteenth-century scholar, Grímur Jónsson Thorkelin. The text of Thomas Malory's *Morte Darthur* depended entirely on William Caxton's 1485 printing until 1934, when Walter Oakeshott found the Winchester Manuscript (London, British Library, MS Additional 59678), while looking for something else. That same year also saw Hope Emily Allen's identification of a complete manuscript for *The Book of Margery Kempe* (London, British Library, MS Additional 61823), which had, up to that point, existed only in excerpts in early print. We would not have the *Alliterative Morte Arthure* were it not for its preservation in Robert Thornton's fifteenth-century compilation of romances, religious texts and medical texts (Lincoln, Lincoln Cathedral Library, MS 91). The works of the *Gawain* (or *Pearl*)-poet, too, have come down to us in one manuscript (London, British Library, MS Cotton Nero A.x). While other canonical Middle English poets, such as Chaucer, Gower, Lydgate and Langland, have more robust manuscript traditions in the

---

[1] It is a great pleasure to contribute to this Festschrift in honour of Kathryn Kerby-Fulton. We first met many years ago, when I was a nervous job-seeker and she was one of the faculty members assigned to shepherd me through my interview day. I did not get that particular job, but Kathryn's kindness was a highlight of the process. Afterwards, whenever we met at conferences, she was unfailingly welcoming and curious about my work. I did not work much on manuscripts when first we met, but once I began to do so, I realized that she was one of those rare scholars who combined technical expertise with an ability to ask the big, 'so what' questions. Whenever I find myself too far down in the material weeds, I try to pull back and think about those bigger questions, and Kathryn is one of my most important role models in that task.

aggregate, individual works by these authors can still depend on a handful of surviving copies.

By contrast, some texts that circulated in medieval Britain have an almost overwhelming number of surviving witnesses, with over 130 copies of the *Prick of Conscience*, or more than 250 of the various versions of the Wycliffite Bibles, or over 180 of the Middle English prose *Brut* (along with almost 50 manuscripts of the Anglo-Norman text). The editorial problems represented by these very different situations are varied. In single-manuscript traditions, editors might have to decide what to do with missing or suspect readings, decisions that sometimes require assessing the value of the various, partial post-medieval witnesses. In the case of richer traditions, attempts to establish reliable base texts can require reckoning with the tendency of some kinds of texts to morph repeatedly as they are copied, not only through scribal error or textual corruption, but also through deliberate addition and accretion built into the genre itself (with historical writing being particularly prone to this kind of process). And even the most indefatigable editor must inevitably set some manuscripts aside, in order to produce an edition. Late manuscripts are more likely to hit the cutting room floor, simply because the process of transmission means their texts are usually less likely to be reliable than those in earlier copies.

But the establishing (and subsequent interpretation) of a text is, increasingly, not the only reason manuscripts, whether single copies or multiple witnesses to a tradition, might receive scholarly attention. Construction, illustration, decoration, scribal practice, readerly attention – these and other features of the material book can all attract discussion, and increasingly, these often separate disciplinary approaches are being brought together in studies that put medieval texts back into their books and those books back into the cultures that produced them. Kathryn Kerby-Fulton's work has been a pioneering and shining example of this kind of approach, and I hope that this essay will demonstrate at least some of my debt to her example.

My tradition is not a vernacular one, but its relationship to important vernacular traditions, both in English and in other European vernaculars, will I hope make it relevant to this collection. Geoffrey of Monmouth's *Historia regum Britanniae*, or, to give it its more recent name, *De gestis Britonum*,[2]

---

[2] Michael D. Reeve uses *De gestis Britonum* in his edition of the work, arguing briefly for its superiority to the more familiar *Historia regum Britanniae* on the basis of its use in a significant cluster of manuscripts in the early tradition: *Geoffrey of Monmouth: The History of the Kings of Britain. An Edition and Translation of De gestis Britonum [Historia Regum Britanniae]*, ed. M. D. Reeve and trans. N. Wright (Cambridge, 2007), p. lix. This title is slowly becoming the preferred usage. For a

survives in well over 220 medieval manuscripts,[3] and in a handful of early modern antiquarian transcriptions. Of all of these manuscripts, some forty or so have been noticed in the editorial tradition, and only about half of those have been treated as primary witnesses.[4] The current standard critical edition by Michael D. Reeve is based on a collation of 'eleven manuscripts ... in full and six in part'. Reeve is of course deeply aware of the whole tradition (he lists 219 manuscripts in his Introduction),[5] and it is not my intention to suggest that his edition is mistaken or inadequate. I am however interested in the

---

lengthier discussion of the title in the manuscript tradition, see S. Echard, 'Whose History? Naming Practices in the Transmission of Geoffrey of Monmouth's *Historia regum Britannie*', *Arthuriana* 22.4 (2012), 8–24.

[3] Julia Crick recorded 217 manuscripts (one of them a collection of excerpts) in her catalogue: see J. C. Crick, *The Historia Regum Britannie of Geoffrey of Monmouth, 3: Summary Catalogue of the Manuscripts* (Cambridge, 1989). The list was supplemented in a series of articles by D. N. Dumville: 'Update: The Manuscripts of Geoffrey of Monmouth's *Historia Regum Britanniae*', *Arthurian Literature* 3 (1983), 113–28; 'The Manuscripts of Geoffrey of Monmouth's *Historia Regum Britanniae: Addenda, Corrigenda, and an Alphabetical List*', *Arthurian Literature* 4 (1985), 164–71; and 'The Manuscripts of Geoffrey of Monmouth's *Historia Regum Britanniae: A Second Supplement*', *Arthurian Literature* 5 (1985), 149–51. The most recent update is J. Tahkokallio, 'Update to the List of Manuscripts of Geoffrey of Monmouth's *Historia regum Britanniae*', *Arthurian Literature* 32 (2015), 187–203. See also J. Tahkokallio, 'Early Manuscript Dissemination', in *A Companion to Geoffrey of Monmouth*, ed. G. Henley and J. B. Smith (Leiden, 2020), pp. 155–80; that essay concentrates on those manuscripts (almost 80) that can be dated to before 1210.

[4] There were two editions that appeared in 1929, E. Faral's *La légende arthurienne, études et documents*, 3 vols (Paris, 1929), and A. Griscom's *The Historia Regum Britanniae of Geoffrey of Monmouth* (London, 1929). These drew on a very small number of manuscripts, and both have been viewed as flawed, though for different reasons. Next came J. Hammer's *Historia regum Britanniae: A Variant Version edited from Manuscripts* (Cambridge MA, 1951); while Hammer had surveyed most of the tradition, with the ultimately unfulfilled goal of producing an edition of the dominant tradition, this work drew on 5 manuscripts, and did not sufficiently work out the relationships between the variant versions. N. Wright, ed., *The Historia regum Britannie of Geoffrey of Monmouth. I. Bern, Burgerbibliothek, MS 568* (Cambridge, 1985) was a single-manuscript edition of the main tradition, which he followed with his new edition of the First Variant Version, this time based on all 7 complete manuscripts of the First Variant version: N. Wright, ed., *The Historia Regum Britannie of Geoffrey of Monmouth. II: The First Variant Version: A Critical Edition* (Cambridge, 1988). The most recent edition is D. W. Burchmore, ed. and trans., *The History of the Kings of Britain: The First Variant Version* (Cambridge MA, 2019).

[5] *Geoffrey of Monmouth*, ed. Reeve, p. xi. For his complete list of manuscripts, see pp. xxxii–l.

question of what happens to manuscripts in large traditions when they are not considered to be textually useful. As I have suggested, other aspects of material transmission can attract attention to a particular copy, but not all manuscripts are visually appealing, or associated with a famous reader, or linked to a known producer. It is easy, in other words, for ordinary manuscripts that find themselves in extraordinary traditions to be overlooked. In what follows, I want to sketch a few ways that some ordinary manuscripts might nevertheless still have something to tell us.

I set as my rule for this essay that none of my manuscripts should be in any way significant, as we traditionally understand the term. None of them, that is, forms the basis for any of the modern editions of the text, and none is considered particularly attractive or impressive. They are, instead, at best plain, and at worst, positively scruffy. I begin at the scruffy end of things with damage, both at point of production and after. Vatican, Biblioteca Apostolica Vaticana, MS Pal. Lat. 962 includes a thirteenth-century copy of the *De gestis* in a compilation that now includes other medieval material and some early modern transcriptions. Early in the text of the *De gestis*, a large chunk of one page has been torn or ripped irregularly, leaving a significant gap at the right margin of folio 121r. Such damage is hardly unusual, and there is in this case no way of telling its origin, but I introduce it here as part of a thought-experiment in material serendipity. The section of the text affected by the damage is the story of Locrinus, Guendoloena and Estrildis, with its account of how the Severn River got its name. Locrinus, the early British king who gave his name to Logres, has been compelled to marry Guendoloena, daughter of Corineus, but maintains a relationship with his lover Estrildis, building a secret chamber where he visits her and where she eventually becomes pregnant with his daughter. When Corineus, his formidable father-in-law, dies, Locrinus divorces Guendoloena and makes Estrildis his queen. Guendoloena retaliates by raising the army of Cornwall against Locrinus, defeating and killing him in battle, and throwing Estrildis and her child into the river. Guendoloena then decides that the river should be named for the daughter, Habren: 'and she gave an order that throughout the whole of Britain, the river should be called by the girl's name; she wanted her to have honour into eternity, because her own husband had engendered her'.[6]

The geographical-etymological stories in the early books of the *De gestis* often attract attention from annotators, both medieval and later. A number of manuscripts of the *De gestis* pick out this particular moment. Sometimes the

---

[6] *Geoffrey of Monmouth*, ed. Reeve, II.25, p. 35: '… fecitque edictum per totam Britanniam ut flumen nomine puellae uocaretur; uolebat etenim honorem aeternitatis illi impendere quia maritus suus eam generauerat'. All translations are my own.

attention is medieval, at or just after the point of production, as for example in Cambridge, Corpus Christi College, MS 414 (p. 437); Cambridge, Trinity College, MS R.7.6 (fol. 7v); or Dublin, Trinity College, MS 172 (fol. 97r). Aberystwyth, National Library of Wales, MS Peniarth 42 has notes in both Latin and Welsh. In this manuscript, the story of Habren spans folios 8v to 9r, with marginal notes in an early modern hand surrounding the moment when the girl is thrown into the river. The marginal notes to this section of the text across the tradition often seem particularly interested in the process by which Habren/Hafren has become Sabrina (Severn). As in some of his other etymologies, Geoffrey attributes changes in the name to the passage of time and to what he calls the *corruptionem* that results. In Pal. Lat. 962, a rough manicule in the left margin picks out the paragraph recounting Habren's death, and because the chunk of the right margin that is missing ends just above this paragraph, a reader can read the full account to which the manicule draws attention. Some of what leads up to this moment has, however, become unavailable. We cannot know when the damage occurred, nor indeed how a reader, encountering it, might react. One can imagine a reader skipping the damaged page; one can also imagine a reader noticing the manicule (and again, we cannot know exactly when it was added or whether or not it precedes the damage) and making an effort to puzzle out what precedes this apparently important moment. What is true, however, is that material damage – perhaps the result of casual excision or perhaps resulting from the passage of time – sits next to a tale that foregrounds both physical violence and linguistic decay. There is no way in which this material-textual juxtaposition is *intended* to make meaning, but a reader who lingers over the material may perhaps make her own.

London, British Library, MS Arundel 319 exhibits a kind of damage that we recognize, as well as another that we might have to look harder to see. As its sparse British Library catalogue entry has it, this thirteenth-century copy is *mutilus*, lacking text at the end.[7] It is also an example of the kind of workmanlike manuscript that conserves as much parchment as possible, so that many of the pages, rather than being perfectly rectangular, show clearly the curves of the neck or shoulder of the sheep. Pages like these remind us of the damage to (destruction of) a living creature that was necessary to create the codex in the first place. Manuscript scholars have become more attuned

---

[7] *Catalogue of Manuscripts of the British Museum. New Series. Vol. 1, Part 1: The Arundel MSS* (London, 1834), p. 93. This (Latin) catalogue description had at the time of writing been transferred to online form in the British Library's Archives and Manuscripts catalogue. As will become clear below, while some British Library manuscripts have been re-described in the process of digitization, many still carry descriptions scanned from nineteenth-century catalogues into the modern catalogue interface.

in recent years to the animality of codices written on skin, so copies like these might have a renewed interest for some modern readers, and again, the accidents and vagaries of materiality have the potential to make new meanings.[8] A case in point is the opening, made up of folios 38v and 39r of this copy; the irregular page on the verso bears, centred in its bottom margin, the stamp of the British Library, while the curved margin of the recto bears a single cross, a reader's mark. There are many such marks in this manuscript: whatever its material faults, it was clearly read and used. As for the stamp, it is repeated several times, apparently fairly randomly, throughout the manuscript. This is a routine practice that declares ownership (and was intended to prevent theft). It is something of a democratizing gesture, in that all manuscripts, whether gorgeous or not, received similar treatment.[9] The unremarkable cross and stamp on this opening, then, point to two different parts of this manuscript's life, while the opening's irregularities might also remind us, should we be so inclined, of the life of the sheep with which the manuscript began: the curves suggest what Hannah Ryley has called the 'nose-to-tail' approach to transforming an animal into the materials for book–making.[10] A particularly dramatic example of this kind of 'waste not want not' manuscript is Dublin, Trinity College, MS 11500, an early fifteenth-century copy that moved into a public collection only in 2014. This is a small manuscript with many irregular pages. The irregularities include holes with the text written around them and pages with curved or diagonal edges. The text is very carefully written on these

---

[8] See for example B. Holsinger, 'Of Pigs and Parchment: Medieval Studies and the Coming of the Animal', *PMLA* 124.2 (2009), 616–23; K. Steel, *How to Make a Human: Animals and Violence in the Middle Ages* (Columbus OH, 2011); S. Kay, *Animal Skins and the Reading Self in Medieval Latin and French Bestiaries* (Chicago, 2017); P. McCracken, *In the Skin of a Beast: Sovereignty and Animality in Medieval France* (Chicago, 2017); and, for a recent overview of book history's engagement with animal skin, N. K. Turner, 'The Materiality of Medieval Parchment: A Response to "The Animal Turn"', *Revista Hispánica Moderna* 71.1 (2018), 39–67.

[9] The Arundel manuscripts came into the British Museum Library collection in 1831. It was the practice at the time in the Museum to stamp manuscripts and books when they were acquired, though large bequests sometimes meant that it took some time to finish the process. For a useful overview of the history of British Library book stamps, see Christina Duffy, 'A Guide to British Library Book Stamps', *Collection Care Blog*, September 23, 2013, accessed November 27, 2023, https://blogs.bl.uk/collectioncare/2013/09/a-guide-to-british-library-book-stamps.html.

[10] H. Ryley, *Re-using Manuscripts in Late Medieval England: Repairing, Recycling, Sharing* (York, 2022), p. 19. She goes on to note that other organic products, such as galls and feathers, were also part of the production of parchment and the writing of books, pp. 24–5.

scrappy pieces, often justified in neat diagonal lines next to the curves of the parchment, visually emphasizing the textual support's origins. Daniel Wakelin has argued recently that, faced with the reality of the imperfect organic matter upon which they had to write, medieval scribes nevertheless had an idea of 'the page as an abstract form – a conventional rectangle – that they try to achieve despite the flaws in the skin'.[11] The neatness and care in a manuscript like Trinity 11500, then, may suggest a kind of medieval aspiration that imagines the page beyond its very visible flaws, at the same time that its curves and holes make it impossible for some modern readers not to think about the animal beneath. While it is merely chance that the first text in this manuscript is an abbreviated Latin version of Aristotle's *On the Nature of Animals*, our current critical moment means this mundane manuscript can be reimagined as a meaningful nexus of text and support.

London, British Library, MS Additional 15732 is another modestly-sized parchment manuscript with some irregular pages. It also has a few openings where the text has been carefully written around large holes. The result is particularly striking on the opening make up of folios 25v–26r. On 25v, a red explicit and green incipit mark the transition from Books III to IV, and Book IV begins with a rough but lively seven-line capital in blue. On the recto, two features of the page catch a reader's eye: the three-line capital on the British king Cassibellaunus's angry letter in response to Gaius Julius Caesar's demand for tribute, and the large hole that truncates five lines of text. Through the hole, one can clearly read a few words from the description of the battle between the Romans and the Britons that follows on folio 27r; the word that is centred in this view is *perem[p]tus*, which signals the death of the Roman tribune Labienus at the hands of the Cassibellaunus's brother Nennius, wielding the sword Yellow Death, captured by Nennius from Julius Caesar. Despite the hole, 26r lacks no text because the scribe has written around the hole; furthermore, because of that hole, a window is opened into more text that telegraphs how the battle initiated by the letter on 26r will develop. I have no way of knowing whether a medieval reader would have made any attempt to decipher the text visible through this fleshy window, but I can say it is the first thing I tried to do. Both the large initial and the hole that captured my attention are routine features of production practice, the latter testifying, again, to the underlying value of the textual support. It is difficult to imagine a modern book deliberately choosing to use, rather than to discard, damaged paper, and it is doubtless also the case that a more deluxe medieval manuscript would not have made

---

[11] D. Wakelin, *Immaterial Texts in Late Medieval England: Making English Literary Manuscripts, 1400–1500* (Cambridge, 2022), p. 28.

use of parchment with holes in it. This page, then, serves as a reminder – as did the library stamp discussed above – that measures of value shift over time.

There is another marker of at least use-value in this manuscript. Like Arundel 319, discussed above, Additional 15732 has lost some of its leaves. In this case, the deficit was remedied with leaves (73r–85v) added in the fifteenth century, suggesting that someone cared enough about the manuscript to need or want the text to be complete. The manuscript also has several neat manicules, as well as early modern annotations, showing how long a life even a modest manuscript could have. Trinity Dublin 11500, discussed above for its willingness to use irregular parchment, is another manuscript that shows signs of continuous engagement over time, from production through to institutionalization. Its irregular pages mix contemporary textual corrections, manicules and the occasional early modern note. Later interventions in the manuscript suggest perhaps a decline in perceived value. There is an eighteenth-century table of contents that remarks on the discrepancies between the text of this copy and that of the 'printed copies'; that is, the manuscript is now being judged according to the quality of its text. There is also a rather acerbic post-medieval note on a flyleaf that Geoffrey 'translated the British history into Latin, or published his own fictions as a genuine history'. Here, the judgment is not merely that this is a bad text of the *De gestis* but also that the *De gestis* itself is suspect, at least when judged in the framework of historical writing. And yet both of these interventions occurred as the manuscript passed from one collection to another (it had seven owners between the Dissolution and its acquisition by Trinity College Dublin in 2014). The disclaimers of its value coexist, in other words, with the manuscript's incorporation into the world of book-collecting and library-building. Trinity Dublin's catalogue record adds another frame to the manuscript, one that is worth unpacking in some detail. It notes that the manuscript derives originally from St Mary's Abbey in Dublin, described as 'the wealthiest monastic house in medieval Ireland'. Its chapter house, the catalogue notes, 'still stands on Meetinghouse Lane'. A reader learns that the Irish parliament often met at St Mary's. A reference to a 1304 fire in Dublin is offered as an explanation for the manuscript's existence, 'as the community set about making good the losses it had suffered'.[12] The willingness to use less than perfect parchment might well align with this apparent goal of refilling the library as quickly as possible.

---

[12] 'St Mary's Abbey manuscript', *The Library of Trinity College Dublin Classic Catalogue*, accessed November 27, 2023, http://library.catalogue.tcd.ie/record=b20697999. See also B. Meehan, 'A Fourteenth-Century Historical Compilation from St Mary's Cistercian Abbey, Dublin', in *Medieval Dublin XV: Proceedings of the Friends of Medieval Dublin Symposium 2013*, ed. S. Duffy (Dublin, 2016), pp. 264–76.

The manuscript is a large compilation, including, alongside Geoffrey's, such texts as *De excidio Troiae* and Gerald of Wales's *Topographia* and *Expugnacio Hibernica*. But the bulk of the catalogue description concentrates on one short text: folios 118r–120r contain 'a preliminary version of the ordinances of 1310, in Anglo-Norman French'. The reference here is to Edward II's Ordinances of 1311. The catalogue note also provides links to published material related to the Ordinances more broadly. In the Trinity catalogue, then, this manuscript is firmly located in local geography and history, and in medieval history more broadly, important for one of the genuine historical texts it contains and even more as a physical artefact that witnesses a vibrant medieval past.

London, Lambeth Palace Library, MS 454 is a peculiar manuscript, containing two copies of the *De gestis*, along with, surprisingly, a manipulable astronomical volvelle. Geoffrey's text bears many signs of use, with later annotation, underlining, reading brackets and marks, and manicules. Folios 42rv are written on a piece of parchment with a large hole at the outer margin. It is possible that the damage occurred at some point after the original copying, because the hole has been repaired and the text rewritten over the patch. On 42v the annotation *de Roma* and the manicule accompanying it are written on the repair, in the somewhat later hand that has also added running titles (in French) to the copy. There are a few similar repairs in this copy, suggesting that in this case there was less tolerance than in some of the other copies discussed here for accommodating flaws in the parchment. The manicule on 42v stands out rather more than some of the others in this manuscript because of the repair, since the patch is somewhat lighter than the original parchment. Many later annotators of the *De gestis* show a particular interest in Rome (the hand here points to the city's founding). In Lambeth 454, material happenstance emphasizes this readerly attention.

As I noted at the outset of this essay, while Galfridian manuscripts tend to be assessed primarily in textual terms, some scholars have focused on annotation, both medieval and modern.[13] Inevitably, however, the sheer size of the corpus has meant that many potentially interesting manuscripts have not yet received attention. It is also true that certain *kinds* of readerly interventions are difficult to work with. I return here to the manicules mentioned briefly in Additional 15732. These carefully-drawn hands pick out the Leir story, the star presaging Arthur's birth, the death of Aurelius and Uther's ascension to

---

[13] For example, G. Henley, 'Reading Geoffrey of Monmouth in Wales: The Intellectual Roots of *Brut y Brenhinedd* in Latin Commentaries, Glosses, and Variant Texts', *Viator* 49.3 (2018), 103–27, has recently examined annotation in Welsh-associated manuscripts of the *Historia* (particularly of the Variant version) to demonstrate how Geoffrey's text was received in Wales.

the throne. They are all in the same hand and clearly later than the text they are marking, but exactly when they were added is difficult to say. Some of them occur alongside the single word *nota*, but this is thin evidence for exact dating. Still, manicules (and other, even less visually informative marks like Xes, brackets and underlining) are often the only record we have of engaged reading.[14] Even when they coexist with annotation, however, they can be difficult to interpret. London, British Library, MS Harley 4003, is heavily annotated, so that the opening across folios 82v to 83r includes both notes and a range of manicules. One of the manicules holds a horn: this is the portion of the text when Brutus sneaks into the Greek leader Pandrasus's camp and signals the general attack with the sound of a horn. The text refers only to a signal, but a contemporary annotation explaining that this is the sound of a horn has been added below the text, and the manicule has been attached by a lone line to that annotation, as if to further clarify it. It is clear, then, that this passage attracted readerly attention, but why? It is one of the goriest battle descriptions in the *De gestis*, and below the horn-manicule, we find the annotation *crudelitas*. We might conclude that the reader's attention is negative, but we cannot be sure. Similarly, Vatican, Biblioteca Apostolica Vaticana, MS Reg. lat. 692, a twelfth-century manuscript, has a later manicule and a doodle of a drinking cup on the section of the text where the origins of Wasseil are explained. This is a very popular passage for annotators, medieval and modern alike. Geoffrey here recounts how the Saxon Hengist sends his daughter Renwein to seduce the British king Vortigern. She offers him a cup and salutes him with the words 'Lauerd king, wasseil'. An interpreter explains the greeting to Vortigern and tells him that the response is Drincheil, and 'from that day until today', Geoffrey says, British drinking custom involves the exchange of Wasseil and Drincheil.[15] Perhaps the readers who mark out this section are taking a kind of anthropological stance, but it is also possible that sometimes the passage is highlighted for its negative content. It becomes clear that Vortigern is drunk, and Geoffrey is forthright in condemning the British king's passion for a pagan woman. But without explicit, negative textual comment, we cannot be sure what most of the readers who mark this passage across the tradition were thinking. We can, however, notice that they noticed it, and the more such annotations we see across multiple manuscripts, the clearer the framework for understanding any particular intervention becomes.

---

[14] W. Sherman, *Used Books: Marking Readers in Renaissance England* (Philadelphia, 2008), devotes a chapter to manicules, their possibilities and their frustrations.

[15] *Geoffrey of Monmouth*, ed. Reeve, VI.100, p. 129: Ab illo die usque in hodiernum mansit consuetudo illa in Britannia quia in conuiuiis qui potat ad alium dicit 'wasseil', qui uero post illum recipit potum respondet 'drincheil'.

The Wasseil passage is picked out in Reg. lat. 692 with both the word and the doodled cup, and doodles are another category of potential information that is sometimes overlooked. Most of the time, as with the manicules, doodles are tantalizing because, while they show us someone was reading, they rarely show us who or when or even how. Harley 4003, whose manicules were discussed above, includes several rough marginal drawings that seem to have been made at the time of production. On folio 86v, a large head is drawn next to the story of Corineus and Gogmagog the giant. Above it are two marginal notes, *Nota Cornubia* and *Gogmagog*. Again, we have information here, but not enough: is the focus of attention the exciting story of Corineus wrestling the giant, Corineus's eponymous founding of Cornwall or both? Folio 110r features a reading bracket doodled into a face next to the story of the massacre at Mount Ambrius, along with a drawing of a knife. Just as many copies pick out Wasseil/Drincheil, this moment – when the Old English phrase *nimet oure seaxas* is the signal for the Saxon treachery – is often a site of reader response, and this is not the only manuscript to doodle a knife at this point. But again, while we might assume that a reader disapproves of this moment in the text, it may be important as well because of what comes next. The textual note in the opposite margin refers to Stonehenge, which, Geoffrey tells us, was built to memorialize the dead of the massacre. One of the manuscripts briefly consulted (that is, not as a main witness) by Reeve for his edition is London, Lambeth Palace Library, MS 503. It belonged to William Lambarde, the early modern antiquarian whose *Perambulation of Kent* (1576) was an example of the popular genre of chorography, which fixed history to geographical places and features. It is not surprising, then, that the manuscript is filled with notes in Lambarde's hand picking out Geoffrey's place-name stories. These include several notes on Stonehenge, one of which is a rendering of the name in Old English letter forms. Lambarde's published works included the use of Old English fonts for certain words and place-names, so it is not surprising to find him deploying his archaizing hand here.[16] Harley 4003's doodles and notes are not as copious as are Lambarde's in Lambeth 503, nor can they be connected to a known figure. What they do show, however, is how neglected manuscripts can be slotted into a matrix within which to understand features we might otherwise overlook or struggle to understand.

Just as there are neglected manuscripts, so too are there neglected *parts* of manuscripts. Leaves at the front and back of the main text block may attract cataloguing and scholarly attention if they have been filled by later users with

---

[16] I discuss early modern antiquarians and their use of archaizing hands and specially-commissioned Old English fonts in S. Echard, *Printing the Middle Ages* (Philadelphia, 2008).

connected text – the *Index of Middle English Verse*, for example, includes items found in these kinds of spaces – or if they bear names that can be traced in order to establish provenance. But these leaves contain many other kinds of material as well. London, British Library, MS Royal 13 D.v is not, unlike most of the manuscripts discussed in this essay, a completely obscure copy. It is a thirteenth-century manuscript from St Alban's. It has some rubrics in the hand of Matthew Paris, and is annotated by Polydore Vergil, the Italian historian whose skeptical *Anglica Historia* of 1534 prompted furious denunciation from John Leland on the matter of the historicity of King Arthur.[17] It is thus linked to an important centre of textual production, and to famous medieval and early modern names. A leaf at the back includes what look to be pen trials (often found on flyleaves), and that same leaf also has an elaborate drawing of Gothic tracery, of the sort one might find in stone- or woodwork in a church, or in an illuminated manuscript. The catalogue treatment of this drawing is interesting. The entry in the online Archives and Manuscripts catalogue has been ported from the 1921 printed catalogue, and while it draws attention to St Alban's, Matthew Paris and Polydore Vergil, it makes no mention of the drawing.[18] The record in the online Digital Catalogue of Illuminated Manuscripts (DCIM), on the other hand, does describe the drawing.[19] Because of its more limited focus, on fewer manuscripts and even more specifically, on illuminated copies, the DCIM could spend some time revisiting manuscript descriptions. The addition of the reference to the drawing might reflect the more art-historical orientation of the DCIM, or simply shifts, with the passage of time, in what is considered important in a manuscript description. It stands as a reminder that even a manuscript with famous associations can have elements in it that are overlooked and that ideas about what matters in a manuscript shift according to both time and context.

London, British Library, MS Arundel 10 is another manuscript that has recently received new cataloguing attention. The three-line Latin description in the 1834 catalogue[20] (these descriptions are still in place for some manuscripts today) has in this case been replaced at least twice. The DCIM included four images (a full page and detail of each of folios 2r and 40v) and

---

[17] The dispute is discussed in J. P. Carley, 'Polydore Vergil and John Leland on King Arthur: The Battle of the Books', *Arthurian Interpretations* 15.2 (1984), 86–100.

[18] *Catalogue of Western Manuscripts in the Old Royal and King's Collections. Volume II: Royal MSS. 12 A.1 to 20 E. X and App. 1–89* (London, 1921), p. 110.

[19] 'Royal MS 13 D.v', *DCIM*, accessed April 23, 2023.

[20] *Catalogue of Manuscripts* (1834), p. 3.

a somewhat expanded but still brief (English) description.[21] This description includes folio 123v: 'Inscriptions including reference to the death of Charles, duke of Burgundy, and the date 1530 (f. 123v)'. This reference picks out a set of notes at the base of what is in fact an end leaf of exactly the sort that was not foliated in Royal 13 D.v (where the new description designates it as 200*). Some foliation practices set front- and back matter apart from the text to which it is attached, either by not foliating at all or by using Roman rather than Arabic numerals. The shift here may reflect changing ideas about foliation, or it may reflect a growing value attached to the end leaf and its historical notes. The description attached to the complete digitization of the manuscript further expands on the note on the end leaf: 'This manuscript testifies to the long-lasting popularity of the *Historia* on the Continent: it was, most likely, written in Northern France, and was owned by Cambrai Cathedral during the fourteenth century. It remained in France until at least 1530, when notes about the death of Charles the Bold (b. 1433, d. 1477), Duke of Burgundy, were added to a flyleaf (f. 123v)'.[22] The accretion of detail in the description indicates how the manuscript is being (re)positioned in the textual tradition and that repositioning intersects with its material reality, in that the flyleaf is now granted full foliation status. However, what even the new descriptions do not indicate is that the flyleaf also features an elaborate doodle of a tree or foliate ornament, along with Latin text which might have been written over the drawing. Of course these features are there to be seen by anyone flipping through the manuscript, physically or virtually, but their discovery would be a happy accident; officially, they remain invisible, a reminder of how much puzzling but potentially rich material remains to be discovered in less-examined manuscripts.[23]

Arundel 10 is a French-associated manuscript, and the French notes, while they seem to have no link to the text of the *De gestis* itself, are connected to that association. But flyleaves often contain material that is apparently completely random. Paris, Bibliothèque nationale de France, MS latin 6040, a

[21] 'Arundel MS 10', *DCIM*, accessed April 23, 2023, https://www.bl.uk/catalogues/illuminatedmanuscripts/record.asp?MSID=1630&CollID=20&NStart=10.

[22] 'Arundel MS 10', accessed April 23, 2023, http://www.bl.uk/manuscripts/FullDisplay.aspx?ref=Arundel_MS_10&index=4.

[23] Dealing with a similarly layered set of additions (that doubtless developed over time), on what he calls a 'busy' flyleaf in a register from Peterborough Abbey, J. Luxford, 'Additaments from Peterborough Abbey and the Problem of the "Busy" Flyleaf', *Journal of the Early Book Society* 23 (2020), 213, makes the case for the value of the kind of reading I have attempted here, arguing that such flyleaves are 'a class of historical artefact that could, if tried, comfortably absorb more scholarly attention than they have to date'.

twelfth-century copy of the *De gestis*, has several grotesques sketched on one of its end leaves. They are reasonably accomplished, suggesting the familiar world of manuscript decoration and illumination in what is otherwise a very plain, undecorated text. The leaf also has pen trials and various mottoes, and the codex has evidently been flipped around to facilitate writing in different directions. Nothing here seems to comment on or speak directly to the *De gestis*, which is the only text in this short manuscript, nor to its production context, about which little is known.[24] In the case of the flyleaf to Cambridge, Fitzwilliam Museum, MS 346, however, contiguity is obviously meaningful, as it records the appearance of Aaron Thompson's 1718 English translation of the *De gestis* and his attempt to prove the truth of the Brutus foundation story. The note at the front of Trinity Dublin 11500 calls out Geoffrey's 'fictions'; the note in Fitzwilliam 346 also speaks to the nature of Geoffrey's endeavour, concluding that Thompson 'endeavours to prove the author to be a more faithful historian, than he is generally esteemed to be'.[25] Indeed, flyleaves of manuscripts of the *De gestis* often contain material that evaluates Geoffrey's work, implicitly or explicitly. Post-medieval tables of contents can signal a framing of the text simply through the words used to title or attribute the text. The *De gestis* is typically called a Historia, and attributed to Geoffrey, in what are usually very workmanlike lists, but London, British Library, MS Stowe 56, has a fairly unusual early modern table of contents. The manuscript, from the late twelfth or early thirteenth century, consists of Baudri of Bourgeuil's history of Jerusalem; an abridgement of William of Jumiège's Norman history; *De excidio Troiae*; the *Historia Apollonii regis Tyri*; Alexander material, including the letters of Alexander to Aristotle and Dindimus; and Geoffrey's *De gestis*. The list is carefully written in an imitation of a medieval script, with a decorative initial on the opening of the *Catalogus librorum* and a filler occupying the bottom half of the page. There are no authors mentioned in this list; apart from the letters in the Alexander material, the contents list is a sequence of 'Historia' titles. Geoffrey's text is 'Historia Brittannica'. The flyleaf, then, is part of the generic sorting of the *De gestis*. A further sorting occurred at another moment in the manuscript's ownership history, as the list now has authorial names, where known, penciled next to each entry.

Early modern scholars sometimes use extra space at the front or back of manuscripts to record biographical information about Geoffrey. In Additional

---

[24] J. Crick, *The Historia Regum Britannie*, p. 270, suggests that the notes on 60v, which is the end leaf with the grotesques, suggest 'English early history'.

[25] I discuss Thompson's translation, with some reference to this manuscript, in S. Echard, 'Remembering Brutus: Aaron Thompson's British History of 1718', *Arthurian Literature* 30 (2013), 141–69.

15732, for example, the *Historia* finishes after 9 lines, leaving the rest of the folio initially blank, but an early modern hand has filled it with notes taken from John Bale's *Index Britanniae Scriptorum* of 1557–9.[26] The same hand writes *nota alias Gaufridus Monumetensis* on folio 77r, next to the personal interjection with which Geoffrey prefaces his account of the final battles between Arthur and Mordred. Another manuscript discussed in this essay, Lambeth Palace 503, features William Lambarde's notes about Geoffrey's text, drawn from Ponticus Virunius (who printed the first, albeit abbreviated, edition of the *De gestis* in 1508), Bale and Leland.

Front- and back leaves can frame the delivery of the text. Even when they do not explicitly comment on or present the text, as the tables of contents and biographical notes just discussed do, they are sometimes accorded attention in the scholarly tradition, as for example when the names or ex libris inscriptions sometimes found there can be used to establish provenance. But they also contain matter, such as mottoes and doodles, which might seem, and indeed might be, completely irrelevant to any locating of the object or reading of the text it contains. And yet, they can nevertheless shape a reading experience. If a reader pauses over a grotesque, manipulates a codex to read an apparently upside-down motto or tries to sort out the order of operations by which layers of material have been added to these leaves preceding and following any text, including that of the *De gestis*, then they become part of the transmission of the text, regardless of their irrelevance to the establishing of a text, a provenance or an intelligible reception history.

I close with one last, unimportant manuscript. Notre Dame, IN, Hesburgh Library, MS 40 is a fifteenth-century historical miscellany that includes the *De gestis*. It has an added sixteenth-century flyleaf constructed as a title page. This page brings together many of the elements discussed in this essay. It is an early modern addition to a medieval manuscript that seeks to mimic aspects of medieval manuscript culture: the page features an elaborate dragon grotesque and a heading in an archaizing hand. It lists the contents of the manuscript, naming both works and authors. It notes that this leaf was added in 1560, when the manuscript was newly bound, in order to avoid it being 'confounded for wast parchement in a chaundeless hand' – to preserve it, that is, from damage. It designates the *De gestis* as 'the notable cronycle of brittayne, written by Galfridus of Monmouth', and in a sense, this essay has been about that word, 'notable'. The sense in the manuscript is well-known, remarkable, famous; this

---

[26] Noted by Crick, *The Historia Regum Britannie*, p. 135, and in the new online catalogue entry, 'Additional MS 15732', accessed April 23, 2023, http://www.bl.uk/manuscripts/FullDisplay.aspx?ref=Add_MS_15732&index=0; the 1864 catalogue did not mention these notes.

essay, however, has been about noting in the sense of noticing. I have been trying to centre the *un*remarkable, the *un*noted. Sometimes doing so might lead to new revelations about Geoffrey's text or his readers; but sometimes, the point is just to recognize that every manuscript is worth careful attention, something Kathy has recognized throughout her own, notable career.

6

A Dream of John Bale? The *Catalogus Vetus* and the Lives of Ralph Strode

THOMAS GOODMANN

O moral Gower, this book I directe
To thee, and to thee, philosophical Strode,
To vouchen sauf, ther neede is, to correcte
Of youre benignitees and zeles goode ...
– Chaucer, *Troilus and Criseyde*, V.1856–9[1]

Radulphus Strodus nobilis poeta fuit et versificauit librum elegiacum voc[atum] Fantasma Radulphi.
– Oxford, Merton College, MCR 4.16 *Catalogus Vetus*, fol. 64v (1422)

We should think of Chaucer, Gower, and Strode as a trio of accomplished London poets.
– Bennett, *Chaucer at Oxford and at Cambridge*[2]

In *The Norton Chaucer* (2019), editor David Lawton's footnote to the lines from the penultimate stanza of *Troilus and Criseyde* identifies 'philosophical Strode' as 'Ralph Strode (d. 1387), scholastic philosopher who was a fellow of Merton College, Oxford, and Common Sergeant (i.e., public prosecutor) of the City of London'.[3] This identification of so-called 'Oxford Strode' with so-called 'London Strode' was not confidently adopted for much of the twentieth century. Nowadays it is. Since the 1980s, this once cautiously advanced and often disputed linkage has yielded to a more commonly held view that records of a Ralph Strode in Oxford and those in London refer to one and the same person. Among other leading scholars, Kathryn Kerby-Fulton asserts the identification in her account of the university community's vital if not direct

---

[1] D. Lawton, ed., *The Norton Chaucer* (New York, 2019), p. 994.
[2] J. A. W. Bennett, *Chaucer at Oxford and Cambridge* (Oxford, 1974), p. 64.
[3] Lawton, *Norton Chaucer*, p. 944 n. 8.

contributions to literary production.[4] She cites this research in her recent study, *The Clerical Proletariat and the Resurgence of Medieval English Poetry*:

> As I have shown elsewhere, Ralph Strode, one of the dedicatees of Chaucer's *Troilus*, moved from a Merton College, Oxford, teaching position to the world of London law practice (for years scholars doubted that it could be the same person). But medieval university jobs were regarded often as 'starter' careers, not career ends.[5]

Likewise Estelle V. Stubbs in a richly detailed account of the literary and scribal networks of the Guildhall also understands Strode as having moved from Oxford to London, associating him closely with the much-studied figures of John Marchaunt and Adam Pinkhurst, as well as with Chaucer and Wyclif.[6]

Such was not always the case in Chaucer studies regarding what I might call 'the two Ralph Strodes'. Scholars such as Thomas Frederick Tout, Carleton Brown and John H. Fisher voiced doubts both early and late in the twentieth century over identifying Ralph Strode of Oxford with Ralph Strode of London.[7] This essay traces the curious history of why such scholars rejected

[4] K. Kerby-Fulton, 'Oxford', *Europe: A Literary History: 1348–1418*, ed. D. Wallace, 2 vols (Oxford, 2016), I, 208–26; see especially pp. 216–17: 'As William Courtenay has shown, using a map of medieval London, scholars from Oxford (including men like Ralph Strode) rubbed shoulders not only with those in the episcopal London *studia*, but also with those in government writing offices and Inns of Court, with the latter gradually eclipsing Oxford in professional and vocational legal training' (p. 216).

[5] K. Kerby-Fulton, *The Clerical Proletariat and the Resurgence of Medieval English Poetry* (Philadelphia, 2021), p. 329 n. 72.

[6] E. V. Stubbs, 'Seeking Scribal Communities in Medieval London', in *Scribal Cultures in Late Medieval England: Essays in honour of Linne Mooney*, ed. M. Connolly, H. James-Maddocks and D. Pearsall (York, 2022), pp. 125–45, esp. 128, 136–43. Stubbs writes, 'The last member of this literate Guildhall ensemble in the late fourteenth century, Ralph Strode, was the most highly qualified of all, a Fellow of Merton College who began work in the Guildhall as Common Serjeant in 1373, giving up that position in 1382 to become public prosecutor for the City. Strode's presence at the Guildhall, his acquaintance with Chaucer, Marchaunt and Wyclif, and his role in civic government in the last decades of the fourteenth century has not yet been adequately considered in the light of recent discoveries' (p. 138). With regard to this nexus of what she calls 'a civic elite', Stubbs cites the extensive research of Maureen Jurkowski; see especially M. Jurkowski, 'Lawyers and Lollardy in the early fifteenth century', in *Lollardy and Gentry in the Later Middle Ages*, ed. M. Aston and C. F. Richmond (Stroud, 1997), pp. 155–82.

[7] T. F. Tout, 'Literature and Learning in the English Civil Service in the Fourteenth Century', *Speculum* 4 (1929), 365–89 (pp. 365–80, 388); C. Brown, 'The Author

the identification or, at least, expressed hesitation that Strode the logician was also Strode the lawyer. Since it now appears to be widely accepted that one is identical with the other, it is useful to examine both the history of scholarly skepticism and implicit intellectual assumptions and investments in such uncertainty, towards reviewing the case for why and how views have shifted regarding the career change of this Oxford master, friend to Chaucer. And what especially of Strode the poet?[8] That ascription in particular lies at the centre of debate a century ago, producing dubiousness over the potential identification for some decades.

I advance such an examination in the spirit of Stephanie Trigg's *Congenial Souls* and its perceptive analyses of the many ways in which Chaucerian discourse becomes part and parcel of the Chaucerian text.[9] Chiefly this essay pays modest tribute to Kathryn Kerby-Fulton's career-long investigations of manuscripts and of documentary evidence to illuminate, as in her most recent work, the complex cultural contexts for the making of poetry in this period, and for those with advanced literacy: 'clerics' in the broadest sense. Such circumstances include the career shortcomings that might occur, particularly during a period of limited employment opportunities for university graduates and clergy in minor orders in the later fourteenth century, as well as occasions for the more fortunate and perhaps more savvy. I mean to trace a history of response to such evidence concerning Ralph Strode as referring to one or more individuals, one known as an Oxford philosopher, the same or another (depending on the scholar) as author of a work named only as 'fantasma Radulphi' and the same or another known as Common Serjeant in London in the 1370s and 1380s. These figures first coalesced into a single individual, philosopher and poet, in the expanded biography (of sorts) composed by John Bale in the sixteenth

---

of *The Pearl* Considered in the Light of His Theological Opinions', *PMLA* 19.1 (1904), 115–53 (p. 148); J. H. Fisher, *John Gower: Moral Philosopher and Friend of Chaucer* (New York, 1964), pp. 61–2.

[8] Toward advancing the view that Oxford Strode is also London Strode, R. Delasanta, 'Chaucer and Strode', *ChR* 26 (1991), 205–18, examined the documentary evidence connecting both Chaucer and Wyclif with Ralph Strode, then living in London. Lately that evidence has been enlarged by new discoveries of E. Roger and S. Sobecki, as discussed below. Delasanta also makes a well-informed case for Chaucer's friendship with Strode as the basis for shared philosophical views, given interests and controversies at Oxford and elsewhere, including Strode's exchanges with Wyclif.

[9] S. Trigg, *Congenial Souls: Reading Chaucer from Medieval to Postmodern* (Minneapolis, 2002).

century, via a curious entry in the *Catalogus Vetus* of the fellows of Merton College, written in 1422 with an addition in a later fifteenth-century hand.[10]

What follows is a summary of the documentary evidence linking Chaucer and Strode, beginning with the entry in the *Catalogus Vetus*, and the biographical entries on Strode by John Leland and by John Bale, including study of his autograph notebook and of both the first (1548–9) and second edition (1557–9) of his *Illustrium majoris Britanniae scriptorum*, where he identifies the logician with the author of the so-called 'fantasma Radulphi'. I am interested, first, in the shift from commonly expressed doubt to near certainty, moving through the early twentieth-century disputes conducted among scholars such as Tout, Brown, Edith Rickert and Israel Gollancz in the *DLB* and *TLS*, among other places. I then chart the subsequent mid-century caution to identify Oxford Strode with London Strode that lasted until the 1980s, when it seems to have evaporated into the current common acceptance that they were one and the same, this latter consensus formed on the fairly recent and well-documented articulation of Chaucer's social and literary circle.

'What man artow?'

Writing in the *Dictionary of National Biography* in 1917 Sir Israel Gollancz summarized what was then known – and what he thought ought to be known – of Ralph Strode from his surviving works of logic; from records at Oxford, where he was Fellow of Merton College in 1359–60; and from Wyclif's two written responses to him over theological questions.[11] No one, however cautious, has ever doubted that this Ralph Strode is named as 'the philosophical Strode' whom Chaucer invokes along with 'the moral Gower' at the close of *Troilus and Criseyde*. While Gollancz took no firm stand in his *DNB* entry on the issue of a Ralph Strode recorded both in Oxford and in London, he offered that it was 'noteworthy that soon after the references to Strode cease in the Merton records, a "Radulphus Strode" obtained a reputation as a lawyer

---

[10] D. Pearsall, *The Life of Geoffrey Chaucer: A Critical Biography* (Blackwell, 1992), p. 133.

[11] *DNB*, 'Strode, Ralph' (1917; repr. 1921–2), v. 19, pp. 57–9, by I. Gollancz. Strode's surviving logical works include the *Consequentiae* and *Obligationes*, both used as textbooks into the fifteenth century on the Continent. The former has been edited as a dissertation by W. K. Seaton, 'An Edition and Translation of the *Tractatus de Consequentiis* by Ralph Strode, Fourteenth-Century Logician and Friend of Geoffrey Chaucer' (Ph.D. dissertation, University of California, Berkeley, 1973). Gollancz's entry may be found at 'Dictionary of National Biography, 1885–1900, Volume 55', accessed May 4, 2023, https://en.wikisource.org/wiki/Dictionary_of_National_Biography,_1885-1900/Strode,_Ralph.

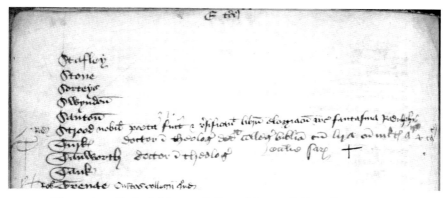

Figure 6.1 Oxford, Merton College, Merton College Register 4.16 (*Catalogus Vetus*), fol. 64v. Reproduced by kind permission.

in London', mentioning that person's office as Common Serjeant of the city, though mistaking his tenure of office as 1375–85, instead of 1373–82.[12] This Strode was given a lease for Aldersgate during the time that Chaucer held one at Aldgate, about a mile and a half apart from one another, both leases likely being consequences of political favour.

Most importantly, Gollancz also includes his opinion, advanced years earlier in his 1891 edition of *Pearl*, that Ralph Strode was the author of that poem and its companion poems in London, British Library, MS Cotton Nero A.x.[13] This contention rests on the entry (cited as an epigraph, above) in the *Catalogus Vetus* of the fellows of Merton College describing Strode not as a logician but as 'nobilis poeta' (a noble poet), author of an elegiacal poem called 'Fantasma Radulphi' (Ralph's Vision).[14] This claim for Strode as poet – but particularly as the possible author of *Pearl* – clouded the question of identifying 'Strode' for years afterward, creating a principal reason for skepticism over identifying Strode of Oxford with Strode of London. (The attribution of Strode as poet still lingers as an attractive possibility.) According to Gollancz, then, three fields of endeavour once marked the points of a triangle for Strode's identity

---

[12] *DNB*, 'Strode, Ralph' (1917), v. 19, p. 59; compare J. D. North, 'Ralph Strode', *ODNB* (Oxford, 2004; 2006), accessed May 4, 2023, https://doi.org/10.1093/ref:odnb/26673.

[13] I. Gollancz, ed., *The Pearl: An English Poem of the Fourteenth Century* (London, 1891), p. lii.

[14] *DNB*, 'Strode, Ralph' (1917), v. 19, p. 58. A facsimile and transcription of the Merton MCR 4.16 (*Catalogus Vetus*) entry may be found in *Merton Muniments*, ed. P. S. Allen and H. W. Garrod, v. 86 (Oxford, 1928), p. 37 and facing plate.

as a man who moved from Oxford to London, changing careers from logician to lawyer, as well as being a poet.

Written on a single line, the entry reads: 'Rad[ulphus] Strood nobilis poeta fuit et versificauit librum elegiacum vocatum Fantasma Radulphi' (Ralph Strood was an eminent poet and composed a book in elegiac verse called *Ralph's Vision*) (Figure 6.1).[15] This catalogue was compiled by Thomas Robert, then a fellow of the college, in or about 1422; the annotations following some of the names listed may have been added by Robert but appear to be in a later fifteenth-century hand.[16] The catalogue lists the fellows alphabetically, according to the reigning king – in this case, of course, '*E*dwardus tercius' (Edward III). Below the entry for 'Strood' on the same leaf, fol. 64v, there is one for 'Wyklyf', describing the latter as 'doctor in theologia, qui tum nimium in proprio ingenio confidebat, vt dicetur' (a doctor in theology, who then trusted too much in his own intellect, as it may be said), and seeming to distance him from Merton, chiming with the times: 'nec erat socius istius Domus, nec annum probacionis habuit plenarie in eadem' (nor was he a member of that House, nor had he a full year of probation in the same).

This entry for 'Strood' remains intriguing, certainly, not only for the absence of any mention of his work on logic or theology, which we know from references elsewhere. But what of the claim for poetic authorship, and the precise meaning of the genre terms, 'librum elegiacum' and 'fantasma'? Gollancz thought these terms described no poem from the period so well as *Pearl*, adding with certainty that 'The poet was clearly from a west midland district and, although Strode's birthplace is not determined, he doubtless belonged to one of the Strode families near that part of the country'.[17] He was reasoning from surviving evidence alone, of course, irrespective of the poem's form and dialect, among other matters, including the fact that Merton fellows, save Wyclif, came largely from the south of England, and not from a dialect region associated with the poems surviving solely in Cotton Nero A.x.

While no one in the modern era takes the sixteenth-century antiquarian, bibliographer and poet John Leland at his word concerning Strode (or anyone else), his entry for 'De Radvlpho Strodaeo' adds substantial allure to the brief ascription in the *Catalogus Vetus*:

> Ralph Strode was a very great credit to the community of Merton College, for he ardently cultivated eloquence and the sweet-voiced muses. In return they loved their disciple so greatly that they poured beauties, graces and wit

---

[15] My thanks to Dr Julia Walworth, Fellow Librarian, and Ms Verity Parkinson, Resource Services and Support Librarian, for their kind assistance.

[16] Pearsall, *Life of Geoffrey Chaucer*, p. 133.

[17] *DNB*, 'Strode, Ralph' (1917).

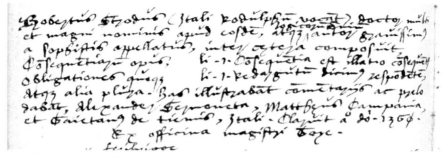

Figure 6.2 Oxford, Bodleian Library, MS Selden Supra 64, fol. 204v.

abundantly into his mouth. Endowed with such gifts, their bard sang elegiac verse with a clear, sonorous, liquid tone and, according to the catalogue of the illustrious scholars of Merton College, called his poem *Phantasma* after its nature.[18]

This account clearly shows Leland's exclusive use of the *Catalogus Vetus* as his source, if floridly embellished. Leland presents Strode solely as a poet, associating him with no other work in logic as a Merton fellow (much less with the law in London). What is evident in the elaboration of the catalogue entry is how very much Leland *wants* Strode to have been a distinguished writer, apparently without ever having seen a word of the phantasmagorical 'Phantasma'.

John Bale, drawing on Leland, writes three entries in his autograph notebook,[19] compiled in the mid-sixteenth century, prior to the two printed editions of his catalogue of British writers. The notebook is extant as Oxford, Bodleian Library, MS Selden Supra 64, and includes two entries for 'Radulphus Strodus' and one for 'Robertus Strodus' seeming to present three separate persons, the first of whom wrote an account of his journey to the Holy Land:

[18] 'Radulphus Strodaeus Maridunensi choro ornamento uel maximo fuit. Coluit enim flagrantissimo amore eloquentiam et musas canoras. Illae rursus cultorem usque adeo redamabant suum, ut ueneres, gratias, et lepores in eius abunde instillarent osculum. Vates autem, tantis donatus muneribus, cantionem elegiacum voce Sonora, liquida, arguta, cecinit; cui et Phantasma nomen a re inditum, teste catalogo illustreis Maridunensis societatis uiros percelebrante', in J. Leland, *De uiris illustribus/ On Famous Men*, ed. and trans. J. P. Carley with C. Brett (Toronto, 2010), pp. 632–3.

[19] In thinking about Ralph Strode for this essay, I revisited transcriptions of the entries in Selden Supra 64 made in Oxford during a summer long ago when I first had the pleasure to meet Kathryn Kerby-Fulton. These have been checked against R. L. Poole and M. Bateson, eds, *Index Britanniae scriptorum*, Anecdota Oxoniensia (Oxford, 1902), pp. 334–5, 334 n. 3.

'Radulphus Strodus scripsit / Itinerarium terre sancte / De quo Chaucerus in fine Troili, Anglicus poeta' (Ralph Strode wrote 'Journey to the Holy Land', regarding whom Chaucer, English poet, at the end of his *Troilus*). Poole and Bateson note that 'Radulphus' has been 'added above the line'. With Bale's typical care (and not yet with antipathy toward drawing on the work of a Catholic predecessor) this entry cites the antiquarian and poet Nicholas Brigham (Nicolao Brigan) as source, himself crucial to the legacy and resting place of Chaucer.[20] Of another, seemingly similar, 'Radulphus Strodus', also known as 'Robert the Wise', Bale writes:

> Radulfus Strodus, alius a Roberto sophista, socius colegij Martonensis in / Oxoniensi gymnasio, poeta nobilis, carmine elegiaco librum edidit, quem / vocabat fantasma Radulphi, / Atque alia nonnulla.[21]
>
> [Ralph Strode, alias Robert the wise, a fellow of Merton College in the University of Oxford, a renowned poet, produced a book of elegiac poems, which he called *The Vision of Ralph*, as well as some other items]

Here of course is the now familiar profile of Strode as poet from the old Merton catalogue. But there is also an entry for 'Robertus Strodus' in Bale's autograph notebook (Figure 6.2):

> Robertus Strodus (Itali Rodulphum vocant) doctor multi et magni nominis apud / eosdem, atque logicorum omnium autor grauissimus a sophistis appellatus, / inter cetera composuit ...[22]
>
> [Robert Strode (the Italians call him Ralph), a doctor of considerable and wide renown among them, and called the greatest author of all logic by logicians, composed among other works ...]

Then follow the titles of several logical works, referencing the Venice edition of the logical texts, adding Bale's source, and closing with 'Claruit A.D. 1360', a date that sorts well with Strode as fellow of Merton, at least according to the *Catalogus Vetus*. There is plainly no mention of him as poet in this entry. But in the three entries there is more than sufficient material to create Strode as poet and philosopher, as Bale would next do, though still not as lawyer.

Strode is not included among the writers listed in the 1548 edition of *Illustrium majoris Britanniae scriptorum*, covering five centuries and printed in Ipswich and Wesel. But he is given a brimful entry as poet, renowned logician

---

[20] On Brigham as antiquarian and 'translator' of Chaucer's body to its present tomb, see T. A. Prendergast, *Chaucer's Dead Body: From Corpse to Corpus* (New York, 2004), pp. 46–8, 50–5, passim.

[21] MS Selden Supra 64, fol. 205r; Poole and Bateson, *Index*, p. 335.

[22] MS Selden Supra 64, fol. 204v; Poole and Bateson, *Index*, p. 389.

and enemy of Christian truth in the much-expanded edition, covering fourteen centuries, printed in Basel in 1557–9, titled *Scriptorum illustriu[m] maioris Brytannie quam nunc Angliam & Scotiam uocant catalogus*. What follows is the better part of a long entry of the sort that earned Bale the epithet 'bilious':

> Ralph Strode, an alumnus of Merton College in Oxford, is called the greatest author of dialectics by Italian and French sophists. In the most burning desire of youth, he strove for eloquence, worshiped the muses and a charming style by which he earned at last the laurels of poetry. After returning from Italy, he began proudly to raise his crests against the Wycliffites for the Papist kingdom, putting great faith in sophistry. By eighteen false arguments and other unjust positions, he strove against God's truth. But overwhelmed by the glory of his own grandeur, he fell into the pit prepared for him, so that thereafter he could never support the false endowment of the clergy, nor the proud dominion of the Pope, sodomitical celibacy, diabolical Masses, useless Hours, empty rituals, or anything of the like, with his frivolous wit. Nonetheless he went down to destruction in posterity … [six works of logic follow in columns] And he published certain other things. The English poet Chaucer names him at the end of his *Troilus* …[23]

No one of course credits this account as factual; as a polemical reading of Strode it is nonetheless remarkable, locating Strode's poetic success in youthful ardor for fame, though without naming any 'phantasma' in elegiacs. Bale explains Strode's downward turn as consequence of his travels to the papist countries of France and Italy, where his work in logic was esteemed, so that thereafter he took up against the Wycliffites – Bale having called Wyclif the 'stella matutina' (morning star) of the Reformation in his earlier *Illustrium*. What we otherwise take as an amicable, if spirited, theological disagreement – from what we

---

[23] Radulphus Strodus, Martonensis collegii apud Oxonienses alumnus, dialectorum grauissimus auctor ab Italorum & Gallorum sophistis appellatur. Iuuenis flagrantissimo desiderio eloquentiam quarebat, musas & lepores colebat: unde laureolam poeticam meruit tandem. Ab Italia reuersus postea, superbas contra Vuicleuum, pro regno Papistico, cristas attollere coepit, elenchis sophisticis magnopere fides. Octodecim argumentis impostricibus, atque aliis positionibus iniquis, Dei veritatem euellere nitebatur. Sed a gloria maiestatis eius oppressus, in foueam cecedit quam parauerat: ita quod deinceps nec cleri dotationem fictam, nec superbum Papae dominium, Sodomiticum coelibatum, diabolicas Missas, Horas superfluas, inanes caeremoniolas, aut simile quidquam fulcire unquam poterat, argutiis suis friuolus. Euomuit tamen ad posteritatis perniciem … [6 works listed] [in ital.] Et alia edidit. Anglicum poetam Chaucerus hunc uocat, in fine sui Troili. Claruit Strodus anno salutis Christian 1370, sub praedicto Edvuardo: & Paganicae temeritatis flagitium esse dicebat, cauteriatus hypocrita, sacerdotes coniuges Christianas (Bale, *Scriptorum*, 1557).

can know, that is, only from Wyclif's responses to Strode – Bale makes into a prideful and doomed misdirection of Strode's energies, a precipitous fall from Parnassus into pernicious and reckless attacks on true Christianity on behalf of Rome. At any rate, it is in Bale's account here, and not in his earlier multiple, and seemingly unpolemical, entries for Ralph/Robert Strode in his notebook, that Strode the poet and Strode the logician come together.

Another triangulation may be drawn among Chaucer, Strode and Wyclif, and some of these points are plainly attested. We have Chaucer's epithet, 'philosophical', for Strode at the close of *Troilus and Criseyde*.[24] As every commentator since Skeat has stated, it is virtually without doubt that the reference is to Strode as associated with Merton College, even if by this time he is also the man who had moved to London and to a legal position. In 1382, as Edith Rickert discovered, Chaucer and Strode – which she took to be the same person as the fellow of Merton College – appeared as mainpernors for the London draper John Hende, lending their assurance, that is, that he would appear in court as summoned.[25] But H. W. Garrod in his reply to Rickert on October 11, 1928, resisted identifying the London lawyer with the fellow of Merton, much less with the person identified as poet in the *Catalogus Vetus*: 'It seems to me likely that Strode the poet and Ralph Strode the dialectician were two distinct persons'.[26] Gollancz rebutted Garrod on October 25, 1928, arguing once again for Ralph Strode as logician, lawyer and poet.[27]

Ernest P. Kuhl, writing more than a decade previous in 1914, presented evidence linking Ralph Strode in London with Wyclif, who was living in Leicestershire in 1374, when the two men were witnesses for Richard Beneger, a fellow of Merton during the same period as Strode. This record seems compelling evidence for identifying Ralph Strode of Oxford and Ralph Strode, living in London, as a single person, rather than as two people.[28] 'That two

---

[24] London, British Library, MS Harley 3943 and Oxford, Bodleian Library, MS Rawlinson Poet. 163 have the variant 'sophistical', for which the *MED* gives a positive sense. For the variants, see R. K. Root, ed., *The Book of Troilus and Criseyde* (1926), p. 564. See also *MED*, s.v. 'sophistical(e', adj., def. c: 'skilled in philosophy, learned, subtle'.

[25] E. Rickert, 'New Life Records of Chaucer – II', *TLS*, October 4, 1928, p. 707.

[26] H. W. Garrod, 'New Life Records of Chaucer. To the Editor of The Times', *TLS*, October 11, 1928, p. 736.

[27] I. Gollancz, 'Response to H. W. Garrod', *TLS*, October 25, 1928, p. 783.

[28] E. P. Kuhl, 'Some Friends of Chaucer', *PMLA* 29 (1914), 270–6. The document is from the *Calendar of Close Rolls* (London, 1913), v. 14 (Edward, years 1374–7), 94. See also A. B. Emden, *A Biographical Register of the University of Oxford to A.D. 1500*, 3 vols (Oxford, 1957–9), 'Benger, Richard', I, 167.

men', reasoned Kuhl, 'not friends, should go bail for a friend is inconceivable'.[29] In 1928 Edith Rickert also cited an item from the *Calendar of Fine Rolls* showing 'Ralph Strode of the City of London' and Robert Rygge, another Merton fellow, as witnesses for John Rioxham, 'warden of the house of scholars of Mertonhalle in Oxford'.[30] These events occurred just after Strode's election as Common Serjeant, well after Strode's time as fellow of Merton, but before Wyclif's two responses to Strode, which Loserth dated as not prior to 1378, given the radical Church reformation Wyclif espoused therein.[31] From Wyclif's addresses to Strode as 'amicus veritatis' (a friend of truth) and 'magister reverende et amice precarissime' (respected teacher and most precious friend), all the same, we may acknowledge a familiarity between the two men, akin to Strode's friendship with Chaucer, and perhaps even closer, given common academic interests if also energized differences.

Chaucer's literary reference to Strode of Merton College in *Troilus and Criseyde* seems clear, even if – and perhaps especially if – this same person had moved to London several years previous. The references in legal documents, meanwhile, seem persuasive in linking a Ralph Strode in Oxford with Chaucer, as well as a Ralph Strode in London,[32] and in establishing the theological exchanges between Ralph Strode, then living in London, and Wyclif in the 1370s.

Recently these legal connections between Chaucer and Strode have been enriched further by the discoveries of Euan Roger and Sebastian Sobecki regarding the charge of *raptus* from which Cecily Chaumpaigne released Geoffrey Chaucer. Among the discoveries is evidence that Strode, along with William Mymms, stood as surety for Chaucer's appearance in response to a writ brought against Cecily Chaumpaigne and Chaucer on October 16, 1379. Roger and Sobecki write straightforwardly that 'Chaucer's association with Strode, the Common Pleader of the City of London with whom he stood surety for John Hend in 1381– and a man he described as "philosophical Strode" in his dedication to *Troilus and Criseyde* (V, 1857) – has long been known. That he acted as surety for Chaucer himself, however, deepens our understanding of the connection between the two men'.[33]

[29] Kuhl, 'Some Friends of Chaucer', pp. 270–6.
[30] Rickert, 'New Life Records for Chaucer – II', p. 707.
[31] J. Wyclif, *Opera Minora*, ed. J. Loserth (London, 1913; repr. 1966), cap. XXXI, XLVII.
[32] M. M. Crow and C. C. Olsen, eds, *Chaucer Life-Records* (Austin, 1966), pp. 146 n., 282, 284, 544 n.
[33] E. Roger and S. Sobecki, 'Geoffrey Chaucer, Cecily Chaumpaigne, and the Statute of Laborers: New Records and Old Evidence Reconsidered', *ChR* 57.4 (2022), 407–37.

Tout's skepticism concerning the possibility of a career change hinges in large part on his reluctance to credit Gollancz's claim that Strode was not only a logician and a lawyer, but also the author of *Pearl*, along with the other remarkable poems in MS Cotton Nero A.x. 'All one can say', concludes Tout, 'is that if the one Ralph Strode did all of these things he was a very remarkable man. But I find it hard to believe that a clerk of established position would leave the university, start a new career as a common lawyer, abandon his clergy for a wife and a family, and find time to write poetry in his leisure'.[34]

No one since Gollancz – who maintained the claim for thirty years and more, from the 1890s forward – has given weight to the argument for anyone named 'Ralph Strode', much less the fellow of Merton, as the author of *Pearl* and its companion poems. No other evidence besides the Merton College *Catalogus Vetus* corroborates the entry that Strode of Merton College was a poet, though it is not impossible that he may have written poetry, as some have since contended. The well-documented life of Chaucer, by comparison, shows someone busy in royal service and in administrative roles; among such records none mentions him as poet, although of course he is acknowledged as such elsewhere.

Diverse folk diversely they seyde

In a 1904 *PMLA* article, published well before both Kuhl and Rickert's respective discoveries of records connecting 'Ralph Strode' and Chaucer in London legal proceedings, Carleton Brown expressed more indignation than Tout over Gollancz's argument, strenuously opposing the identification of Oxford Strode with London Strode:

> Mr. Gollancz makes matters still worse [than John Bale] by attempting to bring into this Strode composite a certain lawyer, Ralph Strode, who lived at Aldersgate, London ... It is too great a strain even for the elasticity of a Strode to stretch him out to cover such a variety of employments. Whether this lawyer Strode was the same as the philosopher is extremely doubtful, but at all events he cannot have been the same as the author of the *Pearl*, for the latter, as I shall undertake to show, was certainly an ecclesiastic.[35]

Again, since no one apart from Gollancz had then maintained that Strode was the author of that poem – notwithstanding that he or another so-named person authored another poem – we may eliminate that point of the triangle. It is unfortunate that Brown did not state why he found it 'extremely doubtful'

---

[34] Tout, 'Literature and Learning', p. 388.
[35] Brown, 'The Author of *The Pearl*', p. 148.

that the logician and the lawyer might have been one and the same.[36] A more temperate skepticism regarding Gollancz's claims characterizes Herbert Workman's view of the question in his study of Wyclif, published in 1926: 'Lawyer, poet, logician – if the identification be correct, Strode was an unusual combination of qualities'.[37]

As a relatively latter-day skeptic on the issue – that is, long after Rickert's documentary discovery and Robinson's cautious affirmation – John Fisher in his study of John Gower discussed Ralph Strode as an associate of the two poets, doubting the identification of the Merton fellow with the London common pleader. In the absence of other evidence, he concluded that 'the transition from Oxford logician to London lawyer was an unlikely one'.[38] But views may change: in his subsequent two editions of Chaucer's works, Fisher annotated the reference to Strode in the *Troilus* by calling him 'the lawyer', contending that he 'had both a university and a legal education'.[39] He does not offer in any detail, however, that Strode was a fellow of Merton, author of texts on logic and later prominent in London legal circles associated with the mayoralty of Nicholas Brembre. In a note to those same concluding lines, R. A. Shoaf in his edition of *Troilus and Criseyde* is hesitant: the 'reference is perhaps to Ralph Strode (the identification is vexed) who was a contemporary philosopher and theologian, a fellow of Merton College, Oxford. He may be the same as the Ralph Strode who is found later practicing law in London and who died in 1387'.[40]

Against the earlier strong detractions of Tout and Brown, and the hesitancy of Workman, Fisher and Shoaf, other scholars across the past century and more have offered cautious affirmation of the identification. G. G. Coulton, writing in 1908, found 'no obvious reason to dissociate the city lawyer from the Oxford scholar', and was ready to entertain the idea of Strode as author of *Pearl*.[41] R. K. Root, citing both Gollancz and Kuhl in his *The Book of Troilus and Criseyde*, published in 1926, not long before Rickert's discoveries, was also credulous of such a resume compiled by a single person named Ralph

---

[36] Brown, 'The Author of *The Pearl*', pp. 146–8.
[37] H. B. Workman, *John Wyclif: A Study of the English Medieval Church* (Oxford, 1926; repr. 1966), pp. 125–7 (p. 127).
[38] Fisher, *John Gower*, p. 61.
[39] J. H. Fisher, ed., *The Complete Poetry and Prose of Geoffrey Chaucer*, 2nd ed. (New York, 1989), p. 540.
[40] R. A. Shoaf, ed., *Geoffrey Chaucer: Troilus and Criseyde, from the Text of A. C. Baugh* (East Lansing MI, 1989), p. 311.
[41] G. G. Coulton, *Chaucer and His England* (London, 1908), pp. 102–3.

Strode: 'There is good ground for believing that the Oxford philosopher and the London lawyer are one and the same person'.[42]

From this point forward, with the removal of the weak argument for attributing *Pearl* to Strode as 'fantasma Randulphi', Oxford Strode increasingly becomes for many students of Chaucer continuous with London Strode as a matter of silent emendation, as it were, in the critical discourse. There is an intriguing richness, for example, in the notes to *Troilus and Criseyde* as presented in successive editions of *The Riverside Chaucer*, edited by F. N. Robinson and Larry D. Benson, respectively. In the first edition, published in 1933 and reprinted in the second edition in 1957, Robinson pens an extended note (running to a column and a half), beginning in familiar terms, 'The *philosophical Strode* is doubtless to be identified with Ralph Strode, fellow of Merton College before 1360, an opponent of Wyclif, though apparently on friendly terms with the reformer', then summarizing what is known of his lost theological writings.[43] Taking up the entry in the 1422 *Catalogus Vetus*, he rejects the notion that the Strode named therein was author of the *Pearl* and the other poems in the same manuscript as 'an unsupported conjecture', citing their West Midland dialect and that Merton was 'a southern college'.[44] (Against this statement, it may be noted that Wyclif, who was from Yorkshire, was a fellow of Merton just a few years prior to Strode.) Likewise, he is dubious about Strode as author of works attributed to him by John Bale and successive cataloguers. All the same, Robinson takes careful note of all the recorded evidence linking Wyclif and the Ralph Strode living in London in 1374: Ralph Strode of London standing as mainpernor in 1377 for one John Bloxham, warden of Merton; the 1375 grant of Aldersgate, following the 1374 grant of Aldgate to Chaucer; and the record of Strode and Chaucer as mainpernors for John Hende in 1382. While Robinson does not state conclusively that the one-time Merton fellow moved to London and practiced law, he doesn't gainsay this suggestive evidence.[45]

The explanatory notes to *Troilus and Criseyde* in Larry D. Benson's third edition (1986), written by Stephen A. Barney, begin, 'Some uncertainty remains as to the identity of **philosophical Strode**' (emphases thus), rehearse what has long been known about him at Oxford and conclude: 'There can be little doubt that Chaucer refers to this Strode'. Barney then revives the potential accuracy

---

[42] Root, ed., *Troilus*, p. 564.
[43] F. N. Robinson, ed., *The Poetical Works of Chaucer* (New York, 1933), p. 951; (repr. 1957), p. 479. Emphasis in the original.
[44] Robinson, *Poetical Works* (1933), p. 951; (1957), p. 479.
[45] Robinson, *Poetical Works* (1933), p. 951; (1957), p. 479.

of what is added to the Merton catalogue entry in that later fifteenth-century hand identifying 'Strood' as 'a noble poet', author of 'a book in the elegiac meter called "Ralph's Vision" (Phantasma Radulphi)'. He continues, 'If this is correct, Chaucer had all the more reason to address him, like Gower, as a fellow poet', even while dismissing Gollancz's ascription of *Pearl* to him. Still, it 'is not certain' whether this Oxford Strode, known to Wyclif, is the same as the London lawyer. Speaking to Tout's doubt, Barney rehearses the legal documentation, coming to rest on the following conclusion: 'It remains possible that there were two or more Ralph Strodes connected with Chaucer, but it is more probable that the Ralph Strode of Oxford, connected with Wyclif and with Merton, is the same man as the Ralph Strode of London, connected with Wyclif and with Merton'.[46]

Likewise presenting all of the documentary evidence then known, A. B. Emden in his *Biographical Register of the University of Oxford to 1500*, argued in the 1950s that the 'biographical particulars do not seem to warrant this dichotomy' between the Merton man and the London lawyer.[47] As editor of *Chaucer's Major Poetry*, Albert Baugh is measured in his note on 'philosophical Strode': 'probably Ralph Strode, a contemporary philosopher and theologian, a fellow of Merton College, Oxford. He may be the same as the Ralph Strode who is later found practicing law in London and who died in 1387'.[48] In 1970 Huling E. Ussery, examining contemporary models for Chaucer's apparently unemployed Clerk, argued energetically for the identification.[49] Alan T. Gaylord, citing Emden for support in a 1979 essay, also affirms the same.[50]

No one since John Bale, however, revived with such enthusiasm the idea of a single Ralph Strode with the tripartite resume of logician, lawyer and poet as J. A. W. Bennett. In a chapter entitled 'The Men of Merton' in his *Chaucer at Oxford and Cambridge*, published in 1974, Bennett advances this claim in no uncertain terms, citing Strode's dwelling at Aldersgate 'at about the same time that Chaucer was leased his house at Aldgate, a few hundred yards off. Strode was then Common Serjeant, or pleader, of the City of London … But before he became a lawyer he had been an eminent logician, Merton favouring the

---

[46] S. A. Barney, in L. D. Benson, gen. ed., *The Riverside Chaucer*, 3rd ed. (New York, 1986), p. 1058.
[47] Emden, *Biographical Register*, III, 1807–8.
[48] A. C. Baugh, ed., *Chaucer's Major Poetry* (New York, 1963), p. 211 n.
[49] H. E. Ussery, 'Fourteenth-Century English Logicians: Possible Models for Chaucer's Clerk', *Tulane Studies in English* 18 (1970), 1–15 (pp. 14–15).
[50] A. T. Gaylord, 'The Lesson of the *Troilus*: Chastisement and Correction', in *Essays on Troilus and Criseyde*, ed. M. Salu (Cambridge, 1979), pp. 23–42 (p. 37, nn. 129–30).

study of law less than logic'.[51] And then, while demurring on the assignment of *Pearl* per se to Strode on generic grounds, Bennett leaps over the absence of other evidence, reasoning from the term 'liber elegiacus' used in the *Catalogus Vetus* that since Gower's *Vox Clamantis* is 'the longest work in elegiacs ever written', then this term may also refer to the same verse form in relation to Strode's composition – assuming, of course, a single Ralph Strode, concluding: 'We should think of Chaucer, Gower and Strode as a trio of accomplished London poets'.[52] As appealing as such a resume (and a poetry circle) may be, the conclusive documentary evidence for such is still lacking. In this case, all that seems certain is that Bennett would like it to be so. It goes without saying that the discovery of such a poem written by Strode would be remarkable.

Who's he when he's at home?

According to P. H. Reaney, the name 'Strode', along with the variants 'Stroud' and 'Strood', has topographic and toponymic roots in Old English strōd, 'marshy ground', first attested in 1206 in the person of one 'Aluina de Strodes'; the editors of *The Oxford Dictionary of Family Names in Britain and Ireland*, published more recently, offer a similar account. The name is found most frequently in southern England, including the counties of Kent, Middlesex, Surrey, Gloucestershire and Berkshire. The etymologically related names 'Strother', 'Struther', and 'Stroder' occur in Northumbria, Durham, the West Riding of Yorkshire and in Cheshire.[53] Although most attestations of the name are recorded after the Middle Ages, as a locative, the name occurs in contemporary medieval records, including the Calendar of Close Rolls.[54] That acknowledged, I have not discovered evidence for anyone else named 'Ralph Strode' apart from known records in Oxford and in London.

What of Chaucer's biographers? In his sometimes fanciful and popularly focused account, John Gardner makes a case for Chaucer's knowledge of

[51] Bennett, *Chaucer at Oxford and Cambridge*, pp. 63–5.
[52] Bennett, *Chaucer at Oxford and Cambridge*, p. 64.
[53] P. H. Reaney, *A Dictionary of English Surnames*, rev. R. M. Wilson, 3rd ed. (Oxford, 1958; 1997); P. Hanks, R. Coates and P. McClure, *The Oxford Dictionary of Family Names in Britain and Ireland* (Oxford, 2016).
[54] For example, naming 'Edmund of Strode': 'Close Rolls, Richard II: February 1381', in *Calendar of Close Rolls, Richard II: Volume 1, 1377–1381*, ed. H. C. Maxwell Lyte (London, 1914), p. 493, *BHO*, accessed November 28, 2023, http://www.british-history.ac.uk/cal-close-rolls/ric2/vol1/p493; naming 'Richard del Strode': 'Close Rolls, Richard II: October 1383', in *Calendar of Close Rolls, Richard II: Volume 2, 1381–1385*, ed. H. C. Maxwell Lyte (London, 1920), pp. 402–3, *BHO*, accessed November 28, 2023, http://www.british-history.ac.uk/cal-close-rolls/ric2/vol2/pp402-403.

current subjects and source manuscripts available not only at Oxford but specifically in the Merton College library, of which Strode was a sometime fellow and Wyclif, too. But he goes further in claiming in more than one place that Chaucer studied at Oxford, filling in the well-noted lack of life records for the years 1361–5. Again – as regarding a poetic composition by one Ralph Strode – this circumstance is not implausible; it simply isn't supported by surviving evidence. On that literary matter, Gardner is somewhat cautious: 'We've spoken already of the Oxford logician Ralph Strode, possibly an influence on Chaucer's inclination toward nominalism and perhaps the same "Rudolphi" [*sic*] celebrated for a long poem in Latin (probably) now lost'.[55]

Donald R. Howard does not speak to the identity of one or more people named 'Ralph Strode' in his more scholarly and well-regarded 1987 biography, noting only the lease on the Aldersgate house as a desirable place to live, like Chaucer's dozen-year tenure of Aldgate (perhaps most appealing due to its free rent).[56] Writing just a few years later in 1992, however, Derek Pearsall has a good deal to say in affirmative terms. Crediting Rickert's discovery that Strode and Chaucer stood as mainpernors for Hende, he adds that 'Strode makes a very interesting addition to the Chaucer circle, one with whom Chaucer could discuss the questions of predestination and free will, of fortune and destiny, that began to preoccupy him in the 1380s, and with whom he could argue about Lollardy'. Entertaining the validity of the *Catalogus Vetus* entry, he adds, 'Strode may have been a poet himself'. And he concludes that the 'presumed shift of the same Ralph Strode from the university to a career offering more opportunity for wealth and public advancement, and perhaps also the opportunity to get married, is many times more plausible that the existence of two Ralph Strodes, more or less exact contemporaries, of equal eminence'.[57]

Paul Strohm has referenced the topic of the two Strodes in a number of places, his *Social Chaucer* having advanced the examination of Chaucer's orbit of courtier-knights and fellow civil servants.[58] Most recently, in *Chaucer's Tale: 1386 and the Road to Canterbury*, he writes in measured terms regarding the 'philosophical Strode':

> Ralph Strode has been identified with a learned Oxford philosopher of the same name, the supposition being that he switched careers in middle age and moved to London, where he became a common pleader – a civil employee and a legal office. There's a possibility that the London Strode

[55] J. Gardner, *The Life and Times of Chaucer* (New York, 1977), p. 225.
[56] D. R. Howard, *Chaucer: His Life, His Works, His World* (New York, 1987).
[57] Pearsall, *Life of Geoffrey Chaucer*, pp. 133–4.
[58] P. Strohm, *Social Chaucer* (Cambridge MA, 1989), pp. 44–5, 58–9, 206–7 nn. 31–5.

simply happens to be the philosopher's namesake and that Chaucer is teasing him with the moniker 'philosophical' ... but, in any case, Strode was a smart and competent professional, a fellow Ricardian factionalist with the city who, like Chaucer, depended on the Brembre faction for advancement, and he even lived nearby, in a city property over another city gate. Whether or not a trained philosopher, he was certainly Chaucer's worthy friend.[59]

Similarly, in a brief introduction to Chaucer's life and work, David Wallace expresses some hesitancy by using a double conjunction and forward slash in referring to Strode as name-checked at the end of *Troilus and Criseyde*: 'The poem is to be sent to John ('moral') Gower, across the water at Southwark, and to "philosophical [Ralph] Strode", Oxford don and/or London lawyer (V, 1856–7)'.[60]

The most recent comprehensive biography of Chaucer is that of Marion Turner, who understands a single Strode: for example, '*Troilus and Criseyde* is also associated with Ralph Strode, common serjeant of London and Chaucer's associate in mainprising John Hende in 1381'.[61] Turner offers a close analysis of Strode's successful balancing act in vexed years, 'exactly the time – late 1382 to early 1383 – when Richard was trying to assert himself'. Like Strohm, she sees Strode as 'smart and competent', a beneficiary of Nicholas Brembre's political largesse in the 1377 grant of a lifetime lease to the apartment at Aldersgate, yet not necessarily of Brembre's party. Having resigned his elected position as Common Serjeant, he likewise gave up Aldersgate under apparent pressure from the king.[62]

---

[59] P. Strohm, *Chaucer's Tale: 1386 and the Road to Canterbury* (New York, 2014), p. 194. Strohm, 'The Social and Literary Scene in England', in *The Cambridge Chaucer Companion*, ed. P. Boitani and J. Mann (Cambridge, 1986), pp. 1–18 (p. 10), numbered Strode among Chaucer's circle 'as a London lawyer, who – unless we are dealing with two persons – enjoyed some standing as an Oxford philosopher-theologian earlier in his career'.

[60] D. Wallace, *Geoffrey Chaucer: A New Introduction* (Oxford, 2017), p. 68.

[61] M. Turner, *Chaucer: A European Life* (Princeton, 2019), p. 281.

[62] Turner, *Chaucer*, p. 279 n. 78, cites S. Lindenbaum, 'London Texts and Literate Practice', in *The Cambridge History of Medieval English Literature*, ed. D. Wallace (Cambridge, 1999), pp. 284–310, for other examples of those trying to maintain equilibrium in circumstances of political precarity: 'the best-known figures employed in the civic secretariat during these years – Ralph Strode, John Marchaunt, William Cheyne and Thomas Usk – all worked at some time for both of the city's major parties' (Lindenbaum, 'London Texts', p. 287). Not all of them managed to do so, of course.

Changing places

No hesitancy colours J. D. North's entry in the *ONDB*, published in 2004 and subsequently updated. North identifies Strode straightforwardly 'as scholastic philosopher and lawyer' with no demurral, nor with any poetic attribution. While he advances no new evidence, he argues implicitly against those such as Brown, Tout or Fisher, who expressed objections on the grounds of that such a career change from logic to law was implausible: 'there are many contemporaries whose lives show this to be simply untrue'.[63] In the absence of utterly conclusive documentary evidence – acknowledging that what we have is more than mildly compelling – it is relevant to examine the likelihood of an Oxford logician and theologian turning himself into a London lawyer, adding a wife and son to his life and enjoying success, at least while Nicholas Brembre was in a position to aid him and until Strode apparently resigned his position voluntarily.[64] Assuming the identification is correct, as many have done and most now do, it is plausible to imagine that, like other academics, Strode had ambitions and sought opportunities beyond Oxford. Wyclif, for example, his friendly disputant, likely had hoped for such, having been cultivated and supported by John of Gaunt in the 1370s, though no bishopric or other such position was ever granted to him.

Prior to North's confident identification of logician with lawyer, historian William Courtenay cites Strode as an example of this contemporary pattern of career changes, if exceptional: 'Secular scholars who made reputations in logic and natural philosophy in the first half of the fourteenth century either became theologians or, in a very few cases, remained simply arts masters before going on to a post-university career. By contrast, Ralph Strode, one of the most prominent logicians of the 1350s, chose a career in law'.[65] As noted above, Kerby-Fulton also cites Courtenay for a map of medieval London to support his extended discussion of what she calls an 'Oxford-influenced, London milieu' of those working in church, civil service and law 'including men like Ralph Strode'.[66]

Though Courtney does not support this assertion with reference to the known documents or with further discussion, he explores the circumstances in the latter half of the century that make such a career change not only plausible, but even likely. Courtenay carefully makes the case for a loss of innovation

---

[63] North, 'Strode, Ralph', *ODNB*.
[64] Kuhl, 'Some Friends', pp. 273–4; Turner, *Chaucer*, p. 288.
[65] W. Courtenay, *Schools and Scholars in Fourteenth-Century England* (Princeton, 1987), p. 318.
[66] Kerby-Fulton, 'Oxford', p. 216 n. 38; see also Courtenay, *Schools*, pp. 91–105.

both in Oxford logic and in scholastic theology, accompanied by a decline in productivity in the latter field, particularly evident with respect to what had been a standard genre, commentaries on the *Sentences*. These had become shorter in the second quarter of the fourteenth century and all but disappeared by the last quarter, along with reference to scholastics, despite a good deal of contemporary satire of masters and doctors.[67] Published *quaestiones de quodlibet* also dwindled markedly after mid-century; Ockham's was one of the last to gain notoriety.[68]

Theological discussion shifted too towards biblical foundations and issues of practical theology, conducted in a more polemical tone than was common among those of earlier generations. Wyclif's writing of course presents the example *par excellence* of such polemicism, and he and Strode were well known to one another, as noted. This quantitative decline in scholastic genres of writing Courtenay locates in 'the degree to which visibility and reputation through academic achievement and publication ceased to be an effective means of attracting a patron and thus ensuring a successful career'.[69] At the same time, as several scholars have argued, the trend at both English universities ran toward legal studies, particularly for Roman or civil law, with evident rewards for those who pursued them.[70]

New, more practical concerns of theology emerged, such as preaching and study of the Bible, accompanied by a greater interest in legal studies under increasingly important aristocratic patronage.[71] Meanwhile, the Oxford arts faculty gave up supposition logic for a simpler form altogether.[72] From the available evidence, John Fletcher has characterized the situation for those at Oxford trained in arts during and after Wyclif's time as being 'confronted by an increasingly assertive and perhaps numerically stronger group of civil and canon lawyers. Outside the university, the artists and theologians saw many of

---

[67] Courtenay, *Schools*, pp. 252–64, 359–61.
[68] Courtenay, *Schools*, p. 251.
[69] Courtenay, *Schools*, p. 367.
[70] Courtenay, *Schools*, pp. 356–68. See further, A. B. Cobban, *The Medieval Universities* (London, 1975), p. 227; R. W. Southern, 'The Changing Role of Universities in Medieval Europe', *Historical Research* 60 (1987), 133–46; J. M. Fletcher, 'Inter-faculty Disputes in Late-Medieval Oxford', in *From Ockham to Wyclif*, ed. A. Hudson and M. Wilks (Oxford, 1987), pp. 331–42; J. Dunbabin, 'Careers and Vocations', in *The History of the University of Oxford*, ed. J. Catto (Oxford, 1984), pp. 565–605.
[71] Courtenay, *Schools*, pp. 365–6, 373.
[72] W. Courtenay, 'Black Death and English Higher Education', *Speculum* 55 (1980), 696–714 (p. 707).

the more prestigious positions in the church falling into the hands of Oxford trained lawyers'.[73]

Strode's fellowship at Merton fell at the end of its preeminence; as a onetime fellow for a brief tenure in 1359–60, Wyclif was in more than one way an exceptional figure associated with the college. The long line of theo-logicians and proto-scientists, including Ockham, Burley, Bradwardine, Kilvington, Dumbleton, Swineshead, among others, had come to an end, seemingly with Strode himself.[74] The later use of his logical works as textbooks on the continent may suggest their nature as primers rather than as current works; we cannot know for certain.

As Common Serjeant Strode remains a notable figure, and there is now no doubt that he could have gained the necessary training in common law. The simple fact that there were practicing 'men of law' in the period (as long prior) means the available education, however formalized, was available to him. In exploring the careers of several men of letters who worked in the growing civil service of the fourteenth century, Tout makes a general point germane to such a potential career change, while expressing hesitation in Strode's case: 'a university-trained clerk could easily renounce his clergy for a lay career … Perhaps already, as certainly in the fifteenth century, he might frequent the London law schools which, I imagine, owed their very existence to the fact that the university had no place for the lay student or for the student of common law'.[75]

Paul Brand too has advanced evidence more recently for the existence of formal training of younger lawyers as early as the thirteenth century.[76] Prior to Fortescue's thorough account in the fifteenth century, senior chancery clerks apparently lectured and organized disputations like those among the faculties of canon and civil law at the universities. As John Baker offers: 'Of the origins of the Inns of Court nothing is known, but we do know that they acquired most of their principal characteristics by the end of the fourteenth century'.[77]

---

[73] Fletcher, 'Inter-faculty Disputes', p. 340.
[74] W. Pantin, *The English Church in the Fourteenth Century* (Cambridge, 1955; repr. Toronto, 1980), p. 138.
[75] Tout, 'Literature and Learning', p. 369.
[76] P. Brand, 'Courtroom and Schoolroom: The Education of Lawyers in England Prior to 1400', *Historical Research* 60 (1987), 147–65. See P. Brand, 'The English Legal Profession in Edward I's Reign (III): Training and Entry into the Profession', *The Origins of the English Legal Profession* (Oxford, 1992), pp. 106–19 and passim.
[77] J. Baker, *The Legal Profession and the Common Law: Historical Essays* (London, 1986), p. 7–23 (p. 7). Baker cites a call of serjeants – likely not the first – in October 1388 as further evidence for the status of the inns during Strode's London career

Strode then with highly advanced skills in logic and disputation could have availed himself of such in the 1360s and early 1370s.[78] Given our benefit of historical perspective, such a career change seems timely, and was certainly successful for Strode, including terms as Common Serjeant and standing counsel of the city, interrupted only by Northampton's re-election to the mayoralty in 1382. Even the subsequent relinquishment of his office and loss of the lease at Aldersgate were recompensed when Brembre returned to office.[79] His new life in the city, as noted above, included a wife, Emma, and a son, Ralph, both of whom survived his death in 1387, likely not long – perhaps a year or two – after Chaucer submitted *Troilus and Criseyde* to his correction and to that of Gower. That he may well have been a poet himself, the author of a long poem in elegiacs called *Fantasma Radulphi*, is an attribution that still haunts the case of Ralph Strode.

I'll end by revisiting what T. F. Tout concluded in 1929: 'All one can say is that if the one Ralph Strode did all of these things he was a very remarkable man. But I find it hard to believe that a clerk of established position would leave the university, start a new career as a common lawyer, abandon his clergy for a wife and a family, and find time to write poetry in his leisure'.[80] That Strode did not write *Pearl* seems certain. What Tout and Brown advanced, all the same, as a practical check on identifying Strode of Oxford with Strode of London has yielded to our more informed understanding of contemporary contingencies for all manner of clerisy.

In this case, all that we know to date points toward a single person: the documentary evidence connecting Chaucer with Strode both via Oxford and in London; the relative shifts in options for those who studied theology versus canon law at the English universities; the dearth of opportunities for graduates as documented by Kathryn Kerby-Fulton, as well as notable circumstances for men such as Strode, along with available training in common law.[81]

(pp. 3–6). Baker revisits speculation that Chaucer may himself have been a fellow of the Inner Temple, which, if true, would add to our sense of rich overlaps and exchanges among those in service to church, chancery, royal court and courts of law (p. 6, n. 16).

[78] Stubbs, 'Seeking Scribal Communities', p. 140, states that indeed he must have done so: 'If Strode began his city career at the Guildhall in 1373 then without doubt he must have had some further legal training, possibly at the London Inns of Court, and he would have been working with John Marchaunt for at least a part of his tenure'.

[79] Kuhl, 'Some Friends', pp. 272–4; Turner, *Chaucer*, p. 288, nn. 72–9.

[80] Tout, 'Literature and Learning', p. 388.

[81] Kerby-Fulton, *Clerical Proletariat*, pp. 1–32; Stubbs, 'Seeking Scribal Communities'.

Any deeper conclusiveness regarding Strode's identity will require further sleuthing in the archives to discover the lifespans and whereabouts of any persons bearing this or a similar name.[82] It is all but certain, nevertheless, if not precisely 'by preeve which that is demonstratif',[83] that Strode left Oxford as a regent master to pursue a more lucrative career in law and public service in London. While maintaining connections with Merton fellows, he was party to London city politics and came to know and to be named by the best-known poet of the age. Examining earlier scholars' skepticism regarding Strode's turn from logician to lawyer sharpens our sense of the assumptions we may make about the exigencies and opportunities of those we study.[84]

---

[82] As Sebastian Sobecki has suggested elsewhere – perhaps in anticipation of his discoveries published with Euan Roger regarding Chaumpaigne and Chaucer, with relevance to Strode – there is indeed more to be found in the archives. (Would that the *fantasma Radulphi* might come to light!) See S. Sobecki, 'Stones Left Unturned (Psst! More New Chaucer Life Records)', NCS blog, October 1, 2019, accessed May 4, 2023, https://chaucerblog.net/2019/10/stones-left-unturned-psst-more-new-chaucer-life-records.

[83] Chaucer, *Summoner's Tale*, III.2272.

[84] My thanks to the anonymous reviewer for helpful suggestions regarding contemporary occurrences of the surname 'Strode' as a check against multiple persons with the same name, and regarding the circumstances for education in common law to support Strode's transition from Oxford to London. Thanks as well to Misty Schieberle as the editor of this volume for her generous guidance, and to Paul Strohm for formative suggestions on this topic at a much earlier stage. Any remaining deficiencies are of course my own.

7

Women's St Edmund: Envisioning a Saint and his Contemplative Legacy

JOCELYN WOGAN-BROWNE

'Either wearied by frequent pilgrims, especially women from England (permission not being granted to any others) who flocked to the tomb of St Edmund, or prompted by greed, [the monks of Pontigny], horrible to tell, with rash audacity cut off the right arm of the saint'.

['vel taedio affecti de frequentia peregrinorum, praecipue mulierum ad tumbam sancti Edmundi Anglicarum (quia aliis non est concessa licentia) catervatim affluentium, vel stimulis agitati cupiditatis, brachium ejusdem sancti dextrum, quod est horrible dictu, ausu temerario absciderunt', *Chronica majora*, V, 113].[1]

Matthew Paris's story of how the Pontigny monks collected pilgrimage revenues by making the arm of St Edmund of Abingdon (Archbishop of Canterbury, 1233–40, canonized 1247) available outside the shrine from which they had banned women is challenged by the contemporary Society of St Edmund (who have custody of the arm of St Edmund in their retreat on Enders Island, Mystic, Connecticut).[2] Certainly, though the arm has been detached for a very long time, Paris's story perhaps testifies less to cupidity at Pontigny than to a Benedictine's regret that a contemporary archbishop and saint of England is buried at a Cistercian house in north-central France.

---

[1] *Matthaei Parisiensis, Chronica majora*, ed. H. R. Luard, 7 vols (London, 1873–83), henceforth cited by volume and page number in the text; *Matthew Paris's English History 1235–1275*, trans. H. A. Giles, 3 vols (London, 1852–4), II, 339 (modifications mine).

[2] The Fathers and Brothers of St Edmund left France in 1903, bringing with them the long-detached arm, which they believe to have come adrift from the body by natural processes. It has been at Mystic since 1954 (pers comm., Edmundites, Burlington VT), and see for example 'Severed Arm of St Edmund', *Atlas Obscura*, accessed July 12, 2022, https://www.atlasobscura.com/places/severed-arm-saint-edmund. I warmly thank the Society of St Edmund for their invitation to give the 2016 St Edmund lecture at St Michael's College, Burlington, VT.

The story also of course witnesses to women's engagement with this saint, an engagement little dealt with in early scholarship but important in shaping Edmund's life and afterlife as a saint and author.

This essay first takes the role of French in transmitting St Edmund of Canterbury's *Mirour de seinte eglyse* as a cue for examining the participation of women in his cult. As is now well understood, no simple equation can be made between vernacular versions of Latin texts and women. Nevertheless, the fact that Edmund's original Latin *Speculum* (1213–1220s?) seems to have survived and multiplied because of its early translation into French[3] – an important language in England for religious writing as for other domains, and especially for women – would prompt consideration of Edmund's audiences and women's roles even were one of its manuscripts not entitled 'Sermon a dames religieuses'. The question of where and for whom the French version may have been made needs to be asked with the roles of women in Edmund's life and cult in mind. Secondly, this essay examines some questions about the twentieth-century editing of Edmund's text to argue that though his *Speculum* is far from being a text 'under suspicion' (to use Kathryn Kerby-Fulton's memorable phrase),[4] neither is it a text in the service of systematic and official

---

[3] The *Speculum religiosorum* is thought to be the original: subsequent French and Latin versions are newer versions not by Edmund himself (though closely identified with him in the manuscripts): *Edmund of Abingdon, Speculum religiosorum and Speculum ecclesie*, ed. H. P. Forshaw (Oxford, 1973); and her 'New Light on the *Speculum Ecclesie* of Saint Edmund of Abingdon', *Archives d'Histoire Doctrinale et Littéraire du Moyen Age*, Annèe 1971 (1972), 7–33; *Mirour de seinte eglyse*, ed. A. D. Wilshere (London, 1982), pp. x–xi and his 'The Latin Primacy of St Edmund's "Mirror of Holy Church"', *Modern Language Review* 71 (1976), 500–12. But oddly, Edmund's *Speculum religiosorum* (1213–1220s) survives only in 7 fifteenth-century manuscripts. As a translation *into* Latin from the French *Mirour de seinte eglyse* (*c.* 1230–50 [?] in 28 thirteenth- and fourteenth-century manuscripts), the *Speculum* becomes the *Speculum ecclesie* (37 fourteenth- and fifteenth-century manuscripts). This transmission history suggests that it is the French *Mirour* that makes the work well known, and that translation from the French as *Speculum ecclesie* in turn prompts fifteenth-century interest in the original Latin *Speculum religiosorum*. This bilingual history makes the text become well enough known to prompt the Middle English prose versions from the late-fourteenth to the sixteenth centuries (24 manuscripts; early prints from 1521 on), and two later-fourteenth-century Middle English verse versions (see further N. Watson, 'The Original Audience and Institutional Setting of Edmund Rich's *Mirror of Holy Church*: The Case for the Salisbury Canons', in *Medieval and Early Modern Religious Cultures: Essays Honouring Vincent Gillespie on his Sixty-Fifth Birthday*, ed. L. Ashe and R. Hanna (Cambridge, 2019), pp. 21–42 (p. 21).

[4] K. Kerby-Fulton, *Books under Suspicion: Censorship and Tolerance of Revelatory Writing in Late Medieval England* (Notre Dame IN, 2006).

distinctions regulating women (or others) as to who should meditate and who should contemplate. Thirdly, the essay looks briefly at the use of Edmund's *Mirour* in para-liturgical books commissioned and/or owned by women, and at the considerable interest this suggests in Edmund's models for meditation and contemplation.

Envisioning St Edmund: Women's Roles and Actions

Edmund's earliest cult documentation, the letters of postulation and the first *vitae*, present his mother Mabilia, wife of the prominent Abingdon citizen Richard 'Rich', as the person who forms Edmund in ascetic piety and practices.[5] By the time of Matthew Paris's *vita* (1247–53), Mabilia is sending Edmund off to study in Paris equipped with a specially rough hairshirt ('asperrimum cilicium'): at her death she leaves him the gift of a lorica, a metal breastplate to be worn in place of or under a shirt (Lawrence, p. 223). This asceticism works to re-trope the mercantile wealth of Edmund's natal family as spiritual wealth, and Mabilia and Edmund are tightly linked in the production of his religious life (though the family's means must also have been important in a career that saw Edmund studying at Oxford, then Paris, before returning to Oxford as regent in Arts).

The letters of postulation and the *vitae* also link Edmund's critical choice of direction with his mother's influence in the womb, his mother's milk and, most of all, her revelatory appearance to Edmund in a vision at Oxford after her death (*c.* 1195?).[6] In the vision, she challenges Edmund's intense attention to arithmetical diagrams: 'Fili, quid legis? Que sunt ille figure …?' (My son,

---

[5] *St Edmund of Abingdon: A Study in Hagiography and History*, ed. C. H. Lawrence (Oxford, 1960), henceforth cited in the text as Lawrence and by page number: for the life produced at Pontigny, *Thesaurus novus anecdotorum*, ed. E. Martène and U. Durand, 5 vols (Paris, 1717; repr. Farnborough, Hants, 1968–9), III, cols. 1775–1826. For Edmund's adoption of the hair shirt, Lawrence, *St Edmund*, pp. 290, 295: for a comparative synopsis of the Latin lives, pp. 100–5.

[6] *Letters of Postulation*, in Lawrence, *St Edmund*, p. 291; Eustace of Faversham, *vita*, pp. 203, 206–7; Matthew Paris, *vita*, pp. 223, 229–30; for the (uncertain) chronology of Edmund's studies in Oxford and possibly in Paris, pp. 110–24. For Edmund's possible commentary on Aristotle's *Sophistici elenchi*, see R. Sharpe, *Handlist of the Latin Writers of Great Britain and Ireland before 1540* (Turnhout, 2001), pp. 106–7. In an Oxford manuscript (*c.* 1247–54) of Aristotle's *De somno et vigilia*, Edmund is represented together with Becket as they watch over two sleeping bishops: N. J. Morgan, *Early Gothic Manuscripts (2), 1250–1285* (London, 1988), no. 146 (a), p. 132: Vatican, Biblioteca Apostolica Vaticana, MS Vat. Urb. lat. 206, fol. 306, accessed November 27, 2023, https://spotlight.vatlib.it/it/latin-paleography/catalog/Urb_lat_206.

what are you reading? What are those figures?) (p. 229). Hearing that they are material for his lecture, she seizes his right hand, draws ('depinxit') three circles in it and writes the names 'Father', 'Son', 'Holy Spirit' in them:

> 'Fili karissime, talibus figuris et non aliis amodo intende'. Quo sompnio quasi per revelacionem edoctus statim ad theologie se transtulit exercicium.
>
> ['My dearest son, to such figures and no others pay attention from now on'. Instructed by this dream as by a revelation, he immediately changed his studies to theology.] (Eustace, *vita*, 206–7; Matthew Paris, *vita*, Lawrence, pp. 229–30)

A scene of many resonances, Mabilia's visionary revelation of Edmund's true career flickers between biography and contemporary socio-religious topoi. It partly expresses the later twelfth- and early thirteenth-century juggling of university and monastic priorities with questions over the value of the liberal arts in their own right or as an *accessus* to theology, and questions of whether a religious life is possible outside religion (Edmund never became a monk). Mabilia's action assimilates her to the long history of mothers with saintly sons (Monica and St Augustine onwards, but also the more recent, highly influential case of Becket d. 1170, canonized 1173, whose sanctity in some *vitae* is revealed to his mother in dreams before his birth). Mabilia's revelation also reiterates the importance of what we might call chaste-matron spiritual influence and leadership as married laywomen saints such as Marie d'Oignies (1177–1213) and Elisabeth of Thuringia (1207–31) became more prominent. The patronage of clerics by women of means had also always been significant in providing livelihoods and producing texts in high medieval England as elsewhere. Mabilia's role in Edmund's *vita* partly gets its place and increasing elaboration in the lives of Edmund because it exemplifies the contemporary importance of chaste matronhood as a style of spirituality and mode of patronage, here, as with Becket's mother, extending from nobility to gentry and townspeople.

A second, much higher-ranking widow was also important for Edmund. Ela, Countess of Salisbury *suo jure* (*c.* 1190–1261) first knew him when he was treasurer at Salisbury Cathedral from 1222–33.[7] Edmund declined a gift of jewels from Ela as Countess but advised her while she created Lacock Abbey (founded 1230), a house of Augustinian canonesses, where she became the

---

[7] Lawrence, *St Edmund*, p. 102. Edmund witnessed Ela's husband's will, the charter by which she carried out her husband's Carthusian canons' move to Hinton, and her covenant for building her abbey with the rector of Lacock: *Lacock Abbey Charters*, ed. K. H. Rogers (Devizes, 1979), nos. 4, 30, pp. 10–11, 18–19.

first abbess in 1238–9.[8] He is also said to have sent a relic of Becket's blood to his friend Ela to cure her of fever.[9] Like many monastic founders, she is said in one of the two surviving Lacock cartularies to have acted *per revelationem*, and later in her life, Matthew Paris credits her with a premonitory revelation of the death of her son William Longespee II at the battle of Mansourah in 1250.[10] Ela is present at the right time and place to have known about Edmund's *Speculum* and to have wanted a text of it in French for her nuns. Initial Latin composition in a male community seems entirely plausible, and Watson makes a strong case that the *Speculum* was originally made not for the canons of Merton with whom Edmund lived from 1213–14, but during his decade with the canons of Salisbury in the 1220s–30s.[11] If the secular canons at Salisbury cathedral make a likely initial audience for the Latin *Speculum religiosorum*, Ela's contemporary establishment of her abbey, with its range of choir nuns, other sisters, estate staff and lay servants makes it a good site for the production of the French text,[12] and, possibly, given the evidence for Lacock's thirteenth-century Latinity, for a copy of the translation's source text, the *Speculum religiosorum* at the abbey. Lacock's books are largely lost, but there is good evidence of its franco-latinate culture, as would be expected for an elite group of Augustine canonesses.[13]

[8] See further 'Houses of Augustinian canonesses: Abbey of Lacock', in *A History of the County of Wiltshire: Volume 3*, BHO, pp. 303–16, accessed April 12, 2023, https://www.british-history.ac.uk/vch/wilts/vol3/; and for Ela as patron of Lacock's thirteenth-century wall paintings, E. Pridgeon and S. Sharp, 'Patronage and Function: The Medieval Wall Paintings at Lacock Abbey in Wiltshire', *Journal of Medieval Monastic Studies* 5 (2016), 113–37.

[9] *Thesaurus*, ed. Martène and Durand, III, cols. 1798–9, and para 43 b.

[10] *Chron. maj.* V, 153–4, 173; S. D. Lloyd and T. Hunt, 'William Longespee II: The Making of an English Crusade Hero, Part II', *Nottingham Medieval Studies* 36 (1992), 79–125.

[11] Watson, 'The Original Audience'.

[12] Forshaw, 'New Light', p. 33, who also proposes Edmund's two sisters at Catesby (on whom see below).

[13] In addition to the two Lacock cartularies and other muniments (see *Lacock Abbey Charters*, pp. 2–6), there survive the Latin Lacock Psalter of c. 1260 (Oxford, Bodleian Library, MS Laud Lat. 114) from the de Brailes workshop in Oxford: a copy of the *Expositiones Vocabulorum Bibliae* by the Franciscan William Brito (Guillaume le Breton), d. 1250, at 'Lacock, Wiltshire', *National Trust*, accessed April 12, 2023, https://www.nationaltrust.org.uk/lacock-abbey-fox-talbot-museum-and-village/features/the-book-that-opens-a-window-on-lacock-abbey/ (composition wrongly attributed to s. xiv). Lacock's copy of this standard work is not included in the 130 manuscripts listed in *Summa Britonis sive Guillelmi Britonis Expositiones Vocabulorum Biblie*, ed. L. W. Daly and B. A. Daly, 2 vols, Thesaurus Mundi, 15–16

If the *Speculum* were translated at or for Lacock, the work could have readily moved into the royal court and to Queen Eleanor of Provence's franco-latinate circle of ladies-in-waiting, baronesses and clerical spiritual advisors.[14] Edmund was certainly welcome at the court of Eleanor's sister, Marguerite of France, where he was received in a private audience by Blanche of Castile, Marguerite's formidable mother-in-law and the mother of Louis IX.[15] At the Westminster court, there is evidence to suggest that Eleanor of Provence and her ladies were readier than Henry III to see the archbishop canonized after his death in 1240 and to forward his cult. In 1245, as Joseph Creamer has shown, court accounts note gifts given to two sisters from the small Cistercian priory of Catesby in Northamptonshire who brought St Edmund's cloak to court ready for the lying-in of Queen Eleanor for the birth of her second son.[16] Powerful relics often supplemented the skills of midwives as did the reading aloud of saints' lives over women undergoing the considerable dangers of childbirth. The two nuns must have been Edmund's birth sisters, Margery (d. 1257) and Alice (d. 1270), whom Edmund had placed in Catesby after their mother Mabilia died. At his own death in 1240, he left them his cloak and a devotional silver tablet, with images of the Virgin and child, and the passions of Christ and Becket.[17] These were treated as relics and began working miracles, Margery was made prioress of Catesby by Grosseteste in 1245

(Padova, 1975), vol. 1, pp. xlii–xlvii. Lacock's third known extant book is now New Haven, Yale University Beinecke Rare Books and Manuscript Library, Osborn a56, *c.* 1300–49 (not in Dean, sold by Lacock at Christies in 2011): I thank Dr Thomas Hinton, University of Exeter, for information on its current whereabouts. The manuscript contains Bibbesworth's *Tretiz* with Middle English interlineations and notes, Bozon's *Les proverbes de bon enseignement*, the *Ordene de chevalrie* sometimes ascribed to 'Hue de Tabarie' (represented as Saladin's prisoner in the text), *Le mariage des ix filles du diable*, here attributed to Sully rather than to Grosseteste.

[14] Among other ties, Ela's husband, William Longespee, third earl of Salisbury (*c.* 1167–1226), the son of Henry II and Rosamund Clifford, was half-brother to Richard I, Henry III's uncle, and remained an important figure in the reign (*ODNB*, 'William Longespee'). Continuing links between Lacock and the English court are also suggested by the fact that Henry and Eleanor paid for the retirement of a beloved but ageing lady-in-waiting to the abbey in 1258: M. Howell, *Eleanor of Provence: Queenship in Thirteenth-Century England* (Oxford, 1998), p. 105.

[15] Lawrence, *St Edmund*, p. 262: L. Grant, *Blanche of Castile: Queen of France* (New Haven, 2016), pp. 122, 134–5.

[16] J. Creamer, 'St Edmund of Canterbury and Henry III in the Shadow of Thomas Becket', *Thirteenth Century England* XIV (2011, online 2013), 129–40 (pp. 130–1).

[17] Lawrence, *St Edmund*, pp. 107–8; Matthew Paris, *vita*, pp. 223, 278–9.

and the little nunnery remained a cult centre for the court.[18] Margery Rich with the assistance of her sister Alice was thus instrumental in establishing Edmund's cult (as it was in establishing her).

Henry III initially opposed Edmund's canonization: the king and the archbishop had clashed several times over church appointments and over the divisions between the king and the barons, and Edmund sent Henry a formal protest in January 1240. In the same year, Edmund left for a papal council in Rome (presented by Matthew Paris as a Beckettian exile, though in fact in response to an un-cooperative papal legate and an intractable quarrel with Edmund's own Canterbury monks).[19] Edmund died later in 1240 while travelling through Soissons near the Cistercian monastery of Pontigny, where he was buried, and where a cult immediately sprang up. This situation was open to political exploitation against Henry III, since Pontigny was where St Thomas Becket had been exiled by Henry's grandfather, Henry II. So it would seem as if either the safe birth of Henry's second son Edmund with the help of the cloak relic in 1245 and/or the political necessity of not being seen to oppose St Edmund's cult won out over Henry's reluctance and brought him to share the women's vision of Edmund as a saint. Certainly, after 1245, Henry claimed to love Edmund and to cherish his memory; and in 1247 and 1250 Catesby received grants of a market and a fair from the king, who himself made a pilgrimage to Edmund's Pontigny shrine in 1254.[20] Given that Edmund's cloak was known about and sent for, the women of the court seem already to have been prepared to cult Edmund, regardless of political embarrassment around the circumstances of his death. To Edmund's sister Margery, custodian of an English shrine to him, the advantages of having her brother's *Speculum* available in French for nuns and the elite lay people who so often shared nunnery reading and interests must have been obvious. Unfortunately, no Catesby books or records survive that enable the possibility

---

[18] William de Mauduit, Earl of Warwick (d. 1267), for instance, had his heart buried at Catesby out of devotion to Edmund; Eleanor de Provence was granted Catesby's advowson in 1279, and Edward II exempted the nunnery from several levies. See 'Houses of Cistercian Nuns: Catesby', *A History of the County of Northampton: Vol. 2, BHO*, pp. 121–5, accessed April 12, 2023, https://www.british-history.ac.uk/vch/northants/vol2/.

[19] C. H. Lawrence, intro. and trans., *The Life of St Edmund by Matthew Paris* (Stroud, 1996), Appendix 1, 'The Alleged Exile of Archbishop Edmund', pp. 168–76.

[20] 'Houses of Cistercian Nuns: Catesby', citing Pat. 31 Hen. III. m. 13; 33 Hen. III. m. 36; pilgrimage, *Chron. maj.* V, p. 475.

to remain more than speculative, but the nunnery offers another plausible location for the French text's genesis.[21]

Evidence of a powerful woman patron with a vision for propagating Edmund's cult exists in Matthew Paris's translation of his own Latin Edmund *vita* (1247 x 1253) into French (1253 x 1259) for Countess Isabella of Arundel. As a baronial patron with monastic rights of advowson and with close court connections, aware of the authoritative status of Latin and equally aware of the importance of vernacular dissemination, Isabella (*c.* 1226/30–79) is a good example of an aristocratic chaste matron's influence across the franco-latinate domain in which Edmund's *Speculum* became more widely known. She was a patron both of Edmund's French life and of the Latin *vita* of his chancellor and follower, St Richard of Chichester (d. 1253, canonized 1262).[22] Edmund died in 1240, but Isabella may have seen or met him at court in her early years as a child bride. A granddaughter of William Marshal (and hence a relative of Ela of Salisbury and Lacock) and born a Warenne,[23] she had been married off in 1234 as a child of eight or younger to Hugh d'Aubigni, Earl of Arundel. By the time Edmund's canonization proceedings were underway in the early 1240s, Isabella, widowed in 1243, was in her teens. She chose thereafter to remain independent till her death in 1279, paying a fine not to be married off again by Henry III, and she founded (but did not enter) the Cistercian nunnery of Marham on her lands in Norfolk in 1249, dedicating it to the Virgin and to St Edmund of Canterbury, and (unusually in England) to St Barbara.[24]

---

[21] Henry VIII's Augmentation Office took church furnishings worth £400 from Catesby, but there is nothing to indicate if this includes any manuscript books, and the TNA's surviving muniments for Catesby record only land ownership.

[22] '*Vita sancti Ricardi Episcopi Cycestrensis*', ed. and trans. D. Jones, 'St Richard of Chichester: The Sources for his Life', *Sussex Record Society* 79 (1995), pp. 83–159 (pp. 83–5).

[23] Not, *pace* Lawrence, *St Edmund*, p. 75, a de Fortibus. For the extensive baronial kinship that included both Ela and Isabella, see L. Lewes Gee, *Women, Art and Patronage from Henry III to Edward III:1216–1377* (Woodbridge, 2002), Appendix B1. Isabella's significance for Edmund and for Matthew Paris's hagiography was not developed by Lawrence in his indispensable and magisterial research on Edmund's Latin *vitae*: see further J. Wogan-Browne, *Saints' Lives and Women's Literary Culture* (Oxford, 2001), pp. 151–88.

[24] 'The History and Cartulary of the Cistercian Nuns of Marham Abbey, 1249–1536', ed. J. A. Nicols (unpublished Ph.D. dissertation, Kent State University, 1974); S. Thompson, *Women Religious: The Founding of English Nunneries after the Norman Conquest* (Oxford, 1991), p. 225 and passim.

As a still young widow in 1252, resolutely defending her rights and property, Isabella publicly tore a strip off Henry III in the king's chamber over his assumption of a wardship attached to one of her sixty knights' fees. Matthew Paris assigns her a speech in his *Chronica majora* for that year, in which she vigorously argues her rights and reproaches Henry for not observing the fundamental liberties enshrined in the Magna Carta signed by his father, King John (*Chron. maj.* V, 336–7) before leaving the court without waiting, as was customary, for the king's permission to go. From letters between Queen Eleanor and Isabella, it seems likely that Eleanor had a hand in the full settlement for which Isabella subsequently pursued the king (what she had said to him must have stung, for a 1254 letter settling the matter, recently discovered by Susanna Annesley sewn into the Fine Roll, contained the proviso that Isabella was not to say anything opprobrious to Henry in court again).[25] However constructed Paris's account of Isabella's speech may have been (and her reproaches to Henry on his treatment of the church and some of her replies to his reported sneers as to whether she had 'a charter to speak for the kingdom's nobles' do suit Paris's own agenda), she is nevertheless presented as a figure who, neatly turning the tables on Henry with an invocation of his father's agreement to Magna Carta, can credibly speak for the political community.

Isabella's engagement in hagiography also had public dimensions. Matthew Paris's translation into French verse of his own Latin Edmund *vita* is not simply a personal favour for the Countess's private use, but part of her campaign to increase the saint's profile and reputation. As a patron of St Albans (she held the advowson of its daughter house Wymondham through her marriage), Paris owes her 'reverence, honour and deference with all my monastic life' (reverence, en tute religiun, en honur et subjection), and he is working to fulfill her intention that Edmund's *beles vertuz et grace* be known to everyone, clerics and laypeople, by the production of a life in French.[26] He has translated his own earlier *vita* 'de latin en franceis apert' (from Latin into clear and understandable French) (v. 33), because

---

[25] S. Annesley, 'Isabella Countess of Arundel's Confrontation with King Henry III', 'Fine of the Month: August 2009', *Henry III Fine Rolls Project*, accessed September 26, 2016, https://finerollshenry3.org.uk/content/month/fm-08-2009.html.

[26] *La Vie de saint Edmund, arcevesque de Canterbire: Prologue and Epilogue*, in *Vernacular Literary Theory from the French of Medieval England: Texts and Translations, c. 1120–c. 1450*, ed. J. Wogan-Browne, T. Fenster and D. W. Russell (Cambridge, 2016), no. 13, pp. 120–7 (vv. 41–2, 47–52), henceforth *VLT*. Citations outside *VLT* excerpts are from A. T. Baker, ed., 'La Vie de seint Edmond, archêveque de Cantorbéry', *Romania* 55 (1929), 332–81; manuscript text online in D. W. Russell, *The Electronic Campsey Project*, accessed April 12, 2023, http://margot.uwaterloo.ca/campsey/CmpBrowserFrame_e.html.

... chascun est de ceo bien cert
[Ke] plus est use[e] et sue
Ke nule launge, et entendue
De clers e lais e la gent tute
Ke le latins ....' (vv. 35–8)

[Everyone knows that [French] is more used and known than any language, and better understood by clerics, the laity and all people, than [is] Latin.][27]

Paris addresses Isabella as a high-profile, exemplary devotee of Edmund: she follows Edmund's footsteps by divine grace ('par la devine grace / De saint Edmund suez la trace') (vv. 1983–4), pledging her service and devotion to the saint. She has also physically followed Edmund's footsteps by going on pilgrimage to his burial place in Pontigny with sea-crossings, long travel and efforts 'beyond the usual strength of women' ('plus ke feminine', v. 58).[28] As one of the Englishwomen whose visits wore down the Pontigny monks, Isabella's efforts may perhaps have included support of relaxing the ban on women at Edmund's shrine.[29] Her activities make her a player on the wider stage of the Plantagenet and Capetian royal courts, for whom Edmund, as an English-born prelate whose relics remained in France, was both object and embodiment of dynastic links and rivalries. Paris presents Isabella as Edmund's agent in England, who, in reclaiming her special relationship with Edmund at his shrine in France, has also reclaimed Edmund's blessings to his country of origin (*VLT*, p. 121 and vv. 113–20). Isabella's own tracing of Edmund's footsteps is amplified by a royal analogy when Matthew Paris concludes the life with Henry III's acquisition of Christ's own footprint in marble (vv. 127–40).

---

[27] In his epilogue, Paris further explains that he has written Edmund's life in two languages for the Countess ('Escrit l'ay en deuz langages/Pur vous cuntesse Ysabele', *VLT*, vv. 99–100; Baker, vv. 1976–7), thus raising the (speculative) possibility that Isabella had prompted him to the Latin *vita* as well as the French (though his phrasing also allows for restriction to the French life).

[28] Perhaps as one of the 'multitude of leading French and English [*Galliæ et Angliæ*] people' present, together with Louis IX and Blanche of Castile, at the 1247 translation at Pontigny (*Annales Monastici*, ed. H. R. Luard, 5 vols (London, 1864–9), II, 339), the second translation in 1249, or perhaps when Henry III made his pilgrimage in 1254.

[29] Exceptions were made for high-ranking women on occasion: Adele, widow of Louis VII had been allowed to visit in 1204 and was buried in Pontigny in 1206 (*Thesaurus*, ed. Martène and Durand, III, cols. 1244–5); Blanche of Castile had a papal privilege allowing her to visit Cistercian houses with twelve of her women (*Chron. maj.* IV, 391).

Paris's emphases in the French life often speak to women's activities and their interest in the cult. For example, (i) he highlights further the women of Edmund's family, (ii) details the texts and procedures of learning in the saint's course of study, especially after Mabilia's visionary intervention, and (iii) heightens the value of Edmund's spiritual charisma in mediating royal and baronial strife.

(i) Paris elaborates Mabilia's nurture of her sons and daughters in a regime at once pious and meritocratic: along with ascetic devotional habits and Latin, French is a key acquisition (Baker, vv. 103–6). Women were often in charge of their children's early education in French, and as Mabilia recognizes, the language was important for both social and ecclesiastical advancement. Although Edmund's celebrated deathbed utterance of an English-language proverb (Baker, vv. 1543–4, Lawrence, p. 266) shows him as bi-lingual, French would have been his main language for relations with the king, the court and secular elites. Mabilia, beautiful and best of Abingdon's matrons ('bele et bone / En trestut icel burc matrone', vv. 123–4), is also a noted lover of God. Edmund's sisters are praised as women of good sense who became nuns (vv. 107–8), in, as noted above, Catesby (like Isabella's own Marham, a Cistercian house).

(ii) Paris's Latin *vita* emphasizes that Edmund seems a model of the religious life when he is among scholars in his sabbatical year with the Augustinian canons at Merton (Lawrence, p. 231), but his French life emphasizes the quality of Merton's library: 'riche d'escrits originals' (v. 546), where Edmund has the books and peace he wants ('Livres et paes ad a pleisir', vv. 549–50). This suggests not only that learning is admired but also that its constituents are a matter of interest to a patroness whose own life is lived in the light of some of the same books and interests as the saint she promotes.

Paris also caters to an interest in the nature of knowledge and the arts of biblical study unsurprising in a culture where women could and did demand a great deal from their chaplains and clerks, where women were often in charge of children's and adolescents' religious education and literacies, and where lay people wanted participation. The thirteenth-century feminization of spirituality is not a matter of simple affectivity or devotion as opposed to cognition: some of its patronesses wanted understanding and intellectual participation. In the French life, just before the scene of Mabilia's visionary appearance, Paris adds thirty-three lines on the liberal arts curriculum Edmund is following. He lists and explains the trivium of grammar, rhetoric, dialectic, and the quadrivium of geometry, arithmetic, music, astronomy and their functions (Baker, vv. 415–48). At the end of the vision, he adds a further twenty lines (Baker, vv. 514–28) explaining how Edmund sets about theology: after acquiring authoritative volumes and the books of the Old and New Testament, together with their explicatory apparatus, the *Glossa Ordinaria* (*la Glose*, v. 520), Edmund gives up the pleasures and the strife of disputation. Euclid and Ptolemy are abandoned for the Gospels and Plato for Augustine and Gregory (Baker, vv. 515–26).

When Mabilia draws her Trinitarian diagram on St Edmund's palm in the vision (p. 147, above), this is not theological dumbing down but a recognized mnemonic device (one used by Grosseteste and illustrated, in its *scutum fidei* form, by Paris himself, and deployed by lay and religious alike in meditation and penitential reading on the Trinity).[30] At Ela of Salisbury's foundation, the Lacock Abbey Psalter's historiated initial of the Trinity with a kneeling Augustinian nun reading in the border further suggests that this was something shared by professed religious and laywomen.[31] The initial is to Psalm 109 in the Lacock Psalter. It shows Jews and others, 'thine enemies' (inimicos tuos) per the psalm, as the 'footstool' (scabellum pedem tuorum) of the Trinity. The image shares in a common representation of the Trinity but has the characteristic tone of thirteenth-century English court spirituality across professed and lay people's religious reading, a high Gothic aesthetic blending the utmost refinement with bellicosity. Mabilia's gesture links her with sophisticated devotional uses of diagrams and meditative aids.

(iii) Paris expands his *vita*'s comment that, as archbishop, Edmund is conscious that 'hatred and strife among magnates imperils their subordinates' (quod a magnatum odio et discordia dependent pericula subditorum) (Lawrence, p. 240). In the French life, Paris creates a mini-Mirror for Magnates such as Isabella of Arundel. Edmund is exemplary in his desire for peace, his counsels to the king and the barons and his deathly hatred (Baker, v. 942) of discord and rivalry between them:

---

[30] M. Evans, 'An Illustrated Fragment of Peraldus's Summary of Vice, Harleian MS 3244', *Journal of the Warburg and Courtauld Institute* 45 (1982), 14–68 (pp. 22–4). A. Kumler, *Translating Truth: Ambitious Images and Religious Knowledge in Late Medieval France and England* (New Haven, 2011), pp. 79–81; J. Wogan-Browne, '"Cest livre liseez … chescun jour": Women and Reading *c*. 1230–*c*. 1430', in *Language and Culture in Medieval Britain: The French of England*, ed. J. Wogan-Browne et al. (York, 2009), pp. 239–53; *VLT*, 20a, pp. 173–8.

[31] For the image see Bodleian Library, MS Laud Lat. 114, fol. 148r, *Digital Bodleian*, accessed August 3, 2022, https://digital.bodleian.ox.ac.uk/objects/5a4fb726-f1ee-4486-9843-a04e89f71afa/surfaces/0dbcbbcb-fc38-4910-af66-bae9cfdd4d21/; Morgan, *Early Gothic Manuscripts (2)*, no. 157. After images of Christ, the Trinity is the most popular image before which thirteenth-century patrons are shown kneeling: N. Morgan, 'Patrons and their Devotions in the Historiated Initials and Full-Page Miniatures of Thirteenth-Century English Psalters', in *The Illuminated Psalter: Studies in the Content, Purpose and Placement of its Images*, ed. F. O. Büttner (Turnhout, 2004), pp. 309–22 (pp. 315, 319).

> Ke il cunust bien lur custumes;
> Si reis u cunte u barun
> Unt entre eus gere u contençun
> La graunt commune de leur gent
> Ke a iceaus sugette apent
> Sunt [tute] a grant destructiun
> Ocise et deseriteisun.
> Kant ke mesprenge le barnage
> Vent a povres [grant] damage.
> Par ceste achesun l'arceveske
> Ne jur ne nuit ne fine jeske
> Pes mette entre les majurs
> Ke [n'en] decent sur les meinurs. (Baker, vv. 944–56)

> [... for he knew their ways very well: if the king or a count or lord engage in war or strife between themselves, the wider community of their people who are subject to them are destroyed, killed and disinherited. Whenever the nobility do wrong, great harm comes to the poor. For this reason the archbishop never ceased striving night and day to achieve peace among the greater men so that [the conflict's effects] did not come down upon the lesser.]

Paris's account of Edmund's brokerage between king and magnates includes interceding for forgiveness for Richard Marshal, killed fighting against the king in Ireland in 1234, and for restoring his younger sibling Gilbert's inheritance; reconciliation between the king and other rebels (Gilbert Basset, Stephen Seagrave and Richard Siward) and between Hubert de Burgh, earl of Kent and justiciar, and the king (Baker, vv. 1019–34: Lawrence, pp. 133–7). These names would have figured in talk around the court, whether or not they were personally known to Isabella (the Marshals were her distant relatives).[32] Such factional strife was not untypical in the constant rebalancing of power between the king and his magnates. Richard Marshal's death, for instance, not only stirred the King's anger but was also the death of a celebrated chivalric figure and a cultivated man (a friend of Grosseteste's), who had spent his earlier career as a liege of Louis VIII: it became the spur to a narrowly overcome baronial rebellion. Edmund's mediation in these and other matters at court is presented by Paris as part of his spiritual charisma (Baker, vv. 983–1018,

---

[32] See further *ODNB*, 'Richard Marshal, sixth earl of Pembroke (d. 1234)'; Lawrence, *Life of St Edmund by Matthew Paris*, pp. 51–5; *ODNB*, 'Hubert de Burgh, Earl of Kent (d. 1243)'; de Burgh, who had risen from relatively lowly beginnings, had married into Isabella's natal de Warenne family near the start of his career.

Lawrence, pp. 240–1) and an argument (expanded from Paris's Latin *vita*, Lawrence, p. 242) for the power of Edmund as an intercessor with God (Baker, vv. 1037–55). There is no separation between politics and sanctity, either in Paris's narrative or in what he chooses to retain or emphasize for Isabella.[33]

Edmund's presentation in the French language of the court and the representation of his sanctity on the model of the pious courtier saint must have helped create demand for his *Mirour* among elite secular and religious women and other patrons. Devotion to Edmund saw the saint as a source of heavenly sweetness, 'nostre pastur' whose name is 'tres duz / A numer suvent'.[34] But for all the sweetness and simplicity admired by some contemporaries, Edmund's life is nonetheless a highly charged one, his sanctity constructed to fit Becket's model of heroic courtier bishops who defend the church and limit the king's power. It is not surprising that magnates like Isabella (who had herself defended her property from the king) culted St Edmund: sweetness, saintly *simplicitas* in tandem with highly disciplined asceticism such as hair shirts and loricas demonstrate courtly-spiritual grace and strength, and hence carry political charisma. It seems unlikely that Edmund would have become so successful a version of this figure without the impact created importantly, though not exclusively, by the engagement of women in court and cloister with the saint and with his legacy.

Envisioning Contemplation in St Edmund's *Mirour*: Could Women Read the Whole Text?

Were women restricted in how far they could follow the contemplative processes articulated in the *Mirour*? This issue arises from the *Mirour de Seinte Eglyses*'s 1982 edition by Alan Wilshere, when he influentially divided the text into versions for religious and for secular people.[35] Wilshere's main criterion was whether the *Mirour*'s chapter 36 on the contemplation of God was revised by partial excisions or not (a subsidiary criterion was how fully the commandments, creeds or sacraments were explained, Wilshere, p. x). This division was

---

[33] On women's devotional reading as a source of political thought, see further J. Wogan-Browne, '"Li poeples est en doloros martire": Reading Social Justice in Women's Devotional Books', in *Engaging Medieval Women Religious*, ed. V. Blanton and P. Stoop (Turnhout, forthcoming).

[34] *Vie de seint Richard evesque de Cycestre*, ed. D. W. Russell (London, 1995), pp. 57–8, vv. 771–2 (a translation, probably of 1276, of the Latin life co-sponsored by Isabella of Arundel, n. 22 above).

[35] Editorial matter cited as Wilshere; *Mirour* text cited by chapter, page and line number.

enticing but problematic from the moment it was made: enticing because it seemed to offer the possibility of an authoritative distinction between the revelatory powers of 'contemplation' versus secular meditation, problematic because it puts great pressure on what Wilshere identifies as the differences between the two versions. Given that Wilshere's base manuscript for his 'religious' version titles itself 'Sermon a dames religieuses' (in a manuscript also containing Latin sermons and associated with Westminster Abbey),[36] could it be that nuns were allowed certain kinds of contemplation discouraged for laywomen? Yet from chapters 6–35, audiences in both Wilshere's versions are offered the same three stages in contemplation of God: in his creatures (chapter 6); his Scriptures (chapter 7 and the following chapters 8–19 of catechetical doctrine); and in his humanity (chapters 20, 21–7). From chapter 28, both are instructed in the contemplation of God in his divine and Trinitarian nature. At the end of chapter 35, both versions invite audiences to 'lift up your heart in the high contemplation of your creator' (levez vostre quer en la haute contemplacion de vostre creatur, ch. 35, pp. 80, 81).

The difference Wilshere's editing sees as determinative in chapter 36 is between being instructed in contemplating God and his created world directly (as in chapters 6–27), or through one's own soul. The latter requires restraint of every corporeal, earthly and celestial 'ymaginacioun', so that sense data from the heart's connection with the created universe is denied and the soul 'may return to itself' and, gathering itself wholly within itself, 'see what it is without its body' (ke ele sey voie tele quele ele est tut sanz sun cors, ch. 36, p. 82, 21–3).[37] This enables the soul to see what it actually is and to be lifted beyond itself to try to look at God its creator in its own nature (p. 82, 15–16). The

---

[36] Wilshere, MS A1, pp. vii.

[37] Contemplation may lift the heart in both figurative and pneumatic ways: one medieval model of the heart (assumed in the *Mirour*'s instructions regarding the images the heart takes in from sense data) sees it as a respiratory organ circulating air, breath, spirit which it uses to concoct blood, sent out from the heart but not circulated; see H. Webb, *The Medieval Heart* (New Haven, 2010). Though not fully apophatic, Edmund's contemplation still requires moving beyond the ordinary behaviour of the heart and mind regarding the forming of images (*ymaginacions*) in the *vis imaginativa* (the faculty of the mind that creates images or concepts, *AND*, s.v. *imaginacion* 1), and makes of this a powerful version of contemplation's mise-en-abysme: 'coment puse jo cunter de boche ço ke ne pus[se] penser de queor? ... pur ço me toys jo, e dreit est ke face, kar ço n'aprent pas launge mes fet sule grace' (How can I recount with my mouth what cannot be thought with the heart? ... therefore I fall silent, and rightly so, for language cannot impart what grace alone can do) (ch. 36, p. 84, 80–3).

perception of how great a thing the soul is then enables some perception of the greatness of its creator (p. 82, 22–32).

By the absence of these instructions from Wilshere's 'lay' text, secular readers would seem to be discouraged from this precise and exalted use of their own soul's nature. Similarly, such users are not instructed to work from the goodness, sweetness and beauty in corporeal creatures to perception of these qualities in a spiritual creature that lives for ever (i.e. humans), and thence to how much greater such qualities are in the creator of all (ch. 36, p. 84, 58–71).[38] The logic here, as Zink comments, is that using the imagination (i.e., the medieval *vis imaginativa*) for images of heavenly things is as dangerous as for earthly, since the only source for either is the bodily senses feeding the imagination, whereas the soul has to see what it is without its body.[39] Both Wilshere's versions nevertheless ultimately direct audiences to

> mettez hors de vostre quer chesqun' ymaginacioun corporele, e lessez vostre nue entendement voler outre chesqun' humayne reason. E la troverez vous si grant doceur e si grant privetée ke nul n'en set fors soul selui qui l'ad esproevé. (ch. 36, p. 84, 72–7; p. 85, 25–30)
>
> [put every corporeal thing out of your heart, and let your naked understanding fly beyond all human reason, and there you will find such great sweetness and such great intimacy that no-one can know it who has not experienced it.]

But the *Mirour*'s differing versions of contemplation are in practice so flexibly instantiated both with regard to its manuscript texts and its audiences as to be circumstantial rather than systematic in their effect. *Mirour* manuscripts – as indeed the editor acknowledges – do not always behave neatly in regard to a lay/religious division: some of the 'secular' version copies take in sentences from the 'religious' version, and some of the 'religious' skimp on their special paragraphs.[40] It is a long leap from recognising a more demanding mode of

---

[38] Both Forshaw's texts, *Speculum religiosorum* and *ecclesie*, nevertheless retain this idea: ch. 29, p. 106, l. 31–p. 108, l. 4 and p. 107, l. 29–109, l. 4.

[39] M. Zink, 'L'Expression de la contemplation dans le *Mirour de seinte eglyse* de saint Edmond d'Abingdon', in *'Plaist vos oïr bone cançon vallant ?' Mélanges offerts à François Suard*, ed. D. Boutet et al., 2 vols (Villeneuve d'Ascq, 1999), I, 1031–40 (I, 1039).

[40] For instance, two of Wilshere's A ('religious') manuscripts omit parts of chapter 36 but have short catechetical chapters: they are declared 'defective rather than revised' and to be classed therefore with A (Wilshere, p. xii); see also his stemma with classes Aa, Ab, Ba, Bb (p. xvii). As Wilshere himself notes, in the mixture of French and Latin titles used for the *Mirour* texts, the address of A1 is to *dames religieuses*, A2's

contemplation to regulation of its practice. The differences in *Mirour* texts are more likely to be a matter of proficiency and audience self-selection: contemplation directly through the soul is for specialists and harder to achieve, but not (at this date in England) a suspicious, potentially heterodox exaltation of one's own capacities and diminishment of the Church's. And contemplation is not necessarily the final aim of the work: the *Mirour* moves from external to interiorized contemplation and, in chapter 37, out again, with contemplation serving as a means to leading the honourable, humble and loving daily spiritual life defined as living perfectly, whether formally professed as a religious or not ('vivre parfitement', ch. 37, pp. 88, 89). Supple and circumstantial variation in how spiritual guidance is applied is a hallmark of thirteenth-century religious guides and pastoralia.[41] There is good reason to believe that religious and laywomen experienced no formal or categorical restrictions on their access to the *Mirour*, until perhaps the restrictions of the later medieval ages.[42]

More recent studies focus on the variety of audiences made visible if we accept and explore manuscript *mouvance*. Cate Gunn and Nicholas Watson have pointed to the varying spectrum of lives, in and outside orders, represented by *religiosi* in the thirteenth century and to the highly variable understandings of what a truly religious life might be, and Cate Gunn's work on the clerical and pastoral functions of the *Speculum religiosorum*, and on the four manuscripts that were possibly or definitely connected with nunneries, has made it clear that no version of the *Mirour* was systematically reserved to nuns or officially withheld from lay or other readers.[43] (How could the

---

to *Frere*, A3 to *Amy*, A5 *Beau frere et beau soer*, A1 *soer*, A6, 7, 9 *treschere soer*. For a valuable account of the varying relations between ascriptions, texts and audiences in *Mirour* manuscripts for women, see C. Gunn, 'Anonymous Then, Invisible Now: The Readers of "Sermon a dames religioses"', in *Nuns' Literacies in Medieval Europe: The Antwerp Dialogue*, ed. V. Blanton, V. O'Mara and P. Stoop (Turnhout, 2017), pp. 251–70.

[41] Notably the early thirteenth-century *Ancrene Wisse* and Angier of Frideswide's extensive options for secular and religious readers in his vernacular textual apparatus for his 1208–13 *Dialogues de saint Grégoire le grand* (*VLT*, no. 24a, p. 235, v. 1; p. 238, v. 151).

[42] See further M. G. Sargent, 'A Ladder for Sisters', in *Women and Devotional Literature in the Middle Ages: Giving Voice to Silence*, ed. C. Gunn, L. H. McAvoy and N. K. Yoshikawa (Cambridge, 2023), pp. 205–22.

[43] C. Gunn, 'Reading Edmund of Abingdon's *Speculum* as Pastoral Literature', in *Texts and Traditions of Pastoral Care: Essays in Honour of Bella Millett*, ed. C. Gunn and C. Parker (York, 2009), pp. 100–14; N. Watson, 'Middle English Versions and Audiences of Edmund of Abingdon's *Speculum Religiosorum*', ibid., pp. 115–31; Gunn, 'Anonymous Then'. On the treatment of the Creed in the different *Speculum*

division in the *Mirour* be policed in a manuscript and patronage culture? Would Matthew Paris or any other cleric have denied a text of the 'religious' version of the *Mirour* to a patron such as Isabella of Arundel, had a text been demanded of them?)

The *Mirour* was composed when Lateran IV had made it explicit that laypeople would need to be entrusted with a great deal more inspection and curation of their own spirituality if they were adequately to prepare their confessions. Even for an era of books under suspicion as so eloquently and richly presented by Kathryn Kerby-Fulton for late medieval England, censorship, as Kerby-Fulton argues, has its work cut out for it.[44] In thirteenth-century England, diocesan bishops and provincial councils exerted control over policy and practice, including over acts and practices deemed heretical, and confessors directed individual penitents, but skepticism and policing of vision saw only some beginnings towards the end of the century in the condemnation by John Pecham (Archbishop of Canterbury, 1279–92) of the Continental visionaries Hildegard of Bingen and Joachim de Fiore.[45] Even in the late Middle Ages, censorship was subject to class-based exemption as well as to the self-thwarting nature of surveillance.[46] The manuscripts of the *Mirour*, as of its yet to be fully edited Middle English counterparts, still have a great deal to tell us, but they suggest that the text was used and freely adapted among religious and secular and female, male and mixed audiences according to opportunity, circumstance and perceptions of need and capability, not according to any strict division between contemplation and meditation.

---

versions, see C. M. Waters, *Translating "Clergie": Status, Education and Salvation in Thirteenth-Century Vernacular Texts* (Philadelphia, 2016), pp. 132–4.

[44] Kerby-Fulton, *Books under Suspicion*, makes the case for the failure of censorship in the fourteenth and fifteenth centuries, pp. 15–20 and passim.

[45] Kerby-Fulton, *Books under Suspicion*, pp. 192–4, and for the (relatively few) actions against heresy in thirteenth-century England in the context of European counterparts, see the tables pp. xx–xxv. For some actions against images and material culture, see P. Binski, *Becket's Crown: Art and Imagination in Gothic England, 1100–1300* (New Haven, 2004), pp. 199–205.

[46] Arundel's 1409 Constitutions prohibit biblical translation *in linguam Anglicanum vel aliam*, but ownership of French texts does not bring readers to trial. The Wycliffite English Bible itself survives in some 250 copies: ownership by royalty, nobility and clergy 'suggests there was scope for the legitimate production of vernacular biblical texts by the mainstream book trade in London and elsewhere': E. Solopova, *Manuscripts of the Wycliffite Bible in the Bodleian and Oxford College Libraries* (Liverpool, 2016), p. 30.

Seeing the *Mirour* in Women's Books

Women's continuing participation in anthologizing and excerpting the *Mirour* in the fourteenth century contributes to the sustained cultural presence of its author. Like Grosseteste, Edmund is one of the rare figures treated as an *auctor* in both Latin and the vernaculars.[47] Some sections of the *Mirour* such as Edmund's commentary on the Pater Noster and how to pray take on a life of their own outside the full text in women's books, as in the Wilton nuns' psalter (London, Royal College of Physicians, MS 409, va–b), or the French prayer ascribed to him in the psalter made for Hawisia du Bois (New York, Morgan Library and Museum, MS M.700).[48] Other texts sometimes enter the *Speculum*'s textual congeries, notably the exquisitely cogent Middle English lyric, 'Nu goth sonne under wode' in the 'Sermon a dames religioses' manuscript of the *Mirour*.[49] An aspect of the *Mirour* that seems to have been of particular interest to women contributed to what Alexa Sand has traced as the development of the feminized devotional book.[50] Edmund's innovative Passion meditation for the contemplation of God in his human nature was designed to be undertaken before each of the canonical hours (*Speculum*, cap. 17–27, pp. 82–101; *Mirour*, cap. 20–7, pp. 56–73) and also became used in preparation for mass. Visual translations of the *Mirour*, working multidimensionally in thought and seeing, text and image, offer a devotional visual

---

[47] *VLT*, pp. 89–90; for London, British Library, MS Harley 1121's framing image of Edmund as *Mirour auctor* see *VLT*, p. 214; for Grosseteste, *VLT*, pp. 40–1 and A. Siebach-Larsen, 'The Materialization of Knowledge in Thirteenth-Century England: Joan Tateshal, Robert Grosseteste, and the Tateshul Miscellany', in *Women Intellectuals and Leaders in the Middle Ages*, ed. K. Kerby-Fulton, K. A.-M. Bugyis and J. Van Engen (Cambridge, 2020), pp. 227–38.

[48] Dean 629, 888, 9 manuscripts, also adapted in the *Manuel dé pechez*, ed. (from Joan Tateshul's manuscript) by D. W. Russell, 3 vols (Oxford, 2019–22), II, vv. 10,823–11,110; III, pp. 70–7, 143 and vv. 10,753 n., 11,059–60 n.). For Hawisia de Bois, see K. A. Smith, *Art, Identity and Devotion in Fourteenth-Century England: Three Women and their Books of Hours* (London, 2003), passim. Smith also notes (p. 58) possible influence from Edmund in the images of the earliest book of hours by William de Brailes, Oxford, *c.* 1240. For an Oxford anchoress, see K. Kerby-Fulton, 'Not So Silent After All: Women Readers and Intellectuals in Medieval Oxford', in *Women and Devotional Literature*, pp. 180–204 (pp. 189–96).

[49] Oxford, St John's College, MS 190, ed. Wilshere, siglum A1, fol. 197r and pp. 68–9, and in 15 further manuscripts of the French, 16 of the Latin and 9 of the English *Mirror*, J. Boffey and A. S. G. Edwards, *New Index of Middle English Verse* (London, 2004), p. 155.

[50] A. Sand, *Visions, Devotion and Self-Representation in Late Medieval Art* (Cambridge, 2014), pp. 1–26.

literacy which also images women's lineal, educational and other social roles in their books.

Edmund's Passion meditations link events of the Passion at appropriate times of the day (Vespers and Compline for the Deposition and Burial, for instance), but they are each paired with an event in Christ's life so do not follow a single narrative sequence (the Resurrection occurs before the Crucifixion in the succession between Prime and Sext, for instance).[51] Their structuring invokes liturgical time and encourages the perception of quasi-figural connections in its pairings. In the return to Gethsemane from Compline to Matins, the sequence embodies the simultaneously time-bound and eternal nature of Christ's life. In their visual-textual life, Edmund's meditations also show a high degree of *mouvance*, marking different desires (and different budgets) for the text from different users.

In their most magnificent visual realization, Edmund's paired meditations from Prime to Compline are interpolated with the daily recital of the Hours of the Virgin in the Nuremberg (Nürnberg) Hours (Nuremberg, Stadtbibliothek, MS Solger 4.4º), of perhaps the early 1290s.[52] The book was designed for the marriage of a woman from the Anglo-French elite, added English-language texts ascribed to St Bridget in the fifteenth century and was ultimately given to Henry V's bride of 1420, Catherine of France.[53] The Nuremberg Hours' lavish gold background for images of the *Mirour*'s meditations signals luxury but also places the scheme out of sequential historical time and into the meaning of time as shaped by God's interventions in salvation history. For example, the opening images of the Nativity and the Arrest (fol. 39v) are opposite Ps 92 (93), 'The Lord reigns, clothed in majesty', underlining the humility of the Nativity and of the ultimate ruler's submission to arrest. Understanding of the

---

[51] H. Forshaw (as Mother Mary Philomena, SHCJ), 'St Edmund of Abingdon's Meditations before the Canonical Hours', *Ephemerides liturgicae* 78 (1964), 35–57 (54–6); Zink, 'L'Expression de la contemplation'; Gunn, 'Speculum as Pastoral Literature', pp. 111–12.

[52] For Edmund's own *Psalterium beatae Mariae uirginis* (a particular devotion, unrelated to the text in the Nuremberg Hours) see *Analecta Hymnica Medii Aevii*, ed. G. H. Dreves and C. Blume, 55 vols, XXXV (1900), 137–52.

[53] E. Simmons (E. Simmons Greenhill), *Les Heures de Nuremberg : reproduction intégrale du calendrier et des images du manuscrit Solger 4.4o de la Stadtbibliothek de Nuremberg, Traduction de l'américain par Charles Scheel* (Paris, 1994). On its possible occasions (Margaret de Clare's 1272 marriage to Edmund of Cornwell or Edward I's 1293–4 negotiations for a daughter of Phillip III of France), see Simmons, pp. 41–3; A. Stones, *Gothic Manuscripts 1260–1320, Part One*, II, Survey of Manuscripts Illuminated in France (London and Turnhout, 2013), Catalogue I–32, pp. 67–9; A. Bennett (review of Simmons), *Studies in Iconography* 38 (1997), 269–74.

way the Nativity implies the Crucifixion for its full meaning is enforced here, but it is not matched with an immediate and graphic image of torture and death, but rather leads to carefully paced stages of betrayal and trial. Together with the pairing for Prime (trial and mockery of Christ's kingship; the Resurrection, fol. 57v), it shows the small blind narrative of human injustice and failure within the frame of God's generosity of response. The artist's visual language emphasizes the quasi-figural effect of Edmund's dual meditations, as well as responding with eloquent figures and their interactions to the events of Christ's life and passion. The intensity of response sought in Edmund's scheme is designed to elicit understanding inclusive of but not limited to affect. The pairings in his austerely gospel-centred but sufficiently detailed and capacious scheme makes comparable demands, beautifully realized in the Nuremberg images.

Alexa Sand has traced the Nuremberg psalter images' influence in the gentry sphere of the combined Ellesmere ('Vernon') psalter-hours of *c.* 1310–25 (San Marino, CA, Huntington Library, MS EL 9.H.17).[54] This is another book designed for a woman (with a laywoman *destinataire* portrayed with an open book at fol. 175v), most probably owned by Isabella de Harcla (married into the Vernons of northern England and d. 1342 at *c.* 80 years) and given by her granddaughter to the Cistercian nunnery of Hampole. The book combines an Hours of post-1323 followed by a Psalter from before 1314, the Psalter with text in Latin, the Hours in French and Latin.[55] Sand's analyses show the Hours quoting and adapting Nuremberg's visual rhetoric and compositions in its images. In Ellesmere, these are juxtaposed with the text of a Short Hours of the Cross text in insular French, a text, Sand argues, that is itself in part a condensation and selection from the *Mirour*'s meditations, with the artist or the designer of the book engaging with the French text as well as deploying the visual opportunities for registering the simultaneity of different times in the *Mirour*'s scheme.[56] Here again, the active understanding of the book's user is sought, and here again women's requirements and commissions play a role in disseminating Edmund's thought and influence.

---

[54] A. Sand, '"Cele houre mesmes": An Eccentric English Psalter-Hours in the Huntington Library', *Huntington Library Quarterly* 75.2 (2012), 171–211. The manuscript is digitized as 'Book of Hours and Psalter [manuscript]', *Huntington Library Digital Library*, accessed April 12, 2022, https://hdl.huntington.org/digital/collection/p15150coll7/id/49172, with a donation inscription of 'Issabella de Vernun' (probably d. 1348/9) to 'Hanpul' on fol. 36.

[55] Sand, '"Cele houre mesmes"', pp. 173, 190.

[56] Dean 966, 985; Sand, '"Cele houre mesmes"', pp. 197, 200–1, 209; p. 190.

Another way in which Edmund's *Mirour* reached audiences of lay as well as religious women was the association of its passion meditations with preparation for mass. Aden Kumler has shown how, in a manuscript made in London in the mid-1320s for an unknown layperson and illustrated by the master of the Queen Mary Psalter (Paris, Bibliothèque nationale de France, MS f. fr. 13342), the text of the *Mirour* (classified by Wilshere as an unrevised text of his 'religious' version, p. vi) precedes a mass treatise and informs the understanding of the mass.[57] Although the *destinataire* of the manuscript is unknown, it is a good example of the numerous variant instructions and treatises extant in insular and continental French, a number in manuscripts commissioned or owned by women. Mass protocols are as important in the elite earthly household as in the heavenly one of which it is supposed to be an image.[58] As Kumler notes, laypeople's contact with the Host was predominantly visual and the miniature of the Host's elevation, with the bleeding figure of Christ appearing above the altar (fols. 46v–47r), constitutes 'a charged visual confrontation, in which a vision of the sacrament involves seeing beyond – or through – the Host to Christ's bleeding body'.[59] By the properly prepared and intent viewer, the second person of the Trinity is thus fully seen in the reality of his human and divine nature. The textual account of this reality is given in the manuscript by the *Mirror*'s meditation for Vespers and Compline which combine the Deposition from the Cross with the Last Supper. The meditator is to think of how blood and water issued from Christ's side and how this is truly ('verrayment') what is consumed at Mass, and yet given in the form of bread and wine to comfort our bodily senses (because there is a natural revulsion ('hidour') to eating human flesh and blood). Through this, the meditator should emerge with a sharpened experience and understanding of transubstantiation, and

---

[57] The manuscript is digitized: 'Mélanges théologiques', *BnF Gallica*, accessed April 12, 2023, https://gallica.bnf.fr/ark:/12148/btv1b105094193/; see Kumler, *Translating Truth*, pp. 128–30. For three other manuscripts with a mass treatise following the *Mirour*, see Dean 720.

[58] For French and Middle English mass treatises, meditations and prayers, see the valuable survey of pastoralia in *Literary Echoes of the Fourth Lateran Council in England and France, 1215–1405*, ed. M. B. M. Boulton (Toronto, 2019), pp. 1–42 (pp. 19–24); Dean 720–35; Boulton, 'French Treatises on Confession, Mass, and Communion in the Thirteenth Century', in *Literary Echoes*, pp. 74–98. On women and the mass treatise, see G. Burger, 'Labouring to Make the Good Wife Good in the *journées chrétiennes* and Le Menagier de Paris', *Florilegium* 23.1 (2006), 19–40; J. Wogan-Browne, '"Parchment and Pure Flesh": Elizabeth de Vere, Countess of the Twelfth Earl of Oxford and her Book', in *Medieval Women and Their Objects*, ed. J. Adams and N. Bradbury (Ann Arbor MI, 2017), pp. 171–98 (pp. 180–3).

[59] Kumler, *Translating Truth*, p. 137, pp. 135–8.

now become able to 'see one thing and believe another' (por ceo ke nous veoms une chose e creoms un'autre) and to receive the sacrament as if from Christ's side (Wilshere, ch. 26, pp. 70/17–72/4 and 71/17–73/30; Paris, Bibliothèque nationale de France, MS f. fr. 13342, fol. 28r).

There is a great deal more to be investigated in late medieval francophone texts in insular and Anglo-French literary culture, particularly with reference to religious instruction, meditation and contemplation, but it is clear from the sampling here that women play a role in the *Mirour*'s continuing circulation in a major pastoral language through books and devotional practices. How this legacy informs and shapes the *Speculum* in later medieval England is not yet apparent, since work on the many variant Middle English *Mirror* texts is at an early stage.[60] Any full account of the *Speculum* will, however, need to consider both the significant francophone element of its eventually trilingual career, and, as with so many medieval matters, women's engagements with writers and their texts.[61]

---

[60] See Watson, 'Middle English Versions and Audiences'; C. Gunn, "'Þis worde of þa apostil longiþ to ȝow men & wymen of cristis Relygyon:" Who Were the Readers of the Mirror of St Edmund?', *Medium Aevum* (forthcoming). I thank Dr Gunn for a pre-publication copy.

[61] To these multilingual aspects of literary history in England, Kathryn Kerby-Fulton's profound scholarship is fully alert, as in everything she deals with: this essay is offered in admiring tribute and gratitude to a peerless all-round scholar and thinker. Hearty thanks also to Misty Schieberle for the warmth and authority of her acute editing and selfless labour for the present volume.

8

Three English Otherworld Visions: Toward a Spirituality of Parish Life

BARBARA NEWMAN

Otherworld visions enjoyed great popularity in England from Bede's *Ecclesiastical History* straight through Edmund Leversedge in 1465. Such texts have been interrogated about conceptions of purgatory, sin and penance, suffrages, anticlericalism, pagan survivals, credulity and skepticism,[1] and much more. The history of the genre has also been well chronicled.[2] In this essay I ask what such visions tell us about relationships among laity, monks and clerics in a genre whose nature is to unite folklore with Latin learning, transmitting 'popular' piety within a deeply monastic milieu.[3] More specifically, I hope to tease out an emerging spirituality of parish life – a difficult task for which otherworld visions provide neglected evidence.[4] I look at three Latin vision-texts

---

[1] On this question see K. Kerby-Fulton, 'Skepticism, Agnosticism and Belief: The Spectrum of Attitudes Toward Women's Vision in Medieval England', in *Women and the Divine in Literature before 1700: Essays in Memory of Margot Louis*, ed. K. Kerby-Fulton (Victoria BC, 2009), pp. 1–17.

[2] For a catalogue see R. Easting, *Visions of the Other World in Middle English*, vol. 3 (Cambridge, 1997). Easting includes Latin texts translated into Middle English. See also P. Dinzelbacher, *Vision und Visionsliteratur im Mittelalter* (Stuttgart, 1981); P. Dinzelbacher, *Revelationes* (Turnhout, 1991); C. Zaleski, *Otherworld Journeys: Accounts of Near-Death Experience in Medieval and Modern Times* (New York, 1987); and C. Carozzi, *Le voyage de l'âme dans l'au-delà d'après la littérature latine (Ve–XIIIe siècle)* (Rome, 1994). *Visions of Heaven and Hell Before Dante*, ed. E. Gardiner (New York, 1989), provides an accessible but not always reliable introduction.

[3] A. J. Gurevich, 'Oral and Written Culture of the Middle Ages: Two "Peasant Visions" of the Late Twelfth-Early Thirteenth Centuries', trans. A. Shukman, *New Literary History* 16 (1984), 51–66; J. Le Goff, 'The Learned and Popular Dimensions of Journeys in the Otherworld in the Middle Ages', trans. V. Aboulaffia, in *Understanding Popular Culture: Europe from the Middle Ages to the Nineteenth Century*, ed. S. L. Kaplan (Berlin, 1984), pp. 19–37.

[4] J. W. Goering, 'The Changing Face of the Village Parish II: The Thirteenth Century', in *Pathways to Medieval Peasants*, ed. J. A. Raftis (Toronto, 1981), pp. 323–33.

composed in England in a single decade (1196–1206) on the cusp of Fourth Lateran.[5] We have substantial information about each of the authors and their connections with the visionaries, so it is possible to situate these texts with rare precision within a social matrix. My analysis shows that even as their monastic writers promote standard doctrine, such as devotion to saints, suffrages and deathbed contrition, they also convey deeply personal glimpses of the laity at work – draining fields, supervising construction sites, buying ornaments for a church – and consecrating their labour with a piety arising directly from the parish world.

Three Seers and their Scribes

My three texts are the *Vision of the Monk of Eynsham* (1196);[6] the visions of Ailsi, a member of the rural gentry from Launceston, Cornwall, transmitted by his grandson Peter of Cornwall (1200);[7] and the *Vision of Thurkill*, an Essex peasant, recorded by the monk Ralph of Coggeshall (1206).[8] Despite their clerical redaction, the visions of Ailsi and Thurkill bring us as close to authentic rural voices as any text from the high Middle Ages, showing in rich detail what it meant to be embedded in village and parochial life – which were more or less coterminous. The Eynsham vision is a long, complex narrative, but I will focus on one section dealing with its most vividly realized character, the goldsmith of Osney. Although the smith appears only as a purgatorial spirit, the novice monk knew him so well that he scarcely needed a vision to describe his old friend's way of life and the manner of his death. A pious alcoholic, the goldsmith presents a moving account of his struggle with drink as well as his last-breath salvation.

For a later period see K. L. French, *The People of the Parish: Community Life in a Late Medieval English Diocese* (Philadelphia, 2000) and *The Good Women of the Parish: Gender and Religion After the Black Death* (Philadelphia, 2007); E. K. Rentz, *Imagining the Parish in Late Medieval England* (Columbus OH, 2015).

[5] This essay is a companion piece to my chapter on 'Visions' in *High Medieval Literary Cultures in England (c. 1066–1300)*, ed. E. Tyler and J. Wogan-Browne (forthcoming).

[6] *The Revelation of the Monk of Eynsham*, ed. R. Easting, EETS OS 318 (Oxford, 2002). This is a facing-page edition of the Latin text (*Visio Monachi de Eynsham*) and its Middle English translation.

[7] R. Easting and R. Sharpe, *Peter of Cornwall's Book of Revelations* (Toronto, 2013), pp. 142–215. This study includes facing-page editions and translations of all Peter's unique material, but not the larger proportion copied from other sources.

[8] *Visio Thurkilli relatore, ut videtur, Radulpho de Coggeshall*, ed. P. G. Schmidt (Leipzig, 1978).

It will be useful to look at the redactors and their textual milieu before considering the visions themselves. The Eynsham text, earliest of the three, is among the longest and most popular vision-texts from the Middle Ages.[9] Eynsham was a Benedictine house five and a half miles northwest of Oxford, where the visionary Edmund as well as his brother and scribe Adam probably studied. Both brothers belonged to the circle of St Hugh of Lincoln, whose diocese included the monastery. At the time of an earlier vision, Edmund was apparently serving as a clerk at St Nicholas, a parish church belonging to Osney Abbey.[10] (Then an island village in the Thames, Osney is now part of Oxford.) This early vision supported the clerical reforms of Bishop Hugh, who encouraged Edmund's decision to become a monk at the age of twenty-five, around Christmas 1194. Edmund was still a novice at the time of his otherworld vision, which took place during the Easter triduum of 1196. At that time Eynsham's abbacy was vacant because of a dispute between Bishop Hugh and the king over the right of election – a vacancy that enhanced Adam's authority in the office of subprior. Soon afterwards, in November 1197, Adam left Eynsham to become Hugh's chaplain, serving in that position until the bishop's death in November 1200. It was Hugh, Adam says, who exhorted him to record his brother's vision, as he did in 1196/7. Adam later composed the *Vita Magna S. Hugonis*, a biography instrumental in Hugh's canonization. He was appointed abbot of Eynsham in 1213 but was deposed in 1228 for mismanaging property and died around 1233.

The *Vision of the Monk of Eynsham* had more currency than the visions of Ailsi and Thurkill. It survives in thirty-four Latin manuscripts, with ten lost copies known. The work also inspired translations: one in French verse (now lost), three independent German versions and a Middle English text from about 1483 – showing that three centuries later, the vision retained its interest. Among historians, Roger of Wendover included excerpts in his *Flores historiarum* and Matthew Paris in his *Chronica majora*. In the fifteenth century, Denis the Carthusian summarized the vision in *De particulari judicio*. Both Ralph of Coggeshall and Peter of Cornwall – the authors of our other vision-texts – also knew *The Monk of Eynsham*. Vincent of Beauvais inserted four of

---

[9] My narrative derives from Easting's extensive introduction to *Revelation*, pp. xvii–c.
[10] For arguments supporting identification of the clerk Edmund with the visionary, see Easting, *Revelation*, pp. xxxiii–xliii. My account of the relationship between Edmund and the goldsmith of Osney strengthens this case. The Norman church of St Nicholas the Confessor – originally a chapel, later a parish – was given to Osney Abbey *c.* 1140: 'Forest Hill, Oxfordshire', *Wikipedia*, accessed August 1, 2021, https://en.wikipedia.org/wiki/Forest_Hill,_Oxfordshire#Churches.

its vignettes (including the drunken goldsmith) in his *Speculum Morale*, from which they went on to enjoy an independent life as exempla.[11]

Despite its widespread and lasting popularity, *The Monk of Eynsham* was among the most controversial works in its genre. The seer Edmund was not yet fully professed and had been ill for fifteen months before his vision. He even admits to having prayed for a sight of the otherworld to prepare for his expected death – a circumstance that might, in some eyes, have compromised his integrity. Moreover, during a two-year abbatial vacancy a community can easily become factionalized. Perhaps the king's party resented Bishop Hugh's party, supported by Edmund and Adam. It did not help that one prominent purgatorial spirit is the late Abbot Godfrey, who denounces four of his monks for sodomy and suffers atrociously for having tolerated their sin.[12] Although the written text suppresses their names, such messages would have been delivered orally and could not have increased Edmund's popularity. Four years later, the earliest manuscript witness to *The Monk of Eynsham* – Peter of Cornwall's massive compendium, the *Liber revelationum* (1200) – shows that the controversy had not yet faded. Peter copies the entire text, crosses it out, then cancels his cancellation, explaining that 'I, Peter, cancelled this vision in this book, thinking it could not be true, but afterwards, via veracious witnesses who knew the matter, I have proved it to be very true'.[13] Nowhere else does Peter display such scruples, so he must have spoken with both factions at Eynsham.

In 1206 the furor was still raging, for at that date Ralph of Coggeshall writes in his preface to the *Visio Thurkilli*:

> Est et alia visio diligenti narratione luculenter exarata, que in monasterio de Einesham anno verbi incarnati MCXCVI contigit, quam domnus Adam supprior eiusdem cenobii, vir valde gravis ac religiosus, eleganti stilo conscripsit, sicut ab eius ore audivit, qui a corpore per duos dies et noctes eductus fuerat. Non credo tantum virum, tam religiosum ac tam litteratum, nisi

---

[11] Vincent of Beauvais, *Speculum Morale* (Douai, 1624), Lib. II, Dist. xi, Pars I ('De morte', col. 739) and Lib. III, Dist. ii, Pars VIII ('De gula', col. 1359C). Vincent, followed by others, wrongly ascribes the anecdote to Peter the Venerable. See also Odo (Eudes) of Cheriton, *Parabolae*, no. 20, ed. L. Hervieux, *Les fabulistes latins: Depuis le siècle d'Auguste jusqu'à la fin du moyen âge*, 5 vols (Paris, 1896), IV, 272; Stephen of Bourbon, *Tractatus de diversis materiis predicabilibus*, Prologus et Prima Pars, I.5.4 and no. 146A, ed. J. Berlioz and J.-L. Eichenlaub, (Turnhout, 2002), pp. 151, 438; F. C. Tubach, *Index Exemplorum: A Handbook of Medieval Religious Tales* (Helsinki, 1969), nos. 1806, 4005. I have been unable to verify the other references in *Revelation*, ed. Easting, p. xxviii.

[12] *Revelation*, ed. Easting, ch. 27, pp. 92–7; introduction, p. lxxxi.

[13] Easting and Sharpe, *Book of Revelations*, p. 57; *Liber revelationum*, I.10, p. 362.

comperta et probabili auctoritate subnixa voluisse scripto mandare, maxime cum tunc temporis extiterit capellanus domni Hugonis Lincolniensis episcopi sanctissimi viri. Interrogatus autem a nobis domnus Thomas prior de Binham, qui illis diebus extitit prior de Einesham, et qui diligenti scrutinio omnia examinaverat de monacho educto et que de eius visione perscrutanda erant, quidnam super his sentiret, respondit se non amplius de veritate huius visionis hesitare quam de domini nostri Iesu Christi crucifixione. Multaque alia nobis retulit probamenta ad commendationem predicte visionis. Hec iccirco dixerim, quia multi contubernalium suorum huic visioni contradicunt, sicut fere de omni revelatione a quibusdam dubitatur.[14]

[There is another vision, brilliantly composed in a painstaking account, that took place in the monastery of Eynsham in the year of the Incarnate Word 1196. Dom Adam, subprior of that monastery, a very serious and religious man, wrote it in an elegant style just as he heard it from the mouth of [the visionary], who had been led out of his body for two days and nights. I do not believe that so great a man, so religious and learned, would have wished to commend it to writing had he not been convinced and supported by proven authority, especially since he was at that time the chaplain of Dom Hugh, bishop of Lincoln, a most saintly man. I also asked Dom Thomas, the prior of Binham – who at the time was prior of Eynsham – what he thought about these things, for with diligent scrutiny he had examined everything to do with the ecstatic monk and the details of his vision. He replied that he would no more doubt the truth of this vision than the crucifixion of our Lord Jesus Christ. He also gave me many more proofs to commend the aforesaid vision. I have said these things because many of his religious brothers oppose this vision – for just about every revelation is doubted by some.]

The fact that both Peter in London and Ralph in Essex took the trouble to investigate the Eynsham vision suggests that such revelations had high stakes. Their credibility was not guaranteed; both the seers' integrity and the content of their visions could be doubted. Because they purported to give accurate knowledge of the state of souls, including many well known to their audience, fabrication could do much harm. Yet for those who believed, each new revelation confirmed the witness of earlier ones and vice versa. Writers of otherworld journeys worked within a well-developed, highly self-conscious tradition.[15] Yet the visionary is never the scribe, so a seer's 'rustic simplicity'

---

[14] *Visio Thurkilli*, pp. 3–4; my translation.
[15] Zaleski, *Otherworld Visions*, p. 85; Carozzi, *Le voyage de l'âme*, pp. 527–8.

(touted as a mark of veracity) often competes with a clerical author's sophisticated learning.[16] Herein lies much of the genre's charm.

Peter and Ralph both took a professional interest in visions and produced their own anthologies, although Ralph's does not survive. Peter (*c.* 1140–1221), the prior of a house of Augustinian canons in Aldgate, states in his prologue that he compiled the *Liber revelationum* to counter widespread skepticism, even atheism: 'there are some who think there is no God; they believe the world has always been as it is now, ruled by chance rather than the providence of God. And many, considering only what they see, do not believe that … the human soul lives on after the body's death, or that there are other spiritual and invisible realities'.[17] On the theory that such doubters could be convinced by a barrage of visions, Peter collected nearly 1100 extracts from 275 works – about 200 otherworld visions and 900 other items. His sources include Augustine, Gregory the Great, the *Vitae patrum*, Bede's *Historia*, saints' lives and recent visions such as *St Patrick's Purgatory* and *The Monk of Eynsham*. In addition he interviewed his friends, including the Cistercian abbots of Ham and Lessness, about visions that occurred in their vicinity. Unlike *The Monk of Eynsham*, Peter's huge collection did not circulate. The only surviving manuscript remained at Holy Trinity, Aldgate, so the work may have been meant more for preaching than for wide readership.

Ailsi's story comes from Peter's family history. Although Peter had not personally known his grandfather, he had heard about his visions from his father. As a landholder in the region of Launceston, Ailsi belonged to what Robert Easting and Richard Sharpe call 'the rural middle class', neither a peasant nor an aristocrat.[18] Since Peter says he was sixty years old in 1200, he must have been born around 1140, which would date his grandfather's visions to the early twelfth century. Ailsi, Peter tells us, had already gained a saintly reputation for his closeness to St Stephen, patron of the parish church, when his youngest son Paganus died at the age of twelve. Ailsi's distress prompted his final, culminating vision of the otherworld, in which Paganus returned to be his guide. This vision is less comprehensive than Edmund's, but its poignant intimacy is rare in the genre.

---

[16] C. S. Watkins, 'Sin, Penance and Purgatory in the Anglo-Norman Realm: The Evidence of Visions and Ghost Stories', *Past & Present* 175 (2002), 3–33.

[17] 'Nonnulli sunt qui Deum non esse putantes mundum semper fuisse sicut nunc est et casu potius quam prouidentia Dei regi estimant, multique sint qui solum ea que uident pensantes, nec bonos angelos siue malos esse, nec animam hominis post mortem corporis uiuere, nec alia spiritualia et inuisibilia esse credant'. Easting and Sharpe, *Book of Revelations*, prologue, p. 74; my translation. See Kerby-Fulton, 'Skepticism, Agnosticism and Belief', pp. 6–9.

[18] Easting and Sharpe, *Book of Revelations*, p. 174.

Finally, we come to Ralph of Coggeshall (d. 1226), a Cistercian historian well known for his *Chronicon Anglicanum*. The history includes a remarkable series of wonder tales, a genre adjacent to vision-texts.[19] An appendix to the *Chronicon* mentions another of Ralph's works: he 'took pains to faithfully record certain visions that he heard from venerable men for the edification of many'.[20] Few medieval peasants have been described as 'venerable', but that honorific must include Thurkill, a farmer from the village of Stisted in Essex, who experienced an otherworld vision not long before All Saints' Day in 1206. Thurkill related his vision orally in his home parish and many others, becoming something of a local celebrity, before it was confided to writing. By the time the vision reached Ralph – whether a few weeks or even a few years later – it was like a dream that had been told many times, revised each time in the telling.[21] So whatever Ralph added, he was not the first to set his stamp on Thurkill's narrative. This vision never reached the Continent but gained modest currency in England; its four extant manuscripts belonged to far-flung monasteries in St Alban's, Dover, Durham and the Isle of Wight.[22] The St Alban's manuscript is an extensive collection of historical works whose scribes included Matthew Paris. Both Paris and Roger of Wendover excerpted *Thurkill's Vision*, like *The Monk of Eynsham*, in their chronicles.

Among Ralph's contributions are elegant literary allusions to Scripture, Horace, Sulpicius Severus, Gregory the Great, *The Vision of Gunthelm* and more. In his preface he sets Thurkill's vision within its generic context, mentioning others recently granted to several monks and the knight Owein in St Patrick's Purgatory. As we have seen, he vigorously defends the authenticity of *The Monk of Eynsham*. Such visions, Ralph asserts, are revealed 'more clearly and frequently' as the end times approach in order to strengthen weak faith and rekindle charity. Like all visions, Thurkill's has its doubters, but he is sure it will be approved by those 'quorum mens est sanior, intellectus acutior, vita religiosior' (who are of sounder mind, sharper intellect, and more religious life).[23]

---

[19] E. Freeman, 'Wonders, Prodigies and Marvels: Unusual Bodies and the Fear of Heresy in Ralph of Coggeshall's *Chronicon Anglicanum*', *Journal of Medieval History* 26 (2000), 127–43.

[20] 'Quasdam visiones, quas a venerabilibus viris audivit, fideliter annotare ob multorum aedificationem curavit'. *Visio Thurkilli*, p. vi.

[21] P. G. Schmidt, 'The Vision of Thurkill', *Journal of the Warburg and Courtauld Institutes* 41 (1978), 50–64 (p. 56). On the collective oral 'authorship' of visionary texts see Zaleski, *Otherworld Journeys*, pp. 85–8.

[22] *Visio Thurkilli*, pp. vii–viii.

[23] Ibid., preface, p. 4.

I have introduced these three texts in order of their composition. But in the discussion to follow I begin with Ailsi, whose visions are the earliest, and continue with Thurkill to juxtapose the two rural seers. Finally, Edmund's anecdote of the goldsmith takes us from rustic villages to the abbey of Eynsham and the 'suburban' parish of Osney, providing us with the fullest account of interactions involving a parish clerk, a monk and a lay parishioner.

The Visions of Ailsi

Our detailed knowledge about Ailsi and his family is exceptional. According to Easting and Sharpe, 'it is only with a few medieval authors from the upper level of society ... that one has so full a picture, not so much of the intellectual formation of the writer but of the home he left behind him, and with which he clearly retained some contact. Every prior and abbot, every writer and scholar, left some kind of home behind; a great many will have come from the same class of local notables – the rural middle class – that Peter [of Cornwall] came from'.[24] A big fish in a small pond, Ailsi had four sons. The eldest, Bernard and Nicholas, became priests and royal scribes under Henry I, enabling us to correlate the deeds Bernard recorded about his family's property transactions with Peter's information. A third son, Jordan (Peter's father), remained a layman and inherited most of Ailsi's land, while the fourth, Paganus, died young and inspired the otherworld vision.

Peter relates thirteen visions and miracles concerning Ailsi and his sons, culminating in the tour of purgatory. One of their overriding themes is *pietas* in both its classical and medieval senses. Filial piety binds father, sons and grandson in a tight bond apparent not only in Peter's affection for his family, but in the very fact of oral traditions passed down through three generations. Peter introduces Ailsi as 'a man simple and upright, fearing God and turning away from evil' (Job 1. 1) – Job-like not in suffering but as an exemplar of lay piety. St Stephen, the patron of his parish, is Ailsi's guardian, guide and healer. He is also something like a feudal lord, for throughout his life Ailsi 'strove to please God and St Stephen'.[25] The whole section on his visions never mentions Christ or Mary. In fact, St Stephen is sufficient for all his needs, spiritual and temporal, so Ailsi's devotion to him is unbounded. 'Blessed Stephen familiarly revealed to him many hidden matters and prophecies, and gently cherished him in all his anxious cares, and often healed his infirmities'. Moreover, the saint frequently appeared in dreams 'in the likeness of a man of venerable

---

[24] Easting and Sharpe, *Book of Revelations*, p. 174.
[25] 'In omni quoque uita sua operum bonorum exhibitione placere Deo et beato Stephano studuit'. Ibid., I.6.2, pp. 186–7; trans. Easting and Sharpe.

aspect, treating him as his faithful and prudent servant'.[26] Ailsi shared these revelations with his neighbours and, so Peter insists, won the reputation of a holy man (*vir sanctus, vir Dei*) for his friendship with the saint.

Much of their contact had to do with a project dear to St Stephen's heart – the building of a tower for his church. Ailsi was not only custodian of the building fund, a position granted him by the canons of St Stephen's, but also responsible for supervising the workmen. It is not clear whether he was a master mason (R. W. Southern's view) or simply an overseer (the position of Easting and Sharpe).[27] In any case, one of the workers charged with hauling stone from the quarry to the building site cheated by secretly transferring stones from his co-workers' piles to his own, earning extra pay, until St Stephen revealed the fraud to Ailsi in a vision.[28] On another occasion, the work had ground to a halt for want of lime, which is extremely scarce in the region. St Stephen came to the rescue again by showing Ailsi a place two miles away from which appropriate stones could be dug, marking its location with two sticks planted in the ground on either side. This hitherto untapped quarry, Peter writes proudly, 'is still generally known in those parts and necessary throughout the region for similar work' – and indeed, it is marked on an ordnance survey map to this day.[29] But as Ailsi and his crew were setting up their lime kiln, the canons objected, fearing that it was too close to their houses and would start a fire. This time St Stephen appeared to *all* the canons in identical dreams, threatening them with death unless they showed up the next day to do Ailsi's bidding. The saint was as good as his word: 'When the kiln was lit, as St Stephen had foretold', the flames and smoke rose straight upward without harming any homes.[30] Having assisted the building process in every way, the saint finally appeared to consecrate the completed work. Ailsi dreamed of a liturgical procession with acolytes holding lighted candles, followed by the saint. Unlike an ordinary procession, though, this one took place not in the nave but on the scaffolding around the tower, which Stephen used to inspect the workmanship. Finding it to his liking, he stretched out his hand to bless Ailsi and thank him for a job well done.[31]

---

[26] 'Beatus itaque Stephanus sepius apparuit ei in specie hominis uenerande forme tanquam fideli seruo suo et prudenti'. Ibid.

[27] R. W. Southern, 'King Henry I', in *Medieval Humanism and Other Studies* (New York, 1970), p. 226; Easting and Sharpe, *Book of Revelations*, p. 156.

[28] Easting and Sharpe, *Book of Revelations*, I.6.2, pp. 186–9.

[29] Ibid., I.6.3, pp. 188–9 and 147.

[30] Ibid., I.6.4, pp. 188–91.

[31] Ibid., I.6.5, pp. 190–1.

These visions show with striking concreteness that the patron saint was no distant figure, but local and near at hand, and the parishioners were happy to accept Ailsi as his representative. Peter indicates the saint's stature as feudal lord when Ailsi, suffering from a painful eye ailment, remonstrates with Stephen: 'If I had served the Count of Mortain, who is now lord of Cornwall, as much as I have long served you, he would have enriched me with many gifts' – yet Stephen lets him suffer torment.[32] Only mildly annoyed, the saint appears that very night to heal the eye. Peter pronounces this a miracle and claims that as a result, all the neighbours hailed Ailsi as a saint and true friend of St Stephen. In fact, the 'miracle' was short-lived, for by the time of his otherworld vision Ailsi had gone completely blind. For that matter, the tower blessed by the saint was also short-lived: the earl of Cornwall pulled it down in 1140 during the war between King Stephen and Matilda, probably to preclude its military use.[33] But Peter suppresses this inconvenient fact in the interest of presenting his grandfather as that rarity, a lay married saint.

As *paterfamilias*, Ailsi passed his values on to his sons, especially his devotion to the parish saint: 'all after their father's example held St Stephen in special and singular affection'.[34] Bernard and Nicholas gave the church an embroidered banner depicting the saint's martyrdom, which in Peter's day was 'still held there in great veneration'. When they retired as scribes, they also donated their ivory writing case and silver inkhorn to serve as reliquaries.[35] Peter's father Jordan died in the arms of Osbert, the prior of St Stephen's.[36] In addition Ailsi had a foster son, a leper. His care for this boy was said to occasion visions and miracles 'pre omnibus miraculis admiranda et stupenda' (to be greatly admired and wondered at before all other miracles).[37] Unfortunately, Peter's memory failed him so he left a lacuna, intending to ask his brother for details – but either he never got around to it or his brother had forgotten too. It's a pity. This was early in the European leprosy pandemic, before many leprosaria had been founded, so it would be useful to know more about a devout layman's care for the afflicted. In any case, Peter thought that even without the

---

[32] 'Si comiti Moretonie, qui modo dominus est Cornubie, tantum seruitii inpendissem, quantum et tibi iam pridem inpendi, multa iam mihi contulisset donaria'. Ibid., I.6.6, pp. 190–1.

[33] Ibid., pp. 156, 161–2.

[34] 'Omnes singularis prerogatiua dilectionis sicut pater eorum beatum Stephanum amplexati sunt'. Ibid., I.6.9, pp. 196–7.

[35] Ibid., I.6.11, pp. 198–9.

[36] Ibid., I.6.12, pp. 200–1.

[37] Ibid., I.6.8, pp. 194–5.

forgotten vision, this act of *pietas* should be revered among his grandfather's saintly deeds.

Finally, we come to the otherworld vision. Surprisingly, Peter tells us that Ailsi's fourth son was called Paganus (eo quod diu paganus fuit), remaining unbaptised until the age of twelve. This seems unlikely,[38] but whatever the case, when the boy died Ailsi became so anxious about the next life that a merciful God sent Paganus to instruct him. The punishments described in his vision need not detain us, for they are standard-issue tortures. Peter knew and compiled so many visions of this type that we cannot safely ascribe the narrative to Ailsi. A few details, however, are unusual and telling. Ailsi dreams that he is on pilgrimage to Jerusalem with others when their path descends into a valley so dark that no one can see another. Arriving at the bottom, Ailsi comes to a great and terrible river. He walks back and forth seeking a bridge, a normal feature of such visions – but finds none and cries to God and St Stephen for help. At this point Paganus appears and, after an exchange of greetings, asks his father to climb onto his back. Ailsi protests that his son is too young and weak to carry him, and they argue, until Paganus simply hoists his father on his shoulders and flies across the river.[39] This simple, non-formulaic scene is moving because of its archetypal elements: a father's grief, a pilgrimage to Jerusalem, the valley of the shadow of death.

At the same time, Paganus's flight over the dark, smoky river cannot fail to evoke *pius Aeneas* fleeing the fires of Troy with his father Anchises on his back. Ailsi could well have dreamed such a flight, but Peter could also have enhanced the vision with a half-conscious reminiscence of Virgil. In fact, a verbal echo follows: the tortured souls in the infernal river 'ad ripam manus suas extendebant' (stretched out their hands toward the shore), trying in vain to clutch at bushes to drag themselves out of the flames. For a Latinate reader, these words cannot fail to evoke Virgil's poignant verse about the dead thronging the shores of the Styx, reaching for Charon's boat: 'tendebantque manus ripae ulterioris amore' (they stretched out their hands for love of the farther shore, *Aeneid* VI.314). A medieval reader, in fact, might have been thinking of that when he scribbled *nota hic* in the margin.[40] At the end of the vision we come to an equally touching moment. Father and son have reached the earthly paradise and Ailsi, unwilling to tear himself away, 'wished to use

---

[38] Ibid., I.6.13, p. 202. Easting and Sharpe refuse to credit this explanation, for it would have been unlike the pious Ailsi to leave a child in such peril. They point out that *Paganus* was the standard Latin form of the English name Pain or Payn. *Book of Revelations*, pp. 176–7.

[39] Ibid., I.6.13, pp. 202–5.

[40] Ibid., p. 204. My translations.

force with his son that he might remain there'. The two dispute again until Paganus vanishes and his father awakens, 'much troubled because he had lost the joys of such great beauty'.[41] At this point Anglophone readers will surely recall the Middle English *Pearl*. Although the poem was written almost two hundred years later, its emotional dynamics are the same: a father, impatient in his longing for bliss, can no longer bear to accept the teaching – nay, command – of his child who has gone before him. Poised between two great poems in such different generic and linguistic traditions, Ailsi's vision gains a resonance that transcends the usual cautionary tortures of the otherworld.

Thurkill's Vision

If Ailsi's vision remains fairly simple, embellishing a family story handed down over a century, Thurkill's is among the most elaborate in the genre. Like Peter of Cornwall and Adam of Eynsham, Ralph of Coggeshall takes pains to situate the visionary within his ordinary life. A peasant from Stisted (diocese of London), Thurkill was hardly rich, yet he was not destitute either. For instance, he could afford modest almsgiving and hospitality. When we first meet him on the evening of October 27, 1206, he is digging ditches to drain a flooded field.[42] In the field Thurkill meets a traveller, who turns out to be St Julian the Hospitaller and promises to take him on a journey the following night. St Julian is a fit guide because Thurkill practices generous hospitality himself. In fact, before recognising his visitor he offers to put him up for the night, but St Julian reveals his saintly identity by telling the peasant something he had not known: his wife had already taken in two lodgers (pauperculas mulieres). When Thurkill returns home, he washes to purify himself, then lies down to sleep apart from his wife because it is Friday.[43] Thus he is already characterized as a devout man and a model parishioner.[44]

In other ways Thurkill was an extraordinary peasant, for he had apparently gone on pilgrimage to both Italy and Santiago de Compostela.[45] Hence,

---

[41] 'Uim facere uoluit pater filio ut ibi remaneret. ... Pater a sompno excussus se in domo sua nimis anxius inuenit, quia tante amenitatis gaudia perdiderat'. Ibid., I.6.17, pp. 212–13.

[42] Schmidt, 'The Vision of Thurkill', p. 64, notes that to this day, if you drive from Stisted to Coggeshall in October, you will pass a sign warning 'Flooded Road'.

[43] For the longer passage summarized here, see *Visio Thurkilli*, pp. 5–6.

[44] On the ideal of *sancta rusticitas* see P. Freedman, *Images of the Medieval Peasant* (Stanford CA, 1999), pp. 204–35.

[45] Schmidt, 'The Vision of Thurkill', pp. 57–9. Pilgrimage by peasants was not unknown: the vision of Gottschalk (from Holstein) mentions that his fellow peasant

along with St Julian, his visionary guides include St James, who refers to him as 'peregrinus meus', and St Domninus. The latter saint was unknown in England; one puzzled scribe even changed his name to Dominicus. But he was the patron of Borgo San Donnino, a popular Italian stop for pilgrims en route to Rome, Bari and Monte Gargano.[46] Thurkill had probably visited at least one and perhaps all three of these destinations – for his better-known saintly guides are Peter and Paul (venerated in Rome), St Nicholas (in Bari) and St Michael the Archangel (at Monte Gargano). Female saints also appear: SS. Catherine, Margaret and Osith grace the entrance to Paradise.[47] This plurality of saints stands in contrast to Ailsi and the goldsmith of Osney, who were both devoted exclusively to their parish patrons, St Stephen and St Nicholas. But this is an exception that proves the rule, for the church of Stisted was dedicated to All Saints – a key point unnoticed by previous scholars.[48] Thurkill lives up to their patronage. While the most typical time for an otherworld vision was the Easter triduum (as with the Monk of Eynsham and Dante), Thurkill has his vision just before the 'fall triduum' of All Hallows' Eve, All Saints and All Souls' Day. For this reason, when St Julian returns in a follow-up dream, he commissions Thurkill to relate his vision in his parish church on All Saints' Day (November 1). As this was the community's patronal feast, the church was packed and the lord of the village, Osbert de Longchamps, was present with his wife. All Souls, of course, was dedicated to prayers for the dead, and the vision abounds in local characters who require specific suffrages for their liberation.

Thus we see the highly unusual figure of a peasant who was well-travelled and, though illiterate, had perhaps acquired some of the wide culture that comes with experience of the world. Moreover, his vision resulted in further travels closer to home. As Ralph of Coggeshall records, when the visionary plowman first recited his narrative on All Saints' Day at the church of All Saints, people were astonished at his sudden eloquence. His account so effectively 'softened hard hearts and … moved them to lamentation and earnest sighing' that it led to further speaking engagements. It is no wonder he found

---

Winido had already been to Jerusalem and vowed a journey to Santiago. *Godeschalcus und Visio Godeschalci* A, ch. 27, ed. and trans. E. Assmann (Neumünster, 1979), p. 102. Chaucer of course includes a Plowman among his Canterbury pilgrims.

[46] Schmidt, 'The Vision of Thurkill', p. 57. Borgo San Donnino is now known as Fidenza.

[47] *Visio Thurkilli*, p. 36. A house of canons near Stisted was dedicated to St Osith, a virgin martyr.

[48] 'Parish Church of All Saints, Stisted', *Historic England*, accessed August 1, 2021, https://historicengland.org.uk/listing/the-list/list-entry/1123870.

a ready audience, for he 'showed everyone the state of their fathers and mothers, brothers and sisters, their relatives and all whom they had known at all in the present life – whether they were still detained in punishment or at rest, and with what suffrages and how many masses they could be rescued from the places of torment and translated to the peace of everlasting bliss'. What news could be more welcome, more sacred, or more practical? So after his initial report, the peasant 'was invited by many people in many churches, communities and religious houses' to share his vision. The text even says that he 'preached' it (predicavit), one of a tiny handful of authorised lay preachers.[49]

The literary polish of the *Visio Thurkilli* and its genre conventions are due to Ralph, but the peasant's own imagination should not be discounted. The star feature of Thurkill's hell, as a travel guide would say, is unique in its genre. This is a vast theatre of cruelty, managed by demons for their own amusement, in which the damned occupy seats of white-hot iron studded with nails, while the fiends enjoy privileged top-tier seating. Grinning and laughing, they haul the wretched souls onstage one by one to reenact their sins. Performances take place every Saturday night. One of King John's justiciars – unnamed, but newly deceased and easily recognisable – mimics the actions of hearing a case while accepting bribes from both parties. As he performs, the coins catch fire and he is compelled to swallow, then vomit the burning money.[50] In another act, illicit lovers obscenely reenact their passion. Then, 'as if driven to frenzy, they mangled one another in turn, gnawing with their teeth, and changed all the superficial love they seemed to have for each other before into fury and cruel hate'.[51] Most commentators assume that the theatre sequence was Ralph's wholesale invention. In one of his sources, *The Vision of Gunthelm*, sinners are likewise forced to reenact their crimes – though not in a theatre and not for

---

[49] 'Ostendit singulis de statu patrum et matrum, fratrum et sororum, parentumque suorum atque omnium illorum, de quibus in presenti vita aliquam habuerat noticiam, utrum adhuc in penis sive in requie detinerentur, quibusve suffragiis et quot missarum officiis a locis penalibus possent eripi et ad requiem eterne beatitudinis transferri.... donec corda obdurata et fere insensibilia emolliret atque ad lamenta et gravia suspiria commoveret. ... Postmodum supradictus vir a multis personis invitatus in pluribus ecclesiis atque hominum conventiculis ac in religiosorum domibus visionem suam constanter predicavit'. *Visio Thurkilli*, p. 9.

[50] Ibid., pp. 23–4. Schmidt, 'The Vision of Thurkill', p. 62, identifies this judge as Osbert fitz Hervey. The same punishment is found in *The Monk of Eynsham* and elsewhere.

[51] 'Deinde quasi in insaniam versi se alternatim dentibus corrodendo lacerabant ac totum illum superficialem amorem, quem prius adinvicem habere videbantur, in furorem et in odii crudelitatem commutaverunt'. *Visio Thurkilli*, p. 25.

devils.[52] One comic scene, the performance of the Proud Man, is lifted almost verbatim from Jean de Hauville's twelfth-century satire *Architrenius*.[53] Some early Christian texts, such as Tertullian's *De spectaculis* and Augustine's *Confessions*, make the theatre a literal haunt of demons.[54] It is possible, though, that Thurkill had seen an ancient Roman amphitheatre, perhaps the Colosseum, in the course of his travels. On learning that martyrs had died in such places, he was unlikely to forget such an awesome sight. So this unique feature could plausibly have involved collaboration between the monk and the plowman.

The vision retains unmistakable signs of its peasant origin. The only punishment Thurkill himself suffers on his journey is exacted for withholding tithes from his harvest. He pleads poverty as an excuse, but St Julian promises that if he pays his tithes in full, his field will produce more abundantly. In his recitation he publicly confesses this sin to warn his fellow parishioners against it.[55] Several punishments involve either sins typical of peasants or those committed at their expense. The thieving miller who steals flour is familiar from Chaucer, but he is rarely considered important enough to show up in otherworld visions, as he does here.[56] Roger Picoth, Thurkill's former lord, is among the souls awaiting suffrages because he had failed to compensate his tradesmen, so he begs his son to pay off his debt of forty pence.[57] An unusual scene puts even corrupt plowmen onstage. To take vengeance on their lords, these peasants had harshly goaded their oxen while reducing their rations until the emaciated beasts died of overwork. In the demonic theatre the oxen, harassed to the point of madness, impale the peasants on their horns.[58] While it may gratify us to see animal abuse pegged as a sin, there is more to this than Thurkill's affection for the sturdy beasts essential to his livelihood. For it was not the peasant, but the lord who owned these expensive animals. Unable to resist manorial oppression directly, the plowmen had adopted a passive-aggressive strategy, making a show of unusually diligent labour and thrifty management. If an ox just happens to die, how can that be the peasant's fault? But Piers the Plowman would not be fooled, and neither is Thurkill's God.

---

[52] Schmidt, 'The Vision of Thurkill', p. 60.
[53] *Visio Thurkilli*, pp. 20–1; Johannes de Hauvilla, *Architrenius*, 5.5, ed. P. G. Schmidt, trans. W. Wetherbee (Cambridge MA, 2019), p. 234.
[54] Cf. Gurevich, 'Oral and Written Culture', p. 59.
[55] *Visio Thurkilli*, pp. 9, 12.
[56] Ibid., p. 26.
[57] Ibid., p. 30.
[58] Ibid., p. 26.

In another scene oriented toward the lower classes, Thurkill meets his own father suffering for crafty frauds he had practised in trade. St Michael says he can be liberated for thirty masses but discounts the rate to ten in view of Thurkill's poverty.[59] Suffrages are clearly priced at what the market will bear. When Thurkill gratefully promises to purchase the ten, his father is liberated at once, before they have even been sung. On the other hand, a lazy priest is damned because he not only failed to instruct his people by preaching or example but also took payment for prayers and masses that he never said.[60] For peasants who worked hard to pay for such suffrages, this sin of omission was a grave betrayal. Otherwise, in contrast to the monk of Eynsham, Thurkill takes little note of clerical sins. His parish priest, however, plays a key role in the frame story. On waking from his trance, the plowman insists on telling the priest about his vision before he will even take food. At first he can speak only haltingly to those around him, 'omitting and withholding many things' (plurimaque omittendo et reticendo). Nor can he give the priest a coherent account 'because of his simplicity and rustic modesty' (pre simplicitate et rusticana verecundia). But after their initial conversation – and another dream visit from St Julian – Thurkill manages to tell his whole story.[61] It seems clear that the priest helped him understand his half-remembered dream, setting the vignettes within a standard religious frame and enabling him to assign meanings to what he had seen.

Thurkill models lay piety in numerous ways, including Friday continence, hospitality, almsgiving, devotion to the saints, pilgrimage, respect for his parish priest and proper tithing (after he has been duly corrected). He is keenly aware of the need to labour honestly and pay debts promptly; failure to do so is invariably punished. If it is wrong for a lord to cheat his workers, it is no less wrong for plowmen to sabotage their lord. Attuned to the devotional calendar of his village, Thurkill chooses – or is chosen for – its annual parish feast as a day of communal revelation. Suffrages loom large, as in most otherworld visions, but especially this one on the eve of All Souls' Day. Above all, the vision vividly recreates the local community, linking its afterlife to the scene of Thurkill's performance and turning the little parish of All Saints Stisted into a microcosm of the universal Church. Yet it is precisely the scenes we have analysed – those that express the seer's familial, parochial and agrarian interests – that Matthew Paris and Roger of Wendover left out of their abridgments.[62]

---

[59] Ibid., p. 32.
[60] Ibid., p. 22.
[61] Ibid., pp. 8–9.
[62] *Visio Thurkilli*, p. x.

They were only interested in the big picture, not local colour, and certainly not in the fate of oxen. So we have reason to be glad that Ralph of Coggeshall, monk though he was, ranked the humble plowman of Stisted among those 'venerable men' whose visions, in all their particularity, would 'edify many'.

The Goldsmith of Osney

The ambitious *Vision of the Monk of Eynsham* owes its origins to both a Latinate seer (Edmund) and a Latinate scribe (Adam), and the brothers were well connected. Accordingly, the clientele Edmund meets in purgatory are of higher rank than the villagers of Stisted. Among the identifiable souls are King Henry II, Baldwin of Ford (late archbishop of Canterbury), five bishops, an abbess, the late abbot of Eynsham and three knights. But the most memorable character is an unnamed goldsmith from Osney, whom Edmund had known for years. Adam preserves his brother's personal narrative: 'I believe you remember that, around the time you had gone down to visit me in the vill [Osney] where I had been stricken with quinsy and was lying half-dead, a certain goldsmith, a citizen of the same place, suddenly died'.[63] The man's narrative fills five chapters, and when he finishes the monk again recalls, 'This man ... passed from the world fifteen months before I spoke with him'.[64] These circumstances would have impressed the goldsmith's death forcefully on the seer's mind, for Edmund had no sooner resolved to become a monk than he was smitten with a life-threatening illness, and at just that moment his old friend passed away. They had been well acquainted: the goldsmith addresses Edmund as 'dilecte mi' or, in the Middle English, 'my dere frynde'.[65] St Nicholas, the visionary's guide, asks whether he knows this spirit and he responds 'notissimum' (ful wele).

But why would an unworldly young cleric about to join a monastery have been so friendly with the local goldsmith? Surely Edmund, the Oxford scholar, was not commissioning jewelry, nor is it likely that the smith needed help with his Latin. Rather, their responsibilities in the parish brought them together. Edmund was the parish clerk, probably assisting the priest as acolyte, while

---

[63] 'Igitur meminisse uos credo ea tempestate qua me sinancia percussum in uillam ubi semineci similis decumbebam uisitaturus descenderatis, aurificem quendam eiusdem loci ciuem subita morte expirasse'. *Revelation of the Monk of Eynsham*, ch. 19, p. 58. Quinsy (*sinancia*), a painful abscess of the throat caused by tonsillitis, can make it difficult to breathe or swallow.

[64] 'Uir ille ... ante .xv. menses quam ipsi sum locutus de seculo migrauit'. Ibid., ch. 23, p. 74.

[65] Ibid., ch. 20, pp. 60–1.

the goldsmith was a kind of churchwarden *avant la lettre*. In his pamphlet on the origins of that office, Charles Drew writes that the wardens' duty was 'to hold and administer any form of property with which the parishioners might be endowed …; should such endowments not exist or suffice, it was their business to provide for the raising of the funds required to meet a particular need; [and] they were responsible for the safe custody of the ornaments and utensils to be provided by the parishioners for the services of the church'.[66] The earliest records of churchwardens appear in 1261. They were known in Oxford by 1270, though such records do not become common until the mid-fourteenth century. Nicholas Orme has more recently shown that from the late thirteenth century, English churchwardens, chosen by the parishioners, were responsible for upkeep of 'the nave, the books, the ornaments, the vestments, the images in the church, the font in the nave, the church tower, and its bells'. One of their most important tasks was to administer and invest the 'church store', or offerings in money and kind to the image of the patron saint.[67]

Although no such formal role can be documented in 1200, the responsibilities evidently preceded the official title, as parishioners gained increasing fiscal responsibility for the maintenance of their churches. When he tells his story, the goldsmith's spirit recalls parochial duties that extended beyond personal devotion to a quasi-public role, which he could exercise only because he possessed considerable wealth as well as the trust of his fellow parishioners.

> In dominum meum … sanctissimum Nicholaum, cuius eram parochianus, talem habui deuocionem, ut nulla vnquam occasione pretermiserim, quin eius ueneracioni quicquid potuissem deuotissime exhiberem. Quantumlibet sero ebrietati indulsissem, matutinas deuote nullatenus pretermittere consueui, sed mox pulsante signo, ipso frequenter ocior capellano accurrebam. Lampadem in oratorio domini mei sancti Nicholai de meo proprio iugiter exhibebam. Que uero ad tocius ecclesie cultum, siue in luminaribus, siue in rebus diuersis, forent necessaria, sedulo quasi familiare ipsius mancipium procurabam, et ubi proprie facultatis minus suppetebant uires, comparochianos mouebam ad conferendum que defore uidebantur. Dona uero conferencium suscipiebam oportunis usibus fidelissime expendenda.[68]

---

[66] C. Drew, *Early Parochial Organisation in England: The Origins of the Office of Churchwarden* (London, 1954), p. 6.

[67] N. Orme, *Going to Church in Medieval England* (New Haven, 2021), pp. 81–2. For churchwardens as doctrinal enforcers in the Reformation era see E. Carlson, 'The Origins, Function, and Status of the Office of Churchwarden, with Particular Reference to the Diocese of Ely', in *The World of Rural Dissenters, 1520–1725*, ed. M. Spufford (Cambridge, 1995), pp. 164–207.

[68] *Revelation of the Monk of Eynsham*, ch. 21, p. 62.

[I had such devotion to my lord St Nicholas, whose parishioner I was, that I never failed to show him all the veneration I could. No matter how late I had been indulging in drink, I used to attend Matins devoutly, never missing it, but as soon as the bell rang I ran to church, often arriving before the chaplain (*parysh pryste*). I kept a lamp burning perpetually in the chapel of my lord St Nicholas at my own expense. Whatever else was needed for the worship (*ornamentys*) of the whole church, whether lights or anything else, I diligently provided as if I were his familiar servant. And where my own resources did not suffice, I moved my fellow parishioners to contribute whatever seemed necessary. I accepted the gifts of those who contributed to be spent faithfully on appropriate uses.]

Given these responsibilities, the goldsmith must have spent a good deal of time in church, where he would often have encountered Edmund performing his own parish duties. (Perhaps it was he who rang the bell that summoned his friend to Matins.) Like Ailsi a century earlier, the goldsmith was entrusted with significant sums of money, which he did not embezzle or squander but spent honestly. Just as Ailsi had been fervently devoted to St Stephen, so the goldsmith was to 'my lord St Nicholas'. Indeed, he saw himself as the saint's personal servant. Edmund includes the touching detail that he himself could not identify his otherworld guide until the goldsmith, recognizing 'my present lorde, Sente Nicholas', joyfully greeted him.[69] Due to the gravity of the goldsmith's sins, Edmund presents his salvation as a miracle of St Nicholas and tells his story to commend devotion to the saints. Yet in other ways, the goldsmith was a model parishioner. For example, he confessed and received communion twice a year at Christmas and Easter, although he died twenty years before Fourth Lateran mandated a single annual confession. He did his best to fulfill his appointed penance, while admitting that he often failed. He even kept a full Lenten fast during Advent, adding extra days to make up forty.

Drink, however, was his nemesis. Speaking for a legion of alcoholics, the goldsmith explains that although he continued in the 'fowle synne of dronkynnes' to his dying day, yet 'hyt was not my wylle, for gretly hyt dysplesyd me, and mekyl Y sorowyde that Y kowde not leue that vyse'. Again and again he swore to stop, but the pleasure of drink and the importunity of his friends ('feleshyppe that Y dranke wyth') dragged him back. On Christmas, as he recalls with 'grete horror and heuynes', after Mass and communion he went out and got drunk again – and the same thing happened the next day and the next. Thus, he lost his 'uirile sobrietatis propositum' (the mighty purpos of soburnes

[69] Ibid., ch. 20, p. 61.

that Y had conceuyd).[70] Finally on the third day he left the tavern, came home and went to bed with his clothes and shoes on. When he rose for Matins, his wife said the bell had not yet rung, so he lay down and went back to sleep, never to rise again. Evidently what he heard was not the church bell but the knell of doom.[71] The smith's posthumous account of his death is hair-raising. A demon, the same one who had long tempted him, entered his mouth like a toad, slipped down his throat, sat on his heart and squeezed it and finally belched out a horrible, poisonous vomit that strangled his dying breath.[72]

Since the man was well known in the parish, the sorry tale spread quickly. He would have been found fully dressed, covered in vomit, having died so suddenly that his wife could not even send for a priest. In fact, his body remained so warm and red from all the wine he had drunk that his household kept him unburied for two days, hoping he might still revive. People said he had sold his life for drink and was surely damned, since he had died in his sins without the last rites. Edmund, lying ill in the same place, must have heard this news with horror. Caught in a liminal state between his old life as parish clerk and his new monastic life, he was too sick at the time for either. He even wondered if it was a sin to pray for his friend because prayers for the damned are of no avail, but only make God angrier. Nevertheless, he prayed at least feebly (licet egre), hoping against hope that the rumour he had heard was false.[73] During the fifteen months that elapsed between the goldsmith's death and the monk's vision, Edmund must have thought often of his comrade. Everything the smith revealed as a purgatorial spirit was already known to the monk except for the fact of his salvation, a cause of immense reassurance.

The inside story is, of course, a deathbed act of contrition. Knowing that his end had come, the goldsmith had only an instant, but he used it to vow a firm purpose of confession and amendment, inwardly calling on St Nicholas to be his pledge (fideiussorem, borowe). At once the demons snatched his soul and dragged it toward hell with terrible torments. Yet St Nicholas, whom he had invoked with all his heart, lifted him powerfully out of their hands and set him in purgatory. There, despite the severity of his pains, he bore them with gratitude in assurance of everlasting joy.[74] There is even a sequel: two weeks after the monk's vision, the goldsmith's son – who had surely heard about it – came

---

[70] Ibid., ch. 21, pp. 63–5.
[71] 'The Vision of the Monk of Eynsham', ed. H. E. Salter, in *Eynsham Cartulary*, vol. 2 (Oxford, 1908), p. 317 n.
[72] *Revelation of the Monk of Eynsham*, ch. 21, pp. 66–7. The Middle English turns the toad into an owl through a confusion of *bufo* and *bubo*.
[73] Ibid., ch. 19, p. 58.
[74] Ibid., ch. 21, pp. 66–9.

to Edmund in tears, saying that his father had appeared to his mother three nights in a row. On the third night he overheard a long conversation between them, though only on his mother's side. She then told the youth that his father was angry: she had neglected a simple thing he had asked of her 'because of the doubtful varieties and uncertainties of visions'.[75] The precise suffrage is not mentioned, but this second vision – aside from authenticating the first – gives Edmund the opportunity to say that he saw no other soul make such rapid progress through purgatory. Finally, the goldsmith urgently begs his wife and son to remain devoted to St Nicholas, 'hys patron and aduocatour', through whose mercy he had escaped the damnation he deserved. Like Ailsi, this loyal parishioner considers it a filial duty to both his family and his lord to sustain their relationship.

As an exemplum, the goldsmith's tale points in two directions. *In malo*, it warns against the perils of drink. Although medieval people thought of drunkenness as a vice, not a disease, the goldsmith's confession rings so true to our understanding of alcoholism that it can only be the story of a real person who struggled mightily against his addiction yet succumbed in the end. He is not unlike the Glutton in Langland's gallery of sins – less a personification than a portrait of the parish barfly. Edmund may have heard his friend's 'firm purpose of amendment' many times in life before he heard it from his spirit in purgatory. *In bono*, the exemplum is a hopeful one, stressing the possibility of salvation even at the point of death and, above all, the value of devotion to saints. Interestingly, the Latin text concludes with a passage on almsgiving, omitted in the Middle English. Adam cites the Gospel verse, 'As you have done it to one of the least of these, you have done it to Me' (Matt. 25. 40). The goldsmith, he says, 'did what he could – not for one of the least, but for one of God's special friends, so he experienced the truth of that saying, "Just as water extinguishes fire, so almsgiving extinguishes sin"'.[76] This special friend of God is St Nicholas, casting the goldsmith's donations to his parish as 'almsgiving' that enabled his speedy progress through purgatory. In this way the text ascribes his salvation at once to grace (deathbed repentance), patronage (the favour of St Nicholas) and merit (the virtue of almsgiving). The two monks responsible for this exemplum make a strong case for the parish, rather than the cloister, as a locus of salvation.

---

[75] Ibid., ch. 23, pp. 72–3. The wife's excuse – she had not acted *propter uisionum incertas uarietates & incertitudines* – may seem ironic in light of the skepticism that greeted Edmund's vision.

[76] 'Hic autem uir predictus vni non quidem de minimis, sed de precipuis amicis Dei, quod potuit fecit, in se expertus sentencie illius ueritatem, *Sicut aqua extinguit ignem, ita elemosina extinguit peccatum*'. Ibid., ch. 23, p. 74.

Conclusion

In his longitudinal study of thirty-four visions from the fifth through thirteenth centuries, Claude Carozzi notes that fifteen of the visionaries were laymen, including poor people, while the remaining nineteen were monks. 'In short, two states of life are favourable [for otherworld journeys]: that of the peasant in his parish and that of the monk in the cloister'.[77] Both cloister and parish, he suggests, afforded a stability absent from the lives of nobles and secular clergy. Moreover, both monks and peasants led penitential lives – monks by their vows, peasants by the lot they were born to – and the visionary universe is a deeply penitential one. But the genre, though steeped in tradition, could also include innovative features.

Even as otherworld visions map the afterlife and skewer the sins of kings, they convey a wealth of humble information about family, village and parish life. Ailsi is guided by his son and memorialised by his grandson; Thurkill liberates his father; Edmund confides in his brother and hears the confession of his friend. All three visions, notwithstanding their otherworld geography, express a remarkably down-to-earth spirituality. Saints can appear while a man is quarrying stone or draining his field. One can be damned for mistreating oxen and saved by faithfully stocking a church with candles. Specific parish roles are highlighted: builders, donors, a churchwarden (before that office formally existed), even a lay preacher. Loyalty to place is paramount. Peter in London fondly remembers his family in Launceston; Thurkill's attention in purgatory centres on his fellow parishioners. In the slightly earlier vision of the German peasant Gottschalk (1189), souls in the city of the dead even seem to be arranged by parishes.[78] Aron Gurevich laments that the perspective of such visions falls short of cosmic grandeur. Indeed, it is 'narrowed to parochialism, thinking on the scale of the church parish'.[79] But why is that a problem? Thurkill was not Dante, nor was meant to be. If our quarry is the emergence of parish spirituality, visions are for that very reason a valuable resource.

Although the genre can seem grim, replete with gruesome tortures, it offers hope by admitting unexpected mercies. C. S. Watkins argues that over the course of the twelfth century, 'the new emerging orthodoxy' of contritionism gradually made its way out of Paris into the parishes. On this view, a good deathbed confession, or even a mere intention – as in the goldsmith's case – could snatch a soul out of hell, though it still had to make satisfaction in

---

[77] Carozzi, *Le voyage de l'âme*, p. 588.
[78] *Godeschalcus und Visio Godeschalci* A, ch. 52, pp. 136–9.
[79] Gurevich, 'Oral and Written Culture', p. 58.

purgatory.[80] Hugh of Lincoln, according to his *Vita* by Adam of Eynsham, taught that 'the Kingdom of God is not confined only to monks, hermits and anchorites', rejecting the once common view that few laypeople would be saved.[81] Hugh believed in the power of deathbed contrition and, as we have seen, influenced Adam and Edmund. Their exemplum of the goldsmith perhaps intentionally promotes this new doctrine, so encouraging for the laity, along with its more conservative emphasis on the power of saints. Everyone presumes that the drunken goldsmith is damned, yet after a dying act of contrition he is freed by St Nicholas, and Edmund complements his tale with that of a prostitute saved by St Margaret.[82] At this pivotal moment of church history, just as the laity were beginning to come into their own, it is instructive to find monks and clerics using the genre of the otherworld vision, traditional yet supple, to show just what lay salvation might look like in the context of ordinary parish life.

---

[80] Watkins, 'Sin, Penance and Purgatory', pp. 4, 25.
[81] Adam of Eynsham, *The Life of St Hugh of Lincoln*, ed. and trans. D. L. Douie and H. Farmer, 2 vols (London, 1961–2), II, 46.
[82] *Revelation of the Monk of Eynsham*, ch. 18, pp. 50–7.

9

Recognizing the Clerical Proletariat: Evidence from Late Medieval London Wills[1]

MISTY SCHIEBERLE

> Item volo et lego omnia predicta terre redditus et tenementa ... Thome filio Willelmi Ocklyfe quondam ciuis et pannarius Londonii *sub tali condicione quod non sit in sacris ordinibus constitutus* ... ad terminum vite sue.
> – Will of Maud Holbech, 1392 (emphasis mine)

> [I will and leave all the aforesaid land, rent and tenement ... to Thomas, son of William Hoccleve, formerly (i.e., deceased) citizen and draper of London, *under such condition that he not be established in sacred orders* ... for the term of his life.][2]

Kathryn Kerby-Fulton has made an excellent case for understanding the precarious employment circumstances of late medieval clerks as central to their poetic identities. Although there had been a shortage of priests following outbreaks of the Black Death, by the later fourteenth century, there

---

[1] When she joined the faculty at Notre Dame, Kathryn Kerby-Fulton generously agreed to co-direct my in-progress dissertation and helped nurture my interests in medieval women and manuscript studies. I am grateful for her keen insights and advice over the years, including about this very article, and I am delighted that my pandemic obsession with reading late medieval wills has given me the chance to be in conversation with her scholarship on the clerical proletariat. I am also grateful to Amanda Bohne and the anonymous press reviewer for encouragement and feedback on this piece.

[2] LMA (City of London), COL/AC/01/015, from the Husting Rolls of Deeds and Wills, roll 122, entry 27 (hereafter, HR, with roll and entry number), emphasis mine. For a summary of Maud's will, see *Calendar of Wills Proved and Enrolled in the Court of Husting, London*, ed. R. R. Sharpe, 2 vols (London, 1889–90), II, 302; hereafter, *Cal. Wills*, with volume and page number. I have consulted digital scans of HR 122(27); otherwise, I consulted the microfilm *Husting Rolls of Deeds and Wills, 1252–1485*, ed. G. H. Martin (Cambridge, 1988). When citing wills, I include their date of composition, not the date of enrollment (usually soon after the testator's death). Translations are my own, unless otherwise noted.

was an employment crisis. Permanent incomes and benefices became increasingly rare, and they often went to men of the upper classes with connections to powerful family members or patrons.[3] As a result, many men expertly trained for and spiritually motivated towards pastoral careers never got the opportunity for stable positions within the Church. Kerby-Fulton traces the way these circumstances impacted late medieval poets and inspired the critiques of benefices and absentee rectors found in the works of Langland, Audelay and Hoccleve, among others. Her portrait of Hoccleve particularly highlights the way that pastoral concerns recur in his poetry, so that even though he was in secular bureaucratic employment and is often thought of as a secular poet, we cannot fail to see how spiritual training and a desire to guide others were integral parts of his identity. Indeed, Hoccleve and others felt keenly alienated from the beneficed clerical class yet superior to uneducated laymen (as Kerby-Fulton's treatment of the *Remonstrance Against Oldcastle* makes clear).[4]

This essay demonstrates that the idea of a clerical proletariat was understood not only by the members of the clerical underclass but also by the broader late fourteenth-century London merchant community, the contemporaries of the poets Kerby-Fulton has analyzed so thoroughly. Chaucer, from a family of vintners, demonstrates an acute sense of the clerical proletariat in his sympathetic portraits of his pilgrim Clerk and of Absolon, but crucially such portraits can be placed in a wider web of sympathies for under-funded clerks and students evidenced in merchant wills. As I have argued elsewhere, the conditional bequest by Maud Holbech, which leaves property and income to Thomas Hoccleve under the condition that he not be in orders, demonstrates her understanding of Hoccleve's career path and that if he were not beneficed or in the ordered clergy, he would need other income, which she sought to provide.[5] Maud, twice married to prominent drapers, provides not just for Hoccleve, with whom she had a close and possibly familial relationship, but also for the support of needy university students at Oxford and Cambridge and of

---

[3] K. Kerby-Fulton, *The Clerical Proletariat and the Resurgence of Medieval English Poetry* (Philadelphia, 2021), pp. 1–32. See also A. K. McHardy, 'Careers and Disappointments in the Late Medieval Church', *Studies in Church History* 26 (1989), 111–30, for demographic evidence on the increasing numbers of unbeneficed clergy from poll taxes of 1377, 1379 and 1381. On the likelihood that the unbeneficed were from middle or lower class, see B. H. Putnam, 'Maximum Wage-Laws for Priests after the Black Death, 1348–1381', *The American Historical Review* 21 (1915), 12–32.

[4] Kerby-Fulton, *Clerical Proletariat*, pp. 125–9.

[5] M. Schieberle, 'Thomas Hoccleve of London: New Evidence of Hoccleve's Family and Finances', *SAC* 45 (2023), 287–311.

poor students in general.[6] While Maud's may be a clear provision of livelihood for a famously un-beneficed clerk, other London wills enrolled in the Court of Husting rolls likewise suggest that London merchants – sometimes but not always family members – recognized the struggles of un-sponsored students or unbeneficed clerks who might otherwise have to cobble together a living in what Kerby-Fulton terms the clerical 'gig economy'.[7] These bequests also add new texture to the notion of a merchant mentality that valued charitable gifts not only for the private benefit to the testator's soul but also for their potential impact on the wider community.[8]

London merchant wills from the 1380s and 1390s demonstrate that although the 'clerical proletariat' or 'clerical precariat' are modern terms, medieval communities were aware that young scholars and underemployed clerks needed support. Bequests to unbeneficed clerks and clerks in training are both spiritual and worldly – they benefit the souls of the faithful by sponsoring prayers but they also mitigate the struggles of the clerical proletariat by financially supporting worthy but underemployed men.[9] These charitable gifts – not unlike dowers for poor women – indicate how widespread the need was, or at least was perceived to be, by medieval Londoners, who show a commitment to support the religious community not only by donating to rectors or churches but also by providing for students, chaplains, disadvantaged chantry priests and other members of the clerical proletariat.[10] While it was common practice to fund chantry priests, some testators arguably acknowledged the additional

---

[6] HR 122(27), *Cal. Wills* II, 302. At a minimum, Hoccleve's father was among the closest family friends and business partners of William Holbech (and an executor of Holbech's estate) and Maud Holbech, with whom he engaged in a variety of real estate dealings after her husband's death. K. Kerby-Fulton, 'Oxford', in *Europe: A Literary History, 1348–1418*, ed. D. Wallace, 2 vols (Oxford, 2015), I, 208–26, acknowledges some issues of needy students.

[7] Kerby-Fulton, *Clerical Proletariat*, p. 3.

[8] A. Appleford, *Learning to Die in London, 1380–1540* (Philadelphia, 2014), pp. 55–97, emphasizes the merchant practice of demonstrating concern for the future of the City by leaving charitable bequests accordingly, with Richard Whittington as the most prominent, remarkable example of community foresight.

[9] See also N. P. Tanner, *The Church in Late Medieval Norwich, 1370–1532* (Toronto, 1984), pp. 105–10.

[10] Chantry priests were a complex category treated in more detail below – some chantries were poor and could be terminated when funding ran out, while others were stable, so some chantry priests would qualify as part of the clerical proletariat, while others might not. See, for example, Kerby-Fulton, *Clerical Proletariat*, pp. 100, 178; and see M.-H. Rousseau, *Saving the Souls of Medieval London: Perpetual Chantries at St. Paul's Cathedral, c. 1200–1548* (Farnham, 2011), pp. 95–7.

complexities and challenges of clerical structures: the expenses of schooling, the scarcity of benefices, the necessity of competent estate management to fund clerical prayers, the importance of selecting worthy chaplains – by name or by descriptive qualities (including mechanisms by which a chaplain might be removed and replaced) – and the need to specifically fund unbeneficed clerks. Such details provide plausible evidence that London merchants were aware of the occupational crises affecting their local churches and the men who operated in and around them.

The most substantial work authored by the average medieval person might be the will that outlines how to dispense with their life's accumulated goods and money. These testaments can be read alongside both praise and critique of clerks in literary authors to demonstrate a wider recognition of clerical crises. Contemporary poets praise poor, unbeneficed priests, express disillusion at how the Church really works and, in the case of Audelay's lyrics, essentially beg readers to endow chantries for or promote poor but talented clerks who have been repeatedly passed over for benefices.[11] The struggles of the clerical proletariat were not just the preoccupation of disgruntled and disadvantaged clerically-trained authors. Those writers offer one view on the circumstances, ecclesiastical records offer another, and, I suggest here, London merchant wills offer yet another valuable perspective on concerns about and sympathies for students, unbeneficed clerks and spiritual labourers.[12]

Wills as Sources

As a disclaimer, this short survey cannot hope to be comprehensive, nor does it contain the data or statistics that often captivate historians. Rather, I evaluate the language choices in wills of London merchants in the latter decades of the fourteenth century in order to call attention to ways they plausibly demonstrate lay awareness of the clerical proletariat; more study will be required, which I hope may be sparked by my present explorations. I have used Sharpe's *Calendar of Wills* as a starting point, but Sharpe is not without limitations: his entries summarize only 'important' bequests (a wildly subjective concept), and for reasons of space, he collapses lengthy portions of wills into

---

[11] Kerby-Fulton, *Clerical Proletariat*, pp. 155–64.

[12] K. Wood-Legh, *Perpetual Chantries in Britain* (Cambridge, 1965), pp. 190–5, demonstrates the limitations of criticism by Chaucer and Gower; see also K. Zieman, *Singing the New Song: Literacy and Liturgy in Late Medieval England* (Philadelphia, 2008), p. 104. To their evidence amassed from ecclesiastical registers, merchant wills add complementary yet new evidence.

'bequests to the church and its ministers', or 'provisions for chantries'.[13] The original documents are often surprisingly varied in their distributions of gifts among clerical recipients and in their guidelines for funding chantry priests and prayers. Sometimes testators list clerks, chaplains and chantry priests by name, when Sharpe does not, and occasionally Sharpe neglects to mention chantries funded by testators or names that later scholars recognize as potentially 'important'. My point is not to criticize Sharpe, since we could hardly demand complete consistency from anyone who embarked on the monumental task he accomplished, but rather to point out that more research is needed to make a fuller assessment.[14] I have targeted wills of interest where Sharpe's truncated summaries suggest there may be richer evidence in order to expose the tip of the iceberg one might uncover with greater attention to the full testaments in the Husting Rolls (or their microfilm copies, which has been my primary means of access). Sharpe's summaries are essential starting points, but they depersonalize the wills, which are often deeply personal documents.[15] By exploring the testators' use of language and terms, I highlight details that point toward their attitudes toward the clerical profession, its potential for precarity and the clerical proletariat.

Medieval wills tended to follow certain formulas: the commendation of the testator's soul to God; the preferred location for burial; bequests to churches, priests (by title and/or name), monastic orders or houses, anchorites and other religious entities, including any funding for chantries or expectations for funeral or memorial services; bequests to family and friends of property and goods, some of which might have conditions attached, like that the rents from a certain property should be expended on a chantry; bequests to servants (if the testator had any) and others, who might include personal chaplains and apprentices; and bequests to charitable beneficiaries, such as unmarried girls, the poor, prisoners, the infirm, improvements to London roads or bridges

---

[13] For Sharpe's methods, see *Cal. Wills* I, xlviii.

[14] For studies by historians analyzing certain types of wills, see E. Kim, 'The Tailors, Drapers and Mercers of London and the London Commissary and Husting Court Wills, 1374–1485' (unpublished Ph.D. dissertation, University of Toronto, 2015); R. A. Wood, 'Life and Death: A Study of the Wills and Testaments of Men and Women in London and Bury St. Edmunds in the late Fourteenth and early Fifteenth Centuries' (unpublished Ph.D. dissertation, Royal Holloway University of London, 2012).

[15] S. Sobecki, *Last Words: The Public Self and the Social Author in Late Medieval England* (Oxford, 2020), pp. 65–73, demonstrates the deeply personal ties revealed in John Bailey's bequests to Thomas Hoccleve.

and so on. However, individual documents vary widely.[16] Some include formal codicils or less-formal seeming afterthoughts; some group gifts to anchorites with religious bequests, while others group them with more general charitable bequests near the will's conclusion; some place chantries among early religious bequests, while others do not mention them until disposing of the properties that will fund them; and some testators make clear that their request for a worthy celebrant is very serious and that there are consequences should that wish not be fulfilled.[17] In these often oddly-specific expressions of last wishes (and contingency plans), testators' personal choices arguably indicate their thoughtful and original approaches, even when they appropriate commonplace formulas.

I focus on wills whose terms can be interpreted to describe unbeneficed individuals – for example, students, stipendiary chaplains, chantry chaplains or anyone essentially contracted to labour spiritually on behalf of the testator's soul. Of course, any bequest left to a church official or religious person carried with it the expectation of being remembered in their prayers, an implied rather than explicit expectation. I am, however, most interested in the documents where that expectation is formally codified in the will, especially when testators seemingly recognize that they are not simply funding a chantry or religious services but also putting funds toward the maintenance (ad sustentationem) of a chaplain, student or clerk – suggesting an awareness that they are supporting spiritual labour, their parish and the well-being of a living person.[18] It is equally important to note that wills only provide evidence of the testator's intent – whether or not chantries were founded or funds were available to be

---

[16] For a primer on testamentary evidence and evaluating formulae, details and omissions, see C. Burgess, *The Right Ordering of Souls: The Parish of All Saints' Bristol on the Eve of the Reformation* (Woodbridge, 2018), pp. 83–118.

[17] The flexibility of medieval wills, despite their formulas, must be emphasized, as must the fact that Sharpe often rearranges bequests to suit a general formula and streamline his summaries. For example, John Seman, HR 123(102), makes no initial arrangements for chantries yet does so later in his will, which Sharpe apparently overlooked (*Cal. Wills* II, 314); Richard of Lincoln, HR 78(12), names his son among the first personal beneficiaries in the will, yet Sharpe names the son last (*Cal. Wills* I, 624–5), obscuring Richard's placement of his son as foremost in his mind, not a later consideration.

[18] *DMLBS*, s.v. *sustentatio*, indicates the term could apply to general support but also sustenance or food. Some testators even leave homes that they clearly expect to be the living places for recipients, displaying a desire to ease the financial and living burdens of beneficiaries. C. Burgess, "'By Quick and by Dead': Wills and Pious Provision in Late Medieval Bristol', *The English Historical Review* 102 (1987), 837–58, details how chantries benefitted both the deceased and the living members of the parish.

distributed at all, much less as specified, is often unknown.[19] Despite these limitations, exploring the wills' representations of clerks and students helps put literary accounts into perspective and describe London merchant assessments of clerical careers, based on their bequests to unbeneficed clerics and students in their communities.[20]

Funding Students, Poor Scholars and Clerks

Maud Holbech includes her bequest to poor students among other general gifts for the maintenance of roads, dowers for honest poor unmarried girls and other pious causes to be determined by her executors. These are gifts designated for the benefit of her soul but that simultaneously benefit society more broadly, which seems to have been part of the formula used by many testators near their wills' conclusions. Maud's husband William, who died in 1367, left funds for repair of religious houses, for mending roads, for decrepit men in hospital and for marriage portions for young or poor needy women (but not for students).[21] Among wills, those broader gifts may vary widely, and only some single out students, scholars and clerks.

Often a family connection can be traced, like the one I posit for Holbech and Hoccleve, and it seems eminently logical for testators to care for family or men with whom they had close relationships.[22] Former mayor John Northampton (dated 1397) bequeaths 100 shillings to 'Henry seruenti clerico meo ad ipsum inueniendo ad scolas' (Henry, my servant clerk, to support him at school).[23] Henry Herbury (dated 1396) leaves a portifory and forty marks sterling to his son Nicholas for his schooling, to be controlled by the boy's

---

[19] C. Burgess, 'Late Medieval Wills and Pious Convention: Testamentary Evidence Reconsidered', in *Profit, Piety and The Professions in Later Medieval England*, ed. E. Hicks (Gloucester, 1990), pp. 14–33, notes the limits of information that can be drawn from wills.

[20] My exploration is broadly in the spirit of the far more wide-ranging and thorough examination of parish wills as evidence of religious practices, devotional preferences and personal connections in C. Burgess, *Right Ordering of Souls*.

[21] HR 95(99). Dates for wills correspond to their year of composition, which may differ from their enrollment year.

[22] Schieberle, 'Thomas Hoccleve of London'. See also A. Bohne, 'Networks of Influence: Widows, Sole Administration, and Unconventional Relationships in Thirteenth-Century London', in *Women Intellectuals and Leaders in the Middle Ages*, ed. K. Kerby-Fulton, K. A.-M. Bugyis and J. Van Engen (Cambridge, 2020), pp. 239–50, who argues that one independent widow had at least an emotional partnership with 'her clerk', and family wills ensured his continued financial security.

[23] HR 126(118).

mother; if Nicholas dies or is promoted to a benefice of worth (which Herbury identifies as £20 per year) before that sum is spent, the money should go toward charitable works.[24] The gift of a portable breviary and mention of benefice indicates if not Nicholas's intentions, then at least Henry's hopes for his son's clerical career.[25] Yet these hopes are tempered by the understanding that Nicholas would be in need as a student and perhaps even afterwards, until he obtains a more substantial, guaranteed income.

Similarly, Reginald Coleman in 1383 leaves his nephew John Coleman 100 shillings 'in aid of his maintenance at school' (in auxilium sustentacionis sue ad scolas). He also leaves to his own son John £200 sterling outright and another £200 to be in his wife's custody for supporting his son's schooling to study whatever he wishes.[26] Of course, both younger men's paths of study are unknown, but the elder Coleman's will indicates his awareness of the needs of young students in his family.

In the wills of two friends, Walter de Berneye (1377) and John Heylesdon (1384), there is evidence that allocating money for student clerks can yield spiritual dividends for the community. Among other bequests to chaplains and clerks, including £20 to the collegiate clerks of 'Baliolehalle', Oxford, Walter singles out Richard de Tasburgh, John de Folsham and Richard son of Ralph Trench to each receive £40 to pursue their studies at Oxford or Cambridge (ad excercendo scolas).[27] By 1384, when Berneye's friend and executor the London mercer John Heylesdon drafted his own will, Richard de Tasburgh is named as the rector of the church of Heylesdon and as one of John's executors tasked with managing his rents and establishing two perpetual chantries with two worthy and honest chaplains (capellanos idoneos et honestos) at his church to pray for the souls of John Heylesdon and his family, Berneye and others, both living and deceased.[28] Berneye's investment in Richard de Tasburgh apparently paid off, and the rector must have seemed the natural choice to fulfill Heylesdon's wishes as someone trustworthy and known to both merchants. After other bequests, Heylesdon also divides his remaining

---

[24] HR 125(41); see also Sharpe, *Cal. Wills* II, 322.
[25] As Kerby-Fulton, *Clerical Proletariat*, p. 187, and Rousseau, *Saving the Souls*, p. 116, note, the portifory was popular among the clerical and liturgical proletariat.
[26] HR 113(54): Et volo quod … summa cc libras sit in custodia Cristine uxoris mee ad inueniendo et sustentando ad dictum filium meum ad scolas ad quam scienciam libera sua voluntas exigerit (damage renders the word following 'quod' illegible).
[27] HR 107(164): Item lego Ricardo de Tasburgh, Johanni de Folsham, et Ricardo filio Radulphi Trench ad excercendo scolas Oxoniensium vel Cantebrigiensium equaliter xl libras.
[28] HR 113(01).

estate into three equal portions, specifying that the third should be used to support poor scholars at school.[29] He does not single out men for scholarship by name as Berneye had, but he continues his friend's investment in poor students and future clerics like Richard de Tasburgh.

Most bequests are more general. Alice de Mordon (the widow of former mayor and stockfishmonger Simon de Mordon) leaves a large share from the sale of her properties to provide marriage portions for poor young women and for the education of poor young scholars (1385).[30] The mercer William Knyghtcote (1382) took a slightly different approach, allotting 10 marks each to support one chantry priest at St Mildred in Bredestrete and one at St Martin Pomery, then allocating a further 10 marks each per year for three additional chaplains to celebrate for two years in the churches of St Laurence in the Jewry, St Martin Pomery and Oxford, 'if one of them chooses to study there' (si studium ibidem excercere voluerit).[31] In addition to rewarding spiritual labours in London, Knyghtcote seems to be offering a portable two-year scholarship to Oxford for a London chaplain.[32] Not all students necessarily became clerks, though the majority often did; we know that Hoccleve and Richard de Tasburgh did, and Nicholas Herbury, Northampton's servant clerk and Knyghtcote's chaplain are also plausible candidates for clerical careers.[33]

Chaplains and Chantries

An examination of how merchants discussed chaplains and chantries in their wills also sheds new light on their views of unbeneficed clerics. Scholars are still working to complicate the negative views offered by Chaucer, Langland and Gower, all fourteenth-century writers who criticize chantry priests. Chaucer's oft-cited commentary praises his Parson for being unlike the absentee priest who 'ran to Londoun unto Seinte Poules / To seken hym a chaunterie for

---

[29] HR 113(01): Et terciam partem inde volo fieri in exhibicionem pauperii scolarii ad scolas.

[30] HR 116(67): in maritagiis pauperum iuuencularum, exhibicione pauperum scolarum ad scolas.

[31] HR 112(08).

[32] See Wood-Legh, *Perpetual Chantries*, pp. 208–9, on chantries functioning as scholarships, which she notes as most common in wills in university towns; the other 'scholarships' I have noted are separate from chantry duties.

[33] Career trajectories for clerks might be religious or fairly secular; see T. A. R. Evans, 'The Number, Origins and Careers of Scholars', *The History of the University of Oxford Volume II: Late Medieval Oxford*, ed. J. I. Catto and Evans (Oxford, 1992), pp. 485–538.

soules' (Gen. Prol. 1.509–10), and Langland similarly gives the impression that chantry priests have deserted a heavier workload for the lighter work of singing chantries in London (*Piers Plowman* C.1.81–4).[34] As Katherine Zieman and Kathleen Wood-Legh have shown, these satirical portraits are more complicated than they appear on the surface, and historical records do not support the notion that priests are leaving beneficed positions for chantries, not least because London chantries would typically have lower incomes than most beneficed positions, and benefices were more secure.[35] Chantry priests might also have additional duties (such as attending masses, visiting the poor or sick, or teaching) and fairly restrictive contracts, depending on the benefactor's stipulations, so not all chantries were necessarily desirable employment for clerks seeking an easy path.[36] Yet chantry priests, especially stipendiary priests who supported themselves on short-term contracts, become a contentious category. For Gower, the idea that a short-term contract priest would fail to meet his obligations is a foregone conclusion. As Zieman has demonstrated, the estates satire of the *Mirour de l'Omme*, ll. 20497–555, depicts annuellers (men who performed chantry duties on a yearly contract) as self-serving opportunists who unethically fail to meet their contracts with the souls of the dead.[37] Zieman further argues that the contractual bases of their labour made the annueller or 'itinerant mass priest' the target of ecclesiastical criticism because it suggested that liturgical labour was separated from a parish's communal structure and long-term community.[38] Zieman's insightful analysis of liturgical labour suggests that unbeneficed clerics and stipendiary contract priests may have been overly criticized because they were visible targets in a changing and newly unstable market for liturgical services. Notably, most evidence for criticism of this category of clerics comes from literary satires, perhaps exaggerated

---

[34] Chaucer, *The Canterbury Tales*, gen. ed. L. D. Benson (New York, 2000); Langland, *Piers Plowman: A New Annotated Version of the C-Text*, ed. D. Pearsall (Exeter, 1994).

[35] Wood-Legh, *Perpetual Chantries*, pp. 190–5, and Zieman, *Singing the New Song*, p. 104, emphasize that not all benefices were lucrative, but most were generally more secure.

[36] Wood-Legh, *Perpetual Chantries*, pp. 65–92, details elements of supervision and restriction on chantry chaplains' behaviours; see also Putnam, 'Maximum Wage-Laws', p. 14 n. 25; see also below.

[37] Zieman, *Singing the New Song*, pp. 109–12; Gower, *The Complete Works of John Gower: The French Works*, ed. G. C. Macaulay, vol. I (Oxford, 1899).

[38] Zieman, *Singing the New Song*, pp. 105–12.

for effect, and ecclesiastical records, which might be interpreted as stemming from frustrated attempts by established clerics to control the market.[39]

Testamentary evidence suggests that lay merchants accepted unbeneficed spiritual labourers and likely shared with Langland and Audelay sympathies for devoted but poor, unbeneficed (or perhaps poorly-beneficed) clerks.[40] The appearance of direct references to members of the clerical 'gig economy' in wills implies that some testators were eager to support underfunded clerks. Such evidence indicates that the relationships between chaplains – even stipendiary ones – and benefactors were not merely transactional parts of a spiritual economy but also demonstrations of a mutual respect and plausibly even of London merchants' sympathy for the career struggles faced by the clerical proletariat.[41]

Unbeneficed clerics within the church structures, according to B. H. Putnam's schema, could fall into three main categories: (1) parish chaplains with cure of souls, acting as assistants to beneficed clergy or as replacements for absentee rectors; (2) private chaplains of important people (sometimes akin to servants, like Northampton's 'servant clerk' above); or (3) chantry priests, contracted to pray for the souls of the departed, sing masses and sometimes, depending on their contract's terms, participate in divine services, minister to the poor and infirm or instruct students.[42] Other employment options existed outside the church, such as secular bureaucratic clerks, secretaries, notaries, schoolmasters, scribes and a range of activities for which clerks were qualified.[43] Most of the time, unbeneficed spiritual labourers were from the middle or lower classes, without the family or social networking connections that might secure them a more permanent position.[44] When we see London

[39] Zieman, *Singing the New Song*, pp. 100–5, usefully interprets annuellers as 'the clerical equivalent of agrarian laborers who had rejected manorial ties to work on short-term contracts' and 'upsetting the socioeconomic order' (p. 105). Putnam, *Wage-Laws*, and Wood-Legh, *Perpetual Chantries*, pp. 190–5, give examples of attempts to control priestly labour prices.

[40] On literary portraits, see Kerby-Fulton, *Clerical Proletariat*, pp. 77–109, 140–74.

[41] For further discussion of the relationships among chaplains, their peers, patrons and founders, see Rousseau, *Saving the Souls*, pp. 93–144.

[42] Putnam, 'Wage-Laws', pp. 13–14. See also Burgess, "'For the Increase of Divine Service'", pp. 51–4, on myriad possible duties for chantry priests, dependent on the founder's wishes. On vicars choral, a category that seem to have been subsumed into Putnam's first group, see *Vicars Choral at English Cathedrals: Cantate Domino. History, Architecture, and Archaeology*, ed. R. Hall and D. Stocker (London, 2005).

[43] On secular employment, see Kerby-Fulton, *Clerical Proletariat*, pp. 2–3.

[44] On influential relatives or other connections as essential to securing benefices, see McHardy, 'Careers and Disappointments'; Rousseau, *Saving the Souls*, pp. 122–3; and Kerby-Fulton, *Clerical Proletariat*, pp. 78–83, 120–3.

merchants' wills funding prayers and establishing chantries to be performed by stipendiary priests or other unbeneficed individuals, there is a sense that they are providing, if not for identified clerical relatives or friends, then at least for clerks of a peer status group or a more needy status group.

Amounts paid for chantries were often healthy but not necessarily perceived by contemporaries as well-paying. Clive Burgess has suggested that Bristol chantry priests could be compensated at a 'relatively high rate of pay' of between five and six pounds, a rate that exceeded the statutory minimum for stipendiary service and was nearly as much as some beneficed clergy earned; most aristocratic Londoners allotted at least £5 annually for each chantry priest, too, according to Joel Rosenthal's detailed study of late medieval aristocratic gift-giving.[45] Most merchant wills fund chantries at a similar rate. However, this 'relatively high' pay is substantially lower than the £20 per year identified by Herbury in 1396 as the income level at which his son would no longer need to draw on his inheritance; it is worth noting, too, that Hoccleve's 1399 annuity from Henry IV is granted for life or until he might be promoted to an ecclesiastical benefice with annual income of £20.[46] My point is that standard chantry rates would not have been comparable to positions deemed 'of worth' from an upwardly mobile or aristocratic perspective, but they could offer opportunities for income to clerks who might have few other options and be affordable ways for merchants to spread out their amassed wealth to fund prayers and priests, increasing personal spiritual benefits and enhancing the broader spiritual community.

There are different types of chantries funded in wills: short-term chantries for a year or a few years following the testator's death; longer term chantries that might run a decade or more; and perpetual chantries expected to be run in perpetuity that often operated as benefices and should be treated as a category separate from chantries with term limits.[47] Testators might also supplement existing perpetual chantries founded by friends or family members, adding their names and estate funds to ensure an unbroken stream of prayers for the

---

[45] Burgess, "'For the Increase of Divine Service'", p. 50; he cautions that Bristol ought not be taken as representative of other locations (p. 47). J. Rosenthal, *The Purchase of Paradise: Gift-Giving and the Aristocracy, 1307–1485* (London, 1972), pp. 37–8.

[46] HR 125(41); J. A. Burrow, *Thomas Hoccleve* (Aldershot, 1994), pp. 34, 39–40.

[47] Wood-Legh, *Perpetual Chantries*, pp. 11–15, 191, emphasizes the perpetual chantry as a separate category marked by stability of employment akin to a benefice but also acknowledges that even perpetual chantries could become impoverished and then be terminated or consolidated (pp. 93–129). See also Rousseau, *Saving the Souls*, pp. 20–4, 195–7. As Zieman, *Singing the New Song*, p. 95, notes, a perpetual chantry 'appropriated [a priest's] entire vocation', even though he might have additional pastoral or parochial duties.

faithful. Many – but not all – testators who found or supplement chantries require 'unum capellanum ydoneum' (a worthy/qualified chaplain).[48] The commonplace formulation may have taken on a particular resonance after the Black Death led to a shortage of priests, when an increased population of unqualified priests – men who would not have been deemed eligible for ordination in previous times – were ordained by necessity to fill positions.[49] Under such circumstances, a testator might well have accepted *any* qualified chaplain and expected the chantry's supervisors to ensure that he fulfilled his duties. After the rises in wages following the Black Death, it might be difficult for supervisors of poorer chantries to find worthy priests who would accept chantry positions rather than positions with less strict regulations governing them.[50] The desire for a 'worthy' chaplain was certainly formulaic, but the surrounding details and regulations in wills demonstrate individual perspectives on chaplains and chantries.

Merchant wills often included instructions for the selection of the chaplain that required good behaviour, but many also went on to describe the conditions under which a chantry priest neglecting his duties should be admonished, removed and replaced. One example can be found in the will of Richard Chaucer (d. 1359), Chaucer's step-grandfather, who trusts the parson and parishioners of two churches to install 'unum capellanum ydoneum' to celebrate mass and all the canonical hours, stating in both cases that if the chaplain fall short or in any way be absent unless the cause were infirmity, he should be admonished and replaced.[51] Richard Chaucer is concerned simply with the chaplain fulfilling his duties, and it is not uncommon for testators to outline the process of replacing a chaplain in cases of illness, infirmity or death, but other testators are far more insistent that the chaplain

---

[48] See *DMLBS*, s.v. *idoneus*. Rousseau, *Saving the Souls*, pp. 35–41, discusses the process of selecting chaplains. Although Rousseau's records of perpetual chantries at St Paul's Cathedral prefer the adjective *honestas* (honest) to *ydoneus*, which she defines as 'suitable', my survey of wills from the 1360s–1400 finds London merchants preferring the term 'idoneus'.

[49] Putnam, 'Maximum Wage-Laws', p. 13, notes the dispensations excusing ordinands from requirements of age, legitimacy, literacy and other traditional expectations. See also Zieman, *Singing the New Song*, pp. 102–4.

[50] Wood-Legh, *Perpetual Chantries*, pp. 93–9. On rising wages and imposed limits, see Putnam, 'Maximum Wage-Laws'.

[51] HR 77(59): si idem capellanus in aliquibus seruiciis diuinas predictus deficerit vel quoquo modo se absentauerit nisi fuerit causa infirmitatis extunc volo et ordino quod dicti parochiani et parsona capellanum predictum remoneant et alii loco suo presentent et instituent. For other clauses describing how patrons might deal with negligent chaplains, see Wood-Legh, *Perpetual Chantries*, pp. 84–90.

also demonstrate good manners and good behaviour (some examples follow below, and although other sources might lead us to assume that stipendiary priests would be the main targets for morality clauses, that is not always the case). Such stipulations give the lie to the assertion by the poet Chaucer's Pardoner that the moral status of the preacher matters little if the message is true.[52] Occasionally, if local churches could not elect a worthy chaplain, a testator would redirect funds entirely away from a particular parish church and toward a chantry at the Guildhall chapel or another location instead.[53] These testators clearly demand a worthy priest to execute their chantries, suggesting that although the term may have been formulaic, it was rooted in a very serious requirement. Such morality clauses for chaplains who cannot or will not perform their duties could be taken to indicate a concern about the quality of chantry priests, but conversely, they – and other contingency plans – may tell us more about the testator's abilities to plan or desire to control their legacy than about their distrust of an entire category of priests.[54]

Indeed, my survey of wills reveals that testators in the 1380s and 1390s are likely to specify that funds be spent on stipendiary priests or chaplains without cure of souls. On the one hand, this detail could be attributed to a testator's desire to ensure that the chantry would not take time away from the primary function of the rector or other parish priests.[55] However, during the times following earlier waves of the Black Death, when priests were in shorter supply, testators seemed unconcerned with whether their bequests might detract from everyday church business; they, like Richard Chaucer, simply sought a worthy chaplain. Perhaps the appearance of ad hoc religious labourers in wills results

---

[52] *Canterbury Tales*, VI, 459–60.

[53] For example, John Northampton, HR 126(118), makes bequests contingent upon recipients fulfilling his wishes, or the income will be redirected to the mayor and citizens of London to fund chantries at the Guildhall and perform charitable works. See also Rousseau, *Saving the Souls*, pp. 40–1.

[54] Rousseau, *Saving the Souls*, p. 41, cautions that such contingency plans in wills regarding chantry management do not necessarily indicate a lack of confidence in chantry supervisors but rather may illustrate a founder's desire to 'maintain some control over their foundation'. I tentatively suggest that contingency plans regarding chantry priests may be read similarly, as estate planning, not necessarily an indictment of chantry priests. Often testators with such contingency plans also have other elaborate plans for the transmission of their wealth to spouses (and others after the spouse dies), family members, apprentices and charitable institutions. Rousseau, *Saving the Souls*, pp. 34, 51–65, notes how wills became increasingly elaborate and individualized in their instructions for chaplains and others managing a chantry's endowment. See also Wood-Legh, *Perpetual Chantries*, pp. 65–92.

[55] Zieman, *Singing the New Song*, p. 95.

from a growing awareness among London merchants that there were underfunded, unbeneficed priests who could use the income.[56]

William Neuport, a prominent fishmonger and former Sheriff and Alderman, in 1390 provides £90 for 'quinque capellanis ydoneis' – five worthy chaplains – to celebrate mass for his soul and the souls of all the faithful departed for three years (£6 each, per year).[57] Neuport also leaves 40 pence for 'cuilibet capellano continue celebranti in eadem ecclesia *excepto rectore et meo proprie capellano*' (any chaplain continually celebrating in that church *except the rector and my own chaplain*).[58] Neuport is supporting worthy chaplains and rewarding celebrants who are not already provided for by the church (the rector) or by Neuport's other bequests (his 'own' chaplain), as are arguably the many other testators who identify unbeneficed chaplains as beneficiaries. Income might not be the only bequest, since late medieval people were becoming aware of the poor housing conditions for many clerks.[59] The knight William Walleworth (dated 1385) endows five 'idoneos capellanos et honestos' to chantries and then designates a tenement he owns in the parish to go to the rector and custodians of the church to provide a residence for the rector, the five chaplains occupying his chantries and other chaplains.[60]

---

[56] C. Burgess, '"For the Increase of Divine Service": Chantries in the Parish of Late Medieval Bristol', *Journal of Ecclesiastical History* 36 (1985), 46–65 (p. 65), suggests that parish clergy may even have encouraged endowments for chantries that would provide their community with 'auxiliary clergy' fully funded by parishioners. But see also J. Rosenthal, *The Purchase of Paradise: Gift Giving and the Aristocracy, 1307–1485* (London, 1972), p. 47, who acknowledges the possibility of conflicts between parish priests and chantry priests.

[57] As Tanner, *The Church in Late Medieval Norwich*, pp. 105–6, has observed, chantries were not 'wholly selfish' and tended to include the testator, his or her family, benefactors, friends and 'all the faithful departed'. See also Rosenthal, *Purchase of Paradise*, pp. 11–30.

[58] HR 119(121), emphasis mine. On Neuport, see A. P. Beaven, ed., *The Aldermen of the City of London Temp. Henry III*, 2 vols (London, 1908), I, 392.

[59] Kerby-Fulton, *Clerical Proletariat*, pp. 218–20.

[60] Walleworth leaves the management of the chantries and the property and rents that will fund them (he does not specify a pay rate) to his wife Margaret during her lifetime and then to the rector and wardens of the church after her death; accordingly, and rather sweetly, his chantry priests should also offer prayers for Margaret's well-being while she lives (pro bono statu eiusdem Margarete dum vixerit). HR 114(70): Item volo quod illud nonum tenementum in predicta parochia Sancti Michelis vbi rector eiusdem ecclesie et allii capellani per ordinacionem meam modo inhabitanti post decessum dicte Margarete remaneat presatis rectori dicte ecclesie Sancti Michelis et custodibus eiusdem ecclesie et eorum successoribus pro habitacione rectoris dicte ecclesie Sancti Michelis qui pro tempore fuerit et dictorum

Walleworth's gift looks beyond his personal spiritual benefit to improve the conditions for priests in his parish community.

According to criticisms of stipendiary priests, one might expect testators to be concerned with their character and fulfillment of their contract, which does occur sometimes, though it seems more common for long-term or perpetual chantries. For instance, Richard de Glemesford (dated 1384) establishes chantries for two worthy chaplains, one for three years and the other for four years, and he decrees that the chaplains be men of good reputation and character and of honest life, or they should be admonished and replaced.[61] In contrast, Simon atte Grene only specifies a worthy chaplain for his twenty-year chantry at 10 marks per year, with no stated terms for the chaplain's removal if needed (dated 1372, enrolled 1389).[62] Juliana Stokesby leaves £15, or 10 shillings each, to fund thirty priests to pray for 30 days after her death for her and her husband's souls, and she specifies that they be 'capellanis honestis qui non sunt curatoribus' (honest chaplains who do not have cure of souls) (dated 1383). Stokesby makes no provision for her short-term cantarists to be negligent, but she allots funds to establish a perpetual chantry, and she there lays out the expectations that 'unus ydoneus capellanus et honestus' be installed by her executors, expected to perform mass and the canonical hours for 10 marks per year and only be excused from his duties for legitimate causes (causa legitima).[63] Further, if he should behave perversely or with iniquity, live dishonestly, fail to serve the aforesaid souls faithfully in the said church or not hold the divine offices as he should, she decrees that he should be admonished and replaced.[64] Likewise, Gilbert atte Mershe (dated 1396) insists that the perpetual chantry he supplements be occupied by a chaplain who is honest of character and conducts himself kindly, and if he misbehave in any way or be reported of bad character or associations, he

---

    quinque capellanorum et aliorum capellanorum prout modo per me ordinatum est et diuisum.

[61] HR 114(22): Volens quod dicti capellani sunt viri bone fame et condicionis ac vite honeste … aut quod se male gesserit contra formam predictam … per executores meos amoneatur … et per eosdem alius capellanus ydoneum loco suo eligatur.

[62] HR 117(99).

[63] HR 112(131).

[64] HR 112(131): Et si capellanus perpetuus predictus peruerse se gesserit et habuerit iniquis aut vixerit inhoneste vel animabus predictis fideliter in dicta ecclesia non deseruerit aut diuinis officiis ibidem vt teneatur debite non interfuerit … volo quod ipsem … amoneatur ac cum appelacione et iuris remedie post positer penitus expellatur et quod eius loco alius capellanus ydoneus et honestius … est ponatur.

should be admonished and replaced.[65] John Fressh (dated 1397) similarly leaves funds to support an existing perpetual chantry but requires that the chaplain be of honest character and kind behaviour, then says that if said chaplain is reported to have behaved dishonestly, he should be admonished and replaced with a worthy chaplain; and if that *next* chaplain should fall short, he, too, should be admonished and replaced.[66] In Fressh's view, the perpetual chantry must be refreshed in perpetuity should any chantry priest fall short of expectations. The concern about whether chantry priests might fulfill their duties thus seems just as likely – if not more likely – to apply to longer-term positions that were like benefices yet not necessarily permanent, since occupants were clearly subject to potential removal.[67]

Some testators name specific priests to their chantries – a move that signals trust in that individual and also suggests a desire to support a friend or family member (though the relationship is rarely identified). Simon Wynchcombe has two separate wills, one covering his property that also earmarks funds for a chantry and one for other goods (dated 1395–6). In the first, he endows 12 marks per year to the perpetual chantry he had established in his lifetime, which is occupied by the chaplains John Wynchcombe and William Caldwell; only in the second document does he identify John Wynchcombe as his son, when he leaves 'my son John the chaplain' (Johanni filio meo capellano) a substantial number of household items or their monetary equivalent.[68] Wynchcombe is for good reason invested in keeping the chantry endowment

---

[65] HR 125(105): sit honeste condicionis et benigne se gerat … Et si huiusmodi capellanus se male gessert et inhoneste condicionis ac conuersacionis repertus fuerit volo et lego quod idem capellanus … amoneatur. The chandler Gilbert atte Mershe instructs the chaplain to pray for not only the souls of his family but also the souls of the vintner William Stokesby and his wife Juliana, whose will similarly addresses chaplain behaviour, suggesting that his will supplements both the funds and contract for the chantry.

[66] HR 127(64): Ita quod sit honeste condiciones et benigne se gerat et si huiusmodi capellanis se male gesserit et inhoneste condicionis et conuersacionis repertus fuerit volo ac lego quod idem capellanus … amoneatur et alius capellanus ydoneus loco suo eligatur quociens necesse fuerit. Fressh then repeats that if *this* next chaplain misbehaves, he should be admonished and replaced.

[67] Wood-Legh, *Perpetual Chantries*, pp. 84–9, notes that contractual chaplains might have wages withheld or be removed at any time for not fulfilling obligations and shows that perpetual chaplains could be removed by ecclesiastical authorities for not fulfilling the duties set out in the foundation deed. K. Veeman, 'John Shirley's Early Bureaucratic Career', *SAC* 38 (2016), 255–63 (pp. 256–9), outlines John Shirley's removal from benefices he held while a clerk in minor orders because he did not move on to the priesthood as required.

[68] HR 128(14) and HR 128(17).

healthy and attuned to the fact that his son may have more need of funds than household goods. William Thornhill (dated 1388) names John Boltoun to his three-year chantry, or another worthy chaplain if Boltoun is deceased – an example of a different contingency plan beyond those governing the moral character of the chaplain.[69] Maud Holbech names 'Roberto Saluen capellano meo' (Robert Saluen, my chaplain) to a seven-year chantry for 10 marks per year but adds 'vel alio capellano honesto in loco suo constituto in casu quo ipse obeirit' (or another honest chaplain appointed in his place in case he dies). Knyghtcote names Ralph Archer to his perpetual chantry for 'totam vitam suam' (all his life) with instructions for his replacement should Archer become infirm.[70] For Wynchcombe and Holbech, the close relationship between benefactor and chaplain is explicitly acknowledged, but a similar relationship can be posited for other testators who name specific chaplains to posts. And these chantry positions are independent of outright gifts to chaplains, which may also have supplemented their income, separate from their chantry duties.[71]

For shorter term chantries or prayers, testators seem to have little concern about stipendiary clerics' fulfillment of duties. Former London mayor John Northampton requests that the prior and religious community charged with maintaining a two-year chantry for him 'eligant et recipiant duos capellanos vel alios duos clericos *non ordinatos*' (elect and receive two chaplains or other clerks *not ordained*).[72] Margery Broun's will (dated 1376) leaves 12 pence for 'cuilibet capellano *stipiendiario*' (any *stipendiary* chaplain) celebrating at her tomb.[73] Christine Coggere (dated 1384) leaves 3 shillings, 4 pence to three

---

[69] HR 116(98): Item lego executoribus meis viginti libras sterlingorum ad inueniendo dominum Johannem Boltoun capellanum divina celebrante in dicta ecclesia pro anima mea et animabus quibus teneor per tres annos prox post decessum meum vt alii ydoneum capellanum si idem Johannes Boltoun infra dictum tempus obierit.

[70] HR 112(08).

[71] I have attempted to keep separate these gifts, much as Simon Wynchcombe did, since gifts may be interpreted as recognition of past services as well as implicit hopes for future remembrances. For instance, Thomas Chapman, in 1394, HR 125(67) leaves money for any priest celebrating in his church except Adam Brekespere, one of his executors to whom he leaves 26 shillings and 8 pence, which I interpret as either as an outright gift or as payment for his labour as executor, not his labour as priest. William Thorp, in HR 125(71), dated 1391, leaves £10 a year to Henry Hamond his chaplain (capellano meo) and entrusts Henry to be an executor and to distribute bows and arrows among servants; he also refers to a Lawrence as 'capellano meo' and leaves him 100 shillings a year (cf. Sharpe's summary in *Cal. Wills* II, 326).

[72] HR 126(118), my emphasis.

[73] HR 109(89), my emphasis. This classification of 'stipendiary' is the exact Marxist definition of the proletariat category, which led mid-twentieth-century British

named chaplains of her church, then 20 pence to 'cuilibet *alii* capellano stipendario' celebrating in the church.[74] The bequest to 'any *other* stipendiary chaplain' suggests that the three priests she named could be gig workers themselves in addition to others she might know less well but still recognizes as essential parts of her parish community. Similar formulations of 'cuilibet capellano stipendario' also appear in the wills of John Halfmark (HR 116–119, dated 1386), Alice Wodegate (HR 117–44, dated 1387), John Strousburgh (HR 117–101, dated 1388), Philip atte Vyne (HR 125–85, dated 1396) and John Clapshethe (HR 126–116, dated 1397) – usually for celebrations at the time of the testator's death. Robert Warwyk (dated 1388) leaves funds to 'cuilibet capellano stipendario et annuylario [*sic*]' (any stipendiary chaplain and annueller).[75] Why recognize the role of the stipendiary priest or annueller at all unless they were becoming far more common, recognizable and respected in the community?[76]

More than one testator leaves money to anyone except the vicar or rector, indirectly perhaps channelling funds to stipendiary priests.[77] John Besouthe (dated 1380) leaves money to the high altar of his parish church, then leaves 12 pence to 'cuilibet capellano continue diuina celebranti in eadem ecclesia *vicario ibidem excepto* ad orando specialiter pro anima mea in diuinis oracionibus suis' (any chaplain continually celebrating holy services in that church *except the vicar* for praying especially for my soul in his holy prayers).[78] John Gille (dated 1380) devotes £21 sterling to establish a chantry at the church of St Christopher for three years, requiring 'unum capellanum bonum probum ydoneum' (one good, honest, worthy chaplain), adding 'et intentio mea est quod capellanus taliter celebraturus sit bone conuersacionis et pro homine bono et laudabilis consciencie reputatus et ex ea causa sibi legam ultra commune stipendium viginti solidi' (and it is my intention that the chaplain

---

historians to adopt the name 'clerical proletariat'; see Kerby-Fulton, *Clerical Proletariat*, pp. 1–25, for an in-depth analysis of the clerical underclass that draws on the work of W. A. Pantin, N. P. Tanner, A. K. McHardy, T. A. R. Evans and others.

[74] HR 113(58), my emphasis.

[75] HR 117(92).

[76] See also Tanner, *The Church in Late Medieval Norwich*, pp. 107–10, who suggests that secular, unbeneficed clerks even seem to have been *preferred* among parish members of a later generation, based on their over-representation in wills.

[77] The category of vicar was also complex: see Kerby-Fulton, *Clerical Proletariat*, pp. 3–5, 163–4, and Zieman, *Singing the New Song*, pp. 62–72. I have not considered vicars or vicars choral because the categories could be too ambiguous (as Zieman, pp. 70–1, points out), and the wills are too vague to hazard a guess as to the role of vicars named.

[78] HR 111(71), my emphasis.

who will celebrate thus be of good character and regarded as a good man and of a praiseworthy conscience, and for that reason, I will bequeath to him 20 shillings beyond the common stipend).[79] In other words, Gille sought to pay above the expected rate for an outstanding chantry chaplain, even though wage laws discouraged such incentives.[80]

Other wills show signs that testators knew that their gifts provided livelihoods for the priests in question. In this way, they emphasize the people involved in the liturgical contract, which, as Zieman puts it, 'guarded against the commodification of masses'.[81] That is, bequests to chantry chaplains were not necessarily one-sided gifts designed exclusively to benefit the testator and souls for whom the chaplain performed his chantry duties; they were also recognized as supporting the chaplain himself. Such a conclusion may be implied when testators specify a named priest or refer to someone as 'my own priest', as testators like those noted above regularly did. But other testators remove any doubt. John Tours (dated 1386) allots a remainder from certain properties to a church rector and the perpetual chaplain Nicholas Oundell to augment a chantry named for William and Isabelle Bukerell.[82] He then explicitly stipulates: 'Et ita quod predictus capellanus qui pro tempore sic fuerit non recipiat aliud salarium quouismodo nisi solummodo de predicta cantaria huius autem testimenti constituo executores meos ... ad ministrando et exequendo hoc testamentum meum in forma pronotata' (And to the extent that the aforesaid chaplain who for the time being shall not receive any salary in any way except from the aforesaid chantry of this testament, moreover, I appoint my executors to administer and execute this my testament in the form proscribed).[83] The implication is that Tours's executors must follow his wishes to the letter because the chaplain's livelihood – not just his unbroken stream of prayers – depends on it. One might read between the lines to see a similar sentiment underpinning the will of Gilbert atte Mershe, which leaves a messuage to the parson and wardens of a church to establish a perpetual chantry, then immediately advises them to manage the property 'competenter'

---

[79] HR 109(67).

[80] Again, the intention of the testator is more important than whether it could be fulfilled. As Putnam, 'Maximum Wage-Laws', p. 22, notes, the maximum wage set for cantarists in 1378 was 7 marks per year, which is less than the £7 per year plus bonus that Gille intended.

[81] Zieman, *Singing the New Song*, p. 95.

[82] The Bukerells lived in the thirteenth century, and as Bohne, 'Networks of Influence', shows, Isabelle was likely involved in what today might be termed a common-law partnership with her chaplain.

[83] HR 115(42).

(competently), since competent management would ensure the property's ability to generate funding for the chantry and its occupant (dated 1396).[84]

Geoffrey Maynard (dated 1386) leaves one part of his estate 'ad sustentacionem tercium capellanorum honestorum' (for the maintenance of three honest chaplains) to celebrate for 'quam diu illa pars monete sufficere poterit et extender' (so long as that part of the money will be able to provide and continue).[85] John Walssh (dated 1384) instructs John Prentice to use funds from property to install a chantry priest for ten years, then adds that if Prentice successfully maintains the priest for that term, then Walssh wishes for the property to be sold and all the money spent to support a(nother?) chaplain in the same church to pray for his soul 'dum diu durare et extendere poterit' (as long as it may last and continue).[86] These London merchants recognized that their wishes were contingent upon the market, and they wished to fund chantry priests for as long as possible – not only for the sake of prayers but potentially also in recognition of the same instability of income for clerics that led John Tours to advocate for attentive administration of his property. Certainly, funding prayers always indicated a testator's desire to reap spiritual benefits, but in some cases, it seems reasonable to consider testators as financing community clerks who may not have had other paths to secure income.

Conclusion

Literary texts by Langland, Hoccleve, Audelay and others alert readers to the laments of the unbeneficed clerk and underfunded student, as Kathryn Kerby-Fulton has so adroitly shown, even when they acknowledge the potential moral problems among this group.[87] Medieval poets were acutely aware of the whole spectrum of moral types who might seek a clerical career, and their views soften the ecclesiastical records that often lean more heavily toward criticism of the clerical underclass.[88] The wills of London merchants give us the additional perspectives of lay men and women who drew on their experiences with parish priests, chaplains and chantry priests in their daily lives. My

---

[84] HR 125(105). On the importance of managing the endowment, see Rousseau, *Saving the Souls*, pp. 33–66.

[85] HR 115(126).

[86] HR 113(32).

[87] Although the entire book is concerned with these broader questions, Kerby-Fulton, *Clerical Proletariat*, pp. 300–4, outlines the broad characteristic attitudes of these literary authors.

[88] Wood-Legh, *Perpetual Chantries*, pp. 189–95, focuses on negative poetic and ecclesiastical portraits.

preliminary conclusions suggest that some London merchants in the 1380s and 1390s recognized the precarity of students and the clerical proletariat, and they took measures, through chantry foundation, bequests and charitable donations to support friends, family and unknown men who had chosen clerical paths. Less interested in critiquing the establishment or particular stereotypes than clerical proletariat authors were, many merchants were committed to endowing temporary or long-term positions to support individuals from their community or other worthy unbeneficed clerks. Institutions such as the Church and government may have been slow to develop alternative models for funding unbeneficed clerks, but it appears that the charity of late medieval Londoners may have mitigated the crisis for at least some underfunded individuals.

10

Langland's Government Scribes at Home and at Work: A Brief Comparison of the HM 114 Scribe and the Fortescue Family

KARRIE FULLER

At one point in the 2010s, Kathryn served on the committees of well over a dozen graduate students. She left us all bewildered. How did she manage to devote so much care and energy to each person, engaging in deep conversations through full days of lengthy in-person appointments and generating copious feedback on draft after draft of dissertation chapters, articles and job materials? Not one of us ever felt short changed, and that mystery remains a part of her legacy. Although probably the most generous human on the planet, she appears to have hoarded this particular superpower for herself, for which we are all grateful.[1]

It is to another indisputable legacy of Kathryn's that the current essay turns, namely her scholarship on civil service scribes generally and, more specifically, their involvement in creating two *Piers Plowman* manuscripts: San Marino, CA, Huntington Library, MS HM 114 and Oxford, Bodleian Library, MS Digby 145.[2] Although unlikely companions for a focused case study, these

---

[1] Little in this world could match Kathryn's love for her students, but William Langland's *Piers Plowman*, manuscripts, William Blake and ballet stand out. I will leave the admirable Blake and the art of dance aside here out of a healthy respect for my own lack of expertise on those subjects. However, *Piers* and manuscripts I joyfully take up. And, although lesser known among medievalists, Kathryn's essays on ballet are listed in her bibliography at the end of this volume.

[2] For decades now, the importance of civil service scribes in the transmission history of *Piers Plowman* has been a prominent theme in Langland scholarship. For a mere handful of examples, see K. Kerby-Fulton, M. Hilmo and L. Olson, *Opening Up Middle English Manuscripts: Literary and Visual Approaches* (Ithaca, 2012); L. R. Mooney and E. Stubbs, *Scribes and the City: London Guildhall Clerks and the Dissemination of Middle English Literature 1374–1425* (York, 2013); S. Horobin, 'The scribe of Bodleian Library MS Digby 102 and the circulation of the C Text of *Piers Plowman*', *YLS* 24 (2010), 89–112; L. R. Mooney and S. Horobin, 'A *Piers*

two books, each strange amalgamations of William Langland's multiple distinct versions of the poem, reinforce Derek Pearsall's point that 'there are no texts that were not embedded in the machinery of their production'.[3] In other words, HM 114 and Digby 145 provide a glimpse into how the unique historical contexts of individual manuscripts shape their production and character, engraving indelible marks on the scribal and reader responses evidenced in their carefully editorialized leaves.[4] In this case, the scribes in question work in legal occupations, lending their services to the government and guilds, and are all therefore connected, in various capacities, to national and city governance. As a result, I argue that this professional and political backdrop influences how and why these scribes share certain reformist tendencies as they express perspectives also adopted by Digby 145's other annotators. The different religious climates of their respective historical contexts put different pressures on these scribes and readers that caused their related but separate strains

---

Plowman Manuscript by the Hengwrt/Ellesmere Scribe and its Implications for London Standard English', *SAC* 26 (2004), 65–112; and L. R. Mooney, 'Chaucer's Scribe', *Speculum* 81 (2006), 97–138. Most recently, K. Kerby-Fulton emphasizes these concerns in *The Clerical Proletariat and the Resurgence of Medieval English Poetry* (Philadelphia, 2021). While not all the scribes treated in this study worked in the formal 'civil service' (in its strictest sense), they all held 'civil' (in its broader sense) positions that placed them in and around the Guildhall and other City offices, if not in direct employment of the king.

[3] D. Pearsall, 'The Text of *Piers Plowman*: Past, Present, and Future', *Poetica* 71 (2009), 75–92 (p. 87). Langland had quite the following in London, but clerks as far as the Dublin Exchequer in Ireland also participated in *Piers*'s transmission history, as seen in Oxford, Bodleian Library, MS Douce 104; see K. Kerby-Fulton and D. L. Despres, *Iconography and the Professional Reader: The Politics of Book Production in the Douce Piers Plowman* (Minneapolis, 1999).

[4] To preserve the integrity of the relationship between the scribal responses embedded in these highly editorialized copies of *Piers* and recorded in the marginal annotations, all passages quoted here are transcribed from the manuscripts themselves but cross-referenced with A. V. C. Schmidt, ed., *Piers Plowman: A Parallel-Text Edition of the A, B, C, and Z Versions*, 2nd ed., 2 vols (Kalamazoo, 2011). An edition of the HM 114 annotations appears in C. D. Benson and L. Blanchfield, *The Manuscripts of Piers Plowman: The B-Version* (Cambridge, 1997), pp. 232–4. An edition of the Digby 145 annotations appears in M. Uhart, 'The Early Reception of *Piers Plowman*' (unpublished Ph.D. dissertation, University of Leicester, 1986). Overall, Uhart makes a valuable contribution to Langland studies, but occasional misattributions of Hand B and Adrian Fortescue occur. For a full account of the A- and C-text passages in HM 114's B-text base, see G. H. Russell and V. Nathan, 'A *Piers Plowman* Manuscript in the Huntington Library', *Huntington Library Quarterly* 26.2 (1963), 119–30.

of reformism to emerge, especially when it concerns an acutely problematic group in Langland's text: the friars.

The Manuscripts: Reading *Piers* in Time and Place

Throughout this first quarter of the twenty-first century, the HM 114 scribe has risen to a new level of stardom in the world of Middle English scholarship because he copied so many popular late medieval texts and worked at the centre of the London book trade. HM 114 alone contains such bestsellers as *Piers Plowman*, Geoffrey Chaucer's *Troilus and Criseyde* and *The Book of John Mandeville*, with three shorter, complementary works interposed among the longer ones – *Susannah*, an excerpt from the *Three Kings of Cologne* and the *Epistola Luciferi ad Clericos*.[5] If, as Linne Mooney and Estelle Stubbs have argued on the basis of paleography, the scribe was the civil servant Richard Osbarn, he would have worked alongside Scribe D (possibly John Marchaunt), Adam Pinkhurst and their many other colleagues in and around the Guildhall, Westminster and insular government offices.[6] As A. I. Doyle has shown, the same hand is found in Letter Book I, a record of business related to the City of London, and in the *Liber Albus*, John Carpenter's compilation of city regulations, so regardless of his identity, the scribe was connected to the Guildhall and some of the City's most important documentary records.[7] Therefore, HM 114, although probably not originally intended for the London book trade, participates in an urban literary culture in which Langland's work

---

[5] Langland's early editors rejected HM 114 because it strays too far from the poem's authorial origins, but more recent interest in scribes and readers has led to foundational studies. On HM 114's background, compilation, literary value and paleographical significance, see R. Hanna III, 'The Scribe of Huntington HM 114', *Studies in Bibliography* 42 (1989), 120–33. Mooney and Stubbs, *Scribes and the City*, pp. 17–37, offer a thorough paleographical study of HM 114. K. Kerby-Fulton, 'Major Middle English Poets and Manuscript Studies, 1300–1450', in *Opening Up*, pp. 39–94 (pp. 65–78), addresses the connection between HM 114 and the Ilchester manuscript. See also J. Bowers, 'Two Professional Readers of Chaucer and Langland: Scribe D and the HM 114 Scribe', *SAC* 26 (2004), 113–46; and J. Thorne, 'Updating *Piers Plowman* Passus 3: An Editorial Agenda in Huntington Library MS HM 114', *YLS* 20 (2006), 67–92.

[6] Mooney and Stubbs, *Scribes and the City*, pp. 17–37; for doubts that nevertheless connect the HM 114 scribe strongly to City and Guildhall productions, see L. Warner, *Chaucer's Scribes: London Textual Production, 1384–1432* (Cambridge, 2018), pp. 72–95.

[7] On Doyle's attributions, see R. Hanna and D. Lawton, eds, *The Siege of Jerusalem*, EETS OS 320 (Oxford, 2003), p. xxii; Horobin and Mooney, 'A *Piers Plowman* Manuscript', p. 99 n. 72; and Mooney and Stubbs, *Scribes and the City*, p. 27.

was popular.[8] This scribe's early fifteenth-century copy, moreover, contains a one-of-a-kind combination of A-, B- and C-text passages likely revised, at least in part, by the scribe himself.[9] The scribe's editorialization coupled with his annotations, which Sarah Wood suggests might derive from manuscript exemplars, reveal a thorough and detail-oriented engagement with the poem, as many scholars, notably Ralph Hanna, have observed.[10]

Given *Piers*'s reputation as a London poem with a strong transmission history connected to scribes with government jobs, it is perhaps not surprising that over a century later, in 1532, at least one government employee with connections to the London court produced his own copy of Langland's work in Digby 145. Although less well known than the HM 114 scribe, Adrian Fortescue (*c*. 1481–1539) lived a life that, as far as the limited documentary evidence suggests, would make a most intriguing historical drama on Netflix or HBO.[11] Fortescue was a distant relative of Anne Boleyn and a loyal Catholic, who was employed for a time by Henry VIII's court, served on various county commissions and later served as a justice of the peace in Oxfordshire.

---

[8] R. Hanna, *London Literature, 1300–1380* (Cambridge, 2005).

[9] P. R. Bart, 'Intellect, Influence, and Evidence: The Elusive Allure of the Ht Scribe', in *'Yee? Baw for Bokes': Essays on Medieval Manuscripts and Poetics in Honor of Hoyt N. Duggan*, ed. M. Calabrese and S. H. A. Shepherd (Los Angeles, 2013), pp. 219–43, examines the French quotations as evidence of the scribe's responsibility for editorializing.

[10] See Hanna, 'The Scribe of Huntington HM 114'. For an argument that the annotations in HM 114 loosely resemble those of genetically related manuscripts, see S. Wood, *Piers Plowman and Its Manuscript Tradition* (Woodbridge, 2022), pp. 154–85. If Wood's theory is correct, these annotations should be read as more of a collaborative effort between the HM 114 scribe and his predecessors. In this case, the scribe exerted his editorial authority when collecting and copying his set of annotations to create the version that best reflects his intentions. For such an active revisionist, it would hardly seem likely that this scribe blindly copied annotations, but rather that he avidly incorporated them into his larger strategy of combining as much material from as many versions of the poem as he could, a habit pointed out by Wood, *Manuscript Tradition*, and Hanna, *London Literature*, among others.

[11] R. Rex, 'Blessed Adrian Fortescue: A Martyr without a Cause?', *Analecta Bollandiana* 115 (1997), 307–53, reconstructs Fortescue's life through excellent documentary research that provides additional context for his scribal activity. See also T. Turville-Petre, 'Sir Adrian Fortescue and His Copy of *Piers Plowman*', *YLS* 14 (2000), 29–48. The reading community evidenced in Digby 145 receives more detailed exploration in K. Fuller, 'Langland in the Early Modern Household: *Piers Plowman* in Oxford, Bodleian Library, MS Digby 145 and Its Scribe-Annotator Dialogues', in *New Directions in Medieval Manuscript Studies and Reading Practices: Essays in Honor of Derek Pearsall*, ed. K. Kerby-Fulton, J. J. Thompson and S. Baechle (Notre Dame IN, 2014), pp. 324–41.

He endured a life punctuated by war as a young knight fighting in France (in 1513, 1522 and 1523), by years of lawsuits as a widower with (angry?) in-laws out to recover lands that belonged to his first wife Anne Stonor (d. 1418) and by (unfair?) arrests and imprisonment as the father-in-law of the rebellious Irish Earl of Kildare (1534–6). Ultimately, he was executed in 1539, according to a Bill of Attainder, for 'dyvers and sundry detestable and abhomynable treasons'.[12] But what treason did Fortescue commit? Did he possess an unrecorded rebellious streak? Or had he simply run afoul of the capricious Henry VIII on a bad day? We know so much more about Fortescue's personal life than the majority of Langland's copyists and yet not nearly enough. We do know, however, that he made a copy of *Piers* and that, as Kathryn Kerby-Fulton discovered, his second, much younger wife Anne Rede helped annotate this manuscript alongside another unknown annotator, Hand B, potentially a blood relative or close family friend.[13]

Coincidentally, these two scribes with connections to London, performing different kinds of legal work for the government, both produced copies of *Piers* most likely intended for personal use by themselves and a small group of readers.[14] However, despite the broad similarities between these scribal contexts, it should not come as a surprise that these manuscripts reflect different reader responses because of their individual historical contexts, which shaped the personal situations of their readers. Unlike the HM 114 scribe, who might have copied his manuscript for a small London audience, Fortescue intended for his manuscript to remain within his household. Moreover, since Fortescue copied and annotated his version of *Piers* (a unique A- and C-text combination) in the years leading up to the Reformation, the turbulent religious climate that led to some of the instability in his own life created a different political context for his work. In both cases, however, these scribes'

---

[12] Quoted in Rex, 'Blessed Adrian', p. 333; Rex, 'Fortescue, Sir Adrian', *ODNB*. Chief Justice of the Bench, Sir John Fortescue (*c.* 1397–1479), was brother to Adrian Fortescue's grandfather Richard.

[13] K. Kerby-Fulton, 'The Women Readers in Langland's Earliest Audience: Some Codicological Evidence', in *Learning and Literacy in Medieval England and Abroad*, ed. S. Rees Jones (Turnhout, 2003), pp. 121–34.

[14] For ideas about the intentions behind the HM 114 scribe's work, see N. Phillips, 'Compilational Reading: Richard Osbarn and Huntington Library MS HM 114', *YLS* 28 (2014), 65–104; Kerby-Fulton, 'Major Middle English Poets', pp. 65–78 and Mooney and Stubbs, *Scribes and the City*, pp. 17–37. There are alternative views as well, but this essay emphasizes the original use rather than the possible later uses for HM 114. Adrian Fortescue's home was in Oxfordshire, but he spent significant time in London at the king's court. Both scribes held different kinds of legal positions, but both served in offices tied to the royal and/or City government.

professional relationship to London government concerns informed how they read Langland's poem. Thus, while the HM 114 scribe revises and annotates his copy to emphasize themes related to work around the Guildhall and in Westminster – mercantilism, documentary culture, the London setting and the king's court – Fortescue and his family read it for more private and theological reasons related to the household, apocalypticism and ecclesiastical reform.[15] Yet, despite reading from disparate historical contexts, these readers' interests in social order, 'inter-clerical polemics' and, oddly enough, marriage and Elde (Old Age) do overlap.[16] The evolution of the reader responses evidenced in the editorialized and annotated versions of *Piers* found in HM 114 and Digby 145 reveal not only the obvious variation caused by the historical gap between them but also the inherent influence of these scribes' professional versus private motives on the physical appearance and textual character of their wholly unique books.

As a result of these scribes' overlapping but distinct readings of *Piers*, their reformist concerns, particularly when it comes to friars, often look quite similar as they express interest in some of the same controversial passages. These concerns begin to take on a different colour, however, when considered within the historical context of each manuscript's editorialized text. Noelle Phillips argues that across the HM 114 manuscript's texts, the evident brand of anticlericalism, which could also be called inter-clerical debate, is at least partly indebted to the Lollard movement. Whether this scribe is specifically a Lollard or not, I agree that HM 114's copy of the *Epistola Luciferi* indicates

---

[15] To clarify, my concern here relates to the copy of *Piers* in HM 114 as read and produced by this active scribe, who chose what and where to copy materials from his multiple exemplars while creating a version of *Piers* that matched his intentions and interests, rather than to the possibility that Wood, *Manuscript Tradition*, pp. 154–85, raises about the annotations' potential transmission from previous exemplars. To what extent this scribe produced original versus copied responses remains a question worthy of continued inquiry, but the final product results from the many decisions the scribe made as a copyist, editor and even revisor, roles we know he assumed even if the details remain a bit murky.

[16] On anticlericalism and inter-clerical polemic, see K. Kerby-Fulton, M. Mayus and K. A.-M. Bugyis, '"Anticlericalism", Inter-Clerical Polemic and Theological Vernaculars', in *The Oxford Handbook to Chaucer*, ed. S. Akbari (Oxford, 2020), pp. 494–526. In short, inter-clerical polemics are produced by clerical employees of the Church who express their dissatisfaction with other ecclesiastical orders; anticlerical discourses are created by lay men and women who express their dissatisfaction with clerics. Both attitudes are at play in HM 114 and Digby 145, whose texts include inter-clerical debates but are produced, read and engaged by lay readers.

the work of a reform-minded intellectual.[17] Influenced by a different series of historical forces, Digby 145's reformist perspectives reflect tensions caused by competing religious groups, including those led by Henry before and during the English Reformation. Both temporally distant readerships highlight problems with Church administration, especially corruption within the higher ranks and among the friars. However, Digby 145's readers display a greater theological engagement with certain abstract concepts, like charity, and their responses reflect a much greater emotional investment in the poem as well.[18] Such extensive interest in subjects like charity contrasts with the HM 114 scribe, who expresses no direct concern with charity or related theological themes in the corresponding B-text passages.[19]

Additionally, taking a step back to view these copies of *Piers* within the context of their larger codices adds depth to our understanding of these scribes' readerly preoccupations. Because of HM 114's compilational character, with its wide range of Middle English bestsellers, the scribe's interests are dispersed across multiple texts that form their own intertextual dialogue through their collection in a single bound volume. Fortescue's Digby 145 reflects an investment in texts more focused on household interests in his personalized copy of *Piers*, the treatise *On the Governance of England* by John Fortescue (Adrian Fortescue's great uncle, which adds to the book's familial character) and some proverbs at the end.[20] The domestic quality of the volume contrasts with some of the larger issues taken up in HM 114. The HM 114 scribe's compilation, and especially his *Piers-Mandeville* pairing, evidences a broader,

---

[17] See Phillips, 'Compilational Reading', and W. Scase, '"Let him be kept in most strait prison": Lollards and the *Epistola Luciferi*', in *Freedom of Movement in the Middle Ages*, ed. P. Horden (Donington, 2007), pp. 57–72. It is unknown whether the HM 114 scribe copied or produced the *Epistola*'s translation.

[18] The HM 114 scribe may have felt emotionally invested, but, if so, he did not display it as openly in the evidence left behind as did the annotations in Digby 145.

[19] The HM 114 scribe annotates passages about money in Passus 15, both in relation to wealth and especially poverty, but he never annotates any mention of charity itself. The closest annotation near a mention of charity is 'lw' next to 'I haue lyuyd in lond quod y my name is longe wille / & fand y neuer ful charite byfor ne behynd' (HM 114, fol. 9v, at B.15.152). The annotation – surely identifying 'Longe Wille' – points to a primary interest in the narrator. Thus, while much of Passus 15 discusses the theological concept of charity, the HM 114 scribe connects instead to the text's narrator and broader discussion of wealth and poverty.

[20] The treatise occurs on fols. 133–59, the proverbs on fols. 160–1. For the treatise and its author, see *Sir John Fortescue: On the Laws and Governance of England*, ed. S. Lockwood (Cambridge, 1997); and J. Simpson, 'Reginald Pecock and John Fortescue', in *A Companion to Middle English Prose*, ed. A. S. G. Edwards (Cambridge, 2010), pp. 271–88.

outward-looking perspective that engages with global and international questions as well as national and local issues. While the scribe might have copied them for personal use, his pairing explores questions about his own nation on a global platform. Together, these two manuscripts show just how much compilational practices can affect the overall character of a manuscript as well as how codicological context can influence readers' interpretations of the same text. Even though both audiences care about issues of national importance, the HM 114 scribe's interest in geography, history and romance does not carry over into Digby 145's more personal perspectives. While inter-clerical polemics appear in the opening and closing texts of HM 114, they do not constitute an overarching theme among all the collected texts. Anticlericalism as expressed by Digby 145's lay readers, however, has a greater presence because *Piers* fills most of the physical space in that volume. The historical gap and the longer view of government scribes afforded by these two examples adds perspective when paired together, and the contrast, at least as much as their commonalities, bring the issues they raise into sharper focus.

Antimendicant Sentiment and Langland's Government Audience

As mentioned above, despite the many contextual differences between HM 114 and Digby 145, both manuscripts exhibit a scribal interest in anticlerical or inter-clerical debates that include some overlapping activity around antimendicant passages in *Piers*.[21] In their respective political and religious contexts, however, Adrian Fortescue and the HM 114 scribe experienced different kinds of external pressures that shaped the precise nature of their anticlerical sentiments. For the Fortescue household, these pressures entered their home and their private lives, meaning that they had more at stake in the political and religious crises of their day, and Fortescue's execution suggests just how serious the stakes were. In many ways, Fortescue's book emphasizes religious and reformist themes to a much greater extent than the HM 114 anthology. Even though reformist arguments like those found in the Lollard movement caused their own set of divisive and dangerous reactions in England, owning and even copying controversial texts did not necessarily lead to serious or life-threatening consequences.[22] HM 114 makes no attempt to

---

[21] In other words, antimendicancy is only one strain of anticlerical and inter-clerical polemic in these manuscripts, not the sole source of their attention.

[22] On Wyclif and Lollardy, see A. Hudson, *Studies in the Transmission of Wyclif's Writings* (Farnham, 2008), especially 'Wyclif Texts in Fifteenth-Century London' and 'The Survival of Wyclif's Works in England and Bohemia' (nos. xv and xvi); and

censor the reformist language of *Piers* and its Middle English translation of the *Epistola*, and the scribe shows no signs of concern over its content. However, remaining Catholic after Henry VIII's break from Rome, especially for a gentry family associated with the court, would have been unquestionably dangerous. Fortescue and his family would have experienced the external pressures of the Reformation, much of which came straight from the Crown, differently than the HM 114 scribe's experience with fourteenth-century controversies being debated under different political circumstances.[23]

As a result of these historical influences, interrogations of political and religious corruption enter each scribe's copy of *Piers* in unique ways. Fortescue, for instance, does not deal as extensively with documentary culture and the London government offices as the HM 114 scribe, which makes sense because not all of his government positions were located in London and because he wrote for his household, rather than within the context of his workplace. Although a great deal changes between the HM 114 scribe's London context and Digby 145's Reformation era, these two historically distant copies reflect a persistent interest in Langland's work as well as the adaptability of *Piers* for audiences with diverse concerns. While these scribes maintain a general interest in anticlericalism, they also reveal particular antimendicant attitudes at the end of the poem. Friars probably constitute Fortescue's strongest source of anticlerical sentiment, and while the HM 114 scribe spends much less time revising later passūs, he annotates some passages with anticlerical themes, and friars become a prominent subject in his marginal commentary in later narrative events.[24] Moreover, some of the annotations made by these two scribes, although produced independently of each other, appear next to the same passages, or even the same lines, strengthening the connections between their interpretations of the poem.

F. Somerset, 'Censorship', in *The Production of Books in England, 1350–1500*, ed. A. Gillespie and D. Wakelin (Cambridge, 2014), pp. 239–58. Although Hudson and Somerset discuss Lollard literature, there were many types of reformist thought in England, and HM 114 contains no definitive evidence of Lollardy, despite the reformist tendencies in *Piers* and the *Epistola*.

[23] See Rex, 'Fortescue, Sir Adrian'; it has been proposed that Fortescue's arrest in 1534 may have involved uncertainty about Henry VIII's role as head of the Church of England, and his inclusion in the act of attainder of 1539 suggests a possible connection to the papacy's movements against Henry. Regardless of Fortescue's personal spirituality, his association with the court exposed him to the pressures of the Reformation.

[24] In HM 114's A-, B- and C- text amalgamation, the A material naturally runs out roughly halfway through the poem, but even the scribe's C interpolations decrease in quantity as the narrative wears on.

Before examining the final passūs in these manuscripts (Passus 20 of the B version and Passus 22 of C), it is important to note the overarching antimendicant sentiment present *throughout* both copies of the poem. These final annotations, therefore, function as the culmination (in some of Langland's juicier passages) of these scribes' antimendicant interests rather than as an isolated occurrence. Fortescue, and his fellow annotator Hand B as well, notes 'freres' often throughout Digby 145, and this word's recurrence makes it as prominent an issue for these two scribes as more personal topics like marriage.[25] Writing 'freres' or a 'nota' in the margins calls attention to one of Langland's most overtly criticized groups; while either could function as a neutral annotation, neutrality feels improbable, especially considering the harsh judgments of friars leveraged in these passages. Fortescue, a Catholic contemplating friars in a period of reformation when they would indubitably be perceived as a problem to be solved, picks up on the continued relevance and significance of Langland's arguments. While the HM 114 scribe's *nota* marks next to passages on friars occur less frequently, they pop up repeatedly in places where he introduces antimendicant content from the C text into his base text. For example, he notes covetous friars in Passus 10 where he adds lines from Passus 5 of the C text: 'And Constantyn shal be koke & couerer of her cherchis / þan freris in þe froytour shul fyndyn a key'.[26] He similarly interpolates a passage on friars from Passus 12 of the C text into his Passus 11: 'For þe frère flaterid me while he fond me riche / Now that y am penyles at litel pris he me settiþ'.[27] In these examples, not only does he introduce references to friars from the C text, but he also places *nota* marks by them to draw attention to these antimendicant ideas, providing a consistent thematic thread throughout. This antimendicant thread, moreover, supports Phillips's argument about the more general anticlerical attitudes present in HM 114. The scribe extends his overt government and documentary interests into a religious context; his interpolated text and annotations highlight and supplement Langland's text about religious law.

Langland casts friars in their most negative role at the end of his narrative when they become some of the Antichrist's most loyal followers, destroying the Church from within it. Their poor behaviour intersects with England's

---

[25] A few examples of his 'freres' annotations include Digby 145, fol. 3r, at Schmidt A.Pr.55; fol. 13r, at Schmidt A.2.172 and 191(annotated by both Fortescue and Hand B); Digby 145, fol. 82v, at Schmidt C.16.288.

[26] HM 114, fol. 62r records 'Prophecia' next to Schmidt C.5.174-5 in Passus 10 of the B text.

[27] HM 114, fol. 65r. The *nota* is next to Schmidt C.12.25-26 in Passus 11 of the B text. He also annotates friars at B.Pr.58 and at B.14.200 among other places.

legal culture and affects the London government in the passages annotated by both Fortescue and the HM 114 scribe. The final section of the poem shows Fortescue reading, at times, like the HM 114 scribe for legal, documentary issues. For Fortescue, this series of annotations constitutes a small part of his extensive running commentary on friars reinforced by his successor, Hand B, but for the HM 114 scribe, these annotations make up a substantial portion of his overall antimendicant commentary. For both scribes, the key themes noted include the impact of the friars' greed on the wider English community, the consequences of this greed for political and religious legal culture and the way that the friars' performance of false confessions maintains both their own greed and the corruption of those who use friars to purchase absolution.

In the first passage addressed here, Conscience welcomingly invites the friars into Holy Church, and their deceit enables the apocalyptic destruction in the poem. Fortescue annotates Conscience's request that the friars who enter Unity Holy Church follow their rule, writing 'conciens conselith / frerres' in the lefthand margin next to the C-text lines,

> holdeth you in vnyte & havith now envye
> To lerdne to lewde but but lyve after your Rewle
> And I wille your borowe ye schold haue bred & clothis
> And other necessarys ynow ...[28]

Only a few lines earlier, Hand B writes 'Conscience to the / Freers' in the opposite margin in a way that further emphasizes Conscience's instruction so that later readers of Digby 145 might see this message as doubly significant to the events unfolding in the narrative.[29] In his B-text copy, the HM 114 scribe places a *nota* in this same passage next to Conscience's use of Francis and Dominic as models for following the friars' rule,

> so þat ʒe leue logyk and lernith for to love
> For for loue left þei lordship boþ londe & stole
> Freris fraunceys ʒ domenyk for loue to be holy
> And if ʒe coueyte cure kynd wil ʒow shewe
> þat in mesure god made al manere thynges ...[30]

Because Francis and Dominic left their worldly positions of high status – their lordships and their lands – for the love of God, Conscience expects his friars to follow suit and abandon worldly status and goods for a higher calling.

---

[28] Digby 145, fol. 127v, at Schmidt C.22.246–9.
[29] Digby 145, fol. 127r, at Schmidt C.22.242–3.
[30] HM 114, fol. 128v; Schmidt B.20.250–4 (*nota* at line 252).

Langland's Government Scribes at Home and at Work 223

Conscience tells the friars that if they live by their rule, abandon logic and learn to love, God will take care of their basic needs. Conscience thereby welcomes them into Unity because he sees their potential to strengthen the foundations of Holy Church. In Conscience's idealized view, friars have a place and purpose in the Church, but in practice, not one of the friars lives up to their potential. The three annotations that appear next to this passage in Digby 145 and HM 114 suggest that both sets of readers recognize, acknowledge and possibly even share Conscience's hope. The passage's emphasis on the friars' rule and the founders of that rule sets the tone for the annotations by stressing the formal set of instructions for the lives the friars commit to when they take up holy orders.

This formal commitment carries with it some legal implications that may have interested the scribes, whose next annotations appear alongside another set of equivalent lines of their C and B texts. The passage in question addresses the religious laws friars are bound to by their rule and uses legal language to identify the friars' corruption as they increase the members of their order beyond what their rule dictates. Fortescue, therefore, responds with 'freres haue no nombre', while the HM 114 scribe contributes his characteristically terse *nota* mark. These two copies read almost identically here, even though the spelling and dialect differ. Fortescue's Digby 145 copy reads:

> her order & her Rewle woll to haue a certeyn nombre
> Of leride & <of> lewde the lawe woll & askyth
> A certeyn for a certeyne save onely of Freres
> For thy quod concyens by cryste kynd witt me tellith
> It is wykkyd & wage you ye wax out of nombre
> For thy I would witterly that ye war in regester
> And your nombre vnder notary sygne neyther more ne lesse.[31]

HM 114's copy reads:

> her ordre & her rule will to have a certeyn nombre
> Of lerid and of lewde þe lawe will & askyth
> A certeyn for a certeyn saf only of freris
> For thy quod conscience by crist kynd wit me telliþ
> hit is wikkyd to wage <ȝow> ȝe wexe out of nombre
> For þi y wold witterly þat ȝe were in þe register
> And ȝour noumbre vndir notarie signe neiþer mo ne lesse.[32]

---

[31] Digby 145, fols. 127v–128r; Schmidt C.22.264–73 (notation at lines 267–8).
[32] HM 114, fol. 129r; Schmidt B.20.265–72 (*nota* at line 267).

The 'lawe' Conscience refers to in this passage designates a 'certeyn' number of friars to fill a 'certeyn' number of jobs. England's friars exceed the number set for them, and Conscience wishes for a legally notarized official register of friars to resolve the problem. Conscience's discussion of the law and a legal document to uphold that law gives his speech a bureaucratic tone that echoes the documentary and administrative tone of the passages revised by the HM 114 scribe earlier in the poem.[33] For the HM 114 scribe, this annotation translates his earlier engagement with London's documentary culture into a religious context, extending those concerns to ecclesiastical law and the moral guidelines by which friars ought to abide. For Fortescue, this passage contributes to his already well-established antimendicant commentary, showing how these sentiments still resonate with early modern readers. The friars' behaviour here converges with Fortescue's larger preoccupation with social order and the spiritual condition of the Church and his nation, and this annotation acknowledges the intersections between Church and state even at a time when that relationship was rupturing.

Both Fortescue and the HM 114 scribe highlight the legal and moral codes of conduct for friars as sanctioned by the Church, and this extension of legal contexts to antimendicant discourse repeats yet again, but in these final examples the scribes mark slightly different passages. Fortescue marks a passage about official documents used to authorize a friar's activity as a confessor, while the HM 114 scribe returns to his earlier preoccupation with Westminster by annotating a simile between the friars' abuse of confession for money with the abuse of Westminster's sanctuary laws by debtors fleeing their creditors. Thus, in one of the many annotations about friars at the end of the poem, Digby 145 records 'frere confessour' beside these lines:

> The fryer here of hard & hiyghid hym fast
> To a lord for a letter leve to have to cure hym
> As he a curatour ware and come with his letter
> boldly to the bysschop and his breeff hold
> In cuntreys there he come confessioouns to here.[34]

Langland describes the process a friar undergoes to gain formal permission to hear confession. The bishop grants this permission based on a letter of support

---

[33] See K. Fuller, 'Repurposing *Piers Plowman*: Literary Geography and the Codicological Remaking of Langland's Work' (unpublished Ph.D. dissertation, University of Notre Dame, 2016), pp. 37–93.

[34] Digby 145, fol. 129r; Schmidt C.22.325–9 (notation at line 325). Fortescue also annotates line 315 about the false confessor (Digby 145, fol. 128v) with 'frere flaterer'.

from an aristocrat, to whom the friar probably owes some debt for this favour. It becomes apparent quickly that this process fails to achieve the Church's desired results of the successful administration of confession. Instead, the friar succeeds in feeding his own greedy appetite, not by curing Contricion of his spiritual illness, but by performing his confession cursorily in exchange for payment. Money, not the cure of souls, is his motivation for entering Holy Church, and confession in the hands of the friar becomes nothing more than an empty gesture. Fortescue notes the formal process by which this friar gains his lucrative position as confessor, and the antimendicant ideas conveyed here contribute to his running commentary on the administrative cracks in ecclesiastical documentary culture.

The failure of officially sanctioned confession performed by friars also captures the attention of the HM 114 scribe, but in a context that hearkens back to the poem's London context. The last *nota* in HM 114's *Piers* occurs alongside a different passage on friar-confessors' greed:

> And al is þis holdyn in þe lond of Ingelond
> For parsons & parish prestis shold þe parisshyns shryve
> Are curatours callid to knowe and to hele
> All þat be her parisshyns penaunce to enioigne
> & shold be ashamyd in her shrift to make hem amende
> And fle to þe freris as folk do to westmestre
> Þat borowiþ and beriþ þider and þan prayeþ frendis
> Fast of foryeuenes or lenger dayes of payng
> But while he is in Westminster he wil be byfore
> And make hym mercy with oþer mennys goodis
> & so hit fariþ by michel folk þat to þe freris shriviþ
> As sisours and executours þei wil ȝeue to freris
> a parcelle to pray for hem & make hem self mery.[35]

Like Fortescue's annotated passage, the HM 114 scribe's *nota* directs the reader's attention to the problems with friar-confessors acting on behalf of their pocketbooks. However, the HM 114 scribe focuses on a passage that involves the London government setting he pays so much attention to throughout the poem.[36] Here several kinds of financial legal corruption ensue as debtors flee to Westminster to evade creditors and live luxuriously. The corruption described also involves executors who pay small wages to friars to pray for the deceased only to keep the rest of the deceased's money for

---

[35] HM 114, fol. 129r; Schmidt B.20.280–92 (*nota* at line 289).
[36] See Fuller, 'Repurposing *Piers*', pp. 94–133.

themselves. These friars, moreover, benefit by receiving payment that would otherwise go to the parish priest and stay in the community rather than going to the itinerant mendicant. This legal context pertains to the secular law in a way that is imbricated with the friars' religious responsibilities, whereas the passage Fortescue annotates pertains to ecclesiastical administration in a way that intersects with the authority of a lord with the power to recommend the friar for promotion to friar-confessor. In these two examples, both Church and nation enable mendicant corruption, although the scribes' annotations differ in emphasis on the administrative sources that allow these mendicants' greed to flourish.

Based on the antimendicant annotations discussed here, Digby 145 and HM 114 overlap in their reading of the political and administrative causes of mendicant corruption as well as the disparity between the idealized rule and actual lives of the friars. Fortescue and the HM 114 scribe agree about the rampant greed plaguing the friar community and its serious consequences for the wider community. Yet, while Fortescue's antimendicant commentary is significantly more extensive than this present analysis conveys, the HM 114 scribe sticks much more closely to administrative critique in a much smaller set of annotations. These different levels of scribal interaction, moreover, show how Digby 145's annotators, with their more involved and precise remarks, guide their readers towards theologically complex interpretations; indeed, the shifting landscape of Reformation England surely required serious reflection on theological distinctions between Catholicism and emergent Protestantism. By contrast, the HM 114 scribe primarily uses *nota* marks that provide only vague guides for capturing readers' attention at moments he views as important. Still, there is continuity between these late medieval and early modern readers, and these examples provide positive evidence of their overlapping readings.

Viewing England Two Ways: A Short Reflection on These Manuscripts' Contents

When stepping back to consider HM 114 and Digby 145 as witnesses to Langland's larger reception history, their differing codicological aims come into sharper focus. HM 114 creates a more global outlook with its geographically and temporally diverse collection of texts, while Digby 145 is characterized by familial household texts, local perspectives and introspective reading practices that it both witnesses and encourages. Their contrasts remind modern readers just how varied Langland's early readers could be, problematizing convenient labels such as 'lay', 'government' or even 'professional' readers. If the HM 114 scribe's collection demonstrates interests in geography, history and romance as well as national issues, by comparison, the Digby 145's scribe and readers maintain more local or regional perspectives through their personal investment in issues relevant to their aristocratic household (even documenting the birth of Adrian's second son Thomas on the second flyleaf) and their place within England. Such inward-looking readings reveal how Digby 145's readers prioritize their personal, familial relationships and the theological foundations of their own spiritual lives with respect to *Piers Plowman* and Fortescue's particular presentation of the text. Both manuscripts' unique interrogation of England's ecclesiastical and political governance, therefore, are shaped by the interconnected historical and codicological contexts in which each readership read. In other words, the personal and historical vantage points from which these readers view England through the lens of *Piers* carries meaning that can only be reached by careful examination of their manuscripts in context.

In terms of their geographical and historical scopes, Fortescue's local perspectives originate in his home and emphasize insular national government and ecclesiastical administration in England; although he extends some attention to Rome, his views are more limited than HM 114's global perspective, which looks far beyond these borders. Digby 145's readers maintain an inward-looking approach to Langland with their private and personal interpretations of marriage themes as well as political and religious corruption. However, HM 114's *Piers-Mandeville* pairing draws readers' attention to geographical sites across the globe so that the audience reads about London and England in relation to the rest of the world and all of the known history it contains.[37] Indeed, the *Mandeville* narrator's introduction announces this worldwide scope:

> I John Mawndevile knyght born yn þe toune of Seynt / Albones in Inglonde passid ouere þe see toward þe holy / londe [...] / and þere have y dwellid longe tyme & / þurgh diuers londis provinces yles and grete kyngdomes þat / is for to sey Turkye Ermenye þe lesse & eke þe more also / þurgh Tartarye Perce Surrye Arabie Egipte þe hye and / eke þe lowe lybie Caldye and a grete parte of Ethiopie / also þurgh Amazone ynde þe more and eke þe lesse also / þurgh meny diuers yles þat longe to ynde [...].[38]

Mandeville's geographical narrative especially invites HM 114's readers to read Langland's allegory for its global significance and England's place within the world instead of looking only at its introspective views of England's governing bodies and crumbling religious structure the way Digby 145

---

[37] For a detailed analysis, see Fuller, 'Repurposing *Piers*', pp. 37–93.
[38] HM 114, fol. 131v. Line breaks marked by a slash '/'.

does. Additionally, Digby 145's localness supports its historical specificity, whereas HM 114's geographical expansiveness – bolstered by its inclusion of *Troilus*, the *Three Kings* and even *Susannah* – supports its universal, historical approach. Unlike the historical flexibility and variety in HM 114, Digby 145 shows little interest in exploring conceptions of history, or in using history as a medium for exploring larger ideas. Rather than depicting the variability and possibility opened up by literary uses of history, Fortescue and his family tended to read Langland for themes that matter to them in England in their precise historical moment, hence the marginal conversations about marriage and the Protestant or Proto-Protestant dialogues found in the margins, which I develop at length elsewhere.[39]

Finally, although Digby 145 expresses little to no interest in courtly love themes connected to the romance genre beyond a general concern for *Piers*'s Mede episode, both manuscripts do respond to marriage-related themes. HM 114's courtly contexts and political interests differ from the personal investment in marriage shared by Anne Fortescue, Adrian Fortescue and Hand B, whose inside jokes and theological commentary on the subject shapes its household quality, even entering the realm of bedroom mishaps when both Adrian and Hand B respond to the narrator's impotence after Elde flies over his head. Adrian Fortescue notes the 'giftes' of age and 'Nota the wyfe' alongside the narrator's complaint about the wife's disappointment; Hand B seems to jokingly respond 'the wief is woo but why', interrupting a private conversation between husband and wife.[40]

In HM 114, on the other hand, the romance genre becomes important as a result of its compilational character, especially with the addition of texts such as *Troilus* and *Susannah* to the *Piers-Mandeville* pairing; the codicological context brings these courtly love themes to the surface in a way that highlights the political setting within which its stories of courtship play out.[41] Thus, Digby 145's marriage commentary contributes further evidence of the manuscript's local, introspective character in a way that also makes its historical moment clear, while marriage themes in HM 114 support the scribe's political commentary on international relations throughout history. Additionally, since Digby 145 expends greater energy on theological issues pertaining to apocalypticism and reformism, its religious interests downplay any responses to the type of courtly love themes that run throughout the romance genre.

---

[39] Fuller, 'Langland in the Early Modern Household'.
[40] Digby 145, fols. 126r–v, at Schmidt C.22.193–7. For more, see Fuller, 'Langland in the Early Modern Household', pp. 335–7.
[41] Fuller, 'Repurposing *Piers*', pp. 37–93.

Thus, while it requires a more in-depth study than this essay permits, reading these manuscripts intertextually, that is, across the compilations designed by their executors, yields further insights into the intentions and priorities of their scribes and readers, a conversation as yet only begun.[42] Moreover, if we expand our definition of medieval intertextuality to include critical evaluation of different manuscript versions of the same text, even when those witnesses appear disparate and distant from each other, as do HM 114 and Digby 145, we can build a fuller history of Langland's readerships that incorporates a wider range of their individual and collective tendencies.

The major differences outlined here reveal how much can change when reading *Piers* within its diverse manuscript and historical contexts. One point, however, remains to be made about the reader responses evidenced in these two manuscripts. While the HM 114 scribe acts as a 'professional reader' who designs his texts as an editor, reviser and annotator for particular kinds of reading, it is impossible to know how contemporary or later readers responded to his attempts 'to govern interpretive activity' without a written record in the margins.[43] In contrast, the marginal conversations in Digby 145 transform this manuscript into a gold mine for modern scholars of reception history because it shows how some of Fortescue's actual readers responded to his edition and interpretations, and it shows to what extent readers can resist a scribe's effort to 'govern' their interpretations as Hand B does when he disagrees with Fortescue's commentary. Digby 145 provides evidence for actual rather than implied readers, and this fact makes reconstructing this Early Modern audience a little bit easier.

This observation points to one of the larger methodological problems faced by scholars attempting to reconstruct literary reception history. That is, how do we understand audiences whose responses are so often absent from or severely limited in the extant material evidence available? Yet, despite the difficulties this problem poses, it is worth following this path of inquiry for the rich interpretative possibilities it opens up. For, such responses, largely unrecoverable but still evidenced to some extent in the manuscript tradition that survives, teach us about the place Langland deservedly holds throughout literary history. Thus, whatever interpretive risks come from working with mere snippets of reader responses, the benefits lead to gains in our understanding of this ever-intriguing, ever-relevant text. Digby 145's unique reader conversations

---

[42] For intertextual readings of HM 114's compilation, see Phillips, 'Compilational Reading', Wood, *Manuscript Tradition*, pp. 154–85, and Fuller, 'Repurposing *Piers*', pp. 37–93.

[43] D. Pearsall, 'The Uses of Manuscripts: Late Medieval English', *Harvard Library Bulletin* 4.4 (1993–4), 30–6 (p. 35).

create their own set of questions for the modern scholar to answer, but its scribal editorializing and textual responses also participate in a long tradition of scribal and readerly commentary on *Piers* that originates in earlier copies of the poem such as that found in HM 114.[44] That is why, over a hundred years after the production of HM 114, scribes and even early printers continued to produce their own editorialized versions to meet the needs of newer generations of readers, a challenge readily taken up by today's coterie of modern editors still adapting Langland's words for continued use and posterity.

---

[44] London manuscripts such as Ilchester offer further useful examples of active scribes. On Ilchester, see D. Pearsall, 'The "Ilchester" Manuscript of *Piers Plowman*', *Neuphilologische Mitteilungen* 82 (1981), 181–93. For further examples, see K. Kerby-Fulton, 'Professional Readers at Work: Annotators, Editors, and Correctors in Middle English Literary Texts', in *Opening Up*, pp. 223–34.

11

Function, Form and *The Lay Folks' Mass Book*

JEREMY J. SMITH

On *The Lay Folks' Mass Book*[1]

The Middle English poem now known as *The Lay Folks' Mass Book* (*LFMB*) was first edited in 1879 by a distinguished Anglican clergyman, Thomas Frederick Simmons.[2] Simmons's edition for the Early English Text Society (EETS) has been criticized over the years, although it has never been replaced. Early in the twentieth century, Gordon Hall Gerould, then a professor at Bryn Mawr and later at Princeton, writing in the philological (and Germanically professional) journal *Englische Studien*, sounded a warning-note of attacks to come: 'It is only fair to say that Canon Simmons, from the antiquarian and ecclesiastical point of view so admirable an editor, may not himself have seen the MS. from which he quotes'.[3] And even aspects of the edition that Gerould

---

[1] Kathryn Kerby-Fulton's delicate attention to the medieval manuscript-record, and how such attention offers new insights into contemporary textual reception, has long been an inspiration; I might refer, for instance, to K. Kerby-Fulton, M. Hilmo and L. Olson, *Opening Up Middle English Manuscripts* (Ithaca, 2012). I am in addition much indebted to Misty Schieberle for her invitation to contribute this paper, and for her ongoing gracious support, and to an anonymous reviewer for very helpful comments on an earlier version. The current paper is part of an ongoing study of *LFMB* and Thomas Frederick Simmons's edition, and their socio-cultural location and significance, involving my colleague David Jasper and myself; I should like to acknowledge David's close assistance throughout its production. Publications in this programme of research so far include D. Jasper and J. J. Smith, '*The Lay Folks' Mass Book* and Thomas Frederick Simmons: Medievalism and the Tractarians', *Journal of Ecclesiastical History* 70 (2019), 785–804; J. J. Smith, 'The Manuscripts of the Middle English *Lay Folks' Mass Book* in Context', *Studia Anglica Posnaniensia* 56 (2021), 361–85; and D. Jasper and J. J. Smith, *Reinventing Medieval Liturgy in Victorian England* (Woodbridge, 2023). The current paper takes issues raised there further than in these publications, notably in relating Simmons's edition to antiquarianism, and in providing deeper analysis in particular of the manuscript containing the B-text of *LFMB*, the most widely-cited version of the poem.

[2] *The Lay Folks' Mass Book*, ed. T. F. Simmons, EETS OS 71 (London, 1879).

[3] G. H. Gerould, '*The Lay-Folks' Mass-Book* from MS Gg V.31, Cambridge University Library', *Englische Studien* 33 (1904), 1–26 (p. 2).

singled out for praise have come to be dismissed as sterner approaches to medieval studies have increasingly dominated the learned landscape. Sue Powell, for instance, one of the best-known and important Anglicists currently working on late medieval English religious texts, has referred in passing to Simmons's 'fey antiquarianism'.[4]

The basis of these attacks is interesting. Antiquarianism has had for many years a bad press, especially since the academisation of learning that emerged – especially in Germany – towards the end of the nineteenth century, but recent work in this field, especially by Rosemary Hill, has recommended a re-evaluation of its achievement.[5] This paper argues that Simmons's edition, notably its aesthetic, antiquarian characteristics, captured – despite its flaws – something important about the medieval manuscript-record that has become occluded in later scholarship, and that his approach flags important insights into both the medieval text and its later reception.

LFMB survives in nine known manuscript witnesses dating from between 1380 and 1500, and is of some 630 lines in its fullest form; it was never printed until the nineteenth century, as far as is known. The manuscripts containing *LFMB* are as follows:

- A = Edinburgh, National Library of Scotland, MS Advocates' 19.3.1, fols. 57–8v
- B = London, British Library, MS Royal 17 B.xvii, fols. 3r–13r
- C = Oxford, Corpus Christi College, MS 155, fols. 252v–268r
- D = Cambridge, University Library, MS Gg.5.31, fols. 1r–5v
- E = Cambridge, Gonville and Caius College, MS 84/166 (Part II), pp. 173–9
- F = Cambridge, Newnham College, MS 900.4 (olim Yates Thompson), fols. 104v–9v
- G = Cambridge, University Library, MS Ii.4.9, fols. 55v–60r
- H = Liverpool, University Library, MS F.4.9, fols. 203v–7v
- I = London, British Library, MS Additional 36523, fols. 88r–93r

---

[4] S. Powell, 'The Transmission and Circulation of *The Lay Folks' Catechism*', in *Late Medieval Religious Texts and their Transmission: Essays in Honour of A. I. Doyle*, ed. A. J. Minnis (Cambridge, 1994), pp. 67–84 (p. 69).

[5] R. Hill, *Time's Witness: History in the Age of Romanticism* (London, 2021).

Of these witnesses, Simmons knew of six (A–F). He presented four versions (B, C, E and F) in what might be termed 'modified diplomatic' fashion, that is, transcriptions, but with 'modern' interpretative punctuation and with suggested readings for manuscript lacunae. Two other copies (A, D) were referenced in textual notes; the A and D texts were subsequently edited in full in the first decade of the twentieth century.[6] The B-text was also re-edited by Carl Horstmann (1896), with slightly different punctuation and a difference in layout that changed the lineation of the text.[7] Horstmann's edition is, however, not really an advance on Simmons's, although he did supply other texts, in lightly edited format, from the same manuscript.

The manuscripts containing B and E are the oldest, datable by script to the late fourteenth century; the other manuscripts all date from the fifteenth century. The poem is written mostly in rough couplets and iambic tetrameter, and it has little literary merit according to present-day canons of taste. *LFMB* – there is no title in any of its witnesses – is a devotional work composed as a gloss or paratext for those attending mass, alternating prayers with descriptions of the distinct actions undertaken by celebrant and congregation; it is thus a kind of vernacular libretto-cum-versified prayer book, presenting materials carefully aligned in sequence with each stage in the liturgy of the mass. There is uncertainty about *LFMB*'s genesis; the poem states at the beginning that it is a translation from French – 'when I vpon þo boke know hit / In til englishe þus I draw hit' (B-text, 31–2) – although no French original has yet been found. Simmons speculates at length about the author of the presumed lost original, referred to in some versions as 'dam Ieremy' who was a 'deuowte mon & a religyus' (B-text, 18–19); however, no 'dam Ieremy' has ever been more precisely identified. Other versions, for example, C, confuse him (absurdly) with 'seynte Ierome', the translator who produced the Vulgate. There is no evidence that the Middle English *LFMB* was composed much before B.[8]

In what follows, a 'double-headed' approach is taken. Following an outline of the principles underpinning Simmons's edition of 1879, discussion turns to how some versions of the *LFMB* functioned in the late medieval period, with

---

[6] Gerould, '*The Lay-Folks' Mass-Book* from MS Gg V.31'; K. Bülbring, 'Das *Lay-Folks' Mass-Book* in der Handschrift der Advocates Library in Edinburgh', *Englische Studien* 35 (1905), 29–33.

[7] *Yorkshire Writers: Richard Rolle of Hampole and his Followers*, ed. C. Horstmann, 3 vols (London, 1896), II, 1–8.

[8] Despite J. Garrison, *Challenging Communion: The Eucharist and Middle English Literature* (Columbus, 2017), p. 32; Garrison follows Simmons, who claimed that *LFMB* was translated from a twelfth-century French original a century later (*LFMB*, ed. Simmons, p. xxxi).

special reference to codicological context; *LFMB* is shown to be part of that extensive body of devotional writing that reached widely across the late medieval English-speaking world. The paper concludes with some observations on editorial practice and on what has come to be called 'cultural mapping'.

The Lay Folks' Mass Book (1879)

Underpinning the modern (and very understandable) charge of 'feyness' is the substantial body of 'Notes and Illustrations' Simmons supplied to accompany the edited texts. This paratextual material is certainly highly informed in Victorian terms, displaying a remarkable range of reference in terms of both contemporary philology and liturgiology. For instance, in his six-page note on the word *rynsande* 'rinsing' (B-text, 575), which starts with an (accurate) account of how the inflexional ending is dialectally significant, Simmons not only engages with the great Victorian editors of the Latin liturgy, William Maskell and William Henderson, but also numerous seventeenth- and eighteenth-century French liturgists still at the time regarded as authoritative, ranging from Jean Mabillon through Edmond Martène to the sieur de Moléon.[9] Simmons even found time to cite a specialist dictionary by Eugène Viollet-Le-Duc, the nineteenth-century architect who built Notre Dame's spire (destroyed in 2019), and who assisted in the construction of the Statue of Liberty.[10]

But the range of reference alone is not, it might be presumed, the main trigger of modern criticism, because some of Simmons's paratextual materials must surely strike a present-day reader as unusual – even unacceptably personal – for a scholarly edition. The discussion of *rynsande* 'rinsing', running over some six pages in the notes, thus includes a description of how Simmons had occasion to examine 'a so-called well, which had lately been uncovered in Beverley Minster … [that] probably served to drain off what was poured into a piscina'.[11] In a footnote to this footnote (the editor enjoys nesting his annotations), Simmons adds a personal element, referring to the building of his own nineteenth-century Gothic Revival church at Dalton Holme in Yorkshire, where he was rector:

> A similar drain or well, about 3 feet deep, and 18 inches across, but lined with rubble walling, was found in the parish where this is written, when we were building the new church, and had to take down the font in the old one.

---

[9] J. Mabillon, *Acta Sanctorum* (Paris, 1685); E. Martène, *De Antiquis Ecclesiae Ritibus* (Rouen, 1700); J. B. Le Brun des Marettes, sieur de Moléon, *Voyages Liturgiques de France* (Paris, 1718).

[10] E. Viollet-le-Duc, *Dictionnaire raisoné de l'architecture française du XIe á XVI siècle* (Paris, 1854).

[11] *LFMB*, ed. Simmons, p. 305.

This information leads Simmons to cite Frederick Lee's extensive revision of John Purchas's *Directorium Anglicanum*:

> The piscina is a stone basin with an orifice and drain to carry away the water which has been used at the washing of the priest's hands in accordance with Psalm xxvi. 6, and for rinsing the chalice after the purifications, and is one of the appurtenances of an altar which in ancient times was never dispensed with.[12]

However, even the reference to the medieval drain displaced by his fine new church can be seen as relevant to the concerns that underpin his edition, for Simmons was attempting to do two things. One was to align *LFMB* with the historical basis for the Church of England's life of worship. Simmons was an acknowledged expert in liturgy, a contributor to leading publications such as the *Contemporary Review*;[13] he was also an important figure in the debates of the recently re-established Northern Convocation of York in the Church of England, where matters of ritual arcane to modern eyes were an urgent topic, notably with reference to Prayer Book reform.[14] After all, in 1877 – a couple of years before Simmons's edition appeared – the Rev Arthur Tooth had been imprisoned for contempt of court, having been accused of practices deemed 'popish' under Disraeli's Public Worship Regulation Act (1874); his arrest was accompanied by riots and fisticuffs. And in 1880, a year after *LFMB*'s publication, the Rev Thomas Pelham Dale found himself briefly in Holloway prison, under a writ of *significavit* triggered by his 'ritualism'.[15] The *Directorium* from which Simmons sourced his discussion of drains was an acknowledged primary point of reference for all such ritualists, something of which many of Simmons's readers would have been fully aware.

Simmons's second concern is demonstrated if we compare his edition of *LFMB* with William Maskell's *Ancient Liturgy of the Church of England* (1844).[16] Maskell, another formidably learned cleric, was, shortly after his book first appeared, to convert from Anglicanism to Roman Catholicism.[17]

---

[12] J. Purchas (rev. F. G. Lee), *Directorium Anglicanum* (London, 1865), p. 10.

[13] For example, T. F. Simmons, 'Standing Before the Lord's Table', *Contemporary Review* 4 (January–April, 1867), 90–109.

[14] See Jasper and Smith, *Victorian Reinvention*.

[15] For details of the careers of both men, see their entries in the *ODNB*, accessed October 21, 2022, https://www.oxforddnb.com.

[16] *The Ancient Liturgy of the Church of England, According to the Uses of Sarum, York, Hereford, and Bangor, and the Roman Liturgy*, ed. W. Maskell (Oxford, 1844).

[17] Maskell's conversion was in the wake of the notorious Gorham Judgment of 1850, in which the Privy Council overruled the Bishop of Exeter on a point of theological controversy concerning baptism. Maskell, as Anglican domestic chaplain to the

Despite their confessional differences, Simmons nevertheless, judging by personal references in his edition of *LFMB*, seems to have been on excellent terms with Maskell. *Ancient Liturgy*, regularly reprinted and appearing in several editions during the nineteenth century, was the first scholarly parallel-text edition of the uses of Sarum, York, Hereford and Bangor, and has still not been fully superseded. And in his formidable set of footnotes Maskell quotes extensively from an English poem to indicate what the lay people were doing in the course of the Latin Mass. This was the B-version of *LFMB*, and it was encountering these verses in Maskell's *Ancient Liturgy* that inspired Simmons to undertake his edition.[18]

Comparison with Maskell's work demonstrates clearly that Simmons was modelling his practice on his friend's monumental piece of Victorian scholarship. Like Maskell, Simmons was evidently an extremely well-read man. His notes and glossary show that he was well acquainted not only with a vast body of liturgiological writing and with canonical literary authors such as Chaucer and Shakespeare but also with the significant body of early English verse and prose that had been published to date, ranging from the *Cursor Mundi* to *The Prick of Conscience*.[19] He was an early subscriber to EETS, recorded in the society's subscription lists from at least 1868 onwards. He had, on the evidence of references in his edition, read not only a complete set of EETS volumes to date but also numerous other medieval English texts published by EETS's precursors, for example the Surtees Society, and he had made himself an expert in matters of English philology; a member of the English Dialect Society, he was also a keen observer of contemporary dialectal usage in his Yorkshire parish, of the kind that would come to its fruition in the later endeavours of Joseph and Elizabeth Wright (1898–1905).[20] Simmons's extensive annotations in his edition drew heavily upon this body of learning, going well beyond anything in terms of range of reference offered even by the editors Richard Morris or Walter W. Skeat. Although these annotations are largely ignored by present-day Anglicist scholarship, closer examination shows that they were a remarkable attempt to treat a comparatively short vernacular work

---

bishop, assisted in the case, but was so affected by it that eventually he converted to Roman Catholicism. For Maskell's career, see in the first instance his entry in *ODNB*.

[18] *LFMB*, ed. Simmons, pp. ix–x.

[19] *Cursor Mundi*, ed. R. Morris, EETS OS 57, 59, 62, 66, 68, 99, 101 (London, 1870–93); *The Prick of Conscience (Stimulus Conscientiae), a Northumbrian Poem by Richard Rolle de Hampole*, ed. R. Morris (Berlin, 1863).

[20] J. and E. M. Wright, *The English Dialect Dictionary* (Oxford, 1898–1905).

with the same care and attention that had been hitherto reserved for liturgical texts in Latin.

Simmons's edition was therefore very much of his time, and, in following Maskell's practice, he also did something else, which again might be considered unusual to present-day scholars. Although he introduced 'modern' punctuation, albeit in a way that present-day editors might regard as more rhetorical than grammatical, he also attempted to capture in his edition elements of textual presentation in his source manuscripts, deploying engrossed letters to flag *litterae notabiliores*, pilcrows to represent paraph marks and bold lettering to indicate rubrication or underlining in the original witnesses.

Comparable 'antiquarian' practices may be detected in, say, Richard Morris's much larger (30,000 lines) multi-volume parallel-text edition for EETS of the Middle English *Cursor Mundi* (1870–93), and indeed in many other contemporary EETS editions. Such attempts to evoke – anachronistically in print – the appearance of the manuscript witnesses had a long pedigree; the earliest printed editions of Old English texts in the sixteenth century were printed in a special font designed to 'counterfeit' insular script, while the gothic blackletter, modelled on medieval textura, became the typeface of choice for the great antiquarians of the eighteenth and nineteenth centuries. Siân Echard has, for instance, drawn attention to Thomas Whitaker's edition of *Piers Plowman* (1813), described by Isaac D'Israeli in 1841 as 'the most magnificent and frightful volume that was ever beheld in the black letter'.[21] And when in 1805 Thomas Johnes published a translation of Jean Froissart's Old French *Chronicle*, he complained to a friend about the (anonymous) critical comments it had received from the *Edinburgh Review*: 'I suspect your reviewer is some young man who has not read much, nor is very learned in books but, smitten with the love of Black letter, sees nothing beautiful but in that'.[22] The 'young man' was Walter Scott, later the author of *The Antiquary* (1816), which he considered to be his best (and favourite) novel.

Elements of these practices persisted for some time in EETS editions, notably in the retention of blackletter for title pages and front covers; a good example is J. R. R. Tolkien's EETS diplomatic edition (1962) of *Ancrene Wisse*, which also reflected in its transcription the *litterae notabiliores* and punctuation of the source manuscript, viz. Cambridge, Corpus Christi College, MS 402.[23] But this practice has since changed, as the society gradually shook off its

---

[21] Cited in S. Echard, *Printing the Middle Ages* (Philadelphia, 2008), p. 12.
[22] Cited in Echard, *Printing the Middle Ages*, p. 12.
[23] *The English Text of the Ancrene Riwle: Ancrene Wisse, edited from MS. Corpus Christi College Cambridge 402*, ed. J. R. R. Tolkien, EETS OS 249 (London, 1962).

antiquarian roots. Eric Dobson's sister-edition of *Ancrene Riwle* (1972), a diplomatic presentation of another manuscript witness, also for EETS and from exactly a decade later, presented the work's title in a modern roman typeface: a discreet acknowledgement of scholarly – and perhaps wider socio-cultural – progress during the intervening years.[24] Significantly, present-day EETS editors tend not only to impose modern punctuation but also, in line with current editorial practice, modern practices of capitalization and layout. It would appear that even editions of the Tolkien/Dobson type are considered to be part of the society's past rather than its present.[25]

Such practices are of course wholly defensible: an edition, after all, is designed for the use of its readers, and must necessarily be constrained by what those readers are looking for. Simmons's edition, however, was aimed at the EETS readership of the late 1870s, and more than a third of that readership was made up of clergy like himself;[26] there is also considerable evidence that such clergy continued to refer to Simmons's edition for their own liturgical purposes for several years.[27] By contrast, the present-day EETS readership consists largely of Anglicist scholars working in universities, with different needs and expectations.

Nevertheless, the achievement of antiquaries of the eighteenth and nineteenth centuries is, as has been flagged already, currently being re-evaluated. Rosemary Hill, for instance, has urged us to retrieve antiquarianism from 'the condescension of posterity':

> Later generations of professional historians have not generally cared to acknowledge their debt to antiquarianism, perhaps because they see the

---

[24] *The English Text of the Ancrene Riwle, edited from BM. Cotton MS. Cleopatra C VI*, ed. E. J. Dobson, EETS OS 267 (London, 1972).

[25] The ongoing production of electronic transcriptions, of course, may change this situation. For a discussion, see J. J. Smith, *Transforming Early English* (Cambridge, 2020), especially chapter 6.

[26] D. Matthews, *The Making of Middle English, 1765–1910* (Minnesota, 1999), pp. 159–60.

[27] See Jasper and Smith, *Victorian Reinvention*, for details. Simmons's edition was regularly referred to by liturgical scholars in the late nineteenth and early twentieth centuries, and fairly often afterwards, for example, in *Walter Howard Frere: His Correspondence on Liturgical Revision and Construction*, ed. R. C. D. Jasper (London, 1954), and in R. Pfaff, *The Liturgy in Medieval England* (Cambridge, 2009). The most recent use of Simmons's edition of *LFMB* for liturgical purposes is the fascinating re-enactment of the medieval mass carried out by John Harper and his team based at Bangor University. See *Late Medieval Liturgies Enacted*, ed. S. Harper, P. Barnwell and M. Williamson (London, 2016).

antiquaries like embarrassing elderly relatives whom one would rather keep out of sight.[28]

Within such a re-evaluation, the 'evocative' element in the editions by Simmons and others deserves, it could be argued, revisiting. In attempting to map the appearance of manuscripts, they were acknowledging the importance of the visual pragmatics of their exemplars, something that is now increasingly recognized as important by researchers.[29] It is to aspects of the manuscript record for *LFMB* that we might now turn.

The Lay Folks' Mass Book in the Late Middle Ages

As Fiona Somerset has pointed out,

> … late medieval religious writing in England more generally had magpie tendencies, prompted or facilitated by the circulation of loose leaves and unbound booklets from which material could readily be recopied or excerpted within other books.[30]

The various versions of *LFMB* are fine illustrations of this characteristic since their contents vary widely. The B- and E-versions are similar and offer the fullest recension of the text. The C-, D- and F-versions, however, offer a shorter form which reduces the material describing the priest's actions and the postures to be adopted by the congregation; this group also reduces formal elements potentially extraneous to the core elements of the mass, dropping the vernacular versification of the Apostles' Creed, the hymn-like 'Ioy be vnto god in heuen' (lines 119–48 in the B- and E-versions) and a prayer that the mass might stand in place of absolution in case of sudden death. The F-version has in addition a shorter, modified opening, '[a]dapted to the practice of smaller churches and chapels in England, where the priest vested before the people', and some extra 'linking' lines.[31] The H- and I-versions, not known to Simmons, resemble this C/D/F group. The A-version, though textually related to C/D/F, is even shorter, its coverage equating to the first 128 lines of C, after the priest's *lavabo*, and ends with an additional couplet. The G-version is another departure from the text recorded in B and E, being a radical revision,

---

[28] Hill, *Time's Witness*, p. 8.
[29] See, for example, *Verbal and Visual Communication in Early English Texts*, ed. M. Peikola, A. Makilahde, H. Salmi, M.-L. Varila and J. Skaffari (Turnhout, 2017), and Smith, *Transforming Early English*. See also the discussion elsewhere in this volume of the manuscript appearance of tail-rhyme poetry.
[30] F. Somerset, *Feeling like Saints: Lollard writings after Wyclif* (Ithaca, 2013), p. 74.
[31] *LFMB*, ed. Simmons, p. 3.

omitting the material of instruction that appears in rubricated form in B, and like the second group excluding the Apostles' Creed and the hymn of joy.[32]

Recent research into manuscripts containing multiple texts – such miscellanies were after all the dominant textual vector in the medieval period – has emphasized the importance of seeing works such as the *LFMB* in their codicological context if we are to establish their 'cultural map'.[33] This insight explains rather well the various modifications the *LFMB* underwent. The G-version, for instance, seems to exclude the versified Apostles' Creed because another version of the Creed appears elsewhere in the manuscript. Indeed, the second section of the volume containing G seems to have been envisaged as a 'devotional kit': reflections on the Ten Commandments, the Seven Deadly Sins, etc., and vernacular versions of the Lord's Prayer, the Ave Maria and the Apostles' Creed, consequent on the initial Easter narrative sequence supplied by the *Northern Passion*, a work with which the book begins.[34] More clearly, the truncated form of the A-version is explicable if the rest of the manuscript's contents are examined. This manuscript, which has received a lot of scholarly attention, brings together a collection of nine booklets that were subsequently bound together. Philippa Hardman has shown how three of these booklets, now Qs. 2, 4 and 5, were once a set of three separate but similar volumes, all written by one scribe, Richard Heege, each focused on a particular romance: *Sir Gowther*, *Sir Ysumbras* and *Sir Amadas* respectively.[35] It seems that the original plan was that each romance should be followed by one further text: *Stans Puer*

---

[32] The G-version appears as item 2205 in the *Digital Index of Middle English Verse* (*DIMEV*), accessed October 23, 2022, https://www.dimev.net/Search.php. The other eight versions are listed as *DIMEV*, item 5537.

[33] For such manuscript miscellanies, see, for example, I. Johnson, 'Theorizing the Miscellaneous and the Middle English Biblical Paratext', in *Late Medieval Religiosity in England: The Evidence of Late Fourteenth and Fifteenth-Century Devotional Compilations*, ed. D. Renevey, M. Cré and D. Denissen (Turnhout, 2020), pp. 83–108. For 'cultural mapping', see J. Thompson, 'The Middle English *Prose Brut* and the Possibilities of Cultural Mapping', in *Design and Distribution of Late Medieval Manuscripts in England*, ed. M. Connolly and L. Mooney (York, 2008), pp. 245–60, and references there cited.

[34] See Smith, 'The Manuscripts', p. 373.

[35] P. Hardman, 'A Mediaeval "Library *in parvo*"', *Medium Ævum* 47 (1978), 262–73; *The Heege Manuscript: A Facsimile of National Library of Scotland MS Advocates 19.3.1*, intro. P. Hardman (Leeds, 2000); see also T. Turville-Petre, 'Some Medieval English Manuscripts in the North-East Midlands', in *Manuscripts and Readers in Fifteenth-Century England*, ed. D. Pearsall (Cambridge, 1983), pp. 125–41. J. Wade, 'Entertainments from a Medieval Minstrel's Repertoire Book', *Review of English Studies* 74 (2023), 605–18, argues that one of the 'booklets' of which the manuscript is composed is a copy by the scribe Heege of a minstrel's miscellany.

ad Mensam (sometimes known as *Urbanitas*), a courtesy-book on table-manners deriving from Robert de Grosseteste's Latin poem, was to accompany *Sir Gowther*, with *LFMB* (referred to as *Þe Masse*) beside *Sir Ysumbras*, and *The Lyttel Childrens Book* – another book on table-manners – alongside *Sir Amadas*. Table-manners – as the well-known poem *Sir Gawain and the Green Knight* illustrates so vividly – were seen as having a moral significance, which accounts for the appearance of the 'holy table' section from *LFMB* being considered appropriate. Although evidence for early provenance (other than linguistic) is comparatively slight, Robert Southey and Walter Scott, when in 1805–6 they secured the manuscript's purchase for the Advocates' Library, were told by the seller's family that the book was saved from 'a parochial house at the reformation'.[36] By contrast, the manuscript containing C, a large and carefully-written volume containing Latin and English texts, has clear indications of a monastic provenance, with the following inscription (fol. 2v):

Liber be*a*te Marie de Rieualle
ex pr*o*curacione d*omi*ni Wille*l*mi
Spenser. Abb*a*tis eiusdem.[37]

This inscription is clear evidence that the manuscript was at Rievaulx, the Cistercian foundation in the North Riding of Yorkshire; William Spenser resigned as abbot in 1448.[38]

Fuller codicological analysis of the manuscript containing the B-version further illustrates the processes involved in cultural mapping; and since the B-text of *LFMB* is the version that is most commonly quoted, and seems to be the earliest (as well as one of the fullest) copy of the poem that has survived, it will be discussed thoroughly here. The *Linguistic Atlas of Late Mediaeval English* (*LALME*), localized (as Linguistic Profile = LP 3) the language of the section of the Royal manuscript containing B to north-east Derbyshire, near Mosborough. This localization would align the text geographically with other versions; the manuscript containing A, for instance, seems plausibly to come from the village of Heage (as implied by the scribe's name) in the

---

For comprehensive discussions of the evidence for provenance of all extant copies of *LFMB*, with references to date, see further Smith, 'The Manuscripts'.

[36] P. Hardman, 'A Note on Some Lost Manuscripts', *The Library* 30 (1975), 245–7 (p. 246); see further Smith, 'The Manuscripts', p. 370.

[37] See further R. Thomson, *A Descriptive Catalogue of the Medieval Manuscripts of Corpus Christi College, Oxford* (Cambridge, 2011); and N. Ker, *Medieval Libraries of Great Britain*, 2nd ed. (London, 1964), p. 159, and A. Watson, *Medieval Libraries of Great Britain: supplement to the second edition* (London, 1987), p. 58.

[38] See Ker, *Medieval Libraries*, p. 149; Smith, 'The Manuscripts', p. 376.

same county, while *LALME* located the hands in the manuscript containing E as 'belong[ing] to Derbys[hire]'; as flagged in the relevant catalogue (James 1907: 79), two of the flyleaves in the Caius manuscript 'are composed of an account roll of a monastery in or near Derby dated 23 Hen. VI' (= 1444). However, early evidence of provenance indicates that the Royal manuscript containing B – if it actually originated in Derbyshire, as suggested by this localization – travelled since.[39] The earliest external evidence of provenance is a fifteenth-century hand that records the name 'Nich. Anger of Hiclilgham de parochia de Halys'. *Hiclilgham* is generally interpreted as Heckingham, and the parish is that of Hales to the south-east of Norwich in Norfolk. The book eventually arrived in the collection of the great Elizabethan book-collector – and, perhaps significantly, recusant – John, Lord Lumley (c. 1533–1609), and only thence to the royal collection: thus its shelf-mark. Other early names include John Carlet, Edward Banyster and John Radclyff, none of whom can be identified with any certainty.[40] Another name, however, is 'Kattryng Houses off Moullyne in Kent' (fol. 107v); it is just possible that *Moullyne* is Malling in Kent, home of an abbey of Benedictine nuns whose library contained both Latin and vernacular materials.[41] Malling is just over 30 miles from Cheam, where Lumley's great palace of Nonsuch was situated.

Analysis of the contents of the Royal manuscript other than *LFMB* reveals the textual network in which it was situated. *LFMB* is the first item in the volume, but fourteen other texts in verse and prose are recorded in its British

---

[39] As I have flagged elsewhere, 'The localization of texts by linguistic typological fit does not prove that texts were produced in the same place: a point which bears repetition, since linguistic evidence is sometimes referred to as proof of, *rather than evidence for*, provenance ... Scribes and authors moved about, and took their language with them; and to say that *LALME* places a text by linguistic means in such and such a location does not mean necessarily that the text was physically produced there'; see J. J. Smith, 'Mapping the Language of the Vernon Manuscript', in *The Making of the Vernon Manuscript*, ed. W. Scase (Turnhout, 2013), pp. 49–70 (p. 54).

[40] The anonymous reviewer of an earlier draft of this chapter, to whom I am much indebted, notes that the name 'Edward Banyster' is associated with Oxford, Bodleian Library, MS Digby 261, a sixteenth-century manuscript of Middle English romances that was apparently modelled on early printed texts. See J. M. P. Donatelli, 'From Script to Print and Back', *Design and Production in Medieval and Early Modern Europe: Essays in Honor of Bradford Blaine*, ed. N. van Deusen (Ottawa, 1998), pp. 88–102; and M. Mills, 'EB and His Two Books: Visual Impact and the Power of Meaningful Suggestion: "Reading" the Illustrations in MSS Douce 261 and Egerton 3132A', in *Imagining the Book*, ed. S. Kelly and J. J. Thompson (Turnhout, 2005), pp. 173–91.

[41] See D. Bell, *What Nuns Read: Books and Libraries in Medieval English Nunneries* (Kalamazoo, 1995), pp. 152–3.

Library catalogue entry.[42] Four Latin texts – two by Richard Rolle – are accompanied by a translation into English of one of Wycliffe's epistles, viz. *Epistola ad simplices sacerdotes*, beginning 'Hit semes medeful to susteyne prestis togedre'. Of the remaining works, a few are not found elsewhere: a short text on the twelve virtues on folios 100r–101r, a quatrain 'Heuen is wonnen with woo and schame' and two poems at the end of the book, 'Of þo flode of þo world' and 'Þo whele of fortune' (these latter both possibly were inspired by the much longer – and very widely circulated – poem *The Prick of Conscience*).[43] Another prose text, an English version of a discourse *De duodecim utilitatibus tribulationis* 'doubtfully attributed to Peter of Blois'[44] is also found otherwise only in Oxford, Bodleian Library, MS Laud Misc. 210.[45] Other texts in the Royal manuscript are, however, more widely attested. *LFMB* is followed by a pair of lyrics – 'a songe of luf longynge' – addressed to Jesus, which might be considered (like many religious lyrics) to be supplementary prayers; these lyrics are recorded in many other manuscripts including three well-known major religious repository-volumes associated with the West Midlands (the Vernon and Simeon manuscripts, and John of Northwood's miscellany).[46] Other witnesses to the text appear in Warminster, Longleat House, MS 29, written in Hiberno-English; Dublin, Trinity College, MS 155, with language located by *LALME* to Staffordshire (LP 215); and the *Processional of the Nuns of Chester*, now San Marino, CA, Huntington Library, MS EL.34.B.7.[47] The *Processional*, interestingly also owned by Benedictine nuns,[48] includes various texts in Latin and English, and a contemporary colophon on folio 85v records that 'This booke longeth to Dame Margery Byrkenhed of Chestre'. Chester's connections to Ireland, as the major English medieval port of the north-west

---

[42] 'Royal MS 17 B XVII', *British Library Digital Catalogue of Manuscripts*, accessed October 23, 2022, http://searcharchives.bl.uk/IAMS_VU2:LSCOP_BL:IAMS040-002107306. For other verse witnesses to the texts in the Royal MS, see *DIMEV*, passim.

[43] See, respectively: P. S. Jolliffe, *A Check-List of Middle English Prose Writings of Spiritual Guidance* (Toronto, 1974), p. 114, item I.39; *DIMEV*, item 1926; *DIMEV*, items 1662 and 402; and R. E. Lewis and A. McIntosh, *A Descriptive Guide to the Manuscripts of the Prick of Conscience* (Oxford, 1982), pp. 12–13.

[44] From the British Library catalogue entry: see n. 43 above.

[45] See Jolliffe, *A Check-List*, p. 166, item J.3(c).

[46] These manuscripts are, respectively: Oxford, Bodleian Library, MS Eng. poet. a.1; London, British Library, MS Additional 22283; and London, British Library, MS Additional 37787.

[47] The text is printed in *The Processional of the Nuns of Chester*, ed. J. Wickham Legg (London, 1899), pp. 30–3. The poem is recorded as *DIMEV* item 5077.

[48] Bell, *What Nuns Read*, pp. 129–30.

Midlands and thus the gateway for Ireland, are well-known, and for this item many of the Royal manuscript's links look west.

The lyrics are followed by the *Speculum Guy of Warwick*, which (despite its title) is a religious poem, in which Guy – a pious layman seeking religious instruction – is advised about various basic points of Christian belief by an imagined (and now legendary) Alcuin, whose *Liber de virtutibus et viciis* (c. 800 CE) is a distant source.[49] Ten copies of this text are now known.[50] It circulated widely in late medieval England, and several copies contain language localized by *LALME*, ranging from Gloucestershire (Oxford, Bodleian Library, MS Additional C.220) to Essex (Cambridge, St John's College, MS 256). A version is found in the well-known Auchinleck Manuscript (Edinburgh, National Library of Scotland, MS Advocates' 19.2.1), generally considered to be a London production.[51] The *Speculum* is followed by another work with a wide circulation, namely the *Stimulus Conscientiae Minor*, considered by Horstman to be 'unquestionabl[y]' by Richard Rolle. Horstman's belief was based on his view – now no longer held – that[52] Rolle was the author of *The Prick of Conscience*, of which the *Stimulus* is a much shorter 'paraphrase'.[53] The *Stimulus* survives in some eight copies.[54] *LALME* offers localizations of the language for several of the manuscripts, ranging from Lancashire and Yorkshire to Leicestershire; one copy (London, British Library, MS Additional 10053), however, is in a manuscript known to have been copied for John Pery, an Austin Canon of the Holy Trinity, Aldgate in London.

What this analysis of contents and the provenance demonstrates is that the texts in the Royal manuscript were part of a 'devotional currency', widely shared across great swathes of late medieval England (and indeed its incipient

---

[49] The original *Liber* was composed for Guido of Tours, whose name led him to be identified with the romance hero. See A. S. G. Edwards, 'The *Speculum Guy de Warwick* and Lydgate's *Guy of Warwick*: the Non-Romance Middle English Tradition', in *Guy of Warwick: Icon and Ancestor*, ed. R. Field and A. Wiggins (Cambridge, 2007), pp. 81–93.

[50] *DIMEV*, item 1782.

[51] See, for example, A. I. Doyle, 'English Books in and out of Court from Edward III to Henry VII', in *English Court Culture in the Later Middle Ages*, ed. V. J. Scattergood and J. W. Sherborne (London, 1984), pp. 163–82.

[52] As with the Vernon Manuscript. See R. Perry, 'Editorial Politics in the Vernon Manuscript', in *The Making of the Vernon Manuscript*, pp. 71–95.

[53] G. Trudel, 'The Middle English "Book of Penance" and the Readers of the "Cursor Mundi"', *Medium Ævum* 74 (2005), 10–33 (p. 15).

[54] *DIMEV*, item 422. *DIMEV* records seven copies; an eighth is Wellesley, MA, Wellesley College, MS 8, for which see Lewis and McIntosh, *A Descriptive Guide*, p. 129.

colonial expansion in the Pale of Dublin). It also seems likely that readership for such vernacular materials varied widely, perhaps more so than has traditionally been considered, ranging from great abbeys (as with the Corpus manuscript containing the C-version of *LFMB*) and noble households through humbler settings, including those in which female readers were dominant.[55] It is possible that the Royal manuscript may have been what is now known as a 'common profit' book, moving – as its inscriptions suggest – between secular and religious locations and intended for sharing vernacular works of devotion. The Royal manuscript may therefore be comparable with John Colop's miscellany, now Cambridge, University Library, MS Ff.6.31.[56] Such texts informed the creative 'imaginative world' of English Catholicism so eloquently described by Eamon Duffy.[57]

However, in reconstructing this imaginative world there is one further step that we might make, where other insights are helpful. Tim Machan argued some time ago, with special reference to medieval manuscript culture, that 'the pragmatics through which a work was articulated included highly expressive features of layout and design that manuscript producers could consciously manipulate', and in a later publication he went on to identify a correlation between linguistic code-switching and deployment of distinct scripts and coloured inks.[58] The term 'pragmatics' is significant; recent research by several scholars, notably those working within the 'Pragmatics of the Page' paradigm, has demonstrated how the analysis of graphic features has opened up new hermeneutic possibilities.[59] It is now possible, at least in principle, to reconstruct not only *who* engaged with these manuscripts, and *where* they did so, but – with greater delicacy than has been achievable hitherto – *how* they did so.

To illustrate the possibilities here we might examine in detail a passage from the B-version of *LFMB*. Passage 1 is a diplomatic transcription from the Royal MS with added lineation; it differs from Simmons's edition in not

---

[55] See D. Watt, 'The Paston Women and Chaucer: Reading Women and Canon Formation in the Fifteenth Century', *SAC* 42 (2020), 337–50.

[56] See W. Scase, 'Reginald Pecock, John Carpenter, and John Colop's "Common-Profit" Books: Aspects of Book Ownership and Circulation in Fifteenth-Century London', *Medium Ævum* 61 (1992), 261–74.

[57] E. Duffy, *The Stripping of the Altars*, 2nd ed. (New Haven, 2005), p. 593.

[58] T. W. Machan, *Textual Criticism and Middle English Texts* (Charlottesville, 1994), p. 165; and 'The Visual Pragmatics of Code-Switching in Late Middle English Literature', in *Code-Switching in Early English*, ed. H. Schendl and L. Wright (Berlin, 2011), pp. 303–33.

[59] For example, *Verbal and Visual Communication*, ed. Peikola et al., and Smith, *Transforming Early English*.

supplying conjectural readings where the manuscript is defective, in deploying <y> where Simmons uses thorn (the figural realizations of the two *litterae* are identical in the manuscript) and in retaining the punctuation of the original. As in Simmons's edition, expansions of contractions are recorded (in italics), and bold is used to flag underlining of the text in red; for typographical reasons engrossed initials are hard to reproduce in the way that Simmons was able to do, so a gap is left to indicate the space occupied (these initials in this passage appear in blue ink in the manuscript). Emendations by Simmons (S) and Horstman (H) are flagged in footnotes.

Passage (1) [fol. 6r]
Bi gods worde welcome to me.[60]
Ioy & louyng lord be to ye.[61]
W hils hit is red speke you noght/.
    bot yenk on him **yt dere ye boght/.**
Sayande yus in **yi [......] mynde.**[62]   185
als you shalt after **wryten fynde.**
I he*s*u m[...]ue gr*a*unt me yi gr*a*ce.[63]
    and of [...]mendme*n*t might & space.[64]
    yi word to kepe & do yi wille.
    yo gode to chese & leeue yo ille.   190
    and yt hit so may be.
    Gode ihe*s*u gr*a*unt hit me. Amen.
R eherce yis oft i*n* yi yoght.
    to yo gosple be don for gete hit noght.
Som where bisyde when hit is done.   195
you make a cros and kys hit sone./
Men oen to saie yo crede som tyme.
when yai saie hore. loke you saie yine.
yis yt folouse in **englishe lett**re**.**
I wolde you sayde hit for yo bettre**.**   200

[60] S considers MS *bi* [*sic*] to be an error, and in a marginal note suggests emending to *be*. H agrees.
[61] An additional letter <o> is inserted by caret before the <o> in *louyng*, as noted by H.
[62] [......] = erasure in MS, not indicated by S; H notes the erasure, but simply suggests that a word is missing, possibly *my*.
[63] S reads *myne* without indicating the erased letters; 3–4 letters seem to be missing between <m> and <n>. H suggests emending to *my loue*, which makes sense in context.
[64] S, H read *amendment* for *[.]mendment*, without indication of damage.

bot yai say hore say you non ellis.
bot do forthe af*er* **als yis boke tellis.**
here to loke you take gode hede.
for here is wryten yin englyshe crede.

  I trow i*n* god fader of might/   205
     yt alle has wroght/
     heue*n* & erthe day & night/
     and alle of noght/
     And i*n* ih*es*u yt gods son is al onely/[65]
     bothe god & mo*n* lord endles/[66]   210

[fol. 6v]

In hi*m* trow I.
thurgh mekenes of yo holy gast.
yat was so milde.
he lyght i*n* mary mayden chast.
be come a childe.   215
vnder pounce pilat pyned he was
vs forto saue.
done on cros & deed he was.
layde i*n* his gr*a*ue.
yo soul of hi*m* went i*n* to helle.   220
yo sothe to say.
vp he rose i*n* flesshe & felle
yo thryd day.

The most obvious feature of Passage 1 is the alternation between plain text and that which is given rubricated underlining, and throughout B – and indeed in several other versions of *LFMB* – the reason for the difference is clear: the sections with rubrication flag commentary and instructions as to actions to be undertaken, whereas the unrubricated sections (in *black letter*: B, line 440) are used for the prayer for grace and for the vernacular creed.

However, there are other less obvious features of the text worthy of comment. Simmons was careful in his edition to reflect the hierarchy of *litterae notabiliores*, and in doing so he was capturing something important about the way the text was to be apprehended. In Passage 1 the engrossed letters introduce the rubricated sections, whereas the larger ones align with prayer and

---

[65] S gives *al onely* a line to itself, thus accounting for an extra line in his lineation, but the MS is as above.
[66] A later hand has repeated this line at the foot of the page, with pen-flourishes.

creed. Such foregrounding was widespread in manuscript books to 'guide the reader around the parts of the text', but the careful correlation here seems to correlate with moments of solemnity, 'mark[ing] the structure of the work to structure readers' responses'.[67]

And there are in Passage 1 yet further 'graphic cues', as Katherine O'Brien O'Keeffe has called them, that might be considered, viz. punctuation.[68] As Malcolm Parkes alerted us,

> Punctuation is not a matter of 'accidentals' but a form of hermeneutics … part of the pragmatics of written language, in that it exacts from readers a contribution from their own ranges of experience to assess the broader significances of various kinds of literary, linguistic and semantic structures embodied in the text.[69]

Most lines in the B-version of *LFMB* conclude with a simple punctus. However, virgules are also deployed on occasion, as follows:

> **I** trow i*n* god fader of might/
> yt alle has wrog*h*t/
> heue*n* & erthe day & night/
> and alle of noght/
> And i*n* ihe*s*u yt gods son is al onely/
> bothe god & mo*n* lord endles/ (ll. 205–10)

In addition, at the end of a few lines, both punctus and virgule appear.

Analysis shows that punctuation in this passage seems to be deployed *per cola et commata*. The terms *colon* (plural *cola*) and *comma* (plural *commata*) used to refer to rhetorical units rather than marks of punctuation, 'meaning something like "by clauses and pauses" … Each unit is probably what a person would read and speak aloud in a single breath'.[70] The punctus commonly found

---

[67] D. Wakelin, *Designing English* (Oxford, 2018), p. 78. See also R. Dahood, 'The Use of Coloured Initials and Other Division Markers in Early Versions of *Ancrene Riwle*', in *Medieval English Studies Presented to George Kane*, ed. E. D. Kennedy, R. A. Waldron and J. S. Wittig (Cambridge, 1988), 79–97, and the essays in Kerby-Fulton et al., *Opening Up*.

[68] K. O'Brien O'Keeffe, *Visible Song: Transitional Literacy in Old English Verse* (Cambridge, 1990).

[69] M. B. Parkes, 'Medieval Punctuation and the Modern Editor', in *Filologia classica e filologia romanza*, ed. A. Ferrari (Spoleto, 1999), pp. 337–49 (p. 338).

[70] C. de Hamel, *Meetings with Remarkable Manuscripts* (Harmondsworth, 2016), p. 20; de Hamel draws a modern parallel: 'Winston Churchill typed his great speeches like this, so that they could be read at a glance and his famous oratorical pauses

at the end of each of the couplet lines in iambic tetrameter is thus in this context unsurprising; as commonly noted by metrists there is a prototypical correlation of syntactic unit with line in iambic tetrameter,[71] as in the following where line and *colon* coincide:

Sayande yus i*n* **yi [……] mynde.**
als you shalt aft*er* **wryten fynde.** (ll. 185–6)

As a result, end-stopping is common in poems written in this metre, and the punctus in the practice of this scribe seems to be used simply to emphasize this characteristic. When, however, there is a departure from the tetrameter measure as in the vernacular creed on the same page, the scribe changes punctuation-practice, using virgules to mark *cola*. This practice changes on folio 6v, however; at the top-left corner of the page the scribe has added a red star of David, presumably to mark the continued foregrounding of the creed; the decorated initial necessarily does not continue onto that side of the leaf. He then ceases to use virgules – the creed covers the entire page, so no disambiguation from other usages is required – replacing them with a simple punctus, save at two points where the *colon* runs over a line, as with the following two examples:

vnder pounce pilat pyned he was
vs forto saue. (ll. 216–17)

vp he rose i*n* flesshe & felle
yo thryd day. (ll. 222–3)

---

were graphically preordained in the layout of his script' (p. 22). A valuable account of the origins of the notion is Thomas Habinek, *The Colometry of Latin Prose* (Berkeley, 1985), especially chapter 1. Habinek shows that the most common view in antiquity – from where medieval (and indeed later) grammarians drew their ideas – was that the colon was a constituent of a sentence, whereas the comma, which originally overlapped in meaning with the colon, came to be regarded as a subdivision of the colon. Both were primarily rhetorical/rhythmical units 'whose boundaries happen to coincide with the boundaries between certain grammatical units' (*Colometry*, p. 11). The sentence (*sententia*) was defined by Malcolm Parkes, in what remains by far the most authoritative discussion of the subject, as 'A thought or opinion: especially the substance or significance expressed by the words of a grammatical "sentence" or a rhetorical period', whereas the period (*periodus*) was 'an utterance or complete rhetorical structure which expresses a single idea' (*Pause and Effect: A History of Punctuation in the West* (London, 1992), pp. 306–7). It will be observed in both cases that the notions were, as was commonly the case in grammatical analysis until towards the end of the last century (and as is still the case in 'popular' understanding of grammar), defined primarily in semantic terms.

[71] D. Attridge, *The Rhythms of English Poetry* (London, 1982), pp. 80–1.

Here, no punctus is needed at the end of the longer line. In sum, the text has been set out in rhetorical units in a way that assists oral delivery and aural perception.

Fascinatingly, therefore, there are aspects of the appearance of the page in the B-version of *LFMB* that are designed for visual apprehension (*litterae notabiliores*, marks of punctuation), and other features that point to oral performance. We might in this context recall the notion of 'speech-like' texts, as formulated by Jonathan Culpeper and Merja Kytö, which emphasizes that the dividing-line between the written and spoken modes is a fuzzy one,[72] and of Brian Stock's argument that the simple oral/literate distinction is too clumsy to deal with cultures where engagement with written texts is frequently mediated, and not dependent on the ability to read.[73] Another useful point to note in this context is Joyce Coleman's, relevant not only to the late medieval and courtly verse with which she was primarily concerned but also to the discourse community engaged with these devotional writings:

> The evidence ... assembled strongly supports the contention that public reading survived well past the announced date of its obsolescence. The strong influences of rising literacy and improving book-technologies, including printing, were countermanded for a considerable period by a simple, persistent preference among elite audiences for the social experience of literature. Such group-listening was synonymous neither with rowdy boorishness nor with paralyzed docility – two extremes frequently mooted by modern scholars. The data suggest, rather, that those who listened to the late medieval texts surveyed here were literate, sophisticated people who participated actively both with their attention and their response. While we can never recover the full experience of such sessions, it behooves us to recognize that they took place.[74]

A book such as the Royal manuscript would seem therefore to have existed as part of what Adam Fox has helpfully described as a 'literate environment'.[75] Fox is referring to the sixteenth and seventeenth centuries, but present-day scholarship increasingly emphasizes the continuities as well as the disjunctions between the medieval and early modern periods.

---

[72] J. Culpeper and M. Kytö, *Early Modern English Dialogues* (Cambridge, 2010).
[73] B. Stock, *The Implications of Literacy: Written Language and Models of Interpretation in the Eleventh and Twelfth Centuries* (Princeton, 1983).
[74] J. Coleman, *Public Reading and the Reading Public in Late Medieval England and France* (Cambridge, 1996), pp. xiii–xiv.
[75] A. Fox, *Oral and Literate Culture in England 1500–1700* (Oxford, 2000), p. 37.

Editions as Maps

It is therefore possible – albeit with a degree of speculation – to get quite close to the practices of the discourse community in which the Royal manuscript, and the earliest surviving copy of *LFMB*, existed in late medieval England: to enter into the imaginative world of the past.[76] In doing so, we are aiming at one of the antiquarian goals expressed by Simmons in the preface to his edition:

> My attention was in the first instance drawn to the British Museum MS. [i.e. the Royal MS containing the B-version of *LFMB*] by Mr. Maskell's extracts from it in the notes of his Ancient English Liturgies. It was one of the first books I asked for on my next visit to the Reading-room, and, besides its curious ritual information, I was much struck by the fact that it was the only document I had met with that enables us to know the prayers which the unlearned of our forefathers used at mass, and by the light it threw upon their inner religious life from a point of view different from that of the many medieval sermons that have come down to us.[77]

Simmons wished, therefore, to reconstruct this 'inner religious life', and to that end his antiquarian approach, however misdirected in modern terms, was nevertheless in its own way illuminating. His attempt (rarely undertaken today) to capture the pragmatic characteristics of the manuscripts he was editing, and his addition of numerous 'Notes and Illustrations' – including editions of numerous other devotional works he considered relevant for reconstructing late medieval religion – may be taken as a precursor of present-day cultural mapping. In so doing he approached his material not only synchronically in terms of the medieval past, but also diachronically in linking it to later practice, including that of his own time: a true descendant of the Romantics, he had a 'lived relationship' with history.[78]

Simmons's edition can also, perhaps, be seen as a useful corrective to some modern notions of the editorial process as an objective exercise. In this context, we might recall Roy Michael Liuzza's words:

> It is true that an edition of a manuscript is no substitute for the manuscript itself – map is not territory, as they say – but on the other hand territory isn't map either; nor do modern readers have the same relationship to text and page that medieval readers or audiences might have had. An edition,

---

[76] See Hill, *Time's Witness*, p. 5.
[77] *LFMB*, ed. Simmons, pp. ix–x.
[78] S. Bann, *The Inventions of History* (Manchester, 1990), p. 102, cited Hill, *Time's Witness*, p. 5.

like a map, is useful precisely *because* it is a model, a representation of a text and its history, an analytical language for reducing artifact to information.[79]

Maps of course change to reflect the cultures and purposes for which they are developed; the fourteenth-century Gough Map, Mercator's Projection (1569), and my *Collins 2022 Road Atlas* all relate to the political biases and practical demands of their times. It is unsurprising that Simmons's edition, therefore, reflected the conditions of 1879. But in addition, like his predecessor antiquarians, he identified something important about how the material forms of a medieval manuscript reflected its devotional functions: something that present-day readers of medieval texts, encountering them only in modern editions, are apt to miss.

---

[79] R. M. Liuzza, 'Scribes of the Mind: Editing Old English, in Theory and Practice', in *The Power of Words: Anglo-Saxon Studies Presented to Donald G. Scragg on his Seventieth Birthday*, ed. H. Magennis and J. Wilcox (Morgantown, 2006), pp. 245–77 (p. 276). See also Machan, *Textual Criticism*, pp. 72–3.

12

Professional Reading Networks and the Reception of Nicholas Love's *Mirror of the Blessed Life of Jesus Christ*: Opportunities and Consequences

JOHN J. THOMPSON

There is much to suggest that a myriad of professional reading habits among the writers, scribes, annotators, artists and patrons who commissioned and produced books in late medieval manuscript culture has profoundly shaped our own twenty-first century reading experience. Wide ranging and often complex networks of professional reading associations can be built up around such intermediary figures. They are intermediary because their interventions stand somewhere between the written text and the original intended readers, as well as between us and our understanding as later readers of the much older written texts before us. And what has not often been clearly or carefully enough acknowledged in the many codicological and textual studies of late medieval reading experience that have recently emerged is that the idea of the professional reader is useful as a corrective to any simplistic assumption that textual evidence regarding what an author said or what a reader was expected to do, drawn down from fifteenth-century books by scholars working more than half a millennium later, can necessarily offer us anything like a completely reliable guide to late medieval reading habits. As Kathryn and her students' important contributions to the field have frequently demonstrated, the motivation for readerly actions in the surviving books is not always readily apparent and requires some careful scholarly excavation.[1]

Previous studies of fifteenth-century professional reading habits regarding Middle English literary writings have focussed on the work of moonlighting

---

[1] Characteristic fruits of such labours appear in *The Medieval Professional Reader at Work: Evidence from Manuscripts of Chaucer, Langland, Kempe, and Gower*, ed. K. Kerby-Fulton and M. Hilmo (Victoria BC, 2001).

scribes whose day-to-day activities were shaped by their engagement in producing documents in late medieval bureaucratic institutions, primarily in urban, legal and governmental settings, or for guilds and larger, often aristocratic, secular and religious households. Little has been said, in this respect, regarding the professional readers who were also spiritual directors and whose religious vocation encouraged them to remain largely cloistered in an institutional space where the idea of advancing the interests of their order by preaching with a pen shaped much of their thinking and became a rule of thumb for much of their scribal activities. In this celebratory essay it therefore seems fitting to review what we think we know regarding how Nicholas Love's *Mirror of the Blessed Life of Jesus Christ* was written, produced and consumed by its earliest readers in the later medieval period. Unlike previous studies of Love's readership, my essay is primarily concerned with the presumed interests and activities of Love's largely anonymous earliest copyists who shared some of the same ambitions for Love's *Mirror* as the Mount Grace prior himself and arranged for the earliest surviving and often expensively-produced written copies to be prepared and made available outside the monastery walls. I hope that this essay will show that it is particularly helpful to consider such early copyists as professional readers and view them as part of the important early reading networks that secured the successful early and continuing dissemination of Love's text.

I have resisted the temptation to place the idea of professional reading in scare quotes in this essay, but there is at least one good reason why it is tempting to do so. That is because Love's *Mirror* is ostensibly directed at an imagined audience of 'simple souls' apparently untutored in the specialised meditative reading tasks associated with the monastic *lectio divina* that his vernacular text recommends.[2] Without at least some additional special pleading, such 'simple souls' can hardly be considered the professional readers of the kind I have in mind who took responsibility for the earliest transmission and promotion of Love's text. Indeed one might well ask where the process of the simple souls actually reading Love's work comes in as he explains the rationale for writing his vernacular text. For example, as an important preliminary to the larger task ahead, Love describes the kind of spiritual direction his intended audience will likely require. It is remarkable that at this early point he manages to characterise the necessary processes of inwardly understanding and being scripturally mindful of Christ's life through using his vernacular writing as a mirror without initially making any explicit reference to the reading process itself.

---

[2] J. J. Thompson, 'Love Reading?', *Poetica* 91–2 (2019), 93–104 (pp. 93–4).

Love's text instead opens with a prologue or *Proheme/Proem* that may well have been largely aimed at his professional readers rather than simple souls. Here he talks about the comfort and promise of words and deeds written about Christ and how the understanding of these by simple souls and the feeding and stirring of the devotional imagination can be accomplished by what he describes as the 'mylke of ly3te doctryne' rather than 'sadde mete of grete clargye and of h[ye] contemplacion'.[3] In this preliminary experience of Love's text, such meditative habits seem to be linked to a lifestyle choice of prayerful meditation that is certainly larger than any such reading process, professional or otherwise. And when the idea of actually reading his text is finally mentioned, at the end of Love's prologue, it is evoked in combination with the idea of hearing his book as part of a request to pray for the author of his Latin source rather than as the primary means by which the intensity of the scriptural experience recommended by the *lectio divina* and Love's text is experienced:

> And amongis oþere who so rediþ or heriþ þis boke felyng any gostly swetnes or grace þereþorth; pray he for charite specialy for þe auctour, & þe drawere oute þereof, as it is writen here in english, to þe profite of symple & deuoute soules ('Proem', p. 13, ll. 25–8).

During the course of his writing, of course, Love expands on this idea of reading, memorising and hearing his text, offering a range of possibilities for immersive and selective meditative reading that can hardly be dismissed as simplistic or elementary.[4] His account obviously builds on and develops the model of repetitive memorised utterances exemplified by the discussion of St Cecilia's meditative habits found in his Latin source and promoted in the *Mirror* prologue.[5] Any claim we might wish to make regarding the possible potential of such 'simple souls' to become professional readers, in the sense that the term is sometimes used to describe scholarly or university-trained readers,

---

[3] All page and line references are to *Nicholas Love, The Mirror of the Blessed Life of Jesus Christ. A Full Critical Edition*, ed. M. G. Sargent (Exeter, 2005); here 'Proem', p. 10, ll. 15–16.

[4] J. J. Thompson, 'Reading Miscellaneously in and around the English Pseudo-Bonaventuran Tradition', in *The Pseudo-Bonaventuran Lives of Christ, Exploring the Middle English Tradition*, ed. I. Johnson and A. F. Westphall (Turnhout, 2013), pp. 127–50 (pp. 131–4).

[5] J. J. Thompson, 'Reading with a Passion: Fifteenth-Century English Geographies of Orthodoxy', in *Cultures of Religious Reading in the Late Middle Ages, Instructing the Soul, Feeding the Spirit, and Awakening the Passion*, ed. S. Corbellini (Turnhout, 2013), pp. 55–69 (pp. 57–61).

will obviously therefore require scare quotes and much further unpacking.[6] A number of recent studies by former members of the Belfast/St Andrews *Geographies of Orthodoxy* project (2007–11) and others have shown that efforts to clarify the terms we should use to identify the later readership of Love's *Mirror* much more precisely than hitherto attempted are already well under way.[7] It remains an attractive prospect to approach Love's *Mirror* from such a variety of perspectives, of course. That is because his later exploration in the text of the different forms of meditative work that might eventually prove beneficial, or that an audience might reasonably be expected to undertake, sometimes sets a fairly high horizon of expectation. That horizon of expectation is likely to have been first encountered by the professional readers and spiritual directors for whom the process of countering *ignorancia sacerdotum* and the Lollard threat remains an institutional imperative that has been publicly voiced in Love's work. And it is perhaps on offer also to some of the simple souls who are deemed ready at a later stage to take on the more inward-looking and personal selection of devotional reading materials such as his *Mirror* offers.[8]

The professional readers that most interest me in this essay, then, are of a different order than Love's imagined audience of simple souls, and they are largely those that show they are fully aware of the opportunities offered by the packaging and consumption of Love's text in preparation for its release to a much broader imagined English readership. Nicholas Love was the first such professional reader, of course, recognizing and exploiting the creative space that existed between his Middle English translated version and its Latin source in the *Meditationes vitae Christi* by adjusting the colouring of his vernacular

[6] For distinctions between 'the scholar or professional man of letters' and 'cultivated' and/or 'pragmatic' late medieval readerships see the seminal study in M. B. Parkes, 'The Literacy of the Laity', in *Literature and Western Civilization: The Medieval World*, ed. D. Daiches and A. Thorlby (London, 1973), pp. 555–77 (p. 555).

[7] See now the approaches taken to questions of pseudo-Bonaventuran readership in essays by S. Kelly, I. Johnson, R. Perry and D. J. Falls, all in *Manuscript Culture and Medieval Devotional Traditions: Essays in Honour of Michael G. Sargent*, ed. J. N. Brown and N. R. Rice (York, 2021). See also the sterling work by A. F. Westphall, 'Textual Profiles', *Geographies of Orthodoxy*, accessed April 6, 2023, https://geographies-of-orthodoxy.qub.ac.uk/. The views expressed in this essay on professional reading are my own and do not necessarily reflect those of other former *Geographies* team members.

[8] For Love's tendency to build upon the examples set by much earlier vernacular pastoralia in this regard see J. J. Thompson, 'Preaching with a Pen: Audience and Self-Regulation in the Writing and Reception of John Mirk and Nicholas Love', in *Preaching the Word in Manuscript and Print in Late Medieval England, Essays in Honour of Susan Powell*, ed. M. W. Driver and V. O'Mara (Turnhout, 2013), pp. 101–16 (pp. 110–12).

translation to meet other often quite specific and apparently sometimes more pressing local concerns.[9] The task of translating and revising the *Meditationes* along such lines may have commenced before Love entered the Carthusian order, and it probably continued for some time during his period at Mount Grace. As rector, Love was head of the community and subsequently became prior when Mount Grace was formally incorporated into the Carthusian Order in April 1410. Michael Sargent's careful research has brought together the evidence showing just what an auspicious time this heralded for the latest English Charterhouse. This was largely because of its success, after a fallow post-Ricardian period, in securing Lancastrian patronage and allegiance.[10]

Love's ongoing *Meditationes* translation work probably played a memorable, perhaps also greatly symbolic, part in that development. At or around the same 1410 period as Thomas Arundel, the Lancastrian Archbishop of Canterbury, was accorded confraternity and officially became a benefactor of Mount Grace, Love submitted his *Mirror* version for examination. Approval was granted in the form of an archiepiscopal 'memorandum of approbation' indicating that Love's text had been professionally read and officially licensed for distribution, 'ad fidelium edificacionem & hereticorum siue lollardorum confutacionem'. The phrasing of the Latin authorisation picks up and echoes how Love's *Mirror* had already set out its stall 'in confusion of alle fals lollardes, & in confort of all trewe louers & wirchiperes', so the Arundel memorandum was hardly pointing Love's work in a direction that he had not already decided to take.[11] Nevertheless, this purposeful coincidence of Latin and English phrasing reinforces the view that the first decade of Lancastrian rule placed a premium on socio-political stability and anti-Lollard religious conformity, features of which early fifteenth-century English professional readers and writers of a conservative reforming cast were probably often aware. Others may perhaps have learned directly about this direction of travel because of the thirteen articles making up Arundel's Lambeth *Constitutions* (dated 1409 but drafted in 1407).[12] At some point well before 1410, it is not inconceivable that Love already recognized how the pages containing his ongoing writing and translation efforts potentially carried a significance and meaning far beyond the pastoral task he had initially set himself as a spiritual adviser for the Mount Grace community. If so, he must have taken the time to adjust the

---

[9] Usefully summarized in Sargent, ed., *Nicholas Love*, 'Introduction', pp. 38–54.
[10] Sargent, ed., *Nicholas Love*, 'Introduction', pp. 27–33.
[11] Sargent, ed., *Nicholas Love*, 'Introduction', pp. 54–75; see also 'Text', p. 7.
[12] See the provocative seminal study in N. Watson, 'Censorship and Cultural Change in Late Medieval England: Vernacular Theology, the Oxford Translation Debate, and Arundel's Constitutions of 1409', *Speculum* 70 (1995), 822–64.

nature and scope of his writing and translation accordingly to match any new ambitions he or other professional readers might have had for his text or to take advantage of other opportunities for Mount Grace and his religious order that might have emerged during his time there as rector and then prior.

Viewed with the benefit of hindsight, Love's *Mirror* offers us a remarkable tale of textual survival across two centuries, and it is attractive to assume that it took on the role of an authorised vernacular response to the perceived Lollard threat, particularly, perhaps, because of the known circulation of the Wycliffite and other vernacular biblical translations that had been so vigorously condemned by Arundel. In addition to its preservation in some form in over sixty manuscript copies, there were nine successive early printings of Love's *Mirror*, all nine of which preserve fully integrated copies of the Arundel memorandum at the head of the main text. These start with William Caxton's prints in 1484 and 1490, and continue with five further by Wynkyn de Worde between 1494 and 1530, and two by Richard Pynson in 1494 and 1506. The prints were not independently derived from manuscript copies but all show differing degrees of dependence on each other and are all based on a single textual tradition – the so-called $α^1$ tradition, which is part of one of three main textual groupings (α, β, γ) identified by traditional stemmatic analysis for the extant copies by Michael Sargent.[13]

Text-critical analysis has enabled something further to be made of the work's earliest transmission patterns. As part of his continuing textual analysis, Sargent has suggested that the earliest representatives of each *Mirror* textual grouping may have simultaneously co-existed within the first few years of the text's existence: broadly speaking the first branch (comprising $α^{1,2,3}$ in the stemma) represents the author's original text, although no holograph manuscript survives; the second ($β^{1,2}$) represents an authorial revision; and the third ($γ^{1,2}$) represents a scribal version. There is remarkably little textual variation, in substantive terms, between α, β and γ texts but much to suggest that the authoritative nature of Love's work remained an important factor in ensuring its careful and organized copying and correction by professional scribal hands.

The degree of care taken in preserving 'accidental' textual features in the scribal copying processes is one indicator of this level of professional interest in Love's text. It has prompted Jeremy Smith, who has found similar patterns in the manuscripts of John Gower's *Confessio Amantis*, to characterise these as 'vectors of textual authority' preserving spelling features that came to be

---

[13] Sargent, ed., *Nicholas Love*, 'Table of Affiliations', p. xvi and passim. For the prints see L. Hellinga, 'Nicholas Love in Print', in *Nicholas Love at Waseda: Proceedings of the International Conference, 20–22 July 1995*, ed. S. Oguro, R. Beadle and M. G. Sargent (Cambridge, 1997), pp. 143–62.

regarded as 'authoritative' among fifteenth-century copyists working in either the Gower or Love writing traditions, or even across both.[14] A particular feature of this linguistic phenomenon is the survival of northern English forms in later non-northern Love texts, a procedure that leaks through into the printed texts and will obviously reward much further analysis and discussion. Lotte Hellinga characterises such usage as 'a conscious wish to preserve the character of the author's language, his "voice", which gives such outstanding individuality to Nicholas Love's translation'.[15]

There may be several reasons why such authoritative linguistic features emerged in the Love writing tradition and why they were sustained for so long by so many copyists and presumably also tolerated by early readers. One major factor that influenced the manner in which Love's *Mirror* gained such an authoritative textual reputation must be related in some manner to the formal archiepiscopal written approval it received early as orthodox religious reading for vernacular English audiences. This is expressed through the memorandum found attached to many Love manuscript copies and across many, but not all, representatives of α, β and γ texts. But precisely how the memorandum worked in practice or what it eventually achieved in terms of countering the perceived Lollard threat remains uncertain. And there are a few oddities that cannot easily be explained by this suggestion. The most significant of these is that none of the earliest manuscripts dated before the first quarter of the fifteenth century originally preserved the memorandum. Instead, it seems to have been a textual addition made after a campaign had already begun to release α and β manuscripts of Love's text into circulation practically simultaneously. Furthermore, although he is the figure most frequently associated with the approval and promotion of Love's *Mirror* and the Lancastrian rehabilitation of Mount Grace, Arundel was dead by 1414. The text of his memorandum would appear to have been variously introduced into the Love textual traditions of the *Mirror* after Arundel's time.[16]

---

[14] J. J. Smith, 'The Afterlives of Nicholas Love', *Studia Neophilogica* 89 (2017), 59–74. I am also particularly grateful to Professor Smith for many informal discussions (both historical and pragmatic) regarding the linguistic value of punctuation as well as other lexical and grammatical features in the study of the 'afterlives' of Middle English texts.

[15] Hellinga, 'Nicholas Love in Print', p. 155.

[16] Questions regarding both the timing and relevance of Arundelian approval or censorship have proved a provocative stimulus for work on Love and other religious writers; see for example the partly allergic reaction to Watson, 'Censorship and Cultural Change', in *After Arundel: Religious Writing in Fifteenth-Century England*, ed. V. Gillespie and K. Ghosh (Turnhout, 2011).

The likely shared preoccupations of some anonymous early Love copyists with producing an authoritative *Mirror* text may well have originated in some general adherence as professional readers to precepts laid down early by some religious orders regarding the importance of maintaining scribal accuracy to create textual authority, chiefly for liturgical and Latin biblical texts or other items deemed important for the order in question. Daniel Wakelin has outlined how many such injunctions are likely to have worked uncertainly in practice with regard to English vernacular texts. In particular, having highlighted Carthusian demands for uniformity in terms of a common concern in the order for accurate wording and pronunciation, he observes that 'some of the most thorough Carthusian efforts at correcting look more like quirky obsessions than the orderly communal control of textual transmission'.[17] On the other hand, the relatively consistent approach to preserving certain linguistic features in Love's *Mirror* as the text was being transcribed may reflect something of its status as an authoritative gospel version approved by Love's order even before it was finally licensed for much wider distribution to counter the Lollard threat.

The role of professional Carthusian reading networks in the earliest dissemination of Love's *Mirror* is suggested by the distribution of some of the most important early manuscripts. Geographically speaking, the earliest extant α, β and γ texts were produced by practised scribal hands that learned their craft a fair distance from Mount Grace and North Yorkshire. But, in considering Love's reputation among his first English readers, I think it is significant that the transmission patterns of the early α and β texts and manuscripts – those most likely to have been authorised personally for release by Love himself – map well on to the evidence of Carthusian institutional presence in Lancastrian England during the first decades of the fifteenth century. The base text for Sargent's edition, Cambridge, University Library, MS Additional 6578, for example, is an $α^1$ text dating from the first quarter of the fifteenth century that we know was once owned by Mount Grace because, in the head margin of folio 2v, an *ex libris* has been added. This reads: 'Iste liber est de domo Assumpcionis Beate Marie in Monte Gracie'. The main text on this page preserves the end of the table of contents for Love's text, immediately followed by the *attende lector* passage that describes how Love has augmented the *Meditationes* version and added or changed details in the Latin source for his translation.[18] In scholarly fashion, the presence of such details is signalled

---

[17] See D. Wakelin, *Scribal Correction and Literary Craft, English Manuscripts 1375–1510* (Cambridge, 2014), pp. 77–83 (p. 79).

[18] Reproduced as colour plate 1 in Sargent, ed., *Nicholas Love*, p. ix.

by marginal insertions in most of the extant copies of some combination of the letters N and B or both. The *attende lector* passage itself now survives along with other Latin marginal apparatus across manuscripts belonging to all three textual groupings and in remarkably consistent form in the earliest and most fully annotated copies, suggesting that it was added professionally, probably originally by Love himself. The information it contained was much recopied and presumably appreciated by later Latinate readers and copyists.

In some of the space remaining on folio 2v in MS Additional 6578, a copy of Arundel's memorandum was then inserted as a late addition by another hand. A Latin note highlighting the difference between northern and southern dialect forms has next been added on the same page by a different hand as yet another late addition. It survives uniquely in this manuscript and reads: 'caue de istis verbis gude pro gode / Item hir pro heere in plurali'. The note advises the reader to beware of finding 'gude' for 'gode' (good) and similarly 'hir' for the plural form 'heere' (their). The warning note on dialect difference suggests that, at some point in its early history, this copy of Love's text may have strayed much further south than the South East Midlands area in which it was copied. Initially, that may have been to allow the book to be decorated or the text checked over by someone in authority, but there is also the possibility that the book was intended to be read or used professionally (perhaps as an exemplar?) by professional readers trained in dialect forms that were distinctively different from Love's northernisms.[19]

Even though the *ex libris* in MS Additional 6578 suggests that this copy of Love's *Mirror* eventually found its way north and back to Mount Grace, dialect evidence suggests that its main copyist came from the Northamptonshire/Oxfordshire border, not far from Coventry. Palaeographical and dialect evidence suggest too that the same hand was responsible for the copy of Love's *Mirror* (an α^1 text) in Cambridge, University Library, MS Additional 6686, where a copy of the memorandum was inserted at the head of the text, and the book was decorated by an East Anglian limner. Both copies were probably made in the second decade of the fifteenth century. Meanwhile, dialect evidence suggests that there was another local α^1 text from the same general area, copied at around the same time. This is the copy in Oxford, Bodleian Library, MS e Musaeo 35, written around 1420 in another professional Midlands hand, this time from northeastern Warwickshire, again close to Coventry, and, similarly

---

[19] Smith, 'Afterlives of Nicholas Love', sensibly makes the point that, if this note was originally directed at later copyists to encourage them to remove northernisms such as those highlighted then they obviously missed the point of it. My own impression is that the note was more likely originally intended in this manuscript as a prompt for non-northern professional readers.

to MSS Additional 6578 and 6686, decorated professionally, although on this occasion more lavishly and probably in a metropolitan setting.[20]

In the case of MS e Musaeo 35, the limner has been identified by Kathleen Scott as a metropolitan artist of considerable standing whose work can be found in at least nine other deluxe manuscripts.[21] The books he worked on include the Bedford Book of Hours and Psalter made for John Duke of Bedford, third son of Henry IV, who was regent of France for his nephew Henry VI from 1422–35. MS e Musaeo 35 contains the arms of the Neville and Beaufort families. The decorative heraldic devices in the manuscript served to remind its first readers of the union (before 1403–4) of Margaret Neville (daughter of Sir Thomas Neville of Hornby) and Thomas Beaufort, half-brother to King Henry IV who was at that time newly on the English throne. In 1412 Beaufort had been responsible for ensuring that the original donation to Mount Grace of the alien priory of Hinckley in Leicestershire was reconfirmed by the king, and a 1417 document associated with the Carthusian motherhouse of the Grande Chartreuse records his foundation and construction of five cells at Mount Grace. Not surprisingly, then, Beaufort's obit surviving in the Carthusian carta for 1427 describes him as 'magnus et continuus benefactor Capituli Generalis et multarum domorum Ordinis' (a great and constant benefactor of the General Chapter and of many houses of the Order).[22]

It is hardly much of a stretch of the imagination to associate this Neville/Beaufort manuscript and the two other authoritative early manuscripts of Love's *Mirror* produced near Coventry that I have so far been discussing, with a disciplined, sympathetic and professional scribal interest in Love's *Mirror* in that general geographical area. The earliest campaign to produce multiple deluxe α¹ texts of Love's *Mirror* cannot as yet be linked too closely to Love himself, of course, or even to Mount Grace and North Yorkshire, but instead seems to reflect the activities and formal work of a cluster of copyists who might more readily be associated with the general South East Midlands area, perhaps as associates of the Carthusian Priory of St Anne in Coventry. It should be remembered in this context that, alongside Richard II, Thomas Holland and other members of the royal affinity, William, Lord Zouche, of Coventry Charterhouse, had been the major co-founder of Mount Grace in

---

[20] Sargent, ed., *Nicholas Love*, 'Introduction', pp. 104–6.
[21] K. L. Scott, 'The Illustration and Decoration of Manuscripts of Nicholas Love's *Mirror of the Blessed Life of Jesus Christ*', in *Nicholas Love at Waseda*, pp. 61–86 (pp. 68, 71–2).
[22] Sargent, ed., *Nicholas Love*, 'Introduction', pp. 28–30.

1381, when the foundation stone was laid, with the link to Coventry continuing into the Lancastrian era.[23]

The β version of Love's *Mirror* represents an authorially-revised version that illustrates a different aspect of the same compelling story regarding Nicholas Love, his first professional readers and Mount Grace's post-Ricardian rehabilitation and slow recovery following a queasy first decade under a Lancastrian king. New Haven, CT, Yale University, Beinecke Rare Book and Manuscript Library, MS Takamiya 8, formerly in Tokyo, stands at the head of the β[1] textual grouping. It is arguably one of the earliest surviving texts of Love's *Mirror*, since its elaborate border decoration has been characterized by Kathleen Scott as being 'in a London style of around 1410'.[24] The manuscript lacks a copy of the memorandum, but, as is well known from previous scholarship, its first owner was Joan Holland, countess of Kent and widow of Thomas, the disgraced Ricardian co-founder of Mount Grace. Sargent has convincingly argued that the book was produced for and presented to Joan when Henry IV granted her permission to take up residence at Beaulieu, a Cistercian House in Hampshire.[25] Joan died in 1442, and her professionally-decorated book shows few signs of use, despite there being evidence that MS Takamiya 8 was part of an intriguing gift-giving culture that obviously thrived on public demonstrations of ecclesiastical and aristocratic patronage and allegiance. On folio 120v, there is a rubricated formal note, decorated with a flourished blue initial and red ink penwork that 'þis booke is ȝyffene to Alyse Belacyse. Be þe ȝiftt of Johane Countesse of Kentt'. This is followed on the next page by another formal note in a near contemporary hand that 'I Alyse Belacyse. ȝyfe þis booke to. Elyzabeth my seruant. With my handys' (fol. 121r).[26]

---

[23] M. G. Sargent, 'The Holland-Takamiya Manuscript of Nicholas Love's *Mirror of the Blessed Life of Jesus Christ*', in *The Medieval Book and a Modern Collector: Essays in Honour of Toshiyuki Takamiya*, ed. T. Matsuda, R. A. Linenthal and J. Scahill (Cambridge, 2004), pp. 135–47 (p. 139). Sargent has also recently discussed how there may be a continuing possible Coventry association through Nicholas Love's family origins; see M. G. Sargent, 'The Transmission by the English Carthusians of Some Late Medieval Spiritual Writings: A Reconsideration of Walter Hilton and Nicholas Love', in *The Capital's Charterhouses and the Record of English Carthusianism*, ed. J. Luxford (Toronto, 2023), pp. 117–51.

[24] Scott, 'Illustration and Decoration', p. 68.

[25] Sargent, 'The Holland-Takamiya Manuscript', pp. 145–7.

[26] See Sargent, 'The Holland-Takamiya Manuscript', p. 146, for colour plates reproducing these donation records. Alice Belacyse/Belasys is identified as a member of the well-established northern family of that name whose piety has been characterized as 'more publicly-oriented' than Joan Holland's in C. Meale, '"oft siþis with grete deuotion I þought what I miȝt do pleysyng to god": The Early Ownership

Love's brand of meditative gospel reading obviously attracted attention to itself both before and after Arundel, so it is easy to see how some of the most authoritative and earliest manuscript copies leaked into wider circulation as formal gifts or were sometimes much less formally passed around among professional readers and copyists, between members of male and female religious communities or, eventually, among other less easily defined and more geographically and socially dispersed groups and networks. As such, MS Takamiya 8 bears comparison to the near contemporary but relatively plain professionally-produced Foyle manuscript, now in private hands.[27] This is the earliest surviving example of the β² textual grouping. Neither MS Takamiya 8 nor Foyle preserve a copy of the memorandum nor do they give much clue as to how or when the early β copies of Love's *Mirror* travelled south. In the Foyle manuscript, however, a rubricated *ex libris* informs us that 'Iste liber constat domine Sibille de ffelton abbatisse de Berkyng' (fol. 4v).

Sibyl de Felton was abbess of the Benedictine convent of Barking from 1393. Her copy of Love's *Mirror* is unusual because it precedes Love's treatment of Christ's Passion with another independent prose translation of the same material from the Latin *Meditationes* source, now known as the Middle English *Meditationes de Passione*.[28] The same idiosyncratic and repetitive sequence of material was once a feature of Oxford, Brasenose College, MS 9 (similarly to MS Takamiya 8, a very early β¹ text from the first decades of the fifteenth century) and is still now found in New Haven, Beinecke Library, MS Takamiya 20 (a β¹ text from the second quarter of the fifteenth century). Perhaps in preparation for its later deployment as a Love exemplar, the quire containing the extraneous Passion account was subsequently torn out of Brasenose College, MS 9, leaving only its opening line and the last few lines of the excised text as evidence that it had ever once existed in that copy. The text of the Middle English *Meditationes de Passione* in the mid-century copy of Love's *Mirror* (β² with traces of selective borrowing from an α² text) in Manchester, Chetham's Library, MS 6690, on the other hand, has been added in place of

---

and Readership of Love's *Mirror*, with Special Reference to its Female Audience', in *Nicholas Love at Waseda*, pp. 19–46 (pp. 35–6). I discuss how similar styles of publicly-oriented friendship and gift giving cultures in the pseudo-Bonaventuran tradition continued to be celebrated and endorsed through the juxtaposition of text and image in the early prints of Love's *Mirror* in Thompson, 'Love Reading?', pp. 100–2.

[27] Sargent, ed., *Nicholas Love*, 'Introduction', pp. 126–8.

[28] M. G. Sargent, 'The Textual Affiliations of the Waseda Manuscript of Nicholas Love's *Mirror of the Blessed Life of Jesus Christ*', in *Nicholas Love at Waseda*, pp. 175–274 (pp. 176–9).

Love's version. Sargent has also now found textual evidence in MS Takamiya 8 and another nine of the sixteen extant β^1 texts that the same seemingly pointless duplication of *Meditationes de Passione* items is likely to have been a feature of the archetype underlying the texts in this grouping that, like Brasenose College, MS 9, had had the offending additional *Passione* item physically removed. He takes this as evidence that the β grouping is ultimately derived from a pre-publication version of Love's *Mirror* – foul papers or a work still in progress – for which the Brasenose 9 copyist and some early readers such as Sibyl de Felton may well have secured privileged and seemingly premature reading privileges. Love's work may well have held some particular attraction for the Abbess, since at some time before her death in 1419, Sibyl de Felton must have had at least some inkling that Nicholas Love had formerly been a Benedictine monk sympathetic to the idea of cenobitic reform in the order and intent on pursuing that goal, probably both before and after his election as Mount Grace prior.[29]

After Sibyl's death, the ownership inscriptions in her book show that it stayed at Barking and came into the possession there of one Margaret Scrope. The Foyle manuscript was then passed on through Margaret's good graces to Agnes Goldwell, who was a gentlewoman in the household of Lady Elizabeth Peche. The latter was Margaret Scrope's sister, and it was in her household that Margaret found a new home upon her retirement following the Henrician Dissolution at Barking and dispersal of the remaining members of the religious community there.[30]

A cluster of three other mid-century deluxe copies betrays further signs that Love's *Mirror* remained susceptible to a later range of professional reading and editing activities. The manuscripts in question are Tokyo, Waseda University Library, MS NE 3691; New York, Morgan Library and Museum, MS M.648; and Edinburgh, National Library of Scotland, MS Advocates' 18.1.7. All three have been prepared by professional readers as aesthetically

---

[29] Love's longstanding complaints against the Benedictines and calls for reform as a former black monk himself must have been widely known among the order and is largely credited with causing Henry V to call a convocation of the English Benedictines in May 1421. See M. G. Sargent, 'Nicholas Love's *Mirror of the Blessed Life of Jesus Christ* and the Politics of Vernacular Translation in Late Medieval England', in *Lost in Translation?*, ed. D. Renevey and C. Whitehead (Turnhout, 2010), pp. 205–21 (p. 220).

[30] M. C. Erler, 'Exchange of Books between Nuns and Laywomen: Three Surviving Examples', in *New Science Out of Old Books: Studies in Manuscripts and Early Printed Books in Honour of A. I. Doyle*, ed. R. Beadle and A. J. Piper (London, 1995), pp. 360–73.

pleasing devotional accessories for their likely earliest aristocratic owners.[31] Their survival hints at the possibility that expensive decorative features on the page can not only act as important readers' aids for simple souls but also might be used to assist the 'showing' of Love's text as an attractive material object to those who might want to appreciate the book form in which the *Mirror* was being presented to them.

In the light of Kathleen Scott's analysis of their decorative and illustrative details, Sargent's patient textual detective work has shown how all three copies were originally drawn from β^1 and γ^2 copies, with Waseda MS NE 3691 used intermittently as an exemplar for parts of Morgan MS M.648 and at least two other copies of Love's text brought into service as exemplars on the occasions when they were available for consultation.[32] Unless all three manuscripts are judged on their own terms, such 'contaminated' texts are of minimal value to the modern editor. Instead, they draw us into the world of professional metropolitan readers and copyists a generation or so after Love had completed his work. In certain respects that world remains a mysterious one. Waseda MS NE 3691 and MS Advocates' 18.1.7 were both copied by the 'Petworth scribe', so called because he was responsible for the Petworth copy of the *Canterbury Tales* (Kent, Petworth House, MS 7) and also the copy of John Gower's *Confessio Amantis* in Cambridge, Pembroke College, MS 307.[33] The Petworth Chaucer text contains the arms of Henry Percy, fourth Earl of Northumberland, while the decoration and illustration in MS Advocates' 18.1.7 suggests that this copy of Love's *Mirror* was written to celebrate the marriage (1444/5?) of Edmund Grey, fourth Lord Grey of Ruthin, to Lady Catherine Percy, daughter of the second Earl of Northumberland.

Sargent argues that the survival of both the Petworth scribal copies of Love's *Mirror* alongside Morgan MS M.648 suggests 'commercial production in a relatively affluent atelier that could afford to have this many exemplars available, and to produce books for which both moderate and very high quality decoration and illumination were available'.[34] At least two of the Love manuscripts under discussion were then sent for finishing by limners working in another metropolitan atelier. Such an idea of 'commercial' London book production suggests a degree of organization in a shared space that brings

---

[31] See discussion of their decorative similarities and differences, particularly in their borderwork, in Scott, 'Illustration and Decoration', pp. 72–6.

[32] Sargent, 'Textual Affiliations', pp. 180–274.

[33] See the most recent profile of this scribe's career and achievement in D. Pearsall and L. R. Mooney, *A Descriptive Catalogue of the English Manuscripts of John Gower's 'Confessio Amantis'* (Cambridge, 2021), pp. 38–45.

[34] Sargent, 'Textual Affiliations', p. 192.

with it connotations of metropolitan scribal workshop interest in deluxe texts of Love's *Mirror*, as well as in two of the most characteristic works by Chaucer and Gower. I think it is necessary to approach this idea with a degree of caution. The complex of scribal activities that created the textual fabric of Love's *Mirror* in all three of the γ^2 copies under discussion was perhaps largely the work of just one professional reader using the quality of resources and multiplicity of exemplars likely to have been available only in some well-resourced religious house, or, perhaps, through London Guildhall connections.[35] Since the Petworth scribe has been identified as clerk of the Skinners' Company in 1441, it is possible to speculate further that, by mid-century, either environment is likely to have encouraged the necessary instincts and editorial interest in the texts being copied that would have prompted such a talented professional reader to undertake and complete the variety of ambitious writing tasks now attributed to him.

We are on securer ground in the search for books concerned with packaging and promoting Love's particular brand of meditative devotion when we turn to examine mid-fifteenth-century Carthusian interest in other manuscript copies of his *Mirror*. One figure stands out as a professional reader in this respect, and that is Stephen Dodesham of Sheen Priory. Dodesham was a prolific copyist and Carthusian monk who wrote Glasgow, Glasgow University Library, MS Hunter 77 (an α^3 text) in the 1474/5 period; he also copied Oxford, Bodleian Library, MS Rawlinson A. 387b (another α^3 text) and Cambridge, Trinity College, MS B.15.16 (a γ^1 text).[36] Apart from his professional interest in Love's *Mirror*, he is known to have written or contributed to at least seventeen other manuscripts before his death in 1481/2, although any connections he may have had to what we might want to tentatively consider the commercial book trade in this period still require further investigation.

The influence of the Carthusian monastery at Sheen on the English Brigittine house at Syon Abbey, particularly in terms of the metropolitan copying and commercial printing of 'orthodox' English religious texts, has been much

---

[35] For a provocative study of the latter as a metropolitan base for professional readers working commercially with Middle English literary texts, see L. R. Mooney and E. Stubbs, *Scribes and the City: London Guildhall Clerks and the Dissemination of Middle English Literature, 1375–1425* (York, 2013). For identification of the Petworth scribe, see J. Griffiths, 'Thomas Hingham, Monk of Bury and the Macro Plays Manuscript', *English Manuscript Studies* 5 (1995), 214–19.

[36] A. I. Doyle, 'Stephen Dodesham of Witham and Sheen', in *Of the Making of Manuscripts, Their Scribes and Readers: Essays Presented to M. B. Parkes*, ed. P. Robinson and R. Zim (Aldershot, 1997), pp. 94–115.

discussed.[37] Henry V had founded Sheen in 1414, with Syon Abbey following in 1415, both seemingly enjoying a reputation as royally-sanctioned centres of religious life with close metropolitan connections, enviable access to books and libraries near and far and a reputation, mid-century, for being central to the production and dissemination of vernacular English translations of Latin works by female religious figures such as Catherine of Siena and Brigit of Sweden, as well as lives of Christ and meditative, mystical and generally devotional guides and approved reading programmes.[38]

Nicholas Love's *Mirror* was certainly not unknown at Sheen to professional readers from at least the early 1430s. At around this time, the anonymous Carthusian writer of the *Mirror to Devout People* states that he had promised the Brigittine sister for whom he was preparing the text 'a medytacyon of the Passyon of oure Lorde whyche promysse I haue not putte fro my mynde but by dyuerse tymys, be the grace of God, I haue parformyd hyt as I myghte' (Preface, ll. 4–6).[39] Ten lines later it transpires that the apology for the delay alluded to here was because he had found out that Nicholas Love had basically beaten him to it in terms of producing such a text. As a result, he admits to almost giving up on his task:

> also I haue besteryd ofte tymys to haue lefte thys bysynesse, bothe for my vnworthynesse, and also for Bonaventure a cardynal and a worthy clerke, made a boke of the same matere the whyche ys callyd Vita Christi. And most of all whenne I herde telle that a man of oure ordyr of charturhowse had iturnyd the same boke into Englyische (Preface, ll. 17–20).

Faced with this dilemma, the Sheen Carthusian consulted his prior, and they both decided he should proceed to write the promised text in a different way, similarly to the manner in which the four evangelists produced complementary Gospel versions, he tells us in his preface. The result, he argues, weaves together a life of Christ that harmonises a variety of European sources, augmenting rather than competing with any earlier pseudo-Bonaventuran reading experience his proposed reader might have had.

---

[37] See, for example, essays by V. R. Bainbridge, V. Gillespie and C. A. Grisé, in *Syon Abbey and its Books: Reading, Writing and Religion, c. 1400–1700*, ed. E. A. Jones and A. Walsham (Woodbridge, 2010).

[38] For the inclusion of Love's *Mirror* in one such reading programme endorsed by Thomas More during the Henrician religious controversies that led to the Dissolution of Sheen and Syon see J. J. Thompson, 'Love in the 1530s', in *Makers and Users of Medieval Books: Essays in Honour of A. S. G. Edwards*, ed. C. M. Meale and D. Pearsall (Cambridge, 2014), pp. 191–201 (pp. 198–201).

[39] *A Mirror to Devout People: Speculum devotorum*, ed. P. J. Patterson, EETS OS 346 (Oxford, 2016).

Viewed in such terms, the *Mirror to Devout People* preface becomes a convenient way for the Sheen Carthusian to be shown to have entered that much larger professional reading network that this essay has built up around the scribes, annotators, artists and patrons who commissioned and produced copies of Love's *Mirror* in late medieval manuscript culture. Such networks are often intriguing and wide ranging, sometimes identifiable only through close textual analysis of surviving copies or the cultural mapping of the many formal and informal points of possible contact hinted at by shared institutional affiliation, diffuse family connections or property ownership and metropolitan living. They do not always offer a straightforward modern scholarly explanation as to the precise motivation for making copies and reading Love professionally or otherwise, of course. On the other hand, the continuing research in this area by a veritable 'fair field' of modern scholars usefully draws attention to the production and dissemination patterns that make Love's *Mirror* such an extraordinary example of English pseudo-Bonaventuran writing.

Kathryn Kerby-Fulton:
The Making of a Medievalist

ROSALYNN VOADEN

There must be something in the water of Humboldt, Saskatchewan. In 1934 George Kane left this small Canadian prairie town, destined to become one of the foremost medievalists of his generation and a preeminent scholar of *Piers Plowman*. Forty years later in 1974, Kathryn Kerby left Humboldt, Saskatchewan to become one of the foremost medievalists of *her* generation and a preeminent scholar of *Piers Plowman*.

Kathryn initially intended to pursue a career in medicine. However, at Glendon College of the University of York, Toronto, fate intervened in the form of a course in Medieval and Renaissance Humanism, taught by John Bruckmann, a magisterial, Latin-speaking medieval historian trained at the Pontifical Institute for Mediaeval Studies, and of the mentorship of Penelope Doob, Professor of English Literature and Women's Studies, and, like Kathryn, a lover of dance. Then Kathryn discovered the brown cloth-covered volumes of the Early English Text Society and, as she says, a whole world opened to her. And so the world lost a physician but gained a medievalist, teacher and mentor whose benign yet uncompromising guidance has influenced hundreds of students and scholars.

Kathryn graduated from York University with an Honours B.A. and B. Ed. *summa cum laude*, and, having been awarded a Royal Society of Canada Scholarship (like George Kane in 1939, before her), headed to Oxford to embark on a D.Phil. Unfortunately, while Oxford offered much, and she passed the M. Phil. qualifying exams, some medievalists at the university were less than enthusiastic about her intended dissertation topic. She had become engaged by *Piers Plowman*, specifically the C-text, which she argued was a neglected text which could be more deeply understood as a work of prophecy and reformist apocalypticism, rather than solely as Estates Satire, an interpretation which then-current scholarship largely supported.

Then, in (another) one of those serendipitous moments which change the direction of a life, a fellow graduate student put her in touch with Derek Pearsall, then teaching at the Centre for Medieval Studies at the University of York, York, England. He read her Oxford dissertation proposal and immediately invited her to York for a meeting. Kathryn says that she learned more about *Piers Plowman* in the first hour of conversation with Derek than she had in two years in Oxford. And the rest is history: Kathryn transferred her scholarships to the University of York to complete her D.Phil. there. She speaks with great fondness and enthusiasm of her time at the Centre for Medieval Studies, and credits Derek as a significant influence on the direction of her future work; she maintained a close relationship with him and with his wife Rosemary all their lives.

Not long after Kathryn arrived at York, the death of faculty member Elizabeth Salter and the funding cutbacks under the then Prime Minister Margaret Thatcher meant that Derek was responsible for the supervision of eighteen D.Phil. candidates – many of whom were to become prominent medievalists. To help remedy the situation, he told them that they would have to learn from each other. Thus ensued a rich experience of collaborative teaching, learning and exploration. In what sounds like a Golden Age of graduate work, Kathryn speaks of going on field trips with fellow graduate students who were specializing in wall paintings, stained glass, archaeology or architecture, and of the rich discussions that followed. This contextual exposure to the breadth of medieval studies, the entanglement of literature and history, art and culture, music and religion, politics and folk lore and science has had a profound influence on her work. It was at this time, also, that she discovered the importance and value – not to mention the excitement – of manuscript studies, which would become absolutely central to her research.

Kathryn completed her degree in 1986, with her D.Phil. thesis 'Latin Religious Prophecy in Medieval England and its Influence on *Piers Plowman*'. This outstanding dissertation became a noted first monograph, *Reformist Apocalypticism and Piers Plowman* (Cambridge, 1990), which won the Medieval Academy of America John Nicholas Brown Prize for a best first book; and, since then, Kathryn has published a succession of important volumes, all informed by her independent and searching scholarship, that have illuminated many previously unexplored corners of the medieval world.

In addition to the wide disciplinary exposure Kathryn experienced at York's Centre for Medieval Studies, the atmosphere of collaborative learning has informed both her research and her mentorship. Her first published article, 'Self Image and the Visionary Role in Two Letters from the Correspondence of Elisabeth of Schönau and Hildegard of Bingen', was co-authored with her colleague Dyan Elliott. Many of her books and articles are written with colleagues or current or former students, and she contributes frequently to edited collections by former students. Kathryn and former student Linda Olson also devised an innovative approach to scholarship in *Voices in Dialogue: Reading*

Women in the Middle Ages (Notre Dame IN, 2005), a volume whose dynamic format pairs each essay with another scholar's response and testifies to rich, ongoing conversations about women and medieval literacy.

Kathryn's scholarly career coincided with, and significantly contributed to, the rise of feminist studies in medieval literature and history, a development which emerged from the burgeoning awareness that the lives of medieval women, what they wrote and what they read had been sadly neglected. Building on work by earlier scholars such as Hope Emily Allen, Peter Dronke, Clarissa Atkinson and Caroline Walker Bynum, Kathryn was part of a generation of scholars, including Barbara Newman, Jocelyn Wogan-Browne and Alexandra Barratt among many others, who helped transform topics previously deemed trivial and relegated to the margins into the important fields of study that they are today.

Kathryn's celebrated teaching career began while she was writing her dissertation. She returned to Canada and took a job as a sessional lecturer at the University of Saskatchewan for a year (1982–3). She then taught at her undergraduate alma mater, York University's Glendon College, while finishing her thesis (1983–5). Then as now, positions for medievalists, let alone tenure-track positions, were few and far between. A position for a medievalist in the English Department at the University of Victoria was one of only two such jobs advertised in 1985. She was asked to apply – and, Reader, she got the job! She taught there for twenty years, rising through the ranks to appointment as Full Professor in 1998. During her tenure at the University of Victoria, she also held positions as Visiting Professor of Religion and Literature at the Yale Institute for Sacred Music (2000–1); as Visiting Scholar at the Department of English, Princeton (1999–2000); and at the Department of English, Harvard (Fall 2002). In 2005 she moved to the University of Notre Dame as an Endowed Chair (The Notre Dame Professorship in English), where she remained until she retired in December 2017. However, although she may have retired from teaching, Kathryn maintains a vigorous program of research and writing and continues to mentor former students.

Kathryn was elected a Fellow of the Medieval Academy of America in 2012 and of the Society of Antiquaries in 2019. During her career, she has held an impressive number of Research Fellowships: two semester-long and one full year fellowship at the Institute for Advanced Study, Princeton; a Guggenheim Fellowship; a fellowship from the National Endowment for the Humanities; and one from the American Council of Learned Societies. She has also received no fewer than eighteen fellowships from the Canada Council (Social Sciences and Humanities Research Council). While these fellowships gave her the time to focus on her research and to visit the great libraries, the residential fellowships in particular, as well as her various appointments as Visiting Scholar, allowed her to continue the intensive and valuable collaboration with other scholars in various disciplines which so enriched her graduate education, and which has always informed her work with a broad contextual understanding. Arguably her best-known book, *Books under Suspicion: Censorship and Tolerance of Revelatory Writing in Late Medieval England* (Notre Dame IN, 2006), an excellent example of the multi-disciplinary nature of her work, was awarded the Charles Homer Haskins Gold Medal in 2010 by the Medieval Academy of America – this prize is generally given to historians.

Kathryn's commitment to her students is evident in her most recent book, *The Clerical Proletariat and the Resurgence of Medieval English Poetry* (Philadelphia, 2021), which in 2022 won the Margaret Wade Labarge Prize for the best book published by a Canadian medievalist. The book is dedicated to her graduate students. In the preface she draws a parallel between the situation of unbeneficed clergy in the Middle Ages and that of 'the young underemployed intellectuals of our day', a situation she blames on 'successive financial downturns, self-interested governments, and corporate models of the university' (p. xviii). It is clear that not enough has changed in academia, as Kathryn's elegant and compassionate account demonstrates.

While Kathryn's research has transformed our understanding of many aspects of written work in the Middle Ages, her teaching and mentorship have also transformed the lives of those fortunate enough to be her students. She is unfailingly generous in sharing ideas, skills and knowledge. I can testify that working with Kathryn in Duke Humfrey's Library at the Bodleian, Oxford was a master class in manuscript studies. Under her tutelage, students learn to burrow deeper into the material, to pull the threads of the tapestry, to follow the clues of the manuscript or text wherever it goes. She communicates the excitement of the quest; the thrill of the discovery of a new piece of knowledge, a different insight into a text, a previously undiscovered link between manuscripts and writers or patrons; and the pleasure of achieving a greater understanding of the women and men who lived, worked and wrote in the Middle Ages.

Since leaving Humboldt, Saskatchewan and discovering those iconic EETS volumes, Kathryn Kerby-Fulton has become one of the most influential medieval scholars of our time and one of the foremost medievalists of her generation. Her research and writing consistently and continually demonstrate that independence of mind and commitment to rigorous scholarship which marked her years at Oxford and York, and which have placed her at the very forefront of contemporary medieval scholarship.

Kathryn Kerby-Fulton: FSA, FMAA Publications

KARRIE FULLER AND MISTY SCHIEBERLE

Books

Reformist Apocalypticism and Piers Plowman (Cambridge, 1990; repr. 2008).
K. Kerby-Fulton and D. L. Despres, *Iconography and the Professional Reader: The Politics of Book Production in the Douce Piers Plowman* (Minneapolis, 1999).
Books under Suspicion: Censorship and Tolerance of Revelatory Writing in Late Medieval England (Notre Dame IN, 2006; repr. 2011).
K. Kerby-Fulton, M. Hilmo and L. Olson, *Opening Up Medieval English Manuscripts: Literary and Visual Approaches* (Ithaca, 2012).
The Clerical Proletariat and the Resurgence of Medieval English Poetry (Philadelphia, 2021).

Edited Collections

S. Justice and K. Kerby-Fulton, eds, *Written Work: Langland, Labour and Authorship* (Philadelphia, 1997).
K. Kerby-Fulton and M. Hilmo, eds, *The Medieval Professional Reader at Work: Evidence from Manuscripts of Chaucer, Langland, Kempe and Gower* (Victoria BC, 2001).
K. Kerby-Fulton and M. Hilmo, eds, *The Medieval Reader: Reception and Cultural History in the Late Medieval Manuscript* (New York, 2002).
L. Olson and K. Kerby-Fulton, eds, *Voices in Dialogue: Reading Women in the Middle Ages* (Notre Dame IN, 2005).
K. Kerby-Fulton, ed., *Women and the Divine in Literature before 1700: Essays in Memory of Margot Louis* (Victoria BC, 2009).
K. Kerby-Fulton and J. Juilfs, eds, *'Something Fearful': Medievalist Scholars on the Religious Turn*, special issue of *Religion and Literature* 42.1–2 (2010).
K. Kerby-Fulton, J. J. Thompson and S. Baechle, eds, *New Directions in Medieval Manuscript Studies and Reading Practices: Essays in Honour of Derek Pearsall* (Notre Dame IN, 2014).
K. Kerby-Fulton, K. A.-M. Bugyis and J. Van Engen, eds, *Women Intellectuals and Leaders in the Middle Age*s (Cambridge, 2020; repr. 2022).
M. Johnston, K. Kerby-Fulton and D. Pearsall, eds, *Poets and Scribes in Late Medieval England: Essays on Manuscripts and Meaning in Honor of Susanna Fein* (Kalamazoo, 2023).

Articles

K. Kerby-Fulton and D. H. Elliott, 'Self-Image and the Visionary Role in Two Letters from the Correspondence of Elizabeth of Schönau and Hildegard of Bingen', *Vox Benedictina: A Journal of Translations from Monastic Sources* 2 (1985), 204–23; repr. in *On Pilgrimage: The Best of Vox Benedictina 1984–1993*, ed. M. H. King (Toronto, 1994), pp. 534–47.

'Hildegard of Bingen and Anti-mendicant Propaganda', *Traditio* 43 (1987), 386–99.

'A Return to "The First Dawn of Justice": Hildegard's Visions of Clerical Reform and the Eremitical Life', *American Benedictine Review* 40 (1989), 383–407.

K. Kerby-Fulton and E. R. Daniel, 'English Joachimism, 1300–1500: The Columbinus Prophecy', in *Il profetismo gioachimita tra Quattrocento e Cinquencento. Atti del III Congresso Internazionale di Studi Gioachimiti, S. Giovanni in Fiore, 17–21 Settembre, 1989*, ed. G. L. Potestà (Fiore, 1990), pp. 313–50.

'"Standing on Lewis's Shoulders": C. S. Lewis as Critic of Medieval Literature', *Studies in Medievalism* 3 (1991), 257–78.

'Langland's Reading: Some Evidence from MSS Containing Religious Prophecy', in *The Uses of Manuscripts in Literary Studies: Essays in Memory of Judson Boyce Allen*, ed. C. C. Morse, P. R. Doob and M. C. Woods (Kalamazoo, 1992), pp. 237–61.

'"Who has Written this Book?": Visionary Autobiography in Langland's C Text', in *The Medieval Mystical Tradition in England: Exeter Symposium V. Papers Read at The Devon Centre Dartington Hall, July 1992*, ed. M. Glasscoe (Cambridge, 1992), pp. 101–16.

'Hilverding (van Wewen), Franz', in *The International Dictionary of Ballet*, 2 vols (London, 1993), I, pp. 667–9.

'LePicq (also Le Picq, Lepic), Charles', in *International Dictionary of Ballet*, II, pp. 846–8.

'The Loves of Mars and Venus', in *International Dictionary of Ballet*, II, pp. 878–9.

'Les Petits Riens', in *International Dictionary of Ballet*, II, pp. 1116–19.

'Song of a Wayfarer', in *International Dictionary of Ballet*, II, pp. 1326–8.

'Subligny, Marie-Thérèse', in *International Dictionary of Ballet*, II, pp. 1354–6.

'The Taming of the Shrew', in *International Dictionary of Ballet*, II, pp. 1384–6.

'Weaver, John', in *International Dictionary of Ballet*, II, pp. 1528–31.

'Hildegard and the Male Reader: A Study in Insular Reception', in *Prophets Abroad: The Reception of Continental Holy Women in Late-Medieval England*, ed. R. Voaden (Cambridge, 1996), pp. 1–18.

'Langland and the Bibliographic Ego', in *Written Work*, pp. 67–143.

K. Kerby-Fulton and S. Justice, 'Langlandian Reading Circles and the Civil Service in London and Dublin, 1380–1427', *New Medieval Literatures* 1 (1998), 59–83.

'Prophet and Reformer: "Smoke in the Vineyard"', in *Voice of the Living Light: Hildegard of Bingen and Her World*, ed. B. Newman (Berkeley, 1998), pp. 70–90.

K. Kerby-Fulton and S. Justice, 'Reformist Intellectual Culture in the English and Irish Civil Service: The *Modus tenendi parliamentum* and Its Literary Relations', *Traditio* 53 (1998), 149–202.

'Piers Plowman', in *The Cambridge History of Medieval English Literature*, ed. D. Wallace (Cambridge, 1999), pp. 513–38.

'James Kudelka', in *Fifty Contemporary Choreographers*, ed. M. Bremser (London, 1999), pp. 128–33.

'Glen Tetley', in *Fifty Contemporary Choreographers*, pp. 212–17.

'Fabricating Failure: The Professional Reader as Textual Terrorist', *Yearbook of Langland Studies* 13 (1999), 193–206.

'Prophecy and Suspicion: Closet Radicalism, Reformist Politics, and the Vogue for Hildegardiana in Ricardian England', *Speculum* 75 (2000), 318–41.

'Professional Readers of Langland at Home and Abroad: New Directions in the Political and Bureaucratic Codicology of *Piers Plowman*', in *New Directions in Later Medieval Manuscript Studies: Essays from the 1998 Harvard Conference*, ed. D. Pearsall (York, 2000), pp. 103–29.

'Langland "in his Working Clothes"?: Scribe D, Authorial Loose Revision Material, and the Nature of Scribal Intervention', in *Middle English Poetry: Texts and Traditions*, ed. A. J. Minnis (York, 2001), pp. 139–67.

'Introduction: The Medieval Professional Reader and Reception History, 1292–1641', in *The Medieval Professional Reader at Work*, pp. 7–13.

K. Kerby-Fulton and S. Justice, 'Scribe D and the Marketing of Ricardian Literature', in *The Medieval Professional Reader at Work*, pp. 217–37.

'Introduction', in *The Medieval Reader*, pp. ix–xiv.

K. Kerby-Fulton and R. Horie, 'The French Version of *the Modus tenendi parliamentum* in the Courtenay Cartulary: A Transcription and Introduction', in *The Medieval Reader*, pp. 225–47.

'The Women Readers in Langland's Earliest Audience: Some Codicological Evidence', in *Learning and Literacy in Medieval England and Abroad*, ed. S. Rees Jones (Turnhout, 2002), pp. 121–34.

K. Kerby-Fulton, M. Hayton and K. Olsen, 'Pseudo-Hildegardian Prophecy and Antimendicant Propaganda in Late-Medieval England: An Edition of the Most Popular Insular Text of "Insurgent gentes"', in *Prophecy, Apocalypse and the Day of Doom: Proceedings of the 2000 Harlaxton Symposium*, ed. N. Morgan (Donington, 2004), pp. 160–94.

'Introduction: The English Illustrated Book and Medieval Ways of Reading: An Archaeology of Images at Work', in M. Hilmo, *Medieval Icons, Images & English Literary Texts: A Study of Illustrated Works from the Ruthwell Cross to the Ellesmere Chaucer* (Aldershot, 2004), pp. ix–xxv.

'When Women Preached: An Introduction to Female Homiletic, Sacramental, and Liturgical Roles in the Later Middle Ages', in *Voices in Dialogue*, pp. 31–55.

'*Eciam Lollardi*: Some Further Thoughts on Fiona Somerset's "*Eciam mulier*: Women in Lollardy and the Problem of Sources"', in *Voices in Dialogue*, pp. 261–78.

'English Joachite Manuscripts and Medieval Optimism about the Role of the Jews in History: A List for Future Studies', in *Confronting the Present with the Past: Essays in Honour of Sheila Delaney*, ed. A. E. C. Canitz and A. Taylor, special issue of *Florilegium: The Journal of the Canadian Society of Medievalists* 23 (2006), 97–144.

'Response: *Books under Suspicion* and Beyond', *Journal of British Studies* 46 (2007), 766–73.

'Preface', in *Women and the Divine in Literature before 1700*, pp. vii–x.

'Skepticism, Agnosticism and Belief: The Spectrum of Attitudes Toward Vision in Late Medieval England', in *Women and the Divine in Literature before 1700*, pp. 1–17.

'Authority, Constraint and the Writing of the Medieval Self', in *The Oxford Handbook of Medieval Literature in English*, ed. E. Treharne and G. Walker (Oxford, 2010), 413–33.

'"The Place of the Apocalyptic View of History in the Later Middle Ages" and the Legacy of Morton Bloomfield', in *The Morton W. Bloomfield Lectures, 1989–2005*, ed. D. Donoghue, J. Simpson and N. Watson (Kalamazoo, 2010), pp. 116–40.

'Hildegard of Bingen', in *Medieval Holy Women in the Christian Tradition, c. 1100–1500*, ed. A. Minnis and R. Voaden (Turnhout, 2010), pp. 343–69.

K. Kerby-Fulton and J. Juilfs, 'Preface', in *'Something Fearful'*, pp. 1–3.

'Introductory Essay: "Something Fearful": Medievalist Scholars on the "Religious Turn"', in *'Something Fearful'*, pp. 5–22.

'James Kudelka', in *Fifty Contemporary Choreographers*, ed. M. Bremser and L. Sanders, 2nd ed. (New York, 2011), pp. 202–11.

'The Vitality of the Past in the Present: A Response to the *Forum on "Acknowledged Convictions"* in *Religion and Literature* 42.1–2', *Religion and Literature* 44.3 (2012), 207–24.

'English Joachimism and its Codicological Content, with a List of Joachite Manuscripts of English Origin or Provenance before 1600', in *Joachim of Fiore and the Influence of Inspiration: Essays in Memory of Marjorie Reeves (1905–2003)*, ed. J. E. Wannenmacher (Aldershot, 2013), pp. 183–230.

'Remembering Kelly Parsons: Medievalist, Buddhist, and Poet', in *For Kelly with Love: Poems on the Abstracts of Carle Hessay*, ed. M. Hilmo (Victoria BC, 2013), pp. xiv–xvii.

'Preface', in *New Directions in Medieval Manuscript Studies*, pp. xvii–xix.

'Confronting the Scribe-Poet Binary: The Z Text, Writing Office Redaction, and the Oxford Reading Circles', in *New Directions in Medieval Manuscript Studies*, pp. 489–515.

'The Fifteenth Century as the Golden Age of Women's Theology in English: Reflections on the Earliest Reception of Julian of Norwich', in *Devotional Culture in Late Medieval England and Europe: Diverse Imaginations of Christ's Life*, ed. S. Kelly and R. Perry (Turnhout, 2014), pp. 573–91.

'The Clerical Proletariat: The Underemployed Scribe and Vocational Crisis', *Journal of the Early Book Society* 17 (2014), 1–34.

'Competing Archives, Competing Languages: Office Vernaculars, Civil Servant Raconteurs, and the Porous Nature of French during Ireland's Rise of English', *Speculum* 90 (2015), 674–700.

'Afterword: Social History of the Book and Beyond: *Originalia*, Medieval Literary Theory and the Aesthetics of Paleography', in *The Medieval Manuscript Book: Cultural Approaches*, ed. M. Johnston and M. Van Dussen (Cambridge, 2015), pp. 243–54.

'Oxford', in *Europe: A Literary History: 1348–1418*, ed. D. Wallace, 2 vols (Oxford, 2016), I, pp. 208–26.

'Foreword', to *Kane from Canada*, ed. M. Kane and J. Roberts (Tempe AZ, 2016), pp. xxix–xxxviii.

A. W. Klein and K. Kerby-Fulton, 'Rhymed Alliterative Verse in *Mise en page* Transition: Two Case Studies in English Poetic Hybridity', in *The Medieval Literary: Beyond Form*, ed. R. J. Meyer-Lee and C. Sanok (Cambridge, 2018), pp. 87–118.

'The Pedagogy of an Oppressed Text: The C Version of Piers Plowman', in *Approaches to Teaching Langland's Piers Plowman*, ed. T. A. Goodmann (New York, 2018), pp. 217–22.

'Taking Early Women Intellectuals and Leaders Seriously', in *Women Intellectuals*, pp. 1–18.

'Preface to Part III: Recovering Lost Women's Authorship: New Solutions to Old Problems', in *Women Intellectuals*, pp. 149–53.

K. Kerby-Fulton, M. Mayus and K. Bugyis, '"Anticlericalism", Inter-clerical Polemic and Theological Vernaculars', in *The Oxford Handbook of Chaucer*, ed. S. Conklin Akbari and J. Simpson (Oxford, 2020), pp. 494–526.

'Making the Early Middle Hiberno-English Lyric: Mysteries, Experiments and Survivals before 1330', *Early Middle English* 2.2 (2020), 1–26.

'Middle Hiberno-English Poetry and the Nascent Bureaucratic Literary Culture of Ireland', in *Scribal Cultures in Late Medieval England: Essays in Honour of Linne R. Mooney*, ed. M. Connolly, H. James-Maddocks and D. Pearsall (York, 2022), pp. 45–64.

K. Kerby-Fulton, A. Minnis, A. S. G. Edwards, 'Memoirs of Fellows and Corresponding Fellows: Derek Pearsall', *Speculum* 97.3 (2022), 945–6.

'Writing Inclusively for Educated Women: Clerical Proletarian-Patroness Relationships and the Shaping of Audelay's Poetry of Beatific Vision and Spiritual Intimacy', in *Poets and Scribes*, pp. 223–55.

'Not So Silent After All: Women Intellectuals and Readers in Medieval Oxford', in *Women and Devotional Literature in the Middle Ages: Giving Voice to Silence. Essays in Honour of Catherine Innes-Parker*, ed. C. Gunn, L. Herbert McAvoy and N. Yosikawa (Cambridge, 2023), pp. 180–204.

'The Art of Light: Romanesque Enamels and the Illumination of Hildegard's *Scivias*', in *Mystics, Goddesses, Lovers, and Teachers: Medieval Visions and Their Modern Legacies: Studies in Honour of Barbara Newman*, ed. S. Rozenski, J. Byron Smith and C. M. Waters (Turnhout, 2023), pp. 37–79.

'Adam Pinkhurst and the Baffled Jury: Assessing Scribal Identifications within the Margin of Error', in special section, 'Communities of Practice: New Methodological Approaches to Adam Pinkhurst and Chaucer's Earliest Scribes', *Speculum* 99.3 (2024), 664–87.

'Administrative and Professional Cultures', in *High Medieval: Literary Cultures in England*, ed. J. Wogan-Browne and E. M. Tyler (Oxford, forthcoming).

Index of Manuscripts

Aberystwyth
  National Library of Wales
    Peniarth 42   109
    Peniarth 392 D   28, 91 n.37, 93, 102
Alnwick
  Alnwick Castle
    82   19

Cambridge
  Corpus Christi College
    402   237
    414   109
  Fitzwilliam Museum
    346   118
  Gonville and Caius College
    84/166   232, 233, 239
    175   33, 43
  Magdalene College
    Pepys 2006   55, 65, 71, 72 n.37, 76 n.9, 77–81, 85, 86
  Newnham College
    900.4   232, 233, 239
  Pembroke College
    215   93, 95
    307   26, 266
  St John's College
    204   23
    256   244
    H.1   9 n.4
  Trinity College
    B.15.16   267
    R.3.2   8, 11 n.11, 21 n.30, 26
    R.3.19   77 n.9
    R.7.6   109
  University Library
    Additional 6578   260, 261–2
    Additional 6686   261–2
    Dd.8.19   24, 25
    Ff.1.6   53, 76 n.9, 77, 78, 95
    Ff.6.31   245
    Gg.4.27   76 n.9, 77, 78, 79, 80, 83, 85, 86
    Gg.5.31   232, 233, 239
    Hh.4.12   76, 77, 78, 79, 80, 81, 82, 83, 86
    Ii.1.38   92–4
    Ii.3.21   92–4
    Ii.4.9   232, 239–40
Cheltenham
  Thirlestaine House
    8192   26 n.47
Chicago
  Newberry Library
    +33.5   25 n.42
Dublin
  Trinity College
    155   243
    172   109
    11500   110, 111, 112, 118

Edinburgh
  National Library of Scotland
    Advocates' 18.1.7   265, 266
    Advocates' 19.2.1   244
    Advocates' 19.3.1   33, 35, 38–9, 232, 233, 240

Glasgow
  Glasgow University Library
    Hunter 77   267

Kent
  Petworth House
    7   266

Lincoln
  Lincoln Cathedral Library
    91   33, 44, 105

Liverpool
  University Library
    F.4.9   232, 239
London
  British Library
    Additional 10053   244
    Additional 12043   26 n.47
    Additional 15732   111, 112, 113, 118–19
    Additional 16165   93 n.38
    Additional 22283   243 n.46
    Additional 24194   9, 23
    Additional 27944   8 n.3, 24
    Additional 36523   232
    Additional 37787   243 n.46
    Additional 59678   105
    Additional 61823   105
    Arundel 10   116–18
    Arundel 38   20
    Arundel 319   109, 112
    C 21c61, Garrick Collection   50 n.72
    Cotton Caligula A.ii   33, 42
    Cotton Nero A.x   105, 125, 126, 132
    Cotton Vitellius A.xv   105
    Egerton 1991   8 n.3, 24, 25
    Egerton 3862   44 n.52
    Harley 978   69
    Harley 1121   162 n.47
    Harley 1239   103
    Harley 2421   92
    Harley 3869   20
    Harley 3943   130 n.24
    Harley 4003   114, 115
    Harley 7026   20
    Harley 7333   76 n.9, 77, 78, 79, 80, 81, 82, 83, 86
    Harley 7334   8, 102
    Royal 13 D.v   116
    Royal 17 B.xvii   232, 233, 236, 239–40, 242, 245, 247
    Royal 18 C.xxii   9 n.4, 24, 25
    Stowe 56   118
  College of Arms
    Arundel 45   25 n.42
  Gray's Inn
    20   33, 34
  Lambeth Palace Library
    454   113
    503   115, 119
  Royal College of Physicians
    409   162
  University College London
    Frag. Angl. 1   10
  University of London, Senate House
    Sterling V.88   8 n.3

Manchester
  Chetham's Library
    6690   264–5

Naples
  Royal Library
    XIII.B.29   33, 41
New Haven, CT
  Yale University, Beinecke Rare Book and Manuscript Library
    Takamiya 8   263–5
    Takamiya 20   264
New York
  Columbia University Library
    Plimpton 265   8 n.3, 24, 25
  Morgan Library and Museum
    M.648   265
    M.690   26
    M.700   162
    M.817   24 n.40
Notre Dame, IN
  Hesburgh Library
    40   119
Nuremberg
  Stadtbibliothek
    Solger 4.4°   163

Oxford
  Bodleian Library
    1119   50 n.72
    Additional C.220   244
    Arch. Selden B.11   25 n.42
    Arch. Selden B.24   77 n.9, 78, 79, 80, 81, 82, 83, 86
    Ashmole 35   25 n.42
    Ashmole 61   33, 36
    Auctarium F.3.5   93 n.39

Bodley 797   93 n.38
Bodley 264   20
Bodley 294   8 n.3
Bodley 628   55
Bodley 638   55 n.4, 65, 71, 76 n.9, 77, 78, 79, 80, 81, 82, 83, 86
Bodley 693   11, 22, 23, 24, 25
Bodley 902   8 n.3, 10, 14, 16, 22
Digby 145   5, 212–13, 215, 217–19, 220–4, 226, 227–30
Digby 181   76 n.9, 77, 78, 79, 80, 81, 82, 83, 86
Digby 261   242 n.40
Douce fragment f 37   50 n.72
Douce 104   213 n.3
Douce 261   32, 50 n.72, 242 n.40
e Musaeo 35   261–2
Eng. poet. a.1   243 n.46
Fairfax 3   19, 20
Fairfax 16   55, 64 n.26, 65–9, 71, 76 n.9, 77, 78, 79, 80, 81, 82, 83, 86
Laud 416   76 n.9, 77, 78, 79, 80, 81, 82, 83, 86
Laud Lat. 114   148 n.13, 155 n.31
Laud Misc. 210   243
Laud Misc. 609   11, 23, 24, 25
Rawlinson A. 387b   267
Rawlinson Poet. 163   130 n.24
Selden Supra 64   127–8
Tanner 346   77 n.9, 78, 79, 80, 81, 82, 83, 86
Brasenose College
  9   9, 264–5
Christ Church
  148   9 n.3, 24, 25
Corpus Christi College
  67   9 n.3, 24, 25
  155   232, 233, 239, 241, 245
  198   9 n.3
Merton College
  Merton College Register
    4.16   125–6
St John's College
  57   76 n.9, 77, 78, 79, 80, 81, 82, 83, 86

  190   162 n.49
  University College
    142   33, 34, 49
Paris
  Bibliothèque nationale de France
    anglais 25   9 n.4
    f. fr. 13342   165, 166
    latin 6040   117–18
Philadelphia
  The Rosenbach
    1083/29   24–5, 26
Princeton, NJ
  Princeton University Library
    Garrett 151   9 n.4, 23
    Taylor 5   9 n.3, 10, 11, 16, 18–21, 23, 25, 26
Salisbury
  Salisbury Cathedral Library
    Sarum 113   92
San Marino, CA
  Huntington Library
    EL 9.H.17   164
    EL 26.A.17   20
    EL 26.C.9   28, 102
    EL 34.B.7   243
    HM 114   5, 212–13, 214–19, 219–26, 227–30
Tokyo
  Senshu University Library
    1   11, 14, 16, 23, 25
  Waseda University Library
    NE 3691   265–6
Vatican
  Biblioteca Apostolica Vaticana
    Pal. Lat. 962   108, 109
Warminster
  Longleat House
    258   76
    29   243

General Index

Adele, queen of France   153 n.29
Aeneid   see under Virgil
Against Jovinian   see Jerome, *Against Jovinian*
Ailsi   *see* Peter of Cornwall, *Book of Revelations*
alcoholism   168, 185–6, 187
Alcuin, *Liber de virtutibus et viciis*   244
Alexander and Dindimus   20, 118
Allen, Hope Emily   105, 272
Alliterative Morte Arthure   45–8, 105
Amis and Amiloun   35
Amtower, Laurel   57
Ancrene Riwle   238
Ancrene Wisse   160 n.4, 237
Anglo-Norman French   106, 113, 145–61
anticlericalism   167, 198–200, 217, 219–20, 221
antimendicancy   5, 219–22, 224–6
antiquarianism   6, 107, 109, 115, 126, 128, 231–2, 237–9, 251–2
Arthur, king   45, 46, 47, 105, 113, 116, 119
Arundel, Thomas, archbishop of Canterbury   257–8, 259, 261, 264
Arundel's Constitutions   161 n.46, 257
auctoritas   55, 56, 58, 61–2, 66, 70, 72
Audelay, John   5, 191, 193, 200, 210
audience   2, 4, 251
   Chaucer   99–100
   Confessio Amantis   19
   contemplative   158–60
   editions   87, 88, 99–100, 251
   elite, 250
   HM 114   219, 220, 227, 229
   House of Fame   59, 62–3, 64
   John Mandeville   218, 227, 229
   Langland, *Piers Plowman*   220, 227, 229
   live   41
   London   216

memorization   35
Mirour de seinte eglyse   145, 158–60, 161, 165
Mirror of the Blessed Life of Christ   254, 256, 259
mouvance   160
narrator, relationship with   42
printers and   51
private reading   33
Ralph of Coggeshall, *Visio Thurkilli*   180
romances   31–2, 33, 35, 41–2, 51
Speculum religiosorum   148
women   165
see also readers, reading
Augustine of Hippo, St   147, 155, 172
   Confessions   181
Augustinian order   148, 155, 172
aurality   30, 31, 32, 36, 48 n.67
The Awentyrs of Arthure at the Terne Wathelyne   45

Baker, John   141–2
Bale, John   4, 123–4, 132, 134, 135
   Illustrium majoris Britanniae scriptorum   124, 128, 129
   Index Britanniae Scriptorum   119, 127–8
Barking Abbey   264, 265
Barney, Stephen   134–5
Barthes, Roland   87–88
Bartholomeus Anglicus, *De proprietatibus rerum*   23–4
Baudri of Bourgeuil   118
Beaufort, Thomas, duke of Exeter   262
Becket, Thomas, St, archbishop of Canterbury   146 n.6, 147, 148, 149, 150
Bede, *Historia ecclesiastica gentis Anglorum*   167, 172

Bédier, Joseph 74
Belasys, Alice 263
Benedictine order 23, 144, 169, 242, 243, 264–5
Bennett, J. A. W. 135–6
Benson, Larry D. 134
Beowulf 105
Berkeley, Sir Thomas 24
Berneye, Walter de 197–8
Bevis of Hampton 41, 43, 44 n.52
Bible 67, 100 n.55, 140, 154–5, 161, 258, 268
    Wycliffite 106
Black Death 190, 202, 203
Blanche of Castile, queen of France 149, 153 nn.28–9
bob-and-wheel 42, 45
Bodleian Library 22, 273
Boece see under Chaucer, Geoffrey
Bohne, Amanda 196 n.22, 209 n.82
Boleyn, Anne, queen of England 215
Boltoun, John 207
Book of the Duchess see under Chaucer, Geoffrey
Book of John Mandeville 214, 218, 227, 228
book production 1, 116, 213, 214, 266–8
    biblical texts 161 n.46
    Gower, *Confessio Amantis* 16 n.15
    damage 110–12
    materials 110–11
    printed books 51
    romances 32, 46
    see also *Lay Folks' Mass Book*; Love, Nicholas, *Mirror of the Blessed Life of Christ*
Brandon, Charles, duke of Suffolk 22
Brembre, Nicholas 133, 138, 139, 142
Brigit of Sweden, St 163, 268
Broun, Margery 207
Brown, Carleton 34–5, 122, 124, 132, 133, 139, 142
Brut 106
Bukerell, Isabelle 196 n.22, 209
Bukerell, William 209

Canterbury Tales see under Chaucer, Geoffrey
Carpenter, John 24–6, 27, 214
Carthusian Order 147 n.7, 257, 260, 262, 267–8
Catesby Priory 148 n.12, 149–50, 151 n.21, 154
Catherine of Siena, St 268
censorship 161, 220
    see also Arundel's Constitutions
Caxton, William 50–1, 52, 55, 69, 105, 258
chantries 192, 193, 194–5, 197, 198–210
    see also clerks
Chaucer, Geoffrey 1, 3, 16, 75–6, 84, 89–90, 105, 122–4, 125, 128, 130–2, 135
    biography 136–8, 191
    Boece 91–4
    Book of the Duchess 72
    Canterbury Tales 3, 5, 55, 76, 83, 88, 98, 102, 135, 191, 203
        Clerk's Tale 41
        General Prologue 198–9
        Melibee 52
        Monk's Tale 97 n.48
        Reeve's Tale 181
        Sir Thopas 3, 28, 29, 32, 38, 49, 51–3
        Wife of Bath's Prologue 54
    glossing practices 3, 54–6
    House of Fame 2–3, 54, 55–6, 56–65, 65–73, 100
    Legend of Good Women 97
    meter 85–6, 98
    Parlement of Foules 76–83, 85–7, 94
    Riverside Chaucer 91–2, 102, 134
    Romance of the Rose 100
    Treatise on the Astrolabe 97
    Troilus and Criseyde 3, 27, 70, 97 n.47, n.50, 99–100, 142, 214, 228
        closing 101, 102–4, 121, 138
        Gower, dedication to 99, 124, 138, 142
        Strode, dedication to 99, 102, 121, 122, 124, 128, 129, 130, 131, 133–4, 138, 142
        glosses in 3, 54, 55–6, 65, 71, 73

284 General Index

see also Manly, John; Chaumpaigne, Cecily; Rickert, Edith; Strode, Ralph
Chaucer, Richard 202–3
Chaumpaigne, Cecily 131, 143 n.82
Cistercian order 144, 149, 150, 151, 153 n.29, 154, 164, 172, 173, 241, 263
clerical proletariat 1, 5, 191–2, 194, 200, 207–8 n.73, 211
clerks 5, 198, 204
 bequests to 194, 196, 197, 198, 200–1, 204, 207, 208 n.76, 210
 chantry employment 190, 199, 201
 precarious employment 190, 191–3, 200, 211
 in *Vision of the Monk of Eynsham* 169, 174, 183, 186
 see also chantries; HM 114 scribe; Hoccleve, Thomas; Strode, Ralph
Coleman, John 197
Coleman, Joyce 31, 250
Coleman, Reginald 197
compilation 33–4, 38–9, 43 n.49, 43–7, 88, 105, 108, 113, 126, 127, 133
'The Complaint of God to Man' 39
confession 161, 185, 186, 187, 188
 abuse of 222, 224–5
Confessio Amantis see under Gower, John
Confessions see under Augustine of Hippo, St
contemplation 4, 146, 157–60, 161, 162, 166, 255
'Contra avaros' 69
Court of Husting 190 n.2, 192, 194
Courtenay, William 122, 139–40
Cursor Mundi 236, 237

De excidio Troiae 113, 118
deathbed contrition 168, 186, 187, 188, 189
dialect 84, 126, 134, 223, 234, 236, 261
Dissolution of the Monasteries 112, 265
 see also Reformation
Dodesham, Stephen 267
Doyle, A. I. (Ian) 8–10, 11 n.11, 214

Dyocliociane 45–8

Early English Text Society (EETS) 231, 236, 237–8, 270, 273
Echard, Siân 237
editing 106
 best text 74, 75, 89, 92 n.37, 94, 96–7, 98–9, 102
 Biblical 100 n.55
 diplomatic 87–9, 98
 eclecticism 3, 74–5, 76, 89–91, 94, 96, 97, 98, 102
 pragmatic 3, 75–6, 94–6, 98–102
 recension 74, 75, 76–87
 stemmatic analysis 74, 78 n.10, 81–3, 86–7, 92–4
Edmund of Abingdon, St, archbishop of Canterbury 144–5
 canonization 150, 151
 and Henry III 150
 Mirour de seinte eglyse 4, 145–6, 146–7, 152–3, 154–7, 162, 163–6
 mother 146–7, 149, 154–5
 sisters 148 n.12, 149–50, 154
 Speculum religiosarum 4, 145–6, 148–9, 150–1, 152–3, 154, 166
 see also Ela, countess of Salisbury; Isabella, countess of Arundel; Lacock Abbey; Paris, Matthew
Edward II, king of England 113, 150 n.18
Edward III, king of England 126
education 38, 122, 133, 140–1, 154, 163, 198
Eglamour 44 n.52, 45, 46, 47, 48
ekphrasis 58, 65, 66, 70
Ela, countess of Salisbury 147–8, 149 n.14, 151, 155
Eleanor of Provence, queen of England 4, 149, 150 n.18, 152
Epistola Luciferi ad Clericos 214, 217–18, 220

de Felton, Sibyl 264–5
Fisher, John 122, 133, 139
Fortescue, Adrian 141
 biography 215–16

Digby 145   216, 217, 218, 219, 220–6, 227–9
  political pressures   219–20
  see also Hand B; Langland, William, *Piers Plowman*
Fortescue, Anne Rede   216, 228
  see also Hand B; Langland, William, *Piers Plowman*
Fortescue, Anne Stonor   216
Fortescue, John, *On the Governance of England*   218
Fressh, John   206
friars   5, 214, 217–18, 220–6

Gardner, John   136–7
Gawain-poet
  see *Pearl*-poet
Geoffrey of Monmouth, *De gestis Britonum* (*Historia regum Britannie*), manuscripts of   4, 106–7
  damaged copies   108, 109–10, 113
  endleaf annotations   115–19
  irregular folios   110–12
  marginal notes in   109, 113–15
  missing leaves   112
  stamped   110
Gerould, Gordon Hall   231–2
Gille, John   208–9
de Glemesford, Richard   205
Glossa Ordinaria   155
glossing   2–3, 22, 54–6, 65–73, 233
  see also marginalia
goldsmith of Osney   see *Vision of the Monk of Eynsham*
Goldwell, Agnes   265
Gollancz, Israel   124–5, 126, 130, 132, 133, 135
Gospel of Matthew   68, 187
Gospels   155, 164, 187, 260, 264, 268
  see also Bible
Gower, John   99, 105, 124, 133, 135, 138, 142, 198, 199, 267
  Confessio Amantis   2, 258–9, 266
    glossing   70–1
    Nebuchadnezzar   18, 20, 22, 23
    scribes   8–11, 14, 16–17, 24–5, 26–7

  Vox Clamantis   136
graphic tail-rhyme   3, 29–30, 32–5, 36, 38–9, 41–53
atte Grene, Simon   205
Griffiths, Jane   72
Griffiths, Jeremy   10 n.8, 11, 23, 25
Grosseteste, Robert   149, 155, 156, 162, 241
Gunn, Cate   160

Hammond, Eleanor   81–2
Hand B, Digby 145   213, 216, 221, 222, 228, 229
  see also Fortescue, Adrian; Langland, William, *Piers Plowman*
Hanna, Ralph   24, 27, 46–7, 91, 92–4, 96, 215
Hardman, Philippa   240
Heege, Richard   38–9, 49, 240
Hende, John   130, 134, 137, 138
Henry II, king of England   149 n.14, 150, 183
Henry III, king of England   149–50, 151–2, 153
Henry IV, king of England   16, 17, 19, 21, 201, 262, 263
Henry V, king of England   163, 265 n.29, 268
Henry VIII, king of England   151 n.21, 215–16, 218, 220
Herbury, Henry   196–7, 201
Herbury, Nicholas   196–7, 198
Heylesdon, John   197
Higden, Ranulph, *Polychronicon*   11, 23, 25
Hildegard of Bingen   161
Hill, Rosemary   232, 238–9
Hilmo, Maidie   1, 11 n.12
Historia Apollonii regis Tyri   118
Historia ecclesiastica gentis Anglorum   see under Bede, *Historia ecclesiastica gentis Anglorum*
Historia regum Britannie   see Geoffrey of Monmouth, *De gestis Britonum*
HM 114 scribe   5, 213, 214–15, 216–19, 219–26, 228–9

General Index

Hoccleve, Thomas 5, 196, 198, 201, 210
   father 190, 192 n.6
   Regiment of Princes 20, 191
   Remonstrance Against Oldcastle 191
Holbech, Maud 191–2, 196, 207
Holbech, William 192 n.6, 196
Holland, Joan 263
Holland, Thomas 262, 263
Horstmann, Carl 233, 244, 246
House of Fame see under Chaucer, Geoffrey
Hugh, St, bishop of Lincoln 169, 170, 171, 189
'The Hunting of the Hare' 39

incipits 35, 37–8, 41, 42, 50, 111
Isabella, countess of Arundel 151–3, 154, 155, 156–7, 161

James I, king of England 22
Jean de Hauville, *Architrenius* 181
Jerome, St, *Against Jovinian* 54
Joachim de Fiore 161
John, duke of Bedford 262
John, king of England 152, 180
John, Lord Lumley 242
Johnston, Michael 35, 46, 48
Justice, Stephen 11, 16–17, 21, 27

Kane, George 74, 83–4 n.14, 89, 90–1, 270
Kempe, Margery, *The Book of Margery Kempe* 105
Kerby-Fulton, Kathryn 1, 2, 3, 5, 7, 106, 123, 166 n.61, 231 n.1, 270–3
   Books under Suspicion 145, 161, 272
   The Clerical Proletariat and the Resurgence of Medieval English Poetry 1, 5, 122, 142, 190–2, 210, 273
   The Medieval Professional Reader at Work 253
   as mentor 28 n.1, 74 n.1, 105 n.1, 190 n.1, 212
   Opening Up Middle English Manuscripts 54, 55–6, 73

Reformist Apocalypticism and Piers Plowman 271
   on Scribe D (John Marchaunt) 11, 16, 17, 21, 27
   on Strode, Ralph 121–2
   Voices in Dialogue 271–2
King, John, dean of Christ Church 22
Knyghtcote, William 198, 207
Kuhl, Ernest 130–1, 132, 133

Lachmann, Karl 74, 91, 92
Lacock Abbey 4, 147–9, 151, 155
Lambarde, William, *Perambulation of Kent* 115
Langland, William, *Piers Plowman* 105–6, 181, 187, 191, 198–9, 270
   antimendicant passages 219–26
   chantries 199
   clerks, unbeneficed 200, 210
   companion texts in manuscripts 214–15, 217–19, 227–9
   editing 84 n.14, 90, 97
   Elde 217
   glossing 71, 72
   marginalia 220, 221–2, 224, 225, 226, 229–30
   Mede 228
   reception history 226
   scribes 5, 213–17
   see also Fortescue, Adrian; Fortescue, Anne Rede; Hand B
   see also marginalia
Lateran IV (Fourth Council of the Lateran) 161, 168, 185
Lawler, Traugott 91, 92–4
Lawton, David 121
The Lay Folks' Mass Book (*LFMB*) 6, 231–4, 235–6, 239–50, 251
lectio divina 254–5
Leland, John 116, 119, 124, 126–7
leprosy 176
Libeaus Desconus 41
Linguistic Atlas of Late Mediaeval English (*LALME*) 241, 242, 243, 244
liturgy 6, 233, 234, 235–6

Liuzza, Roy Michael   251–2
Lollardy   137, 217, 219, 256, 257–8, 259, 260
London
  book production   165
  chantries   199, 201, 203 n.53
  Guildhall   9, 122, 142 n.78, 203, 212–13 n.2, 214, 217, 267
  Inns of Court   122 n.4, 141, 142 n.78
  merchants   5, 191–3, 196, 197, 200, 204, 210
  scribes   2, 8, 24, 26
  wills   5, 192–3, 193–4, 196–8, 200, 201–10
  see also Strode, Ralph
Longespee, William, earl of Salisbury   147 n.7, 149 n.14
Longespee, William II   148
Louis IX, king of France   149, 153 n.28
Love, Nicholas, *Mirror of the Blessed Life of Jesus Christ*   6, 254–6, 257–61, 262
  Carthusian reading networks   260
  licensing   257, 259
  limning   261–2, 266
  linguistic features, authoritative   258–60, 261
  printing history   258
  prologue   255, 269
  readers of   255–6
  transmission   258, 262–5, 266–7
Lovell Lectionary   19–20
Lydgate, John   71, 105
The Lyttel Childrens Book   241

Macaulay, G. C.   10 nn.9–10, 11 n.11, 16 n.15, 17, 20, 22–3, 24–5, 26 n.47, 27
Machan, Tim   94, 245
Magna Carta   152
Malory, Thomas, *Morte Darthur*   105
Mandeville, John   *see Book of John Mandeville*
manicules   109, 112, 113–15
Manly, John   76, 83, 88
Marchaunt, John   10, 16, 17, 19, 21, 22, 24–6, 122, 138 n.62, 142 n.78
marginalia   39, 42, 49 n.70

Digby 145   220, 221, 222, 228, 229
Geoffrey of Monmouth, *De Gestis Britonum*   109, 110, 113, 115
Love, Nicholas, *Mirror of the Blessed Life of Jesus Christ*   260–1
Peter of Cornwall, *Liber revelationum*   177
Piers Plowman   72, 218 n.19, 220
see also glosses, manicules
marriage   54, 163, 196, 198, 266
  Fortescue marriage   217, 221, 227–8
  House of Fame   64, 68
  Isabella, countess of Arundel   151
  Strode, Ralph   132, 139, 142
  Thurkill   178
Maskell, William   234, 235–6, 237, 251
  Ancient Liturgy of the Church of England   235–6
meditation   4, 146, 155, 158, 161, 254–6, 264, 267–8
  on Christ's Passion   162–6
Meditationes vitae Christi   256–7, 260, 264–5
merchants   5, 191–3, 196, 197, 198, 200–1, 202, 204, 210–11
atte Mershe, Gilbert   205, 206 n.65, 209–10
Merton College, Oxford   121–2, 124–32, 134–5, 137, 141, 143, 148, 154
  see also Oxford; Strode, Ralph
meter   86, 98, 101, 102–3, 135, 233, 249
minstrels   30–9, 42, 50, 51–2, 240 n.35
Mirour de l'Omme   199
Mirror of the Blessed Life of Jesus Christ   see Love, Nicholas, *Mirror of the Blessed Life of Jesus Christ*
Mirror to Devout People   268–9
miscellany manuscripts   36, 38 n.35, 49, 119, 240, 243, 245
mise-en-page   31, 44, 45
  rhyming brackets   36, 45
  tail-rhyme   3, 28–30, 31, 39, 42–3, 45, 48–51, 53
Mooney, Linne   214
de Mordon, Alice   198
Morris, Richard   236, 237

288   General Index

Morte Arthure, alliterative   45–8, 105
mothers   146–7, 149, 187, 197
Mount Grace Priory   6, 254, 257–8, 259, 260, 261–3, 265

Neuport, William   204
Neville, Margaret, duchess of Exeter   262
Newman, Barbara   272
Northampton, John   142, 198, 200, 203 n.53, 207

Octavian   43, 46–8
Olson, Linda   1, 37–8, 44, 271–2
orality
   Lay Folks' Mass Book   250
   tail-rhyme   30, 30–4, 35, 36–8, 41–3, 44, 49–52, 53
   otherworld visions   170, 173, 174
Ordinances of 1310–11   113
Osbarn, Richard   *see* HM 114 scribe
Osney Abbey   169
   see also Vision of the Monk of Eynsham
Ovid   59, 65, 69, 70, 72
Oxford   146, 169, 183–4, 191, 197–8, 270–1, 273
   see also Merton College, Oxford

Paris, Matthew   116, 146–7, 148, 150–2, 153, 161, 169, 173, 182
Parkes, Malcolm   8–9, 10, 11 n.11, 248–9
Parlement of Foules   *see under* Chaucer, Geoffrey
parody   28–9, 32, 53
Pearl   125, 126, 132, 133–4, 135, 136, 142, 178
Pearl-poet   105
Pearsall, Derek   16 n.15, 88, 89 n.28, 137, 213
Pecham, John, archbishop of Canterbury   161
penance   167, 185
Percy, Henry, earl of Northumberland   266
Percyvelle   45–6

Peter of Cornwall, *Liber revelationum*   168, 169, 170, 171, 172, 174–8, 179, 188
Petworth scribe   26, 266, 267
Piers Plowman   *see* Langland, William, *Piers Plowman*
piety   146, 174
   lay   5, 167, 168, 174
pilgrimage   5, 144, 150, 153, 177, 178–9, 182
Pinkhurst, Adam (Scribe B)   122, 214
Polychronicon (Higden)   11, 23, 25
Polychronicon (Trevisa)   *see* Trevisa, John, *Polychronicon*
Pontigny Abbey   144, 150, 153
Prick of Conscience   6, 35, 106, 236, 243, 244
print   33, 105, 230, 237, 250, 267
   De gestis Britonum   112, 119
   editing   85, 86, 87, 96, 102
   Love, Nicholas, *Mirror of the Blessed Life of Jesus Christ*   258, 259, 264 n.26
   Isumbras   29, 31, 32 n.15, 33, 49–50, 51
   Lay Folks' Mass Book   232
   Parlement of Foules   76
   romances   242 n.40
   graphic tail rhyme   29, 33, 49–50, 51, 52, 53
   Sir Thopas   49, 51, 52
   see also Caxton, William; de Worde, Wynkyn
Processional of the Nuns of Chester   243
psalms   37, 155, 235
Public Worship Regulation Act (1874)   235
punctuation   12–13, 41, 216, 233, 237–8, 246, 248–50, 259 n.14
Purdie, Rhiannon   29, 30, 32, 34, 43
purgatory   167, 168, 170, 172–3, 174, 183, 186–7, 188–9
Pynson, Richard   258

Ralph of Coggeshall, *Visio Thurkilli*   168, 169, 170–1, 173, 178–83, 188
Rate (scribe)   36–8
readers   1–2, 6, 88–9, 106

capability 4
collaborative 99–101
early modern 224, 226, 227
expert 92
introspective 226
Latinate 177, 261
lay 1, 150, 155, 160
medieval 32, 33, 44, 53, 56, 71, 111, 177, 226, 227, 251, 254, 258, 260
modern 28, 55, 110, 111, 178, 222, 226, 230, 234, 238, 251, 252, 253
nuns 150, 155, 160, 265
performers 36
of *Piers Plowman* 217, 218–19, 223, 226, 227, 229
pragmatic 99
professional 6, 226, 229, 253, 254, 255–6, 257–8, 260, 261, 263, 264, 265–6, 267–8
responses 4, 70, 72, 109, 114, 115, 119, 213, 225, 229, 248
Victorian 238
women 1, 4, 245, 265
see also reading
reading 35, 53, 149, 229
ekphrastic 58, 70
of *House of Fame* 58, 59, 60, 62
meditative 254, 255, 264
mnemonic 58, 59
modern 105, 253
networks 6, 254, 260, 269
polemical 129
private 31, 32–3, 49, 52
professional 253–4, 269
public 31, 32, 42, 48, 49, 50, 250
romances 29–30, 32, 35, 36, 37, 49, 52
see also readers
recipes, medical 41
Recuyell of the Historyes of Troye 69
Reeve, Michael D. 106 n.2, 107, 115
Reformation 2, 5–6, 129, 131, 216, 218, 220–1, 226
see also Dissolution of the Monasteries
Regiment of Princes *see under* Hoccleve, Thomas

Remonstrance Against Oldcastle *see under* Hoccleve, Thomas
Rich, Alice 148 n.12, 149–50, 154
Rich, Margery 148 n.12, 149–51, 154
Richard II, king of England 16, 138, 262
Rickert, Edith 76, 83, 124, 130, 131, 132–3, 137
Robinson, F. N. 85, 92, 93, 102, 133, 134
Roger, Euan 123 n.8, 131, 143 n.82
Roger of Wendover 169, 173, 182
Rolle, Richard 243, 244
Romance of the Rose *see under* Chaucer, Geoffrey
romance *see* graphic tail-rhyme

St Alban's Abbey 116, 152, 173
St Patrick's Purgatory 172, 173
Salisbury Cathedral 147, 148
Sand, Alexa 162, 164
Sargent, Michael 257, 258, 260, 263, 265, 266
Scheerre, Hermann 22–4
Scott, Kathleen 19–20, 23, 262, 263, 266
Scribe D *see* Marchaunt, John
Scribe Delta 9, 23, 24, 25, 27
scribes 1–6, 8, 24, 26, 75, 77, 111, 174, 176
Chaucer 75, 77–8, 83–5, 88, 89–91, 96, 99, 101
Fortescue, Adrian 216, 217, 218, 219, 220–6, 227–9
Fortescue, Anne Rede 216, 228
graphic tail-rhyme 29–36, 37, 38–45, 46, 47–53
Hand B, Digby 145 213, 216, 221, 222, 228, 229
Heege, Richard 38–9, 49, 240
HM 114 scribe 5, 213, 214–15, 216–19, 219–26, 228–9
otherworld visions 168–9, 171, 173, 183
Piers Plowman 5, 72, 213–17
see also glossing, marginalia, Trevisa-Gower scribe
Scrope, Margaret 265
Seaman, Myra 37, 38 n.5
Seint Alex of Rome 41

Sharpe, R. R., *Calendar of Wills* 193–4, 195 n.17
Sheen Priory 267–9
Sherborne Missal 19
Shirley, John 101
Simmons, Thomas Frederick 6, 231–3, 234–7, 238, 239, 245–7, 251–2
Sir Amadas 38, 240–1
Sir Degrevant 45–8
Sir Gawain and the Green Knight 241
Sir Gowther 38, 240–1
Sir Isumbras 3, 29, 30, 31–6, 38–9, 41, 43, 45, 47, 49–52, 240–1
Skeat, W. W. 85, 92, 130, 236
Skinners' Company 26, 267
Slywright, William 35 n.23
Smith, Jeremy 258, 259 n.14, 261 n.19
Sobecki, Sebastian 123 n.8, 131, 143 n.82
Speculum Guy of Warwick 244
Stans Puer ad Mensam 240–1
stemmatics 55, 74, 78 n.10, 81–3, 86–7, 92–4, 159 n.40, 258
Stephen, St 172, 174–6, 177, 179, 185
   see also Peter of Cornwall, *Liber revelationum*
Stimulus Conscientiae Minor 244
Stokesby, Juliana 205, 206 n.65
Strode, Ralph
   career change 4, 121–2, 126, 139
   identification 122–4, 127–30, 136, 137–8, 139, 143
   London career 122 n.6, 125, 130–1, 132–6, 137–8, 139, 141–2
   Merton College fellowship 122, 124, **125 Fig 6.1**, 126–7, 128–9, 130–1, 132–4, 137, 141
   Pearl authorship theory 125–6, 132, 134–5, 142
   as poet 128–30, 135–6
   Troilus and Criseyde 99, 102–3, 124, 128, 130, 131, 133, 138
   Wyclif, John 140
Strohm, Paul 137–8
Stubbs, Estelle 9, 122, 212 n.2, 214
suffrages 167, 168, 179–80, 181, 182, 187
Susannah 42, 214, 228

Syon Abbey 267–8

Taylor, Andrew 36–7, 51
Terrell, Katherine H. 57
'This lovely lady sat and sang' 39
Thompson, John 43
Thornhill, William 207
Thornton, Robert 33, 35, 39, 44–9, 105
Three Kings of Cologne 214, 228
Tolkien, J. R. R. 237, 238
Tours, John 209, 210
Tout, Thomas Frederick 122, 124, 132, 133, 135, 139, 141, 142
translation 100 n.55, 268
   Arundel's Constitutions 161 n.46
   Biblical 100 n.55, 258
   Epistola Luciferi ad Clericos 218 n.17, 220
   Lay Folks' Mass Book 233
   Meditationes vitae Christi 256–7, 258, 259, 260, 264
   Mirour de seinte eglyse 145, 162
   Speculum religiosorum 149
   Paris, Matthew 151, 152
   Trevisa, John, *Polychronicon* 2, 9, 11, 23–4
   Treatise on the Astrolabe see under Chaucer, Geoffrey
   Trevisa, John, *Polychronicon* 2, 9, 11, 23–4
   Trevisa-Gower scribe 2, 9–10, 11, 14–16, 17, 22–7
   Troilus and Criseyde see under Chaucer, Geoffrey

Vergil, Polydore 116
Virgil 61, 63, 70, 72
   Aeneid 58–60, 65, 66–8, 177
Vision of the Monk of Eynsham 168, 169–71, 172, 179, 183–7, 188
Vita Sancti Christofori 46–7

Wade, James 38
Wakelin, Daniel 111, 260
Wallace, David 138
Walleworth, William 204–5

Walssh, John 210
Whitaker, Thomas 237
Whittington, Richard 192
William of Jumiège 118
William of Ockham 140, 141
wills 191, 192, 193–6, 196–8, 200–10
Wilshere, Alan 157–9, 165
Wogan-Browne, Jocelyn 272
women 190 n.1, 192, 196, 198, 217, 272
   House of Fame 70
   readers 1, 4, 158, 160, 162–3, 164, 165, 166
   patrons 146, 152, 164, 165
   and St Edmund of Abingdon 144–6, 147, 149, 150, 153–5
   spirituality 154
   testators 210
Wood, Sarah 71, 72, 215, 217 n.15
de Worde, Wynkyn 29, 51, 258
Wyclif, John 122, 123 n.8, 124, 126, 129–31, 133, 134–5, 137, 139, 140–1, 243
Wycliffism 106, 129, 258
Wynchcombe, Simon 206–7

Zieman, Katherine 199, 200 n.39, 201 n.47, 209

Tabula gratulatoria

Chris Abram and Amy Mulligan
Sarah Baechle
Christopher Baswell
Louise M. Bishop
Siobhain Bly Calkin
Julia Boffey
Amanda Bohne
Matthew Clifton Brown
Julianne Bruneau
Katie Ann-Marie Bugyis
Christopher Cannon
Rebecca Davis
Martha W. Driver
Siân Echard
Nicole Eddy
Susanna Fein
Karrie Fuller
Genelle Gertz
Thomas Goodmann
Megan J. Hall
Marjorie Harrington
Michael Johnston
Jonathan Juilfs
Steven Justice
Andrew W. Klein
Robert J. Meyer-Lee
Robert E. Lerner
Yin Liu
Erica Machulak
Jill Mann
Julia Marvin

Laura Saetveit Miles
Timothy Miller
Alastair Minnis
Linne R. Mooney
Deborah Moore
Barbara Newman
Maura Nolan
Theresa O'Byrne
Kenna L. Olsen
Caroline Palmer
Sarah Rees Jones
Heather A. Reid
Jane Roberts
Misty Schieberle
Elizabeth Schirmer
James Simpson
Jeremy J. Smith
Sebastian Sobecki
A.C. Spearing
Andrew Taylor
John J. Thompson
Michael Van Dussen
Kathryn Veeman
Rosalynn Voaden
Lawrence Warner
Claire M. Waters
Nicholas Watson
Adrienne Williams Boyarin
Jocelyn Wogan-Browne
Hannah Zdansky

YORK MEDIEVAL PRESS

York Medieval Press is published by the University of York's Centre for Medieval Studies in association with Boydell & Brewer Limited. Our objective is the promotion of innovative scholarship and fresh criticism on medieval culture. We have a special commitment to interdisciplinary study, in line with the Centre's belief that the future of Medieval Studies lies in those areas in which its major constituent disciplines at once inform and challenge each other.

Editorial Board (2023)

Peter Biller, Emeritus (Dept of History): General Editor
Tim Ayers (Dept of History of Art): Co-Director, Centre for Medieval Studies
Henry Bainton: Private scholar
K. P. Clarke (Dept of English and Related Literature)
K. F. Giles (Dept of Archaeology)
Shazia Jagot (Dept of English and Related Literature)
Holly James-Maddocks (Dept of English and Related Literature)
Harry Munt (Dept of History)
L. J. Sackville (Dept of History)
Elizabeth M. Tyler (Dept of English and Related Literature): Co-Director, Centre for Medieval Studies
Hanna Vorholt (Dept of History of Art)
Sethina Watson (Dept of History)
J. G. Wogan-Browne (English Faculty, Fordham University)
Stephanie Wynne-Jones (Dept of Archaeology)

All enquiries of an editorial kind, including suggestions for monographs and essay collections, may be sent to pete.biller@york.ac.uk

York Manuscript and Early Print Studies

Series Editors
Orietta Da Rold (Cambridge)
Holly James-Maddocks (York)

YORK MEDIEVAL PRESS PUBLICATIONS
York Manuscript and Early Print Studies

This new series builds on and expands York Medieval Press' Manuscript Culture in the British Isles. It aims to further the study of handwritten and early print sources for literature and intellectual history in the pre-modern period, and champions an interconnected mode of analysis for the textual, material and cultural, whether the focus is local, regional, national or transnational. It welcomes contributions providing critical approaches to manuscript studies, history of the book, cultural history, philology and editing, whether monographs, edited collections, or catalogues.

Series Editors
Orietta Da Rold (Cambridge)
Holly James-Maddocks (York)

Advisory Committee
Alexandra da Costa (Cambridge), Marilena Maniaci (Cassino), Linne Mooney (York), Nicola Morato (Liège), Máire Ní Mhaonaigh (Cambridge), David Rundle (Kent), Elaine Treharne (Stanford)

1 *Manuscript Culture and Medieval Devotional Traditions: Essays in Honour of Michael G. Sargent*, edited by Jennifer N. Brown and Nicole R. Rice
2 *Saints' Legends in Medieval Sarum Breviaries: Catalogue and Studies*, Sherry L. Reames
3 *Scribal Cultures in Late Medieval England: Essays in Honour of Linne R. Mooney*, edited by Margaret Connolly, Holly James-Maddocks and Derek Pearsall
4 *Re-using Manuscripts in Late Medieval England: Repairing, Recycling, Sharing*, Hannah Ryley
5 Piers Plowman *and its Manuscript Tradition*, Sarah Wood
6 *MS Junius and its Poetry*, Carl Kears

Details of other York Medieval Press volumes are available from Boydell & Brewer Ltd

Printed in the United States
by Baker & Taylor Publisher Services